British Social Attitudes

the
5th report

British Social Attitudes

the
5th report

Edited by
Roger Jowell
Sharon Witherspoon
& Lindsay Brook

Gower

Published by
Gower Publishing Company Limited,
Gower House,
Croft Road,
Aldershot,
Hants GU11 3HR
England

Gower Publishing Company,
Old Post Road,
Brookfield,
Vermont 05036,
USA

Cover photograph by Brian Astbury

British Library Cataloguing in Publication Data

British social attitudes: the 5th report.
  1. Public opinion — Great Britain   2. Great Britain — Social conditions
  — 1945–
  I. Jowell, Roger   II. Witherspoon, Sharon   III. Brook, Lindsay
  941.085'8   HD400.P8

ISSN 0–267–6869
ISBN 0–566–05699 2
ISBN 0–566–05771 9 (Pbk)

Typeset in Great Britain by Guildford Graphics Limited, Petworth, West Sussex.
Printed and bound in Great Britain at The Camelot Press Ltd, Southampton

Contents

Introduction

This is the fifth annual volume in this series. In the introduction to the first volume in 1984 we suggested, somewhat defensively, that the findings were sure to become more and more interesting as the years passed. We warned against expecting exciting results too early since changes in people's values were bound to be gradual. As it turns out, we were being over-cautious.

For one thing, movements in public attitudes have been more numerous and more rapid than we had anticipated. Although reporting inertia would have been useful, reporting change has been rather more absorbing. For another thing, some of these movements have been in an unexpected direction and, suspicious as we are of such findings, we cannot escape the fact that surprising results tend to be more exciting than predictable ones.

SCPR's *British Social Attitudes* series aims to monitor public attitudes to a wide variety of social, economic, political and moral issues during the 1980s and 1990s. Its primary source of data is an hour-long annual interview survey, with a self-completion supplement, among a probability sample of around 3000 people nationwide. The cumulated datasets serve as a sort of moving picture, portraying how British people see their world and themselves and, through their eyes, how society itself is changing. Our task is to keep the 'camera' still so that we end up recording rather than creating movement. But we are never able to control the fact that the background keeps shifting. Governments, for instance, insist from time to time on introducing new policies for the nation with little consideration for how they affect social science measurements!

So, however desirable it may be in theory that all questions about all topics should be the same between readings, it is not always possible in practice. And even when the question is the same, we cannot ensure that its *meaning* is constant. Various factors may influence meaning, not least the context within which a particular question appears in the interview: questions *do* tend to be judged by the company they keep, and our questionnaires as a whole change

considerably from year to year, both with the rotation of modules on particular topics and the introduction of new topics. Another factor, as we have suggested, is the wider social or political context within which each survey is conducted. No question or set of questions can be asked in a vacuum; how respondents answer will depend to some extent on what they think a question is actually getting at, not only on what it says.

For instance, suppose we had asked a question about people's attitudes to nationalisation in 1983 and again in 1987. During those four years, circumstances changed radically. The word 'privatisation', let alone the the concept, had barely been invented in 1983, so any question formulated at that time would probably have been couched in the 'old' phraseology, referring – implicitly at any rate – to the 'old' circumstances. By 1987 we had witnessed several widely-publicised privatisations of state-owned enterprises. A question that had been framed four years earlier would by then probably have become little better than a curio. But even if the question itself had not sounded odd in the new circumstances, the chances are that respondents would nonetheless have interpreted it differently in 1987 from the way they had done in 1983. Identical questions may well convey different messages at different times.

We rely on a number of devices, none of them foolproof, for counteracting these sorts of difficulties. First, we try to design questions which will survive the ebbs and flows of political fashion and policy changes. So we concentrate as far as possible on people's underlying values, not on their opinions about topical issues. It is the job of the monthly opinion polls to chart transitory fluctuations in public opinion. The task of this series is to monitor long-term changes in values.

Second, we urge users of the data to be particularly cautious in interpreting differences between one reading and the next. Indeed, the most appropriate initial response to a sudden shift, especially a surprising one, is to look for a more plausible explanation than that attitudes have changed dramatically. For instance, has the context of the item within the questionnaire changed, or has the political climate changed, in a way that is likely to affect answers? Do other answers about the same topic show similar shifts and, if not, why not? Were the two readings based on identical questions, or was there a slight change in wording, perhaps even a misprint in the questionnaire? Only after discounting these and several other possible artefacts should a difference, however large, between two readings be construed as a change. A mere test of statistical significance will not do, since it measures only random sources of error, not these systematic sources of possible bias. 'Tests' of plausibility tend to be the most demanding ones.

Third, we do not always stick steadfastly to particular question wordings come what may. For instance, when questions do not seem to work well, we adjust or discard them in later rounds. When a set of questions begins to date, we try to modernise the items, sometimes by 'splicing' new questions into the existing set with a view to supplanting some of the dated items over time. After all, the slavish repetition of badly-framed questions would thwart rather than assist the development of a robust time-series. On the other hand, there is clearly always a powerful case for staying with the questions we have and, to the extent that we fail, the series is weakened.

A continuing strength of the series is its funding base, now secure until 1991/92.

Core-funding from the Sainsbury Family Charitable Trusts ensures the stability and independence of the series. In addition, fixed-term commitments of funds (usually for three-year periods) are provided by other bodies, mostly government, in support of particular sections of the questionnaire. These funds, like the core funds, are given in the form of grants rather than contracts, in that they carry with them no control over either the questions we ask or the findings we publish. Those decisions remain entirely in SCPR's hands. So our funders cannot be blamed for the series' faults, only thanked for its continuation. In particular, we remain greatly indebted to the trustees of the Sainsbury Trusts and their Director, Hugh de Quetteville, for their continuing consideration, generosity and advice.

We rely too on the regular support of the Departments of Employment and Environment for the modules on labour market attitudes and on housing respectively. The criticisms and suggestions we receive from colleagues in both Departments are always admirably to the point and influential. Three chapters in this volume also owe their existence partly to earmarked funds of this kind. The Department of Trade and Industry is supporting three annual rounds of questions about attitudes to business and industry, and some of the findings are reported in **Chapter 7**. The Countryside Commission has already supported three rounds of questions about attitudes to 'green' issues; the findings are in **Chapter 9**. And the Nuffield Foundation has helped to fund two rounds of questions about public and private morality, which are reported in **Chapter 1**.

We are grateful indeed to all these organisations, and to the individuals within them, who have contributed so much to the series. Long-term funding commitments of this kind ensure not only the series' survival but also its strength, allowing fresh modules and new features to be introduced at planned, rather than at haphazard, intervals, and avoiding the 'stop-go' method of funding which is all too common in social science and is so debilitating.

One new feature to be introduced in 1989 is a cumulative Sourcebook of findings, to be sponsored in the first instance by Shell UK Ltd, and to be published annually – once again by Gower. It will be the only *British Social Attitudes* volume to appear in 1989. Then, in 1990, *The 6th Report* will appear alongside *The 2nd Sourcebook*, and so on in subsequent years.

As we explained last year, the reason for the one-year gap in these Reports is that we decided not to have a *British Social Attitudes* fieldwork round in 1988; thus we do not have the customary annual dataset on which to base a 1989/90 Report. Instead, with the permission of our core-funders and with further support from the ESRC and Pergamon Press, we brought forward the 1988 survey budget and deployed it towards a post-1987 election study, carried out by SCPR and Nuffield College, Oxford as the latest of the *British General Election* studies. We have thus strengthened the numerous links between these two time-series in the belief that there will be considerable mutual benefit. A book on the 1987 election, a sequel to *How Britain Votes*, will appear in 1989, bringing together some of the data on political and social change since 1983.

The proposed annual Sourcebook is intended both as a companion volume to the annual *British Social Attitudes* Report, and also as a stand-alone reference book containing cumulative trend data on literally hundreds of attitudinal questions. The 1989 (introductory) volume will contain a (very sparse) commentary on groups of findings, but thereafter the data will appear on their own, cross-

indexed and fully labelled for ease of reference. Shell UK's generous offer to finance the work in compiling the first volume stems partly from their experience in using the data over the past few years (during which they have also been contributing funders). They felt a clear need for a convenient reference book, fulfilling a role somewhere between that of these annual commentaries and of the datatapes themselves. With five years of data to contend with already, and more in the offing, they believed, as we did, that a Sourcebook was fast becoming a near-necessity. We are, however, particularly pleased that it is being funded by Shell, not least because it demonstrates once again that social science datasets of this kind *are* appreciated beyond the public and academic sectors alone.

Another changing aspect of the series is the consolidation and enlargement of its international links. We helped to found the *International Social Survey Programme* (ISSP) in 1985 as a modest, four-nation exercise (consisting of teams in Australia, Britain, the USA and West Germany). Its aim was to coordinate locally-funded self-completion surveys in each country, containing identical (or equivalent) questions on a mutually-agreed, rotating set of subjects. In each country the objective was to attach the survey, as a supplement, to its annual series. And this is what happened, more or less, in 1985. But by the spring of 1988 we had already been joined in this venture by seven other distinguished national teams (from Austria, Holland, Hungary, the Republic of Ireland, Israel, Italy and Norway), necessitating the development of a constitution, a secretariat and rules of entry! Surprisingly, perhaps, despite this growth rate and bureaucratisation, the ISSP continues to operate smoothly and cordially. More important, it has already begun to produce a rich source of comparative attitudinal data which is archived each year in the West German Data Archive based in Cologne. These combined datatapes are then made available immediately to each participating nation. (In Britain, they are archived with the rest of the *British Social Attitudes* material in the ESRC Data Archive at Essex University.) We have already published one commentary (by Davis in *The 1986 Report*) on these data, and plan to publish others in future volumes.

So the series continues to grow in various planned and unplanned ways and, all the while, our colleagues in SCPR remain indulgent, if somewhat bemused. We are, as ever, grateful to all of them. A particular tribute and vote of thanks goes to our interviewers and coders who once again worked so skilfully on the survey, to the office staff who allocate and control their work, and to the programmers who prepared the data for analysis. These tasks are at the heart of any survey. And right now as we send final copy to the publishers, we are reminded of the debt we owe also to SCPR's highly competent secretarial staff. We wish to single out for special mention, however, the new research assistant, Judith Lewis, whom we are so fortunate to have working on this series, and who has contributed a great deal to the production of this book.

As usual, we end our introduction with a warm salute to our 3000 or so anonymous respondents on whose views all these chapters are based, and to the authors who have described and interpreted these views so faithfully.

RMJ
SFW
LLB

1 The price of honesty

*Michael Johnston**

As Walter Bagehot told us over a century ago, Britain is a nation in which appearances, social perceptions and traditional values count for a great deal. Unlike the USA or France, the values that characterise British society are not derived from any single conflict or event representing the birth of the nation, nor are they laid down in a written constitution. For all that, they seem to be at least as robust.

Almond and Verba (1963) found that Britain exhibited many attributes of what they called the "civic culture". Among these were a respect for traditional values and authority and a trust in the political process. Most British citizens seemed to be content with the current social order and the limits of their role within it – more so than citizens of the other countries they studied. Indeed Almond and Verba saw Britain as the exemplar of this civic culture, which they expected to spread throughout the world. Now, some three decades after their study, observers such as Kavanagh (1980) have not only raised doubts about the assumptions underlying the concept of "civic culture", but have also suggested that Almond and Verba's view of Britain was over-optimistic. Since the early 1960s, Kavanagh observes, various potentially disruptive developments – principally economic difficulties – have served to destabilise traditional attachments. Thus he suggests that the 'image of the law-abiding English' may actually be obsolete. Beer (1982) is even more pessimistic. His account, in the early 1980s, of an unstable Britain in which traditional values and restraint have been lost suggests a British culture in a state of collapse.

Bagehot (1867) portrayed the British culture as "deferential"; more recently, Jessop (1971) argued that it was characterised by "traditionalism" and "civility". But Norton (1984) sees Britons not only as "trusting", but also as "pragmatic". And Heath and Topf, in *The 1987 Report*, argued that while the British support

---

*Associate Professor of Political Science, Colgate University, Hamilton, New York.

the prevailing moral order, they are also politically self-confident and ready
to participate in public life. So most observers now concede that Britain's values
are changing to a degree. What is in dispute is the extent and direction of
these changes.

This chapter investigates a small but important corner of British culture –
the public's assessment of right and wrong in everyday life. In a nation which
places particular emphasis on traditional values and trust, how do people judge
their own actions and those of others? This is a subject we first looked at
three years ago (see Johnston and Wood in *The 1985 Report*); and we now
return to one aspect of it – probity in private transactions – and examine
attitudes in greater detail.

Judging wrongdoing

The 1984 *British Social Attitudes* survey included a group of questions designed
to help us understand standards of right and wrong. We asked respondents
to say, for each of a series of 18 hypothetical actions, how wrong they thought
each one was. The situations ranged from a police officer demanding £50 from
a speeding driver in exchange for "forgetting" the incident, to a householder
offering the dustmen £5 to remove items they were not supposed to take away.
Respondents were invited to say for each type of behaviour whether there was
"nothing wrong" in it, or whether it was "a bit wrong", "wrong" or "seriously
wrong". For some items they were also asked whether they themselves might
do the same thing "if the situation came up".

The results were intriguing. We found that judgements reflected a number
of considerations not addressed by formal rules or by the law, such as the
type and size of gain involved, the role and circumstances of both 'perpetrator'
and 'victim' and the motives attributed to those involved. That these judgements
reflected shared social values was suggested by the fact that the rank-ordering
of items by degrees of 'wrongness' remained almost identical irrespective of
the sex, age group and social class of the respondent. Thus an action regarded
by one subgroup as more wrong than another tended to be judged more wrong
by almost all other groups as well. But while these *rankings* were more or
less constant, respondents did vary in the overall *strictness* of their judgements.
These differences were particularly pronounced in respect of 'private' transactions. While the standards applied to public officials (say, police officers or
council employees) were fairly constant from one group of respondents to the
next, judgements of, say, the householder who 'bribes' the dustmen, or of
someone who pockets extra change, showed more variation. So it was on this
subject of private morality that we decided to concentrate in the 1987 survey.
In addition, three questions asked in 1984 were repeated to give some evidence
as to the stability or change in judgements over time.*

---

*A change in question wording was introduced in 1987. The four categories of 'wrongness'
employed in 1984 were expanded by adding a fifth – "*very* seriously wrong". This was because
the 1984 results suggested to us that the set of only four categories had truncated the range
of responses, denying respondents the opportunity of judging some actions as severely as they
would have wished. The 1987 results support this view. Thus data from the two surveys are
not *strictly* comparable, even when the same answer was given in 1987 as three years earlier,
and we draw attention to this whenever it appears to matter.

Stability over time

The results on those items common to both surveys suggest an overall stability in judgements of right and wrong. The three transactions we asked about again were:

A company employee exaggerates his claim for travel expenses over a period and makes £50.

A householder is having a repair job done by a local plumber. He is told that if he pays cash he will not be charged VAT. So he pays cash.

A man gives a £5 note for goods he is buying in a big store. By mistake, he is given change for a £10 note. He notices, but keeps the change.

Figures for 1984 and 1987 are given below:

	Fiddling expenses		Evading VAT		Pocketing wrong change	
	1984	1987	1984	1987	1984	1987
	%	%	%	%	%	%
Nothing wrong	4	5	31	26	6	8
A bit wrong	17	20	31	29	15	20
Wrong	54	52	32	36	61	58
Seriously wrong	23	15	3	6	16	10
Very seriously wrong	n/a	8	n/a	2	n/a	5

We would not expect dramatic changes in judgements to have occurred in the course of just three years. And indeed such differences as do exist between the two sets of results are very small. But a number of events and controversies during recent years have kept questions of ethics and traditional values very much in the news and, to a degree, in dispute. Viewed in this context, the stability of judgements reported above is important evidence for the continuing strength of "moral traditionalism" (Heath and Topf, 1987).

A similar degree of stability was revealed in the follow-up questions to the 'VAT-dodging' and 'pocketing wrong change' items. Here we asked respondents whether they themselves might take these actions if the occasion arose:

	Evading VAT		Pocketing wrong change	
	1984	1987	1984	1987
	%	%	%	%
I might do it	66	67	18	24
Don't know/no answer	5	6	4	3
I would not do it	27	27	77	73

A somewhat higher proportion of our 1987 sample says that they might keep an extra £5 in change in a big store. But a large majority of our respondents still say that they would not do so. The much larger proportion willing to contemplate VAT-dodging has hardly changed.

These moral dilemmas are of the sort that people encounter every day. Responses to survey questions cannot of course be taken as a definitive statement about how people would react when faced with such dilemmas. But they are a useful guide to basic standards of right and wrong in society – especially when they show overall stability three years apart.

Complexities of judgement

Behind this apparent stability, however, we can glimpse intriguing divergences in people's perceptions of right and wrong. The 1987 survey, like that of 1984, revealed no single boundary between acceptable and unacceptable behaviour. Instead, people make *relative* judgements of degrees of wrongdoing, and respond to a variety of considerations other than (and at times differing from) what may be called 'official' rules of conduct. These sorts of complexities are best illustrated by comparing responses to a number of questions asked in the 1987 survey. We deal first with two features of the 'national morality' that stand out: first, the fact that people's judgements seem to be sharply affected by the size of the stakes (the monetary gain to be made); and second, that judgements depend on the sorts of people involved, and their perceived roles.

Larger and smaller stakes

The notion that right and wrong are moral absolutes is not borne out by our data. They are matters of degree, and the extent of censure which an action attracts depends in part on the size of the stakes involved. This is illustrated by two questions, in which respondents are asked to judge an employee who makes smaller or larger amounts of money by 'fiddling' his travel expenses.

	Amount fiddled	
	£50	£200
	%	%
Nothing wrong	5	2
A bit wrong	20	7
Wrong	52	38
Seriously wrong	15	36
Very seriously wrong	8	17

Formally, and legally, it is wrong for an employee to fiddle his travel expenses, whatever the amount. But in our respondents' eyes, fiddling seems to become more serious as the amount of money goes up. Perhaps this is not surprising in view of the tacit understanding in some organisations that exaggeration of expenses is acceptable, particularly by people whose work is satisfactory (Mars, 1982). In any event, although people often say that 'right is right, and wrong is wrong', they tend nonetheless to judge specific situations on a quite different basis.

Similar contrasts emerge in answers to two questions about exaggerated insurance claims:

> *In making an insurance claim, a man whose home has been burgled exaggerates the value of what was stolen by £100.*

> *In making an insurance claim, a man whose home has been flooded exaggerates the value of what was damaged by £500.*

	Exaggerate burglary claim by £100	Exaggerate flood claim by £500
	%	%
Nothing wrong	9	5
A bit wrong	24	15
Wrong	53	45
Seriously wrong	10	25
Very seriously wrong	3	10

Although these two items are not exactly comparable, since feelings about a flood might well differ from feelings about a burglary, the moral dimension is surely similar. Again, judgements are stricter when larger amounts are at stake. It is also worth noting in passing that respondents judge both these actions almost as harshly as they judge expenses-fiddling, even though the victim in these cases is more distant and impersonal (an insurance company rather than an employer).

Larger stakes may well increase the incentive or temptation to break established rules. But they also lead people to take breaches of the rules more seriously. Responses to another group of questions suggest that this is so even when rule-breaking has no direct 'victim', and when (unlike defrauding an insurance company or one's own employer) there is virtually no chance of being found out. We asked:

> Now, suppose you are alone in an empty street; no-one is likely to come by and see you. There is a £5 note lying on the pavement. Would you leave it there, pick it up and hand it in at the police station, or pick it up and pocket it?

Then we repeated the question, but made the sums involved "a £20 note" and finally "£100 in notes". Our results show that virtually no one would leave *any* sum of money lying in the street; but beyond that, a substantial measure of variation exists among respondents as to what they would do:

	Amount found		
	£5 note	£20 note	£100 in notes
	%	%	%
Leave it	1	1	1
Hand it in to the police	27	48	75
Pocket it	69	48	21

Apart from the unfavoured solution of leaving the money there, the conventionally 'honest' action in such circumstances would be to hand the money in. But the likelihood of this happening seems to depend, at least in part, on the sum of money involved. The motives underlying these responses can only be matters of conjecture. But the larger the sum of money involved, the more seriously breaching the 'honesty rule' is regarded – despite the greater temptation to succumb to dishonesty, and even when there is seemingly no risk of getting caught. Even so one person in five, finding £100 in notes on the pavement, would pocket the money. But from an American perspective, it is perhaps more surprising that three out of four say they would hand it in to the police!

Most people, it seems, regard pocketing a windfall fiver as an inconsequential breach of the 'honesty rule', while they see keeping a larger sum as a much more serious matter. But, as we shall see later, this is not the whole story; regarding things as wrong does not necessarily mean that people won't do them.

Gainers and losers

'Wrongness' is for most people apparently not just a property of an action in itself or of the size of the gain; the context is also crucial. One particularly important part of that context is the identity of the participants. Who gains and who loses? What sorts of roles do they occupy? Do they interact freely as equals, or are they unequal in status or power?

We were of course unable to examine all possible variations on this theme, but several interesting differences emerge when we compare responses to the following three hypothetical transactions, all involving the same amount of financial gain:

> *A company employee exaggerates his claims for travel expenses over a period and makes £200.*

> *A milkman slightly overcharges customers over a period and makes £200.*

> *A shop assistant sometimes rings up less on the till than the customer pays. He keeps the difference and over a period makes £200.*

	Employee fiddling expenses %	Milkman over- charging %	Shop assistant overcharging %
Nothing wrong	2	*	1
A bit wrong	7	4	3
Wrong	38	39	37
Seriously wrong	36	37	39
Very seriously wrong	17	21	21

The differences between these items are not very large, and all three actions attract the disapproval of the great majority of our respondents. But the responses do suggest that, even when the amounts at stake are equal, disapproval is greater when the victims are unsuspecting members of the public than when they are employers.

The importance of who does the taking, and who pays the price, is made even clearer by responses to the following three transactions, again involving the same financial gain:

> *A large firm of car dealers conceals the fact that a used car was in a serious accident. The price they can get increases by about £500.*

> *A man selling his car conceals the fact that it was in a serious accident. The price he can get increases by about £500.*

> *In making an insurance claim, a man whose home has been flooded exaggerates the value of what was damaged by £500.*

	Car dealers conceal accident %	Car owner conceals accident %	Householder over- claims on insurance %
Nothing wrong	*	2	5
A bit wrong	1	2	15
Wrong	14	19	45
Seriously wrong	30	30	25
Very seriously wrong	54	47	10

These differences are stark. When an ordinary individual breaks the rules and

profits at the expense of a distant, impersonal victim – the insurance company – our respondents tend to soften their judgements.* But when the ordinary individual is the *victim* of wrongdoing, it is apparently quite a different matter and it makes little difference who is doing the taking. Both the firm of dealers and the ordinary citizen who misrepresent the condition of their used cars are strongly condemned. Perhaps it is because £500 would be missed more by the average car-buyer than by an insurance company; or perhaps it is because this sort of misrepresentation could jeopardise safety and involves secrecy and deception – factors which themselves seem to contribute to the seriousness of wrongdoing (see Johnston, 1986; Chibnall and Saunders, 1977).

The identities of those involved in wrongdoing – both the perpetrator and the victim – are thus important in shaping the way in which we judge an action. People are more inclined to be tolerant of an 'ordinary person's' wrongdoing than of an organisation's – a result also found in the USA (Johnston, 1986). But they tend nonetheless to be strongly on the side of the victim in all cases, even when the victim is an impersonal organisation.

We put two other questions to respondents to examine the perceived roles of different *dramatis personae*. As already noted, we asked respondents in both 1984 and 1987 to judge the case of a man who pockets £5 extra change accidentally given to him in a big store – a question which produced consistent responses over time. To a degree which this American observer finds surprising, people in Britain regard keeping the extra change as wrong. But we also wanted to assess whether such a transaction might be viewed differently if it took place in a corner shop. So in 1987 we asked about both kinds of shop.

A man gives a £5 note for goods he is buying in a big store. *By mistake, he is given change for a £10 note. He notices but keeps the change.*

A man gives a £5 note for goods he is buying in a corner shop . . .

	Big store %	Corner shop %
Nothing wrong	8	4
A bit wrong	20	12
Wrong	58	64
Seriously wrong	10	15
Very seriously wrong	5	6

Keeping the extra change does not seem to be judged on an altogether different basis in the two different kinds of shop. Most people disapprove of this form of dishonesty rather strongly wherever it takes place. Even so, the judgement is harsher about the wrongdoing in the smaller shop. Perhaps it is because a £5 loss is thought to be less significant to a department store, or because the assistant there is unlikely to be someone we know or will encounter again. In a small shop, the person behind the counter and the customer are more likely to know each other, and the customer is hardly likely to think of the shop as a remote institution. In these circumstances we had expected that our respondents might feel more strongly about 'doing the honest thing' – and on balance they seem to.

---

*We should not however overstate that effect: four out of five people still judge the insurance fraud as at least "wrong", and one in three as "seriously" or "very seriously wrong".

Might you do it?

Social distance between 'taker' and victim thus seems to affect judgements of
right and wrong. It also extends to respondents' views as to what they themselves
might do if the situation came up. For four of our right and wrong items
– paying a plumber in cash to avoid VAT, exaggerating a burglary insurance
claim by £100, and keeping the extra change in a big store, and in a corner
shop – we asked respondents not only to judge the action in terms of the
degree of wrongness, but then added: *Might you do this if the situation came
up?* Results are reported below:

		Yes	No	(Don't know)
Might you ...				
... pay plumber in cash to avoid VAT?	%	67	27	5
... exaggerate burglary claim by £100?	%	26	69	4
... keep £5 extra change in a big store?	%	24	73	3
... keep £5 extra change in a corner shop?	%	10	87	1

These results must be interpreted with some caution. The four questions
intentionally involve different situations and participants; the stakes differ substantially as well. And as noted earlier, answers to survey questions do not
necessarily tell us what a person would actually do in these circumstances.
Even so, the data are intriguing if for no other reason than they tell us something
about how respondents see themselves, or would like to be seen. Many more
people – indeed the majority – say they would take an opportunity to avoid
VAT than say they would keep extra change. Although the VAT saving is
of unspecified size, our other results suggest that it is probably less 'wrong'
to defraud a government office in an indirect way than to defraud another
individual in a face-to-face encounter. There is also the bonus of a convergence
of interests with the plumber: two perpetrators and the (remote) victim may
make the Benthamite calculation easier to justify. But there is apparently more
than just money at stake: the proportions who say they would keep extra change
in a big store, and would defraud the insurance company of a much larger
amount, are virtually the same, while in the case of the corner shop, many
fewer people say they would keep the extra change.

So, in choosing how to respond to these sorts of moral dilemmas we do
not always 'do the honest thing' – but neither do we *simply* ask 'what's in
it for me?' Other factors – circumstantial and social – can alter, and at times
also override, our beliefs about right and wrong. For each of the four transactions
listed above, a sizeable number of respondents say both that the action itself
was wrong *and* that they would go ahead and do it anyway. For example,
some 58% of those who regard VAT-dodging as at least "a bit wrong" say
they would do it themselves, given the opportunity. Among those whose judgements of wrongdoing are harsher, the proportions saying they would do it
themselves tend to decline, but not precipitously. Even among those who judge
VAT-dodging as "seriously" or "very seriously" wrong, a quarter say they
might do it themselves. As for exaggerating an insurance claim by £100, or
keeping change in a large store, around one-fifth of those who judge such
behaviour as at least "a bit wrong" say they might do so themselves, while
the comparable proportion for a corner shop is only seven per cent. So the
correlation between what people consider to be wrong and what they consider

unthinkable for them to do is far from perfect. Full details are given in **Tables 1.1–4**.

Subgroup variations

If Britain's culture is characterised by a high degree of consensus on moral issues, the variations in judgements among different sections of the population are likely to be fairly modest. Uniformity would be reinforced by the nation's moderate geographical size, comparatively homogeneous population, and centralised political parties and news media. Such differences as do exist between subgroups should consequently be matters of degree and of nuance, rather than of sharp cultural divergence.

Apart from inter-generational differences (which we come to later) our data do indeed reveal a great deal of homogeneity in the population's judgements of right and wrong. Such homogeneity is reinforced by another factor: in answering most of our questions, people were applying general standards of morality, legality, or cultural norms, to *others* – indeed, to hypothetical others about whom they were told almost nothing.

But that was patently not the case when we asked people to say what they *themselves* might do in a given situation; and in these cases, subgroup variations are predictably much greater. People should know more, and presumably have stronger feelings, about themselves and their likely reactions and motives, than about others. It is not surprising therefore that many people end up applying different standards to others from those they apply to themselves.

We look first at variations in people's judgements of others.

Judging others

Some subgroup variations emerged from the 1984 data – notably by age. In the 1987 data too, age is the personal attribute most influential in forming judgements of right and wrong: in general, the older the respondent, the stricter the judgements. The following table illustrates the general pattern of age differences.

% of age group who sees "nothing wrong" in each action	Shopper pocketing extra change in store to make £5	Employee fiddling expenses to make £50	Householder exaggerating flood claim to make £500
18–24	25%	15%	18%
25–34	10%	7%	4%
35–54	4%	3%	3%
55+	2%	3%	1%

This general pattern is repeated for most other items as well, whether they involve large or small gains, and personal or more 'remote' transactions. Older

people may have learned their ethical standards in a more censorious era, and simply hold to those beliefs while general social standards have become more lax. Alternatively, individuals may adopt more and more demanding standards as they grow older. We would need comparable data from the same individuals over many years, however, before we could say which of the two explanations was the more correct.

On the strength of the figures above, we might plausibly conclude that individuals become stricter as they age. But there is another possible explanation. Perhaps as we grow older, our stake in society becomes stronger and we become more critical of those who put this stake at risk through deviant behaviour. But if this were true, we would expect income to affect judgements: the higher a person's income, the more censorious we would expect him or her to be. When we hold age constant, however, income differences do not predict answers in a uniform way. We still have much to learn, therefore, about the ways people form and change their judgements of right and wrong.

Analysis of responses by other personal characteristics, such as educational qualifications, social class, and sex reveals few differences. There are tendencies for those who belong to no religion at all or who are non-aligned politically to be less critical, but these relationships are not particularly strong, and can largely be explained by the lower than average age of people belonging to these two groups. **Table 1.5** gives further details.

Setting standards for oneself

When we asked people to say how they themselves might act in a given situation, differences between subgroups were more pronounced. As we have noted, we asked people for some transactions how they themselves might act 'if the situation came up'. For instance, might they keep the extra change in a big store or in a corner shop? Might they exaggerate the value of a burglary insurance claim by £100? Here is a summary of results from these three questions, showing the percentages of various groups who answered "Yes":

	% who might ...		
	... keep extra change in corner shop to make £5	... keep extra change in large store to make £5	... overclaim on insurance to make £100
Sex:			
Men	13%	28%	33%
Women	8%	20%	21%
Age:			
18–24	24%	49%	42%
25–34	16%	34%	36%
35–44	9%	24%	28%
45+	4%	12%	17%

Party identification:

Conservative	7%	20%	28%
Alliance	9%	22%	22%
Labour	14%	30%	27%
Non-aligned	17%	29%	32%

Religious attendance:

Once a week	1%	6%	12%
Once every 2 weeks/month	6%	15%	17%
Less often	8%	16%	23%
Never	12%	29%	30%
No religion	15%	33%	34%

As we can see, the contrasts are often quite sharp – much sharper than when judging others. This was expected. Beliefs about how one might act in a given situation oneself are shaped by many factors: by what other people would consider to be right or wrong, by the likelihood of being found out and the penalties that could follow, and of course, by how one perceives and evaluates the action.

In each of the three transactions above – keeping wrong change and overclaiming on insurance – there are discernible 'victims' of the wrongdoing. Moreover, there is always a chance, however slight, of detection and punishment. But what of cases where there is no discernible victim, and no real chance of detection? These sorts of circumstances are in a sense encounters with one's own conscience. What differences between subgroups do they reveal? As noted, we asked people what they would do if, while walking down a deserted street, they found money lying on the pavement. Would they leave it there, hand in the money at the police station, or pocket it? Here are the percentages who said they would pocket the various sums – £5, £20 and £100 – analysed by the same categories as above:

	% who said they would pocket the money		
	£5 note	**£20 note**	**£100 in notes**
Sex:			
Men	76%	59%	29%
Women	63%	38%	15%
Age:			
18–24	87%	69%	32%
25–34	81%	62%	32%
35–44	71%	53%	24%
45–54	69%	44%	17%
55–64	58%	34%	14%
65 +	45%	26%	8%
Party identification:			
Conservative	66%	45%	17%
Alliance	67%	43%	17%
Labour	75%	55%	28%
Non-aligned	65%	51%	34%

Religious attendance:

Once a week	39%	23%	11%
Once every 2 weeks/month	56%	34%	11%
Less often	68%	41%	16%
Never	71%	50%	19%
No religion	80%	62%	31%

As we have already seen, the larger the sum the greater is the reluctance to pocket it. But within that overall pattern, we find major variations among groups. Women, older persons, Conservative and Alliance supporters and those regularly attending religious services are all *less* likely to say they would keep the money. Increasing age continues to produce the familiar pattern of increasingly strict standards; but even among the youngest respondents, we should note that as the amount of cash increases, so does this group's apparent reluctance simply to keep the money.

These questions are perhaps the hardest of all to evaluate in terms of underlying motives, for what is at stake here is a vague kind of 'honesty rule', rather than legal sanctions, an employer's regulations, or mutual obligations in dealings with specific people or organisations. And the situation described is one involving little or no risk from breaking the 'rule', and no direct reward for following it. The results are tantalising indeed, for they suggest that behind the widely-shared conceptions of right and wrong, there is considerable diversity.

Conclusions

There have been numerous references in this chapter to British 'culture', but of course conceptions of right and wrong are just a small element of it. Values, knowledge and beliefs about society, feelings about its institutions and public figures, and levels of trust, alienation and allegiance are also parts of the culture, as are many other traits, characteristics and interests.

Still, conceptions of right and wrong are important, for they have much to do with the ways people respond to the events and changes around them. When prominent people (or institutions) break accepted social rules and standards, we might expect people to regard this general climate of wrongdoing as justification for breaching the rules themselves. And we might expect trust in institutions and 'deference' to suffer too. It is perhaps for this reason that Beer (1982) wrote, after a difficult two decades for Britain, "it is no exaggeration to speak of the decline in the civic culture as a 'collapse' ".

The data discussed in this chapter, however, do not support such a view, at least to the extent that conceptions of right and wrong illuminate more general trends in the culture. Judgements of the specific actions which are included in both the 1984 and 1987 surveys seem to have remained fairly constant. Results from new questions lend added support to Heath and Topf's assertion in *The 1987 Report* that "moral traditionalism" remains a firm feature of British life. And while sections of the population differ, sometimes to a marked degree, in how they feel they would act in ethically challenging situations, they still seem to agree upon the *relative* seriousness of a range of 'rule-breaking' behaviours. Moreover, there is even less variation between subgroups in the ways they respond to the actions of others – judgements which contribute to

the 'civic' aspect of the culture. Taken together, the evidence hardly portrays a breakdown in British social ethics. In *England, Your England*, Orwell wrote of that "strange mixture of reality and illusion, democracy and privilege, humbug and decency, the subtle network of compromises, by which the nation keeps itself in its familar shape". On our evidence, this description remains essentially true.

References

ALMOND, G.A. and VERBA, S., *The Civic Culture: Political Attitudes and Democracy in Five Nations*, Princeton University Press, Princeton (1963).

BEER, S.H., *Britain Against Itself: the Political Contradictions of Collectivism*, Faber and Faber, London (1982).

CHIBNALL, S. and SAUNDERS, P., 'Worlds Apart: Notes on the Social Reality of Corruption', *British Journal of Sociology*, vol. 28 (June 1977), pp. 138–154.

HEATH, A. and TOPF, R., 'Political Culture', in Jowell, R., Witherspoon, S., and Brook, L. (eds) *British Social Attitudes: the 1987 Report*, Gower, Aldershot (1987).

JESSOP, R.D., 'Civility and Traditionalism in English Political Culture', *British Journal of Political Science*, vol. 1 (1971), pp. 1–24.

JOHNSTON, M., 'Right and Wrong in American Politics', *Polity*, vol. 18 (1986), pp. 367–391.

JOHNSTON, M. and WOOD, D., 'Right and Wrong in Public and Private Life', in Jowell, R. and Witherspoon, S. (eds) *British Social Attitudes: the 1985 Report*, Gower, Aldershot (1985).

KAVANAGH, D., 'Political Culture in Great Britain: the Decline of the Civic Culture', in Almond G.A. and Verba, S. (eds), *The Civic Culture Revisited*, Little, Brown, Boston (1980).

MARS, G., *Cheats at Work: An Anthropology of Workplace Crime*, George Allen and Unwin, London (1982).

NORTON, P., *The British Polity*, Longmans, London and New York (1984).

Acknowledgements

I am very grateful to my 'co-conspirator' in SCPR, Douglas Wood, who helped design the module and devise the questions that gave rise to this chapter, and to the trustees of the Nuffield Foundation for providing funding for the question-naire module.

1.1–4 WHETHER RESPONDENT WOULD TAKE AN ACTION (A91–A94)
by judgement of how wrong it is

HOUSEHOLD PAYS PLUMBER IN CASH TO AVOID VAT (A91a,b)

	TOTAL	Nothing wrong	Wrong Total	Bit wrong	Wrong	Seriously/very seriously wrong
	%	%	%	%	%	%
Might you do it?						
Yes	67	93	58	82	46	25
No	27	3	36	12	46	72
Don't know/not answered	6	4	5	6	7	4
BASE: A RESPONDENTS						
Weighted	1391	362	1016	407	496	113
Unweighted	1437	361	1064	429	515	120

MAN POCKETS £5 CHANGE IN A CORNER SHOP (A93a,b)

	TOTAL	Nothing wrong	Wrong Total	Bit wrong	Wrong	Seriously/very seriously wrong
	%	%	%	%	%	%
Might you do it?						
Yes	10	88	7	22	6	2
No	87	10	91	72	92	97
Don't know/not answered	2	2	1	5	2	2
BASE: A RESPONDENTS						
Weighted	1391	56	1331	164	880	287
Unweighted	1437	55	1377	160	918	299

MAN POCKETS £5 CHANGE IN A BIG STORE (A92a,b)

	TOTAL	Nothing wrong	Wrong Total	Bit wrong	Wrong	Seriously/very seriously wrong
	%	%	%	%	%	%
Might you do it?						
Yes	24	91	18	46	12	3
No	73	7	79	47	85	97
Don't know/not answered	3	2	3	7	3	-
BASE: A RESPONDENTS						
Weighted	1391	106	1284	278	808	198
Unweighted	1437	101	1336	277	853	206

MAN OVERCLAIMS ON INSURANCE TO MAKE £100 (A94a,b)

	TOTAL	Nothing wrong	Wrong Total	Bit wrong	Wrong	Seriously/very seriously wrong
	%	%	%	%	%	%
Might you do it?						
Yes	26	85	21	53	10	3
No	69	8	75	41	85	96
Don't know/not answered	5	6	4	6	5	2
BASE: A RESPONDENTS						
Weighted	1391	126	1258	337	731	190
Unweighted	1437	120	1312	342	769	201

1.5 JUDGEMENT OF HOW WRONG AN ACTION IS (A90a–i) by age, party identification and religious attendance

	TOTAL	AGE				PARTY IDENTIFICATION				RELIGIOUS ATTENDANCE				
		18–24	25–34	35–44	45+	Conservative	Alliance	Labour	Non-aligned	Once a week	Once every two weeks/ month	Less often	Never	(No religion)
	%	%	%	%	%	%	%	%	%	%	%	%	%	%
EMPLOYEE FIDDLES EXPENSES TO MAKE £50														
Nothing wrong/a bit wrong	26	47	38	23	16	22	22	32	37	17	22	19	30	30
Seriously/very seriously wrong	23	13	14	27	27	25	25	19	18	29	27	23	24	18
EMPLOYEE FIDDLES EXPENSES TO MAKE £200														
Nothing wrong/a bit wrong	8	21	13	8	3	4	7	11	24	4	1	4	12	12
Seriously/very seriously wrong	53	40	46	56	58	56	60	48	38	54	63	57	53	48
PLUMBER EVADES TAX TO MAKE £500														
Nothing wrong/a bit wrong	22	38	27	24	14	21	18	24	28	13	11	18	27	25
Seriously/very seriously wrong	32	21	27	29	38	32	37	32	21	38	37	32	32	28
MILKMAN OVERCHARGES CUSTOMERS TO MAKE £200														
Nothing wrong/a bit wrong	4	6	5	4	3	3	2	7	9	2	1	2	6	6
Seriously/very seriously wrong	57	53	54	60	58	59	61	55	48	52	65	56	59	57
SHOP ASSISTANT RINGS UP LESS THAN CUSTOMERS PAY TO MAKE £200														
Nothing wrong/a bit wrong	4	11	5	3	1	2	2	6	12	2	1	2	5	5
Seriously/very seriously wrong	59	50	54	64	62	65	63	55	41	54	69	61	60	57
MAN CONCEALS WOODWORM IN FURNITURE TO MAKE £50														
Nothing wrong/a bit wrong	15	17	19	15	12	17	11	13	17	8	17	13	12	18
Seriously/very seriously wrong	36	29	31	33	41	37	39	37	28	43	44	34	40	32
CAR DEALERS CONCEAL ACCIDENT DAMAGE TO MAKE £500														
Nothing wrong/a bit wrong	2	4	4	1	*	1	*	2	6	1	-	1	1	3
Seriously/very seriously wrong	84	75	79	88	87	89	89	79	68	86	88	85	85	81
HOUSEHOLDER OVERCLAIMS ON INSURANCE FOR FLOOD DAMAGE TO MAKE £500														
Nothing wrong/a bit wrong	19	39	27	18	11	18	12	22	32	9	12	18	22	24
Seriously/very seriously wrong	35	20	28	33	43	37	39	33	24	46	45	35	37	27
MAN SELLING CAR CONCEALS ACCIDENT DAMAGE TO MAKE £500														
Nothing wrong/a bit wrong	4	12	6	2	2	3	2	4	14	1	5	2	5	5
Seriously/very seriously wrong	77	63	71	80	81	81	82	72	62	73	87	76	77	73
BASE: A RESPONDENTS														
Weighted	1391	197	256	282	654	525	260	383	120	157	109	293	339	485
Unweighted	1437	179	261	288	707	552	274	392	112	166	116	307	351	489

2 Education matters

Paul Flather*

In 1976 James Callaghan, then Prime Minister, initiated what he called a "Great Debate" on education. It was to range broadly over a number of issues including standards and quality, what children should be taught, teaching methods and training for jobs. But the debate never really took off, while public expenditure cuts did. It took another decade, another government and a lengthy teachers' dispute over pay, before education re-emerged as a key political issue.

With thousands of classes lost and tens of thousands of children being sent home regularly, education inevitably became one of the main issues in the months leading up to the 1987 general election. The teaching unions, embittered by what they saw as a deliberate rundown of the state education service and by the perceived decline in their own pay levels, maintained various forms of industrial action for three years between 1984 and 1987. The dispute was still in progress although nearing its end during the time of our fieldwork. It was bound to influence people's perceptions of the education service in general and of teachers in particular. And as the results in this chapter suggest, the public's perception was indeed of a service increasingly out of control.

The climate of general disenchantment – critically shared both by those using the service and those providing it – allowed, or perhaps forced, a return to the five key themes of the Great Debate: the curriculum, schools and jobs, standards and assessment, teachers, and the issue of who should control the system. These themes were all under discussion in the run-up to the general election during which the fieldwork for this survey was carried out. Education was indeed a key issue in the campaign, particularly after an apparent public disagreement – quickly patched up – between the Prime Minister and her Secretary of State for Education about one of the planks in the Conservative manifesto.

---

*Educational journalist, and currently Chair of the Further and Higher Education Sub-committee of the Inner London Education Authority.

With the Conservatives re-elected, a new Education Reform Bill was duly produced. Though described by the government as a "charter for better education",* many of its provisions were opposed by virtually the whole of the education establishment, which saw them as retrogressive and centralist. The Bill has five main aims: to provide for a new national curriculum of common subjects for all pupils, with testing at the ages of 7, 11 and 14; to delegate greater budgetary and managerial powers to individual schools and heads; to allow schools to enrol as many pupils as possible until they are full; to allow schools to 'opt out' of Local Education Authorities (LEAs) and be funded directly by the Department of Education and Science; and to establish selective-entry City Technology Colleges. There are also separate and important provisions for higher education.

This chapter reveals a number of shifts between 1985 and 1987 in attitudes towards educational issues, most of which seem to indicate a sense of frustration with the crumbling *status quo* and a feeling that something should be done. As will be seen, many of the solutions which our respondents supported were, if not identical to the government's proposals, at least closer to its position than to that of the opposition. For instance, the survey reveals an increase since 1985 in sympathy towards selection for secondary school entry, a decline in antipathy towards private schooling, and a clear switch in favour of a new nationally devised and controlled curriculum. The most obvious explanation for these shifts is that the government has been winning the arguments over educational policy. This may well turn out to be the case, but there are four other factors which must at least cast some doubt on such a conclusion.

First, the teachers' industrial action had, by the time of our survey, clearly lost whatever sympathy it might have had. As always in such disputes, the rights and wrongs of the case quickly get submerged, leaving only a sense of widespread irritation at both the disruption itself and the people causing it. With the teachers and the government at loggerheads, the government would be likely to benefit.

Second, the media had, in the two years between our 1985 and 1987 surveys, given unprecedented attention to what was dubbed "loony" behaviour by a small number of LEAs (mainly in London). Among the stories run by many tabloids were those about an ILEA 'library book' which portrayed a young girl living happily under the guardianship of two gay men, and the alleged attempt by three London Councils to re-write a 'racist' nursery rhyme, 'Baa baa black sheep!'. These and other reports were denied, or at least heavily qualified, and were ultimately shown to be either fabrications or gross exaggerations. But perhaps the damage had already been done.

Third, the shifts in educational attitudes coincided with a general increase (of around the same scale) in Conservative Party support between 1985 and 1987. So our survey may largely be charting changes in political sympathies rather than differences in educational attitudes over the period. These party political changes did not, however, have a similar impact on other issues, notably the health service, over the same period.

Fourth, the Conservatives were, through their manifesto and their high profile, articulating public concerns over education in a way that Labour was not. Labour's position was perhaps perceived as supporting a *status quo* which in

*DES Press Statement 343/87, 20 November 1987.

important ways was seen to be failing children. Whatever the explanation, the Conservatives seem to have been winning support for their position. When the next round of *British Social Attitudes* goes into the field, far-reaching changes in education will have come into effect. We shall then be able to see, in 1989 and in successive years, whether or not they meet with general public approval.

Most of the topic areas we discuss here have been covered in earlier years of the survey series. So on subjects such as resource allocation, attitudes to private schooling and selectivity, control of the curriculum and multi-cultural education, we can report on trends over the past five years. A series of new questions was, however, introduced in 1987 covering topics such as attitudes to examinations, the status of teachers and classroom behaviour. Some or all of these will be repeated in 1989 and beyond, and are only touched on in this chapter.

Resource allocation

As Chapter 6 shows, when asked to choose between programmes for extra government spending, only about a quarter (24%) of our respondents would give education first priority – exactly the same proportion as in 1983. The proportion of parents* of school-age children who would give highest priority to education spending is only a little higher, at 32%. But, as is apparent from Chapter 6, this probably reflects widespread worries about the condition of the NHS, rather than a lack of concern about education. Forced to make the choice, all main subgroups in our sample – except graduates – name health as their first priority for additional spending. Among those of different political persuasions, there is something approaching a consensus on this issue at least. Rather more than half the sample (55%) name education as first or second priority, next only to health (78%), and way ahead of housing (24%) and social security benefits (12%).

We then asked about priorities *within* education. The latest results show a sharp rise (eight per cent since 1983) in the proportion naming secondary schools as the first priority for extra spending; it is now the most popular choice. This rise has been largely at the expense of children with special needs:

	First priority for extra spending		
	1983	**1985**	**1987**
	%	%	%
Secondary schoolchildren	29	31	37
Less able children with special needs	32	34	28
Primary schoolchildren	16	13	15
Students at colleges, universities or polytechnics	9	9	9
Nursery or pre-school children	10	10	8

Parents of schoolchildren are even more likely to focus on secondary schools as the first priority. Paradoxically, this is especially so if they themselves have

---

*We called respondents with 5–18-year-olds in their households 'parents', although a very few may not be so.

a child currently attending a *private* school (54%), suggesting perhaps that concern for standards in state secondary schools may have prompted them to leave this sector. Equally, though, it might be that parents of children attending private schools, distanced from the 'problem', are more prone to exaggerate its seriousness, especially as to do so also justifies their own choice.

Improving schools

In 1983, and 1985 and again in 1987, we asked respondents which of a number of factors was the most important for improving education in primary schools and in secondary schools. Priorities have not changed much over the years. Little emphasis is placed on the content of the curriculum or on the involvement of parents in the running of schools. As the table below shows, priorities in primary schools are for more teachers and teaching resources: the most popular priority is smaller classes, followed by more resources for books and equipment and the development of the child's skills and interests. For secondary schools, the first priority remains training for jobs, followed by stricter discipline, neither associated with the 'traditional' aims of education:

	Most important factor for improving education in ...			
	primary schools		secondary schools	
	1983	1987	1983	1987
%	%	%	%	%
Smaller classes	31	29	10	9
More resources for books and equipment	15	21	10	14
Developing skills and interests	19	16	13	10
Stricter discipline	11	11	19	19
More discussion between parents and teachers	9	8	5	3
More training and preparation for jobs	1	2	27	25
Preparation for exams	1	2	7	9

The size of primary school classes clearly still concerns our respondents, especially parents of children of primary school age. Despite reductions in primary school rolls, average class sizes (now around 26) have hardly changed since 1983[1] (indeed they are now only expected to grow). It may well be that it is the frustrated *expectation* of smaller classes that has influenced responses.

We also see that, for both primary and secondary schools, there has been a significant increase since 1983 in the proportions opting for more "resources for books and equipment" as their first priority at the expense, for instance, of the development of skills and interests. Over the next few years, we shall see if this signals the start of the sort of discontent that is apparent in attitudes to the NHS – a feeling that the service as a whole is being underresourced.

Certainly, the shift in priorities towards spending on books and equipment (for both primary and secondary schools) is about the same among all types of respondents. Yet the amount spent per pupil on books and equipment by primary and secondary schools actually rose between 1983/84 and 1985/86, though admittedly not in line with the cost inflation of such items.[2] In any

event, the proportion of total local authority spending on books remained virtually constant at 0.7% from 1983 to 1986, and that on equipment increased only very slightly over the same period (DES, 1985, 1987). So the similarities with the NHS are striking: expenditure has not been reduced according to the published figures, but according to 'eye-witness' accounts resources nonetheless appear to be diminishing.

Our sample includes a small number of teachers,[3] and their priorities for primary and, particularly, secondary schools are in some instances sharply different from those of respondents as a whole. For instance, twice the proportion of teachers name reduction of class sizes in both primary and secondary schools as their first priority; far fewer believe that secondary schools should give top priority to providing training and preparation for jobs. It may well be that teachers' views on class sizes are filtering through to, and influencing, parents' anxieties on this issue.

	Most important factor for improving education in ...			
	... primary schools		... secondary schools	
	Total	Teachers	Total	Teachers
	%	%	%	%
Smaller classes	29	58	9	17
More resources for books and equipment	21	12	14	20
Developing skills and interests	16	7	10	12
Stricter discipline	11	5	19	15
More discussion between parents and teachers	8	2	3	2
More training and preparation for jobs	2	2	25	8
Teachers' pay	4	7	4	15

More teachers see the shortage of books and equipment as an issue in secondary (but not primary) schools; and, predictably, more see teachers' pay as an important issue. But given the bitterness of the pay dispute, it is surprising that so *few* teachers choose pay as their top priority. We return to this issue later in the chapter.

Clearly there is increasing concern about some aspects of the state education system, shared by parents, teachers and the public as a whole. Although government claims have been widely disputed, spending on education has remained constant in real terms from 1981 to 1986, despite a nine per cent drop in the school-going population (DES, 1985, 1987). In real terms, between 1981/82 and 1985/86, both primary and secondary schools appear to have benefited much more than has further and higher education (DES, 1987). The figures are now largely accepted, but expectations have been increasing (Crispin and Marslen-Wilson, 1985).[4] A decline in absolute pupil numbers also rarely translates into simple revenue savings. Most costs are fixed, and there are always 'extra' costs in any school closure or rationalisation. Meanwhile public perceptions appear to be that not enough savings (such as they are) find their way back into the system, to be used especially in reducing class sizes and providing books and equipment that teachers and pupils need.

State and private schooling

Between 1983 and 1985 our surveys indicated that the popularity of private schools was suffering. By 1987, however, it had been revived, with the change occurring among people of all ages and social classes, and among Conservative, Labour and Alliance identifiers alike. The rise in the proportion favouring *more* private schools is small: the main reason for the change is that more respondents than in 1985 – now around two-thirds – accept the *status quo*.

	1983	1985	1987
	%	%	%
There should be			
...more private schools	11	9	11
...about the same number as now	67	59	65
...fewer private schools	8	13	11
...no private schools at all	11	16	11

When asked further whether they thought state-maintained schools would benefit from fewer private schools, the proportion of respondents saying "yes" fell from 24% in 1985 to 20%, with a corresponding increase in the proportion saying "no". Again that change is common to all social groups and among identifiers with all parties. Attitudes of parents with school-age children are hardly distinguishable from those without. Not surprisingly Conservatives remain keenest by far on having more private schools, with hostility towards private schooling remaining concentrated among Labour identifiers (see **Table 2.1**).

This general, albeit small, decline in antipathy has coincided with an increase in the numbers receiving private education. Over seven per cent of the total school-aged population now attends private schools, compared with just under six per cent in 1980, and 18% of pupils aged 16 to 18 are now being educated in the private sector. This trend is continuing despite recent annual increases in fee levels of around 11%, well above inflation.* So a small but increasing number of parents are opting out of state education. Having benefited perhaps from various recent tax cuts, it may be that they are now choosing the form of education they have always preferred but could not previously afford. Or, for some parents, it may be that the perceived deficiencies in the state system have driven them away.

Selective education

A similar shift has also taken place in attitudes to selective schooling. In 1985 opinion was evenly divided between a selective secondary system and a comprehensive system. In 1987, a selective system of grammar and secondary modern schools has more support (52%) than a comprehensive system (41%). Again, parents and non-parents held very similar views, and – surprisingly perhaps – a minority (48%) of teachers prefer a comprehensive system. One explanation for the shift may be dissatisfaction with current secondary school standards.

---

*Independent Schools Information Service, *Annual Census* (1988).

Another may be a change in policy preference. The two are in any case closely related.

As we might expect, those respondents who had themselves been to an independent school are particularly keen on selectivity (64%), and if they have children at school in the private sector they are even more so; fewer than one in five of these parents favour a comprehensive system. We have seen that this group is especially concerned about under-resourced secondary schools; dislike of comprehensives is another issue which divides them sharply from other respondents. The shift since 1985 in favour of a selective secondary school system is somewhat greater among older than among younger respondents, and is particularly marked among Conservative identifiers. Alliance and Labour identifiers have changed little or not at all. This does not – as yet, anyway – suggest a widespread popular movement towards selectivity, but rather an erosion of the fragile support for comprehensives.

School examinations

Testing has emerged as a key issue in the current education debate, not least because of a growing feeling that too many youngsters are being 'failed' by the system and leaving without any qualifications. On our self-completion questionnaire, respondents were asked to say whether they thought formal exams were the best way of judging a pupil's ability. Opinion was divided. Forty-four per cent agree that they were, 17% are neutral, and 38% disagree.

In all about 40% of young people leave school nowadays without any qualifications to show prospective employers. It was concern for this "bottom 40%" that led to the introduction of the new GCSE examinations, designed to allow more pupils to leave school with some sort of qualification. After all, qualifications derived from examinations are essentially selection devices for jobs and advanced education; the more information available on each school-leaver the easier it is to place him or her appropriately.

On this issue there is no divergence of view between parents and teachers, nor are there any marked differences by social class, or between identifiers with the three main political party groupings. Surprisingly, even those with higher qualifications (that is, those more successful at passing exams), are indistinguishable from the rest on this issue (see **Table 2.2**).

But there is a very clear age trend, with only a quarter of the under-25s agreeing that exams were the best test of ability, compared with almost two-thirds of the over 64s (again see **Table 2.2**). Despite the fact that older people on the whole have fewer qualifications than younger people, it would appear that age lends enchantment to a system which, in some ways, failed the old more than it fails the young.

We also asked whether too much attention was given in secondary schools to exam results, compared with assessment of "everyday classroom work". Seventy per cent agree, 19% strongly. Again there is the expected age difference, with younger people tending to be more in favour of classwork assessment. But parents of children attending private schools differ markedly, being much more in favour of exams than the rest of the population are; even among this group, however, a majority agrees that exams have too much emphasis. Further details are given in **Table 2.2**.

We asked also about the related question of subject specialisation. The age at which specialisation occurs distinguishes British educational practice from other education systems, both in North America and Western Europe. It might therefore be expected that early specialisation had long been accepted as a cultural norm in Britain. Yet an astonishing 63% of respondents, spread over all demographic subgroups, believe that pupils specialise at too young an age. Had we foreseen this result, we would have added more questions on the subject to explore it further. We aim to put this right in future rounds of the survey series. Meanwhile, it remains an intriguing finding in its own right – and an issue not specifically addressed by the reforms of the Education Bill, although the introduction of the core curriculum may incidentally go some way towards combatting early specialisation. At the time of writing, education ministers have rejected the main recommendation of the Higginson Committee that 'A' Level syllabuses be broadened to discourage specialisation at too early an age. On this issue, as on several others, the government appears to be out of step with majority opinion.

A new compulsory system of national testing at the ages of 7, 11 and 14 has been included in the Education Bill – though, under pressure, the proposed tests are now universally being referred to as "diagnostic" rather than "competitive". This proposal has been criticised by some who see it as the first step to a return of the old 11 + examination, which divided pupils between grammar and secondary schools. Others believe that 7 and 11 are too young an age at which to judge any pupil. As we have seen, there is considerable doubt over even the current emphasis on school exams (even among those educated in, or sending their children to, private schools). A large majority of the population wants to see more emphasis on classroom assessment. So these provisions of the Education Bill do not seem to conform with public priorities. It remains to be seen whether the proposed tests will in fact generate the same sorts of concern that the present examination system apparently does.

Control of the curriculum

In 1985, around half (52%) of respondents thought that local education authorities should decide what is taught in schools, with 40% saying that central government should decide. In 1987, opinion had become almost evenly divided, with 48% expressing support for local control and 47% for central control. The shift in attitude, as with some other key findings, is found almost entirely among Conservative identifiers, suggesting once again that this group – stimulated perhaps by the government's own position on this issue – is becoming distanced from the rest of the population, rather than that any widespread movement in attitudes has taken place.

Control of the curriculum by party identification, 1985–7

	Conservative		Alliance		Labour	
	1985	1987	1985	1987	1985	1987
	%	%	%	%	%	%
Should be decided by:						
Local education authority	42	34	49	51	61	62
Central government	53	62	45	44	32	31
Other answer/don't know/						
not answered	5	4	6	5	7	6

The issue has always been polarised by party identification. Now it is more so. But fieldwork on the survey coincided with a fairly widely publicised debate about the likely benefits of a national curriculum and some very negative media coverage of Labour local authorities and their anti-racist or gay rights policies. All parties, and most educationalists, seemed to agree that some new form of national initiative was needed, though while the government argued for a fairly rigid national curriculum with "core subjects", originally taking up some 90% of class time, critics wanted guidelines which would leave LEAs and teachers the flexibility to take account of special local needs and circumstances. As the government's proposals have been passing through Parliament they have been made more flexible, leaving about 70% of class time to be taken up by core subjects. Controversy continues over what those subjects ought to be.

While parents as a whole are evenly divided on who should control the curriculum, those who had been to a private school – or are sending their children to one – are emphatically in favour of central government control (see **Table 2.3**). It is all the more ironic then that the core curriculum reforms will not apply to private schools. Interestingly, by a small majority (53%), teachers too favour a centrally run curriculum, though our question was probably too blunt to pick up the nuances of teachers' views on such a complex subject. We shall continue to monitor trends in future years, when the content of the new national core curriculum is known.

Teachers and classroom behaviour

Responses to questions asked for the first time in 1987 showed that 71% of respondents think parents, and 88% think pupils, have less respect for teachers than they did ten years ago. Without comparable data from earlier years we cannot say how far these startling figures are an indictment of the legacy of the teachers' dispute. But it is clear from our data that, by the third year of the national dispute, and the classroom disruption it brought, the teachers had little sympathy. For instance, three in five respondents think that teachers are less dedicated to their jobs than they were ten years ago. Even around half of our (small) sample of teachers themselves seem to accept a decline in dedication within the profession. Moreover, parents of secondary school age children are especially likely to regard teachers as less dedicated than in the past. The problem is apparently not confined to the state sector; parents whose children are attending private schools are even more inclined to hold this view than those with children in state schools. Full details are given in **Table 2.4**.

But there is more to the story than this. If respect for teachers and their dedication to their jobs are thought to have declined, so too – in our respondents' opinion – have standards of classroom behaviour. The tendency to believe that things were better in the past is well known, but even so the figures are staggering: 86% think classroom behaviour is worse than it was ten years ago, with most believing it to be *much* worse now. This view of deteriorating behaviour is broadly held with equal force by all age groups, parents and non-parents, private sector and state sector parents. Moreover, on this issue there are no divisions along party political lines.

It is not surprising then that 62% of respondents also think that the job

of a state secondary school teacher is more difficult now than it used to be. This view – predictably, perhaps – is shared by teachers themselves. If teachers' dedication is perceived to have declined, here then is a possible cause: their jobs are perceived to be much more fraught than in the past.

In this matter, our respondents are echoing anxiety that is already deep, and indeed several recent surveys have indicated that worries may be well-founded. For example, a poll carried out by NOP for the National Union of Teachers showed that one in two secondary, and one in three primary, school-teachers thought that indiscipline was a regular or frequent classroom problem.[5] In response to this problem, and to the rising concern about it, the Home Office has set up the Elton Enquiry which is to examine and report back on violence in schools by the end of 1988.

Teachers' pay

Figures supplied by the National Union of Teachers Research Unit show that since 1974 teachers' pay has declined by 16% against average earnings and by 23% against other salaries, even though teachers' pay has risen by eight per cent more than the Retail Price Index in that same period.* In any event, most of our respondents think that teachers are better paid now than they were ten years ago: 31% think that they are much better paid, a further 25% that they are a little better paid. Only 24% think that they are worse off. Moreover, as we have already seen, teachers' pay has not been seen by the public – since 1983 at any rate – as a priority for extra education spending.

A majority of the teachers in our sample take a different view, with 66% saying pay was worse or much worse now. They remain discontented, although strike action is not at present being considered. Overall, however, our data suggest a failure on the part of the teaching unions to generate any real support among the public in general – or even among parents – for their cause. This is despite the fact that sympathy for their general difficulties (for instance, with classroom behaviour) is very high.

Multi-cultural education

There has been hardly any shift in attitudes towards multi-cultural education over the last four years. The majority supports cultural diversity but opposes cultural separatism. They feel that multi-cultural teaching is a good thing, as long as everyone gets it; they do not like special provision for minorities nearly so much, except for those sorts of provision, such as English language teaching, which reduce rather than emphasise differences. The question, asked on the self-completion supplement, was posed like this:

> There has been a lot of debate among teachers about how British schools should cater for children whose parents come from other countries and cultures. Do you think in general that schools with many such children should . . .

---

*Following the pay deal imposed in 1987, the average teacher's pay at the time of our survey was £12 237 p.a.

	% agreeing	
	1983	**1987**
. . . provide special classes in English if required?	77%	80%
. . . teach *all* children about the history and culture of these countries?	74%	74%
. . . allow those for whom it is important to wear traditional dress at school?	43%	45%
. . . teach children (from different backgrounds) about the history and culture of their parents' countries of origin?	40%	40%
. . . provide separate religious instruction if their parents request it?	32%	37%
. . . allow these children to study their mother tongue in school hours?	16%	17%

So we see that while 58% of respondents reject the idea that pupils from ethnic minority groups alone should be taught about the history and culture of their parents' country of origin, about three-quarters approve the idea that *all* children in schools should be taught about these countries. There is no significant divergence among parents or by party allegiance. On these issues, our respondents' views largely coincide with the recommendations of the Swann Report (1983) which looked at achievement levels of pupils from ethnic minorities. Any movement since 1983 has been towards a more liberal stance, for example in allowing separate religious instruction. In any event, although many people remain opposed to some of the policies now being adopted in a range of LEAs from Inner London to the shire counties, our time-series data show that there has been no backlash against cultural diversity in the past few years. The Macdonald Enquiry, commissioned by Manchester City Council to investigate the apparent failure of the particular anti-racist policies in Burnage High School, had not, of course, reported at the time of our survey.

It should be noted that teachers are much more liberal on these issues than is the population at large. Almost all support extra English language classes if needed, 75% are in favour of allowing traditional dress, 56% are in favour of teaching pupils the history of their parents' countries, and 41% support mother-tongue teaching in school hours.

The transition from school to work

There is a strong all-round feeling that schools could do better in preparing children for the world of work. More than two-thirds feel that Britain's schools fail to teach the kind of skills that British industry needs, and that state secondary schools fail to prepare young people for work. This feeling is even stronger among those in non-manual occupations and among parents of secondary school age children. All this may well reflect a number of reported claims by employers that schools and colleges are not providing school leavers and students with the necessary skills. Certainly there is no consensus of opinion among the public about whether the problem is now more or less serious than it was ten years ago. Overall, there appears to be a sort of resigned acceptance that school and work are far apart and that the gap seems more or less unbridgeable. In any event, there is just as little consensus about the value of government schemes as a bridge. As many think they are good as think they are counter-productive.

Nonetheless, a majority (57%) of respondents consider that state secondary schools perform well in teaching so-called basic skills (like reading, writing and maths), though significantly teachers are generally rather more sceptical. Again, and not unexpectedly here, there are marked age differences, with only 37% of the over 64s feeling such skills are taught well, compared with 78% of the under 25s. So those closest to the education system seem to be most appreciative of its ability to communicate basic skills to schoolchildren. Labour identifiers (66%) are more positive than Alliance identifiers (54%) and Conservatives (49%). Once again, Conservative identifiers seem to be responding more than other groups in the population to the government's emphasis on supposed failings within this area of the curriculum. Full details are shown in **Table 2.3.**

Higher education

There has been a steady shift in favour of increasing opportunities for young people to go on to higher education. In 1983 44% agreed, in 1985 49%, and in 1987 53%, that opportunities for higher education should be increased. All the main population subgroups share this view. Not surprisingly, parents of secondary school children are the keenest.

British universities continue to have to limit student intake in the face of financial restrictions. Indeed, enrolment of 18–24-year-olds in higher education is lower in the UK than in any other OECD country (DES, 1987). The rising support shown by our data for an increase in university and polytechnic places may reflect anxieties expressed in many quarters that Britain may soon be faced both with a graduate shortage and a labour force whose skills fail to match those of our main trading competitors. But the fact that parents are apparently more worried than others suggests that the cause of the anxiety is that their own children will be 'locked out' of the system.

Identifiers with all three main political groupings have increased their support for opportunities in higher education since 1983, though the rise is steepest among Alliance identifiers.

	1983	1987
% saying that opportunities for higher education should be increased		
Party identification:		
Conservative	38%	45%
Alliance	44%	56%
Labour	54%	61%

Despite various efforts by the government since 1980 to promote the idea of a loans system rather than grants for students, the public appears to have moved even more in favour of grants – up from 57% in 1983 to 65% in 1987. Teachers are particularly keen on grants (73%), as are parents of school-children (72%). Again this is an issue that divides those of different party political allegiance. Although Conservative identifiers (least enthusiastic about grants in 1983) have increased their support slightly, the gap between them and Labour and Alliance identifiers in 1987 is wider than ever.

% saying that students should get grants	1983	1987
Party identification:		
Conservative	51%	56%
Alliance	58%	68%
Labour	66%	77%

A marked preference for grants comes, not surprisingly, from the 'traditional student age' sector (with 74% of 18–34-year-olds preferring them). Among the older age groups support for grants dips, with only 45% of those aged over 64 preferring loans.

The case for maintaining the current grants system, on the basis of equal opportunities for all, has been well put in a recent report by the National Union of Students (1985). The case against grants is based both on the high cost of grants and the notion that higher education is a privilege which ought to be paid for by those who benefit. Moreover, the UK is far more generous than other OECD countries in terms of student support.

Our survey did not deal with attitudes towards a mixed system of grants and loans, which the government now appears to favour. Proposals expected in summer 1988 were to contain safeguards for those on low incomes and for those studying less vocational subjects, the two main concerns of critics of 'loans-only' schemes. These proposals have now again been postponed. We hope to gauge attitudes towards this issue in future rounds of the series.

Conclusions

We have shown that there are widespread worries about a number of aspects of state education. Among the most pressing are large class sizes (in both primary and secondary schools), shortages of books and equipment, classroom behaviour in secondary schools, early specialisation, and the respect for and commitment of teachers. There is some concern too that schools are not doing enough to prepare children for work, and a growing feeling that there are insufficient opportunities for pupils to go on to higher education. Many of these concerns are expressed, with even greater force, by parents and teachers too.

This unease about education has not, however, led to any increased antagonism towards private education – if anything, the reverse seems to be true. There is also greater support than before for a selective secondary school system, and a clear trend in favour of a national curriculum. On all these issues, party political allegiance clearly influences attitudes, with Conservative identifiers more sharply divided from Labour and Alliance than they used to be and more influenced, it seems, by the government's own agenda.

The provisions in the new Education Bill may go some way to alleviate public anxieties about certain parts of the system. But most of the measures do not seem to address the most widespread anxieties, and this could turn out to be embarrassing for the government. Future reports in this series will attempt to monitor reactions to at least some of the changes as they come into effect.

Notes

1. In 1983 the average number of children in a state primary school class was 25.1, and in 1986 it was 25.9. In state secondary schools, the average class size was 24.8 in 1983, rising to 25.5 in 1986 (DES, 1985, 1987).
2. In 1983–84, *per capita* expenditure on books and equipment in primary schools was £23, and in secondary schools £39; the equivalent figures in 1985–86 were £25 and £45 (DES, 1985, 1987).
3. We have defined 'teachers' as those respondents who are currently in, or who have retired from, occupation groups with codes 031, 032, 033, 034 and 053 (teachers at universities, further education establishments and primary and secondary schools; those teaching occupational skills at evening institutes and so on). For full details see *Classification of Occupations 1980*, OPCS (1980), especially Coding Index, p. 4, note (7).
4. A detailed study by Crispin and Marslen-Wilson (1985) has also shown that although the amount spent on each pupil has increased over the last few years, so have real costs per pupil. Also they show that the demand per pupil in terms of, for example, curricula development, special needs and the knock-on effects of high youth unemployment have absorbed much of the extra resources – at the expense mainly of supplies of books and equipment and of the upkeep of school buildings. See also David (1988).
5. Another survey in 15 LEAs, carried out on behalf of the National Association of Head Teachers and published in June 1988, found that teachers face one assault every four minutes; and overall 18,000 acts of violence annually, with 30,000 children suspended each year for bad behaviour. However, the findings of other recent surveys have been disputed by bodies such as the Children's Legal Centre, and by the National Children's Bureau in its evidence to the Elton Enquiry.

References

CRISPIN, A. and MARSLEN-WILSON, F., *Changes in Education Provision, 1980–1985*, Association of Metropolitan Authorities, London (1985).

DAVID, R., 'The Funding of Education', in Morris, M. and Griggs, C. (eds), *Education – the wasted years? 1973–1986*, Falmer, London (1988).

DES, *Statistical Bulletins*, 14/85 (December 1985); 14/87 (December 1987).

Education for All. The Report of the Committee of Enquiry into Education of Children from Ethnic Minority Groups, ['The Swann Report'], Cmnd 9453, HMSO, London (1983).

NATIONAL UNION OF STUDENTS, *Student Loans – the Costs and Consequences*, NUS, London (September 1985).

Acknowledgement

We have depended heavily on the assistance of Harvey Goldstein who not only helped to think up the initial questions but also contributed substantially to early drafts of this chapter. The editors and I are very grateful for his advice and help.

2.1 ATTITUDES TOWARDS PRIVATE EDUCATION (Q73a, b) by party identification within year (1983, 1985, 1987)

	1983				1985				1987			
	TOTAL	PARTY IDENTIFICATION			TOTAL	PARTY IDENTIFICATION			TOTAL	PARTY IDENTIFICATION		
		Conservative	Alliance	Labour		Conservative	Alliance	Labour		Conservative	Alliance	Labour
	%	%	%	%	%	%	%	%	%	%	%	%
THERE SHOULD BE ...												
... more private schools	11	19	7	4	9	17	7	4	11	19	4	5
... about the same number as now	67	73	74	59	59	71	63	48	65	69	74	53
... fewer private schools	8	3	9	14	13	5	15	20	11	5	9	19
... no private schools at all	11	4	8	20	16	6	12	25	11	3	9	21
Other answer/don't know/not answered	2	2	2	2	3	2	3	3	3	3	3	2
IF THERE WERE FEWER PRIVATE SCHOOLS IN BRITAIN TODAY ...												
... state schools would benefit	18	12	18	25	24	13	24	34	20	11	21	32
... state schools would suffer	18	26	16	12	12	19	13	6	16	23	13	10
... it would make no difference	59	59	63	57	58	65	58	54	60	63	63	53
Other answer/don't know/not answered	4	3	2	5	6	3	4	7	5	3	3	6
BASES: ALL RESPONDENTS IN EACH YEAR												
Weighted	1719	664	252	565	1769	545	311	645	2766	1051	517	804
Unweighted	1761	676	258	584	1804	564	317	649	2847	1095	533	824

2.2 ATTITUDES TOWARDS SCHOOL EXAMINATIONS (A203a, d) by age, highest educational qualification obtained and private schooling

	TOTAL	AGE						HIGHEST QUALIFICATION OBTAINED				PRIVATE SCHOOLING	
		18-24	25-34	35-44	45-54	55-64	65+	Degree	Pro-fessional	'A' level/ 'O' level/ CSE	Foreign/ Other/ None	Respondent attended private school	Respondent's child(ren) at private school
	%	%	%	%	%	%	%	%	%	%	%	%	%
FORMAL EXAMS ARE THE BEST WAY OF JUDGING THE ABILITY OF PUPILS													
Agree strongly	9	4	6	9	8	10	14	9	8	8	10	11	13
Agree	36	21	28	35	38	46	49	34	39	29	42	37	31
Neither agree nor disagree	17	13	19	16	18	17	18	12	13	16	20	12	19
Disagree	31	45	40	30	31	23	16	36	36	38	22	30	23
Disagree strongly	7	17	6	9	4	3	1	10	4	9	4	8	14
Don't know/not answered	1	1	*	-	1	1	3	1	*	-	2	1	-
SO MUCH ATTENTION IS GIVEN TO EXAM RESULTS THAT A PUPIL'S EVERYDAY CLASSROOM WORK COUNTS FOR TOO LITTLE													
Agree strongly	19	26	21	17	13	19	16	18	17	20	18	16	17
Agree	52	53	53	49	58	49	46	39	47	54	53	44	36
Neither agree nor disagree	12	10	13	10	10	15	16	18	11	10	14	12	13
Disagree	15	11	11	21	16	16	15	24	22	15	12	24	35
Disagree strongly	1	-	2	2	2	1	2	-	3	1	1	2	-
Don't know/not answered	1	-	-	-	-	-	4	-	1	-	1	2	-
BASE: A RESPONDENTS													
Weighted	*1243*	*174*	*238*	*252*	*202*	*181*	*195*	*98*	*169*	*476*	*500*	*160*	*48*
Unweighted	*1281*	*158*	*241*	*254*	*223*	*195*	*207*	*102*	*177*	*485*	*514*	*164*	*51*

2.3 CONTROL OF THE CURRICULUM AND TEACHING OF BASIC SKILLS (Q71, A204b) by age, party identification, whether or not schoolchild(ren) in household and private schooling

	TOTAL	AGE						PARTY IDENTIFICATION				SCHOOLCHILD(REN)		PRIVATE SCHOOLING	
		18-24	25-34	35-44	45-54	55-64	65+	Conservative	Alliance	Labour	Non-aligned	In house-hold	Not in household	Respondent attended private school	Respondent's child(ren) at private school
	%	%	%	%	%	%	%	%	%	%	%	%	%	%	%
DO YOU THINK WHAT IS TAUGHT IN SCHOOLS SHOULD BE UP TO ...															
... the local education authority to decide	48	48	49	43	49	51	49	34	51	62	50	48	48	36	28
or - should central government have the final say?	47	47	46	53	48	43	42	62	44	31	38	47	46	58	67
Other answer/don't know/not answered	6	5	6	4	4	7	9	4	5	6	13	5	6	6	4
BASE: ALL RESPONDENTS Weighted	2766	371	532	556	424	425	454	1051	517	804	208	842	1323	359	113
Unweighted	2847	347	538	564	460	457	482	1095	533	824	205	860	1987	364	120
HOW WELL DO YOU THINK STATE SECONDARY SCHOOLS NOWADAYS TEACH YOUNG PEOPLE BASIC SKILLS, SUCH AS READING, WRITING AND MATHS?															
Very well	10	19	11	12	7	7	7	9	10	15	11	10	10	7	8
Quite well	46	59	58	47	45	37	30	40	45	51	55	54	43	34	36
Not very well	31	14	24	31	36	41	42	36	38	26	16	28	33	42	42
Not at all well	11	8	7	9	12	15	17	14	7	7	16	6	13	17	14
Don't know/not answered	1	-	*	*	*	1	3	1	*	1	2	1	1	-	-
BASE: A RESPONDENTS Weighted	1243	174	238	252	202	181	195	483	242	331	100	393	851	160	48
Unweighted	1281	158	241	254	223	195	207	505	254	337	93	394	886	164	51

2.4 ATTITUDES TOWARDS TEACHERS IN STATE SECONDARY SCHOOLS (A205d, e, f) by age, whether or not schoolchild(ren) in household, private schooling, and whether or not teaching professional

	TOTAL	AGE						SCHOOLCHILD(REN)		PRIVATE SCHOOLING		RESPONDENT IS ...	
		18-24	25-34	35-44	45-54	55-64	65+	In house-hold	Not in household	Respondent attended private school	Respondent's child(ren) at private school	teaching profess-ional	not teaching pro-fessional
	%	%	%	%	%	%	%	%	%	%	%	%	%
TEACHERS IN STATE SECONDARY SCHOOLS													
Compared with ten years ago, <u>parents</u> have ...													
... much more respect for them	1	-	3	1	1	2	1	1	1	1	(-)	-	1
... a little more respect	4	6	4	4	2	3	4	4	4	4	(2)	2	4
... about the same amount	23	28	20	25	18	24	22	24	22	16	(20)	19	23
... a little less respect	41	44	45	33	43	42	42	41	41	41	(46)	45	41
... much less respect for them	30	21	26	37	36	28	29	28	31	38	(32)	34	30
(Don't know/not answered)	1	1	*	1	-	1	1	1	1	1	(-)	-	1
Compared with ten years ago, <u>pupils</u> have ...													
... much more respect for them	*	-	*	-	-	2	-	-	*	-	(-)	-	*
... a little more respect	2	5	2	1	1	2	1	2	2	2	(-)	-	2
... about the same amount	9	13	9	12	7	9	7	10	9	5	(12)	11	9
... a little less respect	32	34	36	29	32	30	30	32	31	34	(35)	38	31
... much less respect for them	56	48	52	58	60	57	60	55	56	59	(52)	52	56
(Don't know/not answered)	1	1	*	*	-	1	2	1	1	-	(-)	-	1
Compared with ten years ago, <u>teachers</u> are ...													
... much more dedicated to their jobs	1	*	1	1	*	4	2	2	1	1	(-)	1	1
... a little more dedicated	4	8	5	3	2	3	5	4	5	4	(-)	9	4
... about the same	33	42	43	30	30	28	26	32	34	24	(30)	39	33
... a little less dedicated	36	35	34	37	38	39	33	37	35	43	(43)	32	36
... much less dedicated to their jobs	24	15	16	28	29	26	31	25	24	28	(27)	19	25
(Don't know/not answered)	1	*	*	1	-	1	3	1	1	1	(-)	-	1
BASE: A RESPONDENTS													
Weighted	1243	174	238	252	202	181	195	393	851	160	(48)	59	1158
Unweighted	1281	158	241	254	223	195	207	394	886	164	(48)	67	1183

3 Trends in permissiveness

*Stephen Harding**

"A morality is, at the very least, the regulation of the taking of life and the regulation of sexual relations, and it also includes rules of distributive justice, family duties, almost always duties of friendship, also rights and duties in respect of money and property" (Hampshire, 1978).

Over the last five years the *British Social Attitudes* series has included a number of questions on moral issues, all of which fall well within this definition. In this chapter we re-examine the first two aspects of morality that Hampshire listed; other areas are discussed elsewhere in this Report (see especially Chapter 1) or have been covered in earlier reports in this series.

There is much survey evidence to suggest that respondents tend to treat most issues of sexuality in a conceptually similar manner. Individuals who are censorious of extra-marital sex or divorce, for example, tend also to be critical of homosexuality and pornography. As we shall see, these differences vary predictably within the population, with older people, and those with religious commitment, for example, being more censorious than average. Cross-nationally, over a range of such 'personal–sexual' issues, the British emerge as close to the West European average: more censorious than the Danes, French and Dutch, less so than the Irish (in both North and South), Italians and Spaniards (Harding and Phillips, 1986).

What makes monitoring issues like these so pertinent to Britain is that there have been enormous changes, both in individual behaviour and in legislation over the past few decades. Divorce, abortion, homosexuality, the death penalty, *in vitro* fertilisation, surrogate motherhood, censorship, are all issues which are firmly on the public agenda and which have been the subject of legislative reform. The 1960s and early 1970s in particular saw a period of extensive liberalising reforms, seen by some as eroding traditional values and legitimising a

---

*Senior Lecturer in Psychology, Nene College, Northampton.

'permissive Britain' (see Davies, 1975, 1980). Since then, debate on many of these moral issues has remained vigorous, with recent parliamentary attention directed towards curbing or qualifying previous liberalising measures. The most recent instances are Clause 28 of the Local Government Act which limits councils' activities in 'promoting homosexuality', and a private member's bill which sought, but failed, to reduce the number of weeks during which abortions would be legal. We examine here whether or not such moves are in line with public attitudes on moral issues, and to what extent they reflect broader ideological influences.

Sexual relationships

Attitudes towards pre-marital, extra-marital and homosexual relationships have been investigated using a set of questions (similar to the ones used in the US General Social Survey). Respondents are given a choice of five options ranging from "not wrong at all" to "always wrong" for each sort of relationship.

In *The 1986 Report* (Chapter 9), we reported that responses in respect of pre- and extra-marital sexual relationships had remained largely unchanged between 1983 and 1985, but that there had been an increase in the proportion saying that *homosexual* relationships were "always" or "mostly" wrong (Airey and Brook in *The 1986 Report*). Two years later our data reveal continued stability in attitudes towards sex before marriage, but a sharp increase in the proportion censuring sex outside marriage and a further climb in the proportion critical of homosexuality.

	1983	1985	1987
	%	%	%
"Always" or "mostly" wrong			
Pre-marital sexual relationships	28	23	25
Extra-marital sexual relationships*	83	82	88
Homosexual relationships	62	69	74

*The item wording in 1983 referred to husband and wife separately. The answers were almost identical, so averaged responses are given here.

Pre-marital sex is viewed with the greatest leniency by the age group most likely to participate in it. Thus, 79% of those aged 18–24 regard pre-marital sex as "rarely wrong" or "not wrong at all", compared with only 22% of the over 64s. This is a striking difference, made more so by the fact that extra-marital sex is regarded in an altogether stricter light, by all age groups alike, with almost 90% of the sample (and including over 80% of the 18–24 age group) regarding it as 'always' or 'mostly' wrong. We must be careful, however, to distinguish attitudes from behaviour. Disapproval of a certain kind of behaviour does not necessarily mean that people will refrain from it (see Chapter 1); adultery is still one of the most widely cited grounds for divorce in Britain. In any event, censoriousness of extra-marital sex seems to be increasing.

But it is in attitudes to homosexual relationships that the most marked shift has occurred, with a steady increase in censoriousness since 1983. Then 62% of the population took the view that sexual relations between two adults of the same sex were 'always' or 'mostly' wrong; by 1987 the proportion had risen to 74%. In *The 1986 Report*, we speculated that the increase in censoriousness towards homosexuality could have been related to a rapidly rising concern

about AIDS, because of its association in the public's consciousness with the gay community. This is a theme that we return to in Chapter 5 of this Report, where we show in which sections of the population the main changes have occurred.

As we have noted, responses to our questions allow comparison with those given on the US General Social Survey (GSS). Data from the United States running back to 1973 reveal a liberalisation of attitudes towards sexual relationships during the ten-year period up to 1982. Since then little change has occurred. The views of Americans on sexual *mores* started off somewhat more censorious than those of the British, but have remained virtually constant during the last five years. Now, except on pre-marital sex, British and American attitudes are similar:

% saying "always"/"mostly"* wrong	1983	1984	1985	1986	1987
Pre-marital relations:					
US	36%		36%	36%	
Britain	28%	27%	23%		25%
Extra-marital relations:					
US		87%	87%		89%
Britain	83%	85%	82%		88%
Homosexual relations:					
US		75%	77%		78%
Britain	62%	67%	69%		74%

*In America, "almost always". *Source: GSS Cumulative Codebook 1972-1987*. Not all the questions were asked every year.

In *The 6th Report* we shall show whether or not these trends have continued.

Pornography

Attitudes towards pornography have been investigated once before in the *British Social Attitudes* series, in 1983. Since then efforts have been made to restrict the availability of sexually explicit material. In 1986, and again in 1987, private members' bills were introduced (both without success) to bring television programmes within the scope of the Obscene Publications Act, and another MP sought to bring in legislation banning 'page 3' photographs in tabloid newspapers. Now the government has set up a new Broadcasting Standards Council which, at the time of writing, is pressing for powers to preview television programmes bought from abroad.

In 1983, by a small majority (52%), our respondents thought that pornographic magazines and films should be available, but only in special adult shops and not on public display. Then only one-third favoured an outright ban, and almost half as many favoured less restriction than already exists. Since then, there has been a clear shift in favour of an outright ban, in preference to special adult shops. From being a poor second choice in 1983, an outright ban is now almost as popular as adult shops.

Views on the availability of pornographic magazines and films

	1983	1987
	%	%
They should be ...		
... banned altogether	33	38
... available in special adult shops but not displayed to the public	52	42
... available in special adult shops with public display permitted	7	8
... available in any shop for sale to adults only	7	8
... available in any shop for sale to anyone	1	1

Less censorious than average are those without any religious affiliation and those in Social Classes I and II (professional and managerial). But as in 1983, it is age that produces the most striking variations in attitude, with only 16% of 18–24-year-olds favouring an outright ban, compared with 72% of those aged 65 and over. On this issue, as on all sexual matters (except homosexuality), men tend to be more liberal than women, although the movement towards increased censoriousness of pornography has served to close the gender gap somewhat and – except among younger men – the age gap too:

% saying that pornographic material should be banned altogether	1983	1987	% change 1983–1987
Men:			
Total	25%	33%	+8
18–34	6%	11%	+5
35–54	18%	30%	+12
55+	52%	61%	+9
Women:			
Total	40%	43%	+3
18–34	11%	23%	+12
35–54	35%	39%	+4
55+	70%	70%	–

We show in Chapter 5 a similar pattern in respect of extra-marital and homo-sexual relationships, the net result being that men and women, and people of different ages, are now generally less distinct in their views on moral issues than they were in 1983. Nonetheless, subgroup differences in attitudes towards pornography in particular remain quite large. Examples are given in **Table 3.1**.

Conception, contraception and abortion

The topics discussed so far consider sexuality outside any reproductive context. However, the survey series has also covered three aspects relating to conception and its prevention: artificial fertility measures, contraception and abortion.

Artificial fertility measures

Questions on artificial insemination by husband (AIH) or by another donor (AID) were first asked in the 1985 survey, as a means of ascertaining public

attitudes towards some of the issues raised by the Warnock Report (1984). We also included questions about the acceptability of *in vitro* ('test tube') fertilisation and surrogate motherhood.* Repetition of the items in 1987 shows first that there is little change in the widespread acceptance of AIH and *in vitro* fertilisation using AIH: both are regarded as acceptable practices by the vast majority. Among older people (aged 55 +) enthusiasm is somewhat more muted, but there is still majority support among all population subgroups. Details are given in **Table 3.2**.

However, where the problem of infertility is addressed by involving someone outside the immediate family, respondents are generally far less sympathetic, and are becoming less so.

	Should be allowed by law	
(No 'outside' person involved)	1985	1987
Artificial insemination by husband	90%	89%
'Test-tube' embryo implanted	83%	85%
('Outside' person involved)		
Artificial insemination by donor	53%	50%
Unpaid surrogate motherhood	46%	36%
Paid surrogate motherhood	27%	23%

In the case of a couple trying to have a child using AID, respondents continue to be evenly divided, although again it is younger people (particularly 25–34-year-olds) and graduates who are more sympathetic, with around two-thirds of these groups in favour (see **Table 3.2**).

Far less favoured is the much newer practice of surrogate motherhood, where (using AIH) a woman agrees to bear a child for a couple, either with or without payment. This has remained a contentious issue. Concern has been expressed over possible exploitation, and widespread media coverage has been given to cases where the bearing mother has reneged on the contract and refused to hand over the child. Support for both types of surrogacy has diminished, particularly among younger people, and even more steeply among younger women:

	Unpaid surrogacy			Paid surrogacy			
	1985	1987	% change 1985–1987	1985	1987	% change 1985–1987	
% saying should be allowed by law							
Men:							
18–34	62%	49%	−13	42%	35%	−7	
35–54	53%	42%	−11	33%	29%	−4	
55+	38%	32%	−6	19%		23%	+4
Women:							
18–34	57%	33%	−24	35%	20%	−15	
35–54	42%	37%	−5	20%	20%	−	
55+	23%	19%	−4	12%	9%	−3	

In 1985 young people (aged 18–34) were more in favour of than against non-commercial surrogacy (*The 1986 Report*, p. 158). This is no longer true (see **Table 3.2**).

*These were asked on the self-completion questionnaire (A216). For the exact wording, see Appendix III.

The Warnock Committee recommended that both profit- and non-profit-making surrogacy agencies should be outlawed. Under the 1985 Surrogacy Arrangements Act, commercial surrogacy agencies were banned, but the Act did not actually prohibit individuals from themselves entering into surrogacy agreements, even if the bearing mother was paid. According to our data, there is increasing public disapproval of the practice, whether paid or unpaid. Indeed, the fall in support among 18–34-year-old women for surrogate arrangements is precipitous. Could it owe something to the adverse publicity which some cases in Britain and the US have attracted, or even to the recent change in the law? Or might it even be connected with the increasingly widespread fear of AIDS? We cannot tell.

Contraception

In the first *British Social Attitudes* survey in 1983, respondents were asked to agree or disagree with the statement: *Contraceptive advice and supplies should be available to all young people, whatever their age.* On balance (46% as opposed to 40%), they disagreed. Further interest in the issue was aroused following the lengthy campaign (spearheaded by Mrs Victoria Gillick) to ban GPs from giving contraceptive advice or supplies to people under 16 without their parents' consent. Hence, a more specific question was asked in the 1985 and 1987 self-completion questionnaires:

> *Doctors should be allowed to give contraceptive advice and supplies to young people under 16 without having to inform parents.*

	1985	1987
	%	%
Agree strongly	12	7
Agree	23	24
Neither agree nor disagree	13	9
Disagree	33	34
Disagree strongly	17	26

It is evident that, on this issue also, there has been a shift towards a more censorious stance. Five per cent fewer in 1987 agree strongly that GPs should be allowed to give contraceptive advice and supplies to those under 16; nine per cent more are strongly against the proposition. Among young people aged 18–24, however, a bare majority (54%) is still in agreement (see **Table 3.1**).

Abortion

Abortion is perhaps more passionately contested than any other moral issue. It has been the subject of intense public debate and political lobbying, with well-organised and vociferous protest groups on each side. Most recently (but well after our survey) the debate has focused on a private member's Bill, introduced by David Alton MP, designed to reduce the period of time (from 28 weeks to 18) during which a pregant woman may be allowed by law to have an abortion. This constitutes only the latest of many attempts in the past 20 years to reform the 1967 Act.

The *British Social Attitudes* questions are designed to focus on the personal and social circumstances in which abortion might be considered permissible,

rather than to examine the time limit involved. The same questions have been asked in the self-completion section of the questionnaire in 1983, 1985 and 1987. The results paint an unequivocal picture: unlike surrogacy and contraceptive advice to young people, and despite the various attempts at legislative reform, public support for allowing abortion in all circumstances has increased significantly among all demographic groups over the four-year period.

% agreeing that abortion should be allowed by law when...	1983	1985	1987
... the woman decides on her own she does not wish to have the child	37%	49%	54%
... the woman is not married and does not wish to marry the man	44%	54%	56%
... the couple agree they do not wish to have the child	46%	55%	59%
... the couple cannot afford any more children	47%	58%	58%
... there is a strong chance of a defect in the baby	82%	87%	89%
... the woman became pregnant as a result of rape	85%	89%	93%
... the woman's health is seriously endangered by the pregnancy	87%	91%	94%

In 1983, less than half the population was in favour of abortion for any of the reasons of preference. By 1987 a majority held this view on all the items. On grounds of health, although large majorities have been consistently in favour, attitudes have also shifted markedly towards greater acceptance of abortion. Even among Catholics, 79% now favour abortion in the case of rape and 78% when the mother's health is endangered. Agreement that foetal abnormality should be grounds for abortion has also grown dramatically in this group, from 51% in 1983 to 68% in 1987. Respondents within other religious denominations (including C. of E.) do not differ from the national average on these items. These and other breakdowns are shown in **Table 3.3**.

There are only two circumstances in which the attitudes of women differ to any extent from those of men. Men are rather more willing than women to condone abortion on social grounds in the two circumstances we presented in which *the couple* is specifically mentioned. Surprisingly, however, men are just as likely as women to support the *woman's* right to decide:

% agreeing that abortion should be allowed by law when	Men	Women
... *the couple* agree they do not wish to have the child	63%	55%
... *the couple* cannot afford any more children	61%	54%
... *the woman* decides on her own she does not wish to have the child	54%	54%
... *the woman* is not married and does not wish to marry the man	57%	55%

Overall, the change in attitudes over the previous four years has been greatest among those aged 55 and over. Combining all the circumstances in which an abortion should be allowed, increase in approval since 1983 ranges between 10% among the 18–34-year-olds and 18% among the over 54s. But there is still a substantial level of disapproval of abortion for reasons of preference among women and older people (again see **Table 3.3**). Of course, even in the most recent survey, the young are more approving of abortion than the old, but the gap between them has narrowed; on this issue it is almost as if the older generation has been 'catching up' with the young.

The trend towards more liberal attitudes to abortion stands out from trends on other sexual issues. One reason could be that abortion has increasingly come to be seen more as a matter of women's rights than of sexual morality. On the other hand it can be seen that the largest part of the shift towards more liberal views about abortion, particularly for reasons of preference, took place between 1983 and 1985. But, as has been noted by Airey and Brook in *The 1986 Report* (p.155), attitudes towards abortion are particularly volatile. So we shall have to wait to see what effect the renewed debate within and outside Parliament has on future public opinion on this still controversial issue.

Ideology and sexual morality

Attitudes towards moral issues do not find expression in a vacuum; they are shaped by individuals' cultural, social and personal experiences. Clearly certain groups within the population share a common experience; older and younger people, for example, were brought up in different moral climates; people at different stages in their life cycle are likely to have differing views on sexual conduct. Religious commitment, level of education, gender, and even where they live, can influence people's views.

What of people's political views? Do they influence attitudes in these matters? After all, a strict moral outlook is often described as 'conservative', whereas more permissive attitudes are often described as 'liberal'. Moreover, on questions of declining morals, it is usually those who represent the political right who are the most vociferous. Nonetheless, in Parliament, moral issues have traditionally been subject to a free vote, suggesting that they have not been at the core of any one party's policies. And this corresponds broadly with public attitudes, the association between party identification and one's attitudes to personal–sexual issues being rather loose. For example, although Conservative identifiers are more likely to disapprove of homosexuality and of a GP giving contraceptive advice or supplies to an under 16-year-old, they are *less* likely to disapprove of abortion on grounds of preference than either Labour or Alliance voters are. In each case, however, the percentage differences are fairly small.

Authoritarian and libertarian values

The problem is that, as a measure of ideology (on all sorts of matters), party identification is simply inadequate. A more revealing strategy is to explore some of the values which are thought to underlie political preferences, and which tend to be seen as the more important determinant of the way in which people actually vote (Heath, Jowell and Curtice, 1985). Much survey research has tended to focus exclusively on measures of left *versus* right. Such measures, however, oversimplify the political agenda; for example they have difficulty in accounting for the distinction between economic concerns on the one hand, and matters of law and order, or the emergence of new political issues, such as the environment, on the other (see Chapter 4). Several researchers have proposed a two-dimensional model of political ideology, with one dimension representing political views differentiated in terms of a left–right continuum, where the left stands for egalitarian values and the right stands for free market forces. This axis represents the key political conflicts over ownership of the means of pro-

duction and the distribution of income, and it is the axis along which most of the established political parties in Western Europe have traditionally been aligned. Almost independent of this dimension is an axis which characterises what might be called 'authoritarian' values at one end, and 'libertarian' values at the other (Himmelweit, Humphreys and Jaeger, 1985; Billig, 1982). This dimension is concerned more with civil than with economic liberty – the desire for freedom of expression as against the conviction that law, discipline and 'traditional values' must be maintained if society is to remain orderly. According to this model, an adequate explanation of political preference will need to account for positions on *both* dimensions, as political parties may have varying appeal on each. Moreover the relative political saliency of issues falling on each dimension may vary across time (see Heath and Topf in *The 1987 Report*).

Some researchers working within this framework have proposed that greater affluence, general stability and increased access to education in the last 30 years or so have led to the development of new, more libertarian, values. It is argued that the young and well-educated particularly tend to be less preoccupied with the traditional class-based conflict over economic issues, and also far less deferential towards authority (Inglehart, 1977, 1988; Flanagan, 1987). These trends are seen to explain the recent emergence of new 'non-economic' political issues (such as civil liberties and environmental issues) and support for grass-roots movements to help promote them. All this has been held to challenge traditional 'moral' conventions of behaviour, and so has led to greater permissiveness, expressed politically by groups advocating such causes as gay and lesbian rights, women's rights, abortion on demand, and so on. This shift towards libertarian values is said further to have provoked a backlash from those claiming to represent more traditional, 'moralist' values; they in turn have their own campaigns against too much sex or 'bad language' or violence on TV, against liberal abortion laws, against some aspects of sex education, and against unfettered embryo research (Kavanagh, 1987; Davies, 1980). So do these two dimensions in fact discriminate on these personal–sexual issues? According to the model proposed, we would expect the moral–traditional scale to be far more predictive of people's sexual *mores* than either the egalitarian scale or party identification would be.

Measures of egalitarian and morally traditional values

Two scales have already been developed and used in analyses of *British Social Attitudes* survey data.* The first is a measure of egalitarianism (the political 'left–right' dimension) concerned primarily with issues of redistribution and equality. The scale is very effective in distinguishing party identification.

The second scale is a measure of authoritarian–libertarian values. Here the key dichotomy is the need for society to maintain a state of order and security *versus* the right within a democracy for individuals to maintain their own civil liberties. Thus, some of the items focus on questions of dutifulness and discipline and support for traditional moral values, whereas others tap respondents' attitudes to various types of lawful political protest[†] (see **Table 3.5**). Again on this scale there is an association with party, but not such a strong one.

Broadly speaking, as we would expect, on the egalitarian dimension Labour

---

*The scales aim to be general, deliberately excluding items referring to specific policies and concentrating on underlying values (see **Tables 3.4** and **3.5** and Note 1).
†Here responses have been aggregated to form a three-point scale.

identifiers tend to be strongly egalitarian and Conservatives anti-egalitarian, with Alliance identifiers coming somewhere in between. On the libertarian dimension, the same pattern occurs but not as strongly: all three groups of identifiers tend to fall more towards the middle of that scale (conformism rather than either libertarianism or authoritarianism), but Labour identifiers are the least likely and Conservatives the most likely to fall at the authoritarian end. Even so, 24% of Labour identifiers are 'authoritarian', compared with 31% of Alliance identifiers and 49% of Conservatives.

Egalitarian values also relate strongly and predictably to social class, increasing consistently from Classes I and II (professional and managerial), through Class III to semi- and unskilled workers in Classes IV and V. Although social class has less of an influence on libertarian values, the trend is in the opposite direction, with least authoritarian responses coming from Social Classes I and II. Other demographic differences on the two dimensions reveal conspicuously more libertarian responses among graduates and (to a lesser extent) young people in general. Differences according to religious affiliation are not especially pronounced. A figure showing these patterns will be found at the end of the chapter

As we had anticipated, the libertarian scale is much more predictive of people's attitudes to sexual issues than is the egalitarian scale. The table below shows the consistent differences between people at one end of this scale and those at the other on the various issues covered in this chapter..

	Authoritarians	Libertarians	Index of dissimilarity*
% endorsing the censorious option			
Premarital relations always/ mostly wrong	33%	4%	29
Extra-marital relations always/ mostly wrong	91%	74%	17
Homosexual relations always/ mostly wrong	86%	24%	62
Ban pornography outright	48%	19%	29
Disagree with GP giving contraceptive advice and supplies to under 16s	70%	25%	45
AIH should not be allowed by law	11%	3%	8
AID should not be allowed by law	52%	24%	28
'Test-tube' fertilisation should not be allowed by law	14%	6%	8
Unpaid surrogacy should not be allowed by law	62%	49%	13
Paid surrogacy should not be allowed by law	76%	61%	15
Abortion should not be allowed by law (average across all items)	24%	22%	2

*The index of dissimilarity, a device used in earlier *British Social Attitudes* reports, is the sum of the differences (of the same sign) between the percentage of one group in each response category and the percentage of the other group in each category. Of course it tells us nothing about the *level* of support for each attitudinal item, merely about the extent to which the two groups *differ* on that item. The index ranges between 100 and nil, with 100 being the biggest possible difference.

The pattern confirms the important impact of underlying values on attitudes towards sexual conduct and behaviour. Those endorsing libertarian values are far less likely to be censorious of the personal behaviour of others; the reverse tends to be true among authoritarians. Naturally, the differences do vary: on issues which command widespread support (such as AIH), the influence of libertarian values is far smaller than it is on a more contested issue such as homosexuality. The one exception to the trend is again seen on the abortion items. On none of these does the libertarian scale differentiate to any degree. This lends some support to our earlier suggestion that abortion tends not to be judged so much on a personal–moral dimension, but on a rather more 'political' basis.

So permissiveness on sexual matters is more likely to be found among those who value civil liberties highly. It is not closely related to party identification or to the left–right dimension of politics.

Conclusions

We do not have trend data on all these measures over the survey series, but the pattern of results which has emerged in this chapter suggests that permissiveness on most issues seems, for the moment at least, to be somewhat in decline. With the exception of abortion, such changes in attitudes to sexual issues that have occurred have been consistently in the direction of increased censoriousness. The message of those advocating a return to 'traditional values' seems thus to have found a sympathetic audience. But, at the risk of being proved wrong in future volumes, we believe that the liberalising trend over the past few decades on these issues is unlikely to suffer more than a short-term setback. The attitudes of young people on all these issues are so much more permissive than those of older people that their influence is bound to seep through both by means of cohort replacement (young people carrying their more permissive values with them into middle age), and by means of parental transmission of values to the next generation.

Note

1. The two scales were derived from factor analyses carried out by Heath, Jowell, Curtice and Witherspoon (1986). Their results showed both scales to be highly reliable. On the egalitarianism (left–right) scale, the internal consistency (Cronbach's alpha) was 0.84 and the Pearson test–retest correlation was 0.79; on the moral traditionalism (authoritarian–libertarian) scale, the internal consistency was 0.66 and the test–retest correlation was 0.83. The scale items are shown in **Tables 3.4** and **3.5**.

References

AIREY, C. and BROOK, L., 'Interim Report: Social and Moral Issues', in Jowell, R., Witherspoon, S. and Brook, L. (eds), *British Social Attitudes: the 1986 Report*, Gower, Aldershot (1986).

BILLIG, M., *Ideology and Social Psychology*, Blackwell, Oxford (1982).

DAVIES, C., *Permissive Britain: Social change in the Sixties and Seventies*, Pitman, London (1975).

DAVIES, C., 'Moralists, Causalists, Sex, Law and Morality', in Armytage, W., Chester, R. and Peel, J. (eds), *Changing Patterns of Sexual Behaviour*, Academic Press, London (1980).

FLANAGAN, S., 'Changing Values in Advanced Industrial Societies Revisited: Towards a Resolution of the Values Debate', *American Political Science Review*, vol. 81 (December 1987), pp. 1289–319.

HAMPSHIRE, S., (ed.) *Public and Private Morality*, Cambridge University Press, Cambridge (1978), p. 7.

HARDING, S. and PHILLIPS, D., with FOGARTY, M., *Contrasting Values in Western Europe*, Macmillan, London (1986)

HEATH, A. and TOPF, R., 'Political Culture', in Jowell, R., Witherspoon, S. and Brook, L. (eds), *British Social Attitudes: the 1987 Report*, Gower, Aldershot (1987).

HEATH, A., JOWELL, R. and CURTICE, J., *How Britain Votes*, Pergamon Press, Oxford (1985).

HEATH, A., JOWELL, R., CURTICE, J. and WITHERSPOON, S. *End of Award Report to the ESRC: Methodological Aspects of Attitude Research*, SCPR, London (1986).

HIMMELWEIT, H., HUMPREYS, P. and JAEGER, M., *How Voters Decide*, (rev. edn), Open University Press, Milton Keynes (1985).

INGLEHART, R., *The Silent Revolution. Changing Values and Political Styles among Western Publics*, Princeton University Press, Princeton (1977).

INGLEHART, R., *Culture Shift in Advanced Industrial Society*, Princeton University Press, Princeton (1988, in press).

KAVANAGH, D., *Thatcherism and British Politics: the End of Consensus?*, Oxford University Press, Oxford (1987).

Report of the Committee of Inquiry into Human Fertilisation and Embryology ['The Warnock Report']; Cmnd 9314, HMSO, London (1984).

3.1 ATTITUDES TO PORNOGRAPHY (A217) AND CONTRACEPTION FOR YOUNG PEOPLE UNDER 16 (A207f)
by age within sex, social class and religion

	TOTAL	AGE WITHIN SEX						SOCIAL CLASS				RELIGION			
		MALE			FEMALE			I/II	III non-manual	III manual	IV/V	Roman Catholic	C of E/ Anglican	Other Christian	Other (No religion)
		18-34	35-54	55+	18-34	35-54	55+								
	%	%	%	%	%	%	%	%	%	%	%	%	%	%	%
VIEWS ON THE AVAILABILITY OF PORNOGRAPHIC MAGAZINES AND FILMS															
They should be banned altogether	38	11	30	61	23	39	70	31	40	39	42	42	42	46	29
They should be available in special adult shops but not displayed to the public	42	52	51	26	54	46	21	47	40	40	42	38	42	37	47
They should be available in special adult shops with public display permitted	8	14	10	4	12	7	1	12	9	7	4	11	7	4	10
They should be available in any shop for sale to adults only	8	18	8	5	10	4	5	7	8	10	9	6	7	8	10
They should be available in any shop for sale to anyone	1	5	*	-	1	-	1	1	*	-	1	-	1	2	2
VIEWS ON WHETHER DOCTORS SHOULD BE ALLOWED TO GIVE CONTRACEPTIVE ADVICE AND SUPPLIES TO YOUNG PEOPLE UNDER 16 WITHOUT HAVING TO INFORM PARENTS															
Agree strongly	7	13	7	6	9	5	1	9	4	8	7	7	6	4	9
Agree	24	39	26	13	36	19	10	29	25	22	18	11	18	21	35
Neither agree nor disagree	9	10	7	9	9	9	8	7	9	9	9	7	10	9	8
Disagree	34	23	31	34	32	41	41	30	39	32	33	37	37	36	28
Disagree strongly	26	15	29	37	15	25	37	25	22	28	32	38	27	30	20
BASE: A RESPONDENTS															
Weighted	*1243*	*195*	*213*	*179*	*217*	*241*	*196*	*326*	*292*	*254*	*286*	*124*	*441*	*220*	*441*
Unweighted	*1281*	*184*	*225*	*191*	*215*	*252*	*211*	*339*	*309*	*264*	*291*	*124*	*463*	*228*	*445*

3.2 ATTITUDES TO ARTIFICIAL FERTILITY MEASURES (A216) by sex, age within sex and religion

SHOULD THE LAW ALLOW A MARRIED COUPLE TO USE THE FOLLOWING METHODS?	TOTAL	SEX		AGE WITHIN SEX						RELIGION				
		Male	Female	MALE 18-34	35-54	55+	FEMALE 18-34	35-54	55+	Roman Catholic	C of E/ Anglican	Other Christian	Other religion	(No religion)
	%	%	%	%	%	%	%	%	%	%	%	%	%	%
Artificial insemination: husband as donor														
Allowed by law	89	89	89	90	93	82	96	92	78	82	88	87	93	
Not allowed by law	9	10	7	9	6	16	3	6	13	15	9	11	5	
Other/Don't know	2	1	4	*	1	2	1	2	9	3	4	2	2	
Artificial insemination: anonymous donor														
Allowed by law	50	53	47	64	57	36	61	49	27	40	46	45	58	
Not allowed by law	47	45	48	34	41	61	38	47	62	56	49	52	39	
Other/Don't know	4	2	5	1	2	3	1	4	11	4	5	3	3	
'Test-tube' embryo implanted														
Allowed by law	85	84	86	90	87	75	93	90	73	78	84	84	89	
Not allowed by law	12	13	10	9	10	22	6	7	19	17	12	15	8	
Other/Don't know	3	2	4	1	3	3	1	4	8	5	5	2	2	
'Surrogate mother': without payment														
Allowed by law	36	41	31	49	42	32	33	37	19	24	33	31	43	
Not allowed by law	61	57	65	49	56	65	66	59	70	73	63	66	55	
Other/Don't know	4	2	5	2	2	3	1	4	10	3	5	3	2	
'Surrogate mother': paid														
Allowed by law	23	29	17	35	29	22	20	20	9	16	20	20	27	
Not allowed by law	74	69	79	63	69	75	79	77	81	81	76	78	70	
Other/Don't know	3	2	5	2	2	3	2	3	10	3	5	2	2	
BASE: A RESPONDENTS														
Weighted	1243	587	636	195	213	179	217	241	196	124	441	220	441	
Unweighted	1281	600	680	184	225	191	215	252	211	124	463	228	445	

3.3 CIRCUMSTANCES IN WHICH ABORTION SHOULD BE LEGALISED (A215)
by sex, age within sex, religion and marital status

SHOULD THE LAW ALLOW AN ABORTION IN EACH CASE?	TOTAL	SEX		AGE WITHIN SEX						RELIGION				MARITAL STATUS		
				MALE			FEMALE									
		Male	Female	18-34	35-54	55+	18-34	35-54	55+	Roman Catholic	C of E/ Anglican	Other Christian	(No religion)	Married now	Separated/ divorced/ widowed	Never married
	%	%	%	%	%	%	%	%	%	%	%	%	%	%	%	%
The woman decides on her own she does not wish to have the child	54	54	54	62	49	53	57	57	45	34	55	49	61	53	50	59
The couple agree they do not wish to have the child	59	63	55	71	60	59	63	57	43	38	57	55	67	58	50	66
The woman is not married and does not wish to marry the man	56	57	55	62	55	56	60	58	47	32	56	54	64	56	52	58
The couple cannot afford any more children	58	61	54	59	62	61	59	54	50	37	57	53	66	59	53	54
There is a strong chance of a defect in the baby	89	88	90	90	87	88	94	91	85	68	92	92	91	91	85	85
The woman's health is seriously endangered by the pregnancy	94	94	93	95	95	91	97	95	88	78	95	94	97	95	90	92
The woman becomes pregnant as a result of rape	93	94	93	95	94	92	97	92	90	79	94	93	97	94	88	93
BASE: A RESPONDENTS Weighted	1243	587	656	195	213	179	217	241	196	124	441	220	441	887	140	217
Unweighted	1281	600	680	184	225	191	215	252	211	124	463	228	445	905	165	210

3.4 ITEMS COMPRISING THE 'LEFT-RIGHT' SCALE (A227a–e/B238)
by party identification

% AGREEING WITH EACH STATEMENT

	TOTAL	PARTY IDENTIFICATION		
		Conservative	Alliance	Labour
	%	%	%	%
There is one law for the rich and one for the poor	66	46	73	86
Ordinary working people do not get their fair share of the nation's wealth	64	41	70	89
Management will always try to get the better of employees if it gets the chance	61	45	61	80
Big business benefits owners at the expense of the workers	51	32	57	70
Government should redistribute income from the better-off to those who are less well-off	45	21	53	70
BASE: ALL RESPONDENTS				
Weighted	2424	947	466	683
Unweighted	2493	985	479	699

3.5 ITEMS COMPRISING THE 'AUTHORITARIAN-LIBERTARIAN SCALE' (A227f–n)
by party identification

% AGREEING/DISAGREEING WITH EACH STATEMENT

	TOTAL	PARTY IDENTIFICATION		
		Conservative	Alliance	Labour
	%	%	%	%
AGREE — Schools should teach children to obey authority	83	91	81	76
People who break the law should be given stiffer sentences	80	86	69	75
For some crimes, the death penalty is the most appropriate sentence	74	84	67	65
Censorship of films and magazines is necessary to uphold moral standards	71	78	71	60
Young people don't have enough respect for traditional British values	66	77	61	57
The law should always be obeyed, even if a particular law is wrong	46	56	47	34
DISAGREE — People should be allowed to organise public meetings to protest against the government	61	53	67	72
People should be allowed to publish leaflets to protest against the government	58	53	63	67
People should be allowed to organise protest marches and demonstrations	54	49	60	59
BASE: A RESPONDENTS				
Weighted	1243	482	242	331
Unweighted	1281	505	254	337

Figure 3.1

Variations in 'authoritarian' and 'egalitarian' values

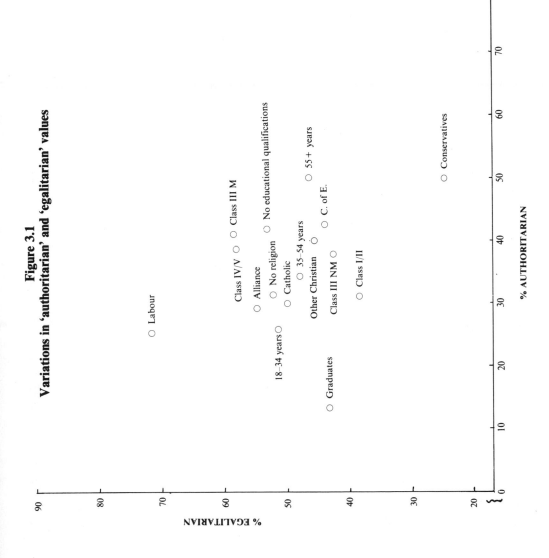

4 Working-class Conservatives and middle-class socialists

*Anthony Heath and Geoff Evans**

In this chapter we examine the links between people's class, attitudes and party allegiance, with particular reference to those people whose party attachments seem to be against their 'natural' class interests. Specifically, why do some members of the middle classes identify with the Labour Party, especially at a time when the Conservatives' taxation policies, for instance, are particularly beneficial to the better off? Similarly, what is it that leads almost half the working class to identify with the Alliance or the Conservatives rather than with their 'natural' class party?

Previous reports in this series have examined the general relationship between attitudes and political partisanship. In *The 1986* and *1987 Reports*, John Curtice showed that the issues which most divided Labour and Conservative partisans were the 'traditional' ones – attitudes towards trade unions, redistribution and economic policy generally. These economic issues are, of course, the traditional substance of British politics, dividing not only the parties but also the classes, just as religion, language or region divide people in other countries.

However, in recent years a second group of non-economic issues concerning women's rights, gays, ethnic minorities, nuclear policy and 'green' concerns have come to the fore. They are not issues which divide the classes in the same way as the old economic ones do; they tend to divide people more on the basis of education, and are sometimes referred to as 'new agenda' issues. One possibility is that these new agenda issues will help to explain variations – in values and in characteristics – *within* rather than between the classes, in party support. Thus middle-class Labour identifiers may be people who take 'left-wing' positions on non-economic as opposed to economic issues (see Parkin, 1968 and Inglehart, 1971). Conversely, among the working class, the Conserva-

---

*Anthony Heath is Official Fellow, and Geoff Evans is a Research Officer, at Nuffield College, Oxford.

tive Party might appeal particularly to those who are unsympathetic to Labour's apparent concern with, for instance, women's, gay and black issues. These sorts of people, along with those who favour, say, strong policing, have sometimes been referred to as working-class 'authoritarians" (Lipset, 1959). If these explanations hold, it might be that the Labour Party has been losing more working-class adherents than it has been gaining middle-class ones through its championship of some of the new agenda issues; or it might work the other way around.

An alternative explanation would stress the continued importance of the old economic issues. Thus, those among the middle classes who vote Labour might simply be the less well-paid section of the middle class – people who have not shared so much in the general affluence and who might thus be attracted to the Labour Party more on traditional economic grounds. This has been referred to as a 'disguised working-class vote' (Rallings, 1975). Similarly, working-class Conservatives may turn out simply to be the more affluent members of the working class who do not think of themselves as having working-class interests, who aspire to individual economic advancement and who reject the collectivist approach of, say, trade unionism. If this explanation holds, the Conservative Party will appeal particularly to the new working class of affluent home-owners and share-owners, who might be referred to analogously as a 'disguised middle class'.

To investigate these issues we have used a selection of questions from the 1987 survey which represent some of the key elements of the 'old' (economic) and 'new' (non-economic) agendas. To represent the old agenda we have selected questions which deal with the distribution of wealth; unemployment and inflation; taxation and government spending; the power of trade unions; and reliance on individual effort rather than state provision of benefits. For the new agenda, we have selected questions on nuclear defence; homosexuality; equal opportunity legislation for women; and ethnic minorities. Amongst these new agenda items we have also included two longstanding libertarian issues: rights of political protest and the death penalty.[1]

To distinguish the different social classes we use a version of the schema devised by John Goldthorpe, which should by now be familiar to regular readers of this series. There are five classes:

Class 1 – The salariat. In this class are salaried professionals and semi-professionals, managers and administrators, together with large employers and self-employed professionals. People in these occupations tend to have a secure basis of employment, typically affording a high income.

Class 2 – Routine non-manual workers. In this class are clerks, salesworkers and secretaries – those in subordinate positions with relatively low levels of income. This group constitutes a kind of white-collar labour force.

Class 3 – The petty bourgeoisie. In this class are farmers, small proprietors and own-account manual workers – the self-employed but not self-employed professionals.

Class 4 – Foremen and technicians. In this class is a sort of blue-collar elite, its members being set apart from the mass of wage labour by their supervisory functions or greater amount of discretion and autonomy.

Class 5 – The working class. In this class are rank and file manual employees in industry and agriculture.

Class cleavages and attitudes

We show below, for each of the 11 selected items, the percentage of the salariat on the one hand and of the working class on the other, who hold 'left-wing' attitudes. We have omitted from this table the other classes, but show their distribution in **Table 4.1** at the end of the chapter (where the complete question wording is also given).

% adopting 'left-wing' position on 'old agenda' (economic and welfare) issues	Salariat	Working class
1. Inequality of wealth (A227c)	53%	78%
2. Unemployment *v.* inflation (Q.13a)	64%	77%
3. Trade union power (A211)	10%	17%
4. Tax cuts *v.* social spending (Q.61)	53%	51%
5. Welfare *v.* self-help (A227s)	48%	48%

% adopting 'left-wing' position on 'new agenda' (non-economic) issues	Salariat	Working class
6. Nuclear defence (Q.7)	25%	27%
7. Sex discrimination (A82)	79%	69%
8. Right to protest (A227h)	72%	59%
9. Cultural diversity in schools (A206e)	43%	39%
10. Homosexuality (A88c)	20%	9%
11. Death penalty (A227i)	27%	11%

Items 1 to 3 on the list above are issues that are central to the 'old' agenda – inequality of wealth, unemployment, and trade unions. Here we see a clear class gradient with the working class, particularly in the case of inequality, being well to the 'left' of the salariat (and incidentally of all the other classes too – see **Table 4.1**).

Items 4 and 5 are issues on which the salariat and the working class have an almost identical distribution of response. Affection for the welfare state is as common among the middle classes as among the working classes. On these issues it is the petty bourgeoisie (see **Table 4.1**) which is different from all other classes, displaying much less enthusiasm for welfare spending and income support. It is of some interest that the divisions between working class and salariat are not as great on state spending items as on inequality, but the explanation is not hard to find. First, many members of the salariat are employed in the public sector and stand to gain from greater government spending; second, the middle classes have been shown to be particular beneficiaries of state spending on services such as health and education (Le Grand, 1987); third, while redistribution of wealth tends to favour the working classes especially, tax cuts are more widespread in their effects, certainly reaching working-class people on average incomes.

Finally, when we come to the non-economic issues of the 'new' agenda (items 6–11), the salariat in most cases tends to be more 'left-wing' than the working class. Among these are issues, such as the death penalty, which have tended to give the working class its reputation for 'authoritarianism', although it is only right to point out that, on this issue as well as on homosexuality, all the classes are rather illiberal.

Working-class authoritarianism

The term 'authoritarianism' first came to prominence in the study of the authoritarian personality by Adorno and his colleagues (1950). This work had its theoretical roots in psychoanalytic theory and involved many assumptions that we ourselves do not make (nor would we wish to) in this context, particularly as the term has many negative connotations. The questions in our survey, while designed to tap items on the new agenda, do not allow us to measure authoritarianism in the sense described by Adorno. Instead we talk about "moral traditionalism" (see Heath and Topf in *The 1987 Report*), or for simplicity here – a 'right-wing' position.

Let us test then whether the working-class Conservative is someone who adopts a 'right-wing' position on the items of the new agenda – such as nuclear defence and sex discrimination, as well as on traditional issues to do with law and order.

Attitudes within the working class

	Conservative	Alliance	Labour
% adopting a 'left-wing' position on:			
Nuclear defence	9%	21%	38%
Sex discrimination law	71%	72%	68%
Right to protest	47%	59%	70%
Cultural diversity in schools	31%	34%	46%
Homosexuality	9%	15%	7%
Death penalty	5%	13%	15%

The evidence is by no means clear-cut, and does not permit us to draw decisive conclusions about the working class in general. At one extreme we find high levels of censoriousness about homosexuality and high support for the death penalty, and these attitudes are shared by Conservative, Labour and Alliance identifiers more or less alike. At the other extreme, we find high levels of support for sexual equality and for civil liberties. A simple characterisation of the working class as 'authoritarian' or 'morally traditional' simply will not do.

Nor is there evidence which would allow us to conclude that working-class Conservatives are consistently more right-wing on these new agenda items than working-class Alliance or Labour identifiers are. On two of the six items, for instance, differences between the parties are small indeed. Only on nuclear defence do we find a major difference, which is not surprising, perhaps, in view of the fact that it is by far the most 'politicised' of these items. Party positions are surely more likely to influence supporters' positions on issues upon which the Party takes a distinctive public stand.

We can put these differences into perspective by looking at working-class attitudes to the conventional economic issues that form the old agenda.

Attitudes within the working class

	Conservative	Alliance	Labour
% adopting 'left-wing' position on:			
Inequality of wealth	52%	81%	93%
Unemployment *v.* inflation	61%	82%	87%
Trade union power	2%	11%	29%
Tax cuts *v.* social spending	35%	57%	61%
Welfare *v.* self-help	30%	49%	66%

Here we see differences between Conservative and Labour identifiers ranging from 26 to 41 points.[2] With the exception of nuclear defence, none of the new agenda items rivals the old agenda items in explaining differences in party support among the working class. In short, working-class Conservatives cannot be distinguished so much from other people in the working class by their attitudes to gays, ethnic minorities or women's issues. It is the traditional economic issues that mainly explain working-class Conservatism.

Multi-variate analysis of the relationships between Conservative party identification and attitudes within the working class underlines the dominance of these economic issues. In such an analysis the issues which discriminate significantly between working-class Conservatives and non-Conservatives are (in descending order of importance) trade union power, inequality of wealth, unemployment and inflation, nuclear defence, and welfare *versus* self-help. Once these issues have been taken into account, attitudes to homosexuality, equal opportunities for women and so on add nothing to the analysis.[3] Moral traditionalism, therefore, fails as an explanation of political differences within the working class.

The social bases of working-class Conservatism

The failure of the thesis of working-class authoritarianism leads naturally to the alternative thesis that working-class Conservatives are simply a 'bourgeois' section of the working class distinguished from their Labour peers by their affluence, home ownership, education, origins, social relationships and so on.

There is certainly truth in this, as we can see if we compare the characteristics of the working class as a whole with those of working-class Conservatives and salariat Conservatives.[4]

	Working class		Salariat	
	All	Conservatives	Conservatives	All
% with...				
...income under £5000	41%	32%	9%	10%
...rented accommodation	47%	33%	13%	15%
...no qualifications	65%	63%	12%	11%
...working-class father*	67%	56%	27%	33%
...working-class spouse	36%	29%	14%	10%
...working-class identity	68%	54%	17%	20%
...father who voted Labour*	56%	40%	28%	37%

Source: British General Election study, 1987.

As this table shows, working-class Conservatives are indeed likely to be better paid than working-class people in general, and they are much less likely to live in rented accommodation. However, on both these criteria, they fall well short of the levels found in the salariat. These working-class Conservatives may be in the process of becoming 'bourgeois', but they still have a long way to travel. This is even clearer if we look at their educational qualifications. Here we see that they are little different from the rest of the working class in their low level of qualification and fall a long way short of the education that is typical of the salariat.

In their patterns of social relationships and social identities, too, working-class Conservatives seem to lie part-way between the working class as a whole and

the salariat. They are less likely to have working-class social origins, to be married to a working-class spouse, or to describe themselves as working-class, but they are still a long way from the salariat in these respects. Overall then, despite the fact that working-class Conservatives are almost identical to salariat Conservatives in their political attitudes, they are still markedly different from them in their social position and relationships. One interpretation is that they are an 'aspiring middle class' who are some way towards achieving their aspirations.

The one characteristic, however, on which working-class Conservatives are close to salariat Conservatives is in their political origins. The proportion reporting that their father voted Labour when they were young is much lower than that in the working class as a whole and, in this case only, actually approaches the proportion found in the salariat as a whole. This suggests a rather different interpretation of the patterns we have found. The causal link may be the opposite of what has been assumed. Perhaps it is not so much affluence that leads to Conservatism – rather that Conservative political origins lead to the pursuit of individual advancement.

Middle-class libertarianism

While the theories of working-class authoritarianism and middle-class libertarianism are neatly symmetrical, there is no empirical reason to suppose that the findings will also be symmetrical. And when we turn from the working class to the salariat, we find that there are much bigger party differences within the salariat on the new agenda than were apparent among the working class. Labour identifiers are more radical on all these items than are Alliance identifiers; Conservative identifiers are the least radical of all of them.

Attitudes within the salariat			
	Conservative	Alliance	Labour
% adopting 'left-wing' position on:			
Nuclear defence	7%	27%	65%
Sex discrimination law	70%	85%	93%
Right to protest	62%	83%	85%
Cultural diversity in schools	31%	44%	69%
Homosexuality	9%	29%	43%
Death penalty	12%	36%	58%

When we examine the figures further we find another striking contrast. Whereas on all but one of these new agenda issues, working-class and salariat Conservatives give almost identical answers, Labour identifiers in different classes display large differences (see **Table 4.4**). With few exceptions, salariat Labour identifiers are much more radical on these new agenda issues than are working-class Labour identifiers. Indeed Labour's working-class identifiers are closer on these issues to Conservative identifiers than they are to Labour's middle-class identifiers. For example, seven per cent of working-class Labour identifiers are tolerant of homosexuality, as are nine per cent of working-class Conservatives and nine per cent of salariat Conservatives. Among the Labour salariat, however, the percentage is 43%. This general pattern holds true for most of these new agenda items. Salariat Labour identifiers, then, are well to the left of their Conservative counterparts in all classes, as well as to the left of working-class Labour identifiers on these new agenda items.

We might expect, however, that salariat Labour identifiers would be well to the *right* of working-class Labour identifiers in their attitudes to the old agenda *economic* issues. After all, their 'class interests' here would coincide more with those of salariat Alliance and Conservative identifiers, than with those of working-class Labour identifiers. So while we might expect them to be more left-wing than others in the salariat, the effect would surely be less marked than on the new agenda issues.

That expectation was simply wrong. As the table below shows, salariat Labour identifiers are indeed 'left-wing' on the old agenda 'economic' items too.

Attitudes within the salariat

% adopting 'left-wing' position on:	Conservative	Alliance	Labour
Inequality of wealth	32%	64%	88%
Unemployment *v.* inflation	47%	77%	89%
Trade union power	1%	12%	37%
Tax cuts *v.* social spending	34%	72%	80%
Welfare *v.* self-help	30%	66%	71%

On four of these economic issues the proportion of salariat Labour identifiers who adopt a 'left-wing' position is higher than the proportion in the working class, and on the fifth items it is almost as high; thus on tax cuts *versus* social spending 80% of salariat Labour identifiers want higher taxes and more government expenditure, compared with 61% of the working class. On welfare benefits too, where similar proportions of working-class and salariat Labour identifiers give broadly 'left-wing' answers, the salariat identifiers are more likely to express strong views on the issue (see **Table 4.3**).

Following Robertson (1984) the picture can be sketched in the following diagram, where we have grouped the old and new agenda items respectively to form two scales.[5]

As we can see, salariat and working-class Conservatives lie quite close together, particularly on the new agenda. In contrast, salariat and working-class Labour identifiers, while close together on the old agenda, lie much further apart from each other on the new agenda. Meanwhile the Alliance is a pale reflection of Labour – its salariat and working-class identifiers being close together on the old agenda but some way apart on the new.

The social bases of middle-class socialism

Given these attitudinal differences between salariat and working-class Labour identifiers, we would not expect to find great similarities in their social characteristics and relationships. In other words, we would *not* expect the salariat Labour identifiers to be a 'disguised working class', consisting of relatively unsuccessful salaried people.

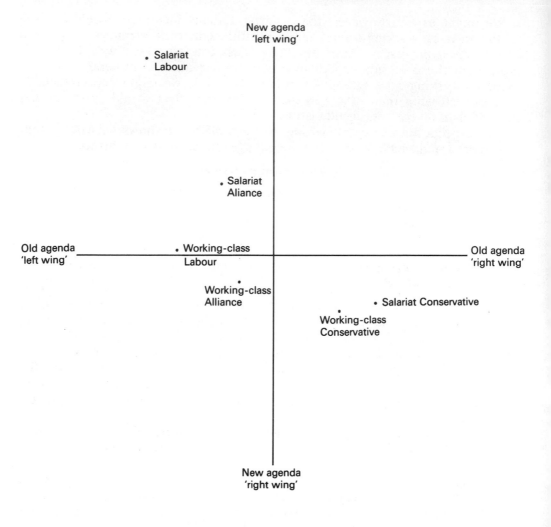

	Old agenda	New agenda
Salariat Conservative	+0.77	+0.37
Salariat Alliance	−0.39	−0.53
Salariat Labour	−0.96	−1.50
Working-class Conservative	+0.56	+0.43
Working-class Alliance	−0.25	+0.22
Working-class Labour	−0.73	−0.03

| | Working class | | Salariat | |
% with ...	All	Labour	Labour	All
... income over £10 000 p.a.	15%	14%	60%	62%
... rented accommodation	47%	54%	22%	15%
... degree	–	–	43%	28%
... working-class father*	67%	74%	47%	33%
... working-class spouse	36%	41%	8%	10%
... working-class identity	68%	75%	33%	20%
... father who voted Labour*	56%	74%	60%	37%

Source: British General Election study, 1987

As we can see, this is largely borne out. The income levels of salariat Labour identifiers are typical of the salariat as a whole, and their educational levels are actually higher, with nearly half of them holding degrees.

They are, however, different from the salariat in their social origins and in the class they identify with. Nearly one half of them have working-class origins and might thus fit the label of 'yuppies' (young upwardly mobile professionals); indeed, 55% of them are aged under 35, compared with 32% of the salariat generally. But we do not imply from this that they conform to the popular and largely pejorative image of yuppies. On the contrary, their social and political attitudes hardly match the 'yuppie' stereotype of aggressive consumerism.

As with working-class Conservatism, we find that political traditions within the family are most influential in party identification. Indeed a majority of these salariat Labour identifiers report that their father voted Labour when they were growing up, and in this respect they are much closer to the working class generally, and to Labour identifiers in the working class, than they are to the salariat.

These young, highly educated and salariat Labour identifiers are patently not even remotely a disguised working class. What they share with the working class is a family tradition of Labour voting, which in turn may help to explain their left-wing economic attitudes and their similarity to working-class Labour identifiers on the 'old' political agenda. An even more likely explanation of why they differ from working-class Labour identifiers on 'new' agenda issues is their high level of education, in which respect they resemble Alliance identifiers. Still, Labour identifiers are to the left of their Alliance counterparts on most of these new agenda items too.

If we are to find a disguised working class, then, it is not among this highly educated group of salariat Labour identifiers. The obvious place to look for one is not in the salariat itself but among the routine non-manual workers (Class 2). Their terms and conditions of employment make them more analogous in many ways to the working class than to the salariat proper. The following table compares the social characteristics of all Class 2 respondents with those of Labour Class 2 identifiers in order to see whether we can find a disguised working class.

| % with | Routine non-manual workers | |
	All	Labour
... income over £10 000 p.a.	10%	14%
... rented accommodation	23%	29%
... degree	2%	6%
... no qualifications	34%	39%
... working-class father*	42%	56%
... working-class spouse	25%	35%
... working-class identity	42%	63%
... father who voted Labour*	41%	68%

Source: British General Election study, 1987

The story of this table is a mixed one. For example, Labour identifiers in this class are not unlike the class as a whole in several respects, such as pay and qualifications. Lowish pay and middling qualifications are typical of white-collar workers as a whole and distinguish them as a genuine lower white-collar class, rather than as working-class respondents who have been misclassified. Labour identifiers in this class are, however, closer to working-class Labour identifiers than to salariat Labour identifiers in their likelihood of being married to a working-class spouse and of having a working-class self-image.

Routine non-manual work is of course largely done by women workers, and what we may have here is a group that is linked to the working-class proper through marriage and other social relationships. In that sense it *is* a disguised working class. Not surprisingly, then, they come much closer to working-class than to salariat Labour identifiers in their attitudes to the new agenda items.

| | Labour identifiers who are ... | | |
| | .. salariat | .. routine non- | .. working |
% adopting 'left-wing' position on:		manual	class
Inequality of wealth	88%	84%	93%
Unemployment *v.* inflation	89%	94%	87%
Trade union power	37%	33%	29%
Tax cuts *v.* social spending	80%	64%	61%
Welfare *v.* self-help	71%	71%	66%
Nuclear defence	66%	43%	38%
Sex discrimination law	93%	75%	68%
Right to protest	85%	72%	70%
Cultural diversity in schools	69%	54%	46%
Homosexuality	43%	15%	7%
Death penalty	58%	20%	15%

This table confirms that, as far as the new agenda goes, salariat Labour identifiers are not only different from their class but also from most of their own party. It is perhaps relevant to note that they have many similarities, both in attitudes and social position, to supporters of the Green Party in Germany (Burklin, 1981).

Conclusion

It is no wonder then that some of Labour's perennial problems of disunity do not seem to be shared by the Conservatives. As the diagram on p. 60 shows,

the Conservative Party is ideologically united; its working class and salariat identifiers are similar in their attitudes, both to new and old agenda issues, despite the wide divergences in their social positions. But the Labour Party is more of a coalition between groups; in some other countries these groups might even be in separate parties. It is a tribute to the Labour Party that it is so robust, given the divergent interests it has to satisfy.

However, the great differences between salariat and working-class Labour identifiers in their attitudes to new agenda issues do not imply that the Labour Party actually loses potential working-class votes because of its policies on these issues. On the contrary, our analysis suggests that, with the exception of the nuclear issue, the new agenda is rather unimportant in influencing how working-class people vote. It is the old agenda which is still central to working-class politics. And on the old agenda, as we have seen, salariat and working-class Labour identifiers do not differ greatly.

It is on the issue of nuclear defence that Labour faces its greatest dilemma. This is the single issue, of all the ones that we have considered, which not only distinguishes working-class and middle-class Labour identifiers, but which also distinguishes *within* the working class between Labour and Conservative identifiers. We must be careful about drawing causal inferences from cross-sectional data but nuclear defence, unlike the other new agenda issues, may well lose Labour votes within the working class. Yet it is also an issue on which a major change in the Party's position might lose it support among its middle-class identifiers. On the other hand, we cannot tell from these data whether the nuclear defence issue is not just a proxy for 'nationalism' – a subject we have not tackled in this study, but will look at in future rounds. Nationalism may be a further separate dimension, distinguishing working-class Conservatives from other members of the working class and distinguishing working-class and middle-class Labour identifiers – in other words behaving much as the defence issue itself behaves.

Meanwhile the working class is slowly contracting in size while the salariat is expanding. So it may be in the Labour Party's long-term interests not to risk antagonising its salariat supporters. But Labour has much greater support at present, and many more potential recruits, in the working class proper, than it has in the salariat; and it probably always will have as long as class politics survive in Britain. So the Labour Party cannot afford to antagonise its working-class supporters either.

Whichever way we look at it, the message seems to be the same. Whereas the Conservative Party is *par excellence* a party of conviction, its policies uniting its different class elements, the Labour Party – at present, anyway – is not. Its different class elements have different attitudes and different perspectives. That they remain in the same party is impressive, but it does not make for an easy life.

Notes

1. The items have been chosen to reflect a diverse range of issues rather than those which scale most conveniently. However, they are more or less interchangeable with a range of other similar issues in each category. In other words, the items we have chosen are indeed exemplars of the sorts of issue they are supposed to represent. Other analogous items could do the same work.

2. Strictly speaking it is not appropriate to compare the raw differences (between those giving 'left-wing' answers) across questions since there will be 'ceiling' and 'floor' effects. In other words, on a question such as that of the death penalty where few people give a left-wing answer, the 'floor' effect will tend to reduce the observed differences. An odds ratio or logit coefficient is a more appropriate measure. So while the difference between Labour and Conservative is only 10 points on the death penalty compared with 22 points on the right to protest, we find that the odds ratio is actually larger for the death penalty. This affects the detailed comparison between questions, but does not affect our overall comparisons between new and old agenda issues, since 'ceiling' and 'floor' effects operate on both sets of issues.

3. In the multivariate analysis we took the dichotomy of Conservative *versus* non-Conservative identification as our dependent variable. With a dichotomous dependent variable, logistic regression is appropriate (because of the ceiling and floor effects mentioned in note 2) and this is what we have used. We initially entered all 11 items as independent variables but several of them proved to have coefficients which were not significantly different from zero. We then successively deleted the items which had the least significant coefficient until we reached a model in which all independent variables made a significant contribution. The ratios of the coefficients to their standard errors for the five remaining independent variables were as follows: trade union power 5.2:1; inequality of wealth 5.0:1; unemployment and inflation 3.2:1; nuclear defence 2.3:1; welfare *versus* self-help 2.3:1. Similar results were obtained when Conservative versus Labour identification was taken as the dependent variable.

4. Working-class identity is defined as the response "working" in answer to question 76a (see Appendix III). The response "upper working" is not included.

5. The diagram is a rough summary of the findings of this chapter and, like all summaries, it loses information. We should note in particular that a two-dimensional map of issues is a considerable oversimplification. Issues such as inequality of wealth, trade union power and unemployment *versus* inflation do tend to 'go together' and a reasonable scale can be formed for this dimension (which we can call an egalitarian dimension). At the other extreme, issues such as the death penalty, homosexuality, and cultural diversity also go together and the dimension which they form (which we can call a libertarian dimension) is almost orthogonal to the egalitarian dimension (that is, the two dimensions are only weakly correlated). The other issues, however, come somewhere in between. For example, attitudes to self-help are associated *both* with the egalitarian dimension and with the libertarian dimension. It would in fact be preferable to construct further scales to represent welfare state items and nuclear defence items respectively, but a four-dimensional diagram would not be easy to understand.

    It is important to recognise, therefore, that the two scales representing the old and new agendas are not orthogonal to each other. One further complication which we should note is that the two scales have a somewhat higher correlation in the salariat than they do in the population as a whole. This reflects our finding that salariat Labour identifiers take left-wing positions on *both* old and new agendas.

References

ADORNO, T. *et al*, *The Authoritarian Personality*, Harper, New York (1950).
BURKLIN, W., 'Die Grünen und die Neue Politik', *Politische Vierteljahresschrift*, 22 (1981), pp. 359–83.
CURTICE, J., 'Political partisanship' in Jowell, R., Witherspoon, S. and Brook, L. (eds), *British Social Attitudes: the 1986 Report*, Gower, Aldershot (1986).

CURTICE, J., 'Party Politics' in Jowell, R., Witherspoon, S. and Brook, L. (eds), *British Social Attitudes: the 1987 Report*, Gower, Aldershot (1987).

HEATH, A. and TOPF, R., 'Political Culture', in Jowell, R., Witherspoon, S. and Brook, L. (eds), *British Social Attitudes: the 1987 Report*, Gower, Aldershot (1987).

INGLEHART, R., *The Silent Revolution: Changing Values and Political Styles among Western Publics*, Princeton University Press, Princeton N.J. (1977).

LE GRAND, J., 'Mrs Thatcher, the Welfare State and the Middle Classes', *LSE Quarterly*, vol. 1, no. 3 (Autumn 1987), pp. 255–71.

LIPSET, S.M., 'Democracy and Working-class Authoritarianism', *American Sociological Review*, vol. 24 (1959), pp. 482–501.

PARKIN, F., *Middle-class Radicalism*, Manchester University Press, Manchester (1968).

RALLINGS, C.S., 'Two types of middle-class Labour voter?', *British Journal of Political Science*, vol. 5 (1975), pp. 107–28.

ROBERTSON, D., *Class and the British Electorate*, Basil Blackwell, Oxford (1984).

4.1 PROPORTIONS ADOPTING 'LEFT WING' AND 'RIGHT WING' POSITIONS ON 'OLD AGENDA' ISSUES by compressed Goldthorpe class schema

% ADOPTING 'LEFT WING' AND 'RIGHT WING' POSITIONS ON 'OLD AGENDA' (ECONOMIC AND WELFARE) ISSUES	TOTAL	COMPRESSED GOLDTHORPE CLASS SCHEMA				
		Salariat	Routine non-manual workers	Petty bourgeoisie	Foremen and technicians	Working class
	%	%	%	%	%	%
+Inequality of wealth (A227c/B238c)						
Agree strongly or agree that ordinary working people do not get their fair share of the nation's wealth	64	53	61	54	72	78
Disagree/disagree strongly	17	25	20	23	14	9
*Unemployment v. inflation (Q 13a)						
If the government had to choose ... it should give highest priority to keeping down unemployment	73	64	80	62	70	77
... it should give highest priority to keeping down inflation	23	31	17	35	27	19
**Trade union power (A 211)						
Trade unions in this country have too little or far too little power	13	10	10	8	10	17
... have too much/far too much power	48	46	55	64	48	43
*Tax cuts v. social spending (Q 61)						
If the government had to choose, it should increase taxes and spend more on health, education and social benefits	50	53	50	41	47	51
... it should reduce taxes and spend less on health, education and social benefits	3	3	2	4	3	4
**Welfare v. self-help (A227s)						
Disagree or disagree strongly that if welfare benefits weren't so generous, people would learn to stand on their own two feet	45	48	41	31	48	48
Agree strongly/agree ...	33	31	29	52	38	33
BASES: *ALL RESPONDENTS (INTERVIEW)						
Weighted	2766	651	604	206	127	1002
Unweighted	2847	674	633	216	133	1026
+ALL RESPONDENTS (SELF-COMPLETION)						
Weighted	2424	591	541	170	116	834
Unweighted	2493	614	568	176	119	853
**A RESPONDENTS (SELF-COMPLETION)						
Weighted	1243	302	273	90	63	431
Unweighted	1281	319	290	94	64	440

4.2 PROPORTIONS ADOPTING 'LEFT WING' AND 'RIGHT WING' POSITIONS ON 'NEW AGENDA' ISSUES by compressed Goldthorpe class schema

	TOTAL	COMPRESSED GOLDTHORPE CLASS SCHEMA				
		Salariat	Routine non-manual workers	Petty bourgeoisie	Foremen and technicians	Working class
% ADOPTING 'LEFT WING' AND 'RIGHT WING' POSITIONS ON 'NEW AGENDA' (NON-ECONOMIC) ISSUES	%	%	%	%	%	%
*Nuclear defence (Q.7)						
Britain should rid itself of nuclear weapons while persuading others to do the same	25	25	23	18	19	27
... keep its nuclear weapons until we persuade others to reduce theirs	72	73	75	80	81	69
+Sex discrimination law (A82)						
Support a law against sex discrimination	75	79	82	70	74	69
Oppose ...	22	21	16	28	25	27
**Right to protest (A227h)						
Agree strongly or agree that people should be allowed to organise public meetings to protest against the government	61	72	52	61	60	59
Disagree or disagree strongly ...	12	10	16	12	10	13
**Cultural diversity in schools (A206e)						
Schools with many children from different backgrounds should teach them about the history and culture of their parents' country of origin	40	43	38	40	47	39
Should not teach them ...	58	57	62	60	53	60
+Homosexuality (A88c)						
Sexual relations between two adults of the same sex are rarely wrong or not wrong at all	13	20	14	12	7	9
... always or mostly wrong	74	65	72	79	75	81
**Death penalty (A227i)						
Disagree strongly or disagree that, for some crimes, the death penalty is the most appropriate sentence	17	27	16	14	6	11
Agree strongly/agree ...	74	66	74	81	83	79
BASES: *ALL RESPONDENTS(INTERVIEW) Weighted	2766	651	604	206	127	1002
Unweighted	2847	674	633	216	133	1026
+A RESPONDENTS (INTERVIEW) Weighted	1391	328	301	102	67	496
Unweighted	1437	347	317	108	70	507
**A RESPONDENTS (SELF-COMPLETION) Weighted	1243	302	273	90	63	431
Unweighted	1281	319	290	94	64	440

4.3 PROPORTIONS ADOPTING 'LEFT WING' POSITIONS ON 'OLD AGENDA' ITEMS by party identification within compressed Goldthorpe class schema

PARTY IDENTIFICATION WITHIN COMPRESSED GOLDTHORPE CLASS SCHEMA

% ADOPTING 'LEFT WING' POSITIONS ON 'OLD AGENDA' (ECONOMIC AND WELFARE) ISSUES	SALARIAT			ROUTINE NON-MAN. WORKERS			PETTY BOURGEOISIE			FOREMEN AND TECHNICIANS			WORKING CLASS		
	Conservative	Alliance	Labour	Conservative	Alliance	Labour	Conservative	Alliance	Labour	Conservative	Alliance	Labour	Conservative	Alliance	Labour
	%	%	%	%	%	%	%	%	%	%	%	%	%	%	%
+Inequality of wealth (A227c/B238c) Agree strongly or agree that ordinary working people do not get their fair share of the nation's wealth	32	64	88	44	67	84	31	(72)	(96)	61	(95)	(86)	52	81	93
*Unemployment v. inflation (Q13a) If the government had to choose ... it should give highest priority to keeping down unemployment	47	77	89	71	88	94	44	(11)	(83)	62	(78)	(88)	61	82	87
**Trade union power (A211) Trade unions in this country have too little or far too little power	1	12	37	5	7	(33)	-	(8)	(27)	(3)	(21)	(17)	2	12	29
*Tax cuts v. social spending (Q61)															
If the government had to choose, it should increase taxes and spend more on health, education and social benefits	34	72	80	40	58	64	33	(39)	(51)	33	(70)	(61)	35	57	61
**Welfare v. self-help (A227e) Disagree or disagree strongly that if welfare benefits weren't so generous, people would learn to stand on their own two feet	30	66	71	29	39	(72)	18	(38)	(57)	(34)	(64)	(50)	30	49	66
BASES:															
*ALL RESPONDENTS (INTERVIEW) Weighted	320	152	123	263	135	132	112	(28)	(35)	55	(23)	(32)	257	155	417
Unweighted	330	158	128	282	138	134	121	(29)	(36)	57	(23)	(33)	263	160	429
+ALL RESPONDENTS (SELF-COMPL.) Weighted	291	140	109	238	119	116	91	(25)	(27)	51	(22)	(28)	219	131	346
Unweighted	301	145	114	255	122	120	98	(25)	(28)	53	(22)	(28)	223	135	356
**A RESPONDENTS (SELF-COMPL.) Weighted	152	76	52	129	56	(45)	(45)	(13)	(15)	(29)	(14)	(12)	108	69	176
Unweighted	159	80	55	138	59	(46)	(50)	(14)	(15)	(30)	(13)	(12)	109	74	180

N.B. Some of the bases on this table are very small, and the data should be treated with particular caution.

4.4 PROPORTIONS ADOPTING 'LEFT WING' POSITIONS ON 'NEW AGENDA' ITEMS by party identification within compressed Goldthorpe class schema

		SALARIAT			ROUTINE NON-MAN. WORKERS			PETTY BOURGEOISIE			FOREMEN AND TECHNICIANS			WORKING CLASS		
% ADOPTING 'LEFT WING' POSITIONS ON 'NEW AGENDA' (NON-ECONOMIC) ISSUES		Conservative %	Alliance %	Labour %	Conservative %	Alliance %	Labour %	Conservative %	Alliance %	Labour %	Conservative %	Alliance %	Labour %	Conservative %	Alliance %	Labour %
*Nuclear defence (Q.7)	Britain should rid itself of nuclear weapons while persuading others to do the same	7	27	66	8	31	43	7	(18)	(40)	11	(13)	(34)	9	21	38
+Sex discrimination law (A82)	Support a law against sex discrimination	70	85	93	81	84	75	68	(79)	(81)	(73)	(86)	(71)	71	72	68
**Right to protest (A227h)	Agree strongly or agree that people should be allowed to organise public meetings to protest against the government	62	83	85	47	50	(72)	(60)	(69)	(73)	(55)	(71)	(75)	47	59	70
**Cultural diversity in schools (A206e)	Schools with many children from different backgrounds should teach them about the history and culture of their parents' country of origin	31	44	69	28	44	(54)	(28)	(38)	(60)	(43)	(43)	(42)	31	34	46
+Homosexuality (A88c)	Sexual relations between two adults of the same sex are rarely wrong or not wrong at all	9	29	43	10	25	15	9	(14)	(13)	(10)	(-)	(7)	9	15	7
**Death penalty (A227i)	Disagree strongly or disagree that, for some crimes, the death penalty is the most appropriate sentence	12	36	58	10	20	(20)	(4)	(38)	(20)	(-)	(14)	(8)	5	13	15
BASES:																
*ALL RESPONDENTS (INTERVIEW)	Weighted	320	152	123	263	135	132	112	(28)	(35)	55	(23)	(32)	257	155	417
	Unweighted	330	158	128	282	138	134	121	(29)	(36)	57	(23)	(33)	263	160	429
+A RESPONDENTS (INTERVIEW)	Weighted	166	80	58	136	61	55	53	(14)	(16)	(30)	(14)	(14)	122	75	203
	Unweighted	174	85	62	146	64	55	59	(16)	(16)	(31)	(13)	(15)	123	81	208
**A RESPONDENTS (SELF-COMPL.)	Weighted	152	76	52	129	56	(45)	(45)	(13)	(15)	(29)	(14)	(12)	108	69	176
	Unweighted	159	80	55	138	59	(46)	(50)	(14)	(15)	(30)	(13)	(12)	109	74	180

N.B.　Some of the bases on this table are very small, and the data should be treated with particular caution.

5 The public's response to AIDS

*Lindsay Brook**

On no other topic covered by this series so far has there been more continuous publicity, campaigning and media coverage. Since 1983, when the series began, it is as if a searchlight has been more or less continuously focused on a new disease and – because of its associations – on a particular community, gay men. Increasingly, however, expert knowledge (or opinion) about the spread of the disease has broadened this focus: the groups now publicised as being most at risk are not only gay men, but also people who are sexually active with more than one partner, or whose partner is. 'Safer' sex with one stable partner is now recommended practice to minimise risk. So it is one of those issues on which practical advice coincides perfectly with moral exhortations. As we shall show in this chapter, it is no wonder then that public attitudes to AIDS are so infused with a highly moralistic flavour.

The *British Social Attitudes* series had no questions on AIDS *per se* between 1983 and 1986. We rectified that omission in the 1987 survey when we developed and included a special module on the subject. The questions, as always, are devised for repetition, certainly in 1989 and probably at intervals thereafter. They covered five particular themes which correspond with later sections of this chapter. First, we asked a number of questions about which groups in society were thought to be most at risk from AIDS. This was in an attempt to find out whether AIDS is (still) thought of as a specifically 'gay' disease, or perceived as becoming more widespread. Second, we asked about the likely spread of AIDS. Amidst reports of an epidemic growth in the disease, we wanted to find out how people view the size of the threat. Third, we included questions that would enable us to gauge changing levels of public sympathy for victims of the disease, and in particular how they should be treated by society. Fourth, we asked about the extent to which resources should be devoted both towards

*Senior Researcher at SCPR and Co-director of this survey series.

treatment and the search for a cure. Finally, we included three items about the wider moral questions which AIDS raises, such as whether the onset of the disease is regarded as an inevitable consequence of society's declining standards – a sort of retribution – or as just a tragic coincidence.

Before going on to describe these findings, we first describe here the moral climate in which attitudes to AIDS ought to be placed. Whereas specific questions on AIDS were introduced into the series only in 1987, other questions covering permissiveness and censoriousness towards sexual matters have been included since 1983. The trends are reported fully in Chapter 3 and touched on here only briefly.

The moral climate

As Chapter 3 shows, disapproval both of extra-marital sex and of homosexual relationships has increased since 1983. The growth in censoriousness of homo-sexuality was already apparent from the results of earlier rounds and we speculated then that it was probably associated with anxieties about AIDS (Airey and Brook in *The 1986 Report*). The continuation of the trend lends weight to that thesis, especially now that censoriousness of extra-marital sex has also increased. Our data cannot, of course, prove the link but they certainly imply a clear connection. Either that, or we are witnessing a selective return to more puritanical values, coincidentally on just those issues that are connected strongly in the public mind with AIDS.

Although the growth in censoriousness is apparent among all subgroups of the population, it is faster among some sections than among others. In earlier reports, we have noted that on these issues age is by far the most important discriminator, with older people substantially more likely than younger people to disapprove of both types of sexual relationship. Attitudes differ too by educa-tion and, to a lesser extent, by gender. These three variables account for most of the differences in people's views on sexual morality. So we looked at them for evidence of change. Were all subgroups changing their views at a similar pace?

Examining first attitudes towards extra-marital sex, we find that men, having been slightly more permissive than women in 1983, are now equally censorious and that the age differences are also less noticeable.

	1983*	1987	Increase
Extra-marital sex 'always' or 'mostly' wrong			
Men: total	82%	89%	+7
18–34	76%	86%	+10
35–54	79%	90%	+11
55+	89%	91%	+2
Women: total	86%	88%	+2
18–34	80%	85%	+5
35–54	83%	84%	+1
55+	92%	96%	+4

* The item wording in 1983 referred to husband and wife separately. The answers were almost identical, so averaged responses are given here.

The move towards something approaching a consensus is also apparent among those of different levels of education. Two years ago, those with degrees stood out as conspicuously more permissive than those with lower or no qualifications. Now their views are scarcely different (see **Table 5.1**).

In the light of these findings, we expected to see a similar movement towards consensus in attitudes to homosexual relationships; and we did. The views of men and women, different age groups, and people with varying levels of education are indeed coming closer together, with a general tendency towards greater censoriousness. It is true that women are still more likely than men to hold permissive attitudes in respect of homosexual relationships, but noticeably less so than four years ago. The young are still more likely than older people to be permissive, but also noticeably less so – the biggest movements having occurred among people aged between 25 and 64: all four groups seem to have shifted (almost as if in unison) to being more disapproving than they were, and have now nearly caught up with the two age groups, the youngest and oldest, on either side.

		1983	1985	1987	Increase 1983–87
Homosexual relationships 'always' or 'mostly' wrong					
Sex:	Men	67%	71%	77%	+ 10
	Women	57%	67%	72%	+ 15
Age:	18–24	59%	62%	60%	+ 1
	25–34	44%	56%	61%	+ 17
	35–44	52%	59%	68%	+ 16
	45–54	62%	74%	80%	+ 18
	55–64	70%	84%	89%	+ 19
	65+	82%	85%	92%	+ 10

Graduates, too, conspicuously more permissive in 1985 (we do not have comparable figures on graduates for 1983), are now moving closer to non-graduates, rather than the other way around, in their feelings of censoriousness.

	1985	1987	Increase
Homosexual relationships 'always' or 'mostly' wrong			
Highest educational qualification:			
Degree	39%	51%	+ 12
No degree	71%	76%	+ 5

Full details are given in **Table 5.1**.

We expected this trend towards increasing disapproval of homosexual relationships to be mirrored by a similar trend towards denying gays and lesbians access to positions of authority – especially ones which brought them into contact with young people. We repeated a series of questions asked in earlier years:

> *Now I would like you to tell me whether, in your opinion, it is acceptable for a homosexual person to . . .*
> *. . . be a teacher in a school?*
> *. . . be a teacher in a college or university?*
> *. . . hold a responsible position in public life?*

In *The 1986 Report*, we noted that rather fewer people in 1985 than two years earlier were "willing to accept homosexuals in these sorts of jobs, and rather more were inclined to say 'it depends' " (Airey and Brook in *The 1986 Report*,

p.153). Here we report, with some surprise, that this apparent trend towards discrimination has *not* been sustained.

Is it acceptable for a homosexual person...	1983	1985	1987
... to be a teacher in school?	%	%	%
Yes	41	36	43
No	53	54	50
It depends/other answer	6	10	7
... to be a teacher in college or university?	%	%	%
Yes	48	44	51
No	48	48	44
It depends/other answer	4	8	5
... to hold a responsible position in public life?	%	%	%
Yes	53	50	54
No	42	41	39
It depends/other answer	5	9	7

It remains the case, however, that half the population regards it as unacceptable for homosexuals to teach in schools, and not far short of that proportion would bar them from teaching at colleges or universities and from positions of authority in public life. Nonetheless, attitudes seem to be *marginally* less discriminatory than they were four years earlier: the movements, compared with some presented elsewhere in this Report, are small but they offer at least a little encouragement to those who feared more of a 'gay backlash' in response to events of the past few years.

All these findings should be viewed against the higher profile of the gay community, criticism by some politicians and many sections of the national press of the stance adopted by various local councils towards gay rights and above all, perhaps, the early tabloid press reports of AIDS as a "gay plague" that could be caught by "merely associating with sufferers" (Connor and Kingman, 1988). In that context, although people are expressing mounting disapproval of homosexual relationships, derived perhaps from their anxieties about AIDS, they have *not* become more inclined to bar people from areas of public life merely on the grounds of their sexual preference.

People in Social Classes IV and V – the least tolerant in the past – have become markedly less discriminatory, as have Labour identifiers. Londoners, always more permissive than those elsewhere in their attitudes towards homosexuality, have remained so, as have the other more permissive groups, such as young men, women in the middle-age group (35–54) and graduates (see **Table 5.2**).

In another respect, however, attitudes towards homosexuals – especially *male* homosexuals – seem resistant to liberalisation. We asked in 1985 and again last year, whether or not female and male homosexual couples should be allowed to adopt a baby under the same conditions as other couples. There was always massive resistance to this idea and, if anything, opinion has hardened: 86% would forbid lesbians and a decisive 93% would forbid gay men. It is rare in the *British Social Attitudes* series to find such near-unanimity.

It is in the climate of increased censoriousness towards extra-marital and homosexual relationships, accompanied by a marginally greater tolerance of homosexuals as teachers and in public life, that we turn to the public's response to the growing threat of AIDS.

Groups at risk

Our survey took place in the weeks following the national advertising campaign on television and in the press, warning people not to "die of ignorance". It was certainly not our intention to monitor the results of this campaign: the Central Office of Information had commissioned a series of market research surveys to gauge its effectiveness in, for example, raising awareness of how HIV can be transmitted, and of which sexual and drug-related practices were low- and high-risk. These results are reported in DHSS (1987). Our interest was to find out which groups in the population were perceived to be most at risk from AIDS. Respondents were asked, about eight groups of people in turn, whether they were "greatly" at risk, "quite a lot", "not very much" or "not at all". Over half the sample identified five of the eight groups as "greatly" or "quite a lot" at risk:

Types of people		Greatly at risk	Quite a lot at risk	Not very much/ not at all
People who inject themselves with drugs using shared needles	%	93	6	*
Male homosexuals – that is, gays	%	87	11	1
People who have sex with many different partners of the opposite sex	%	71	24	3
Female homosexuals – that is, lesbians	%	43	17	32
Married couples who occasionally have sex with someone other than their regular partner	%	12	52	34
People who have a blood transfusion	%	12	24	62
Doctors and nurses who treat people who have AIDS	%	5	18	75
Married couples who have sex only with each other	%	*	*	99

As the table shows, the two groups generally regarded as most exposed to the AIDS virus are almost universally recognised as such. Moreover, the message that promiscuous heterosexual behaviour places people at risk seems to have been received by an overwhelming majority. We were surprised by the finding that three out of five people see lesbians as "greatly" or "quite a lot" at risk,[1] since their lifestyles are believed by expert opinion to put them in the "very low" or "low-risk" categories (Terrence Higgins Trust, 1987). Also unexpected was that over a third of respondents saw blood transfusion as risky, even though the so-called 'competitive test' developed by British scientists has reduced the risks to negligible proportions. The continuing plight of haemophilia sufferers, who became infected with HIV in the early 1980s, has clearly left its legacy. It looks, however, as if further public education might be necessary to restore full confidence in Britain's National Blood Transfusion Service. Doctors and nurses, though regarded widely as low-risk groups, are nonetheless identified as high-risk by nearly a quarter of the sample, while faithful heterosexual couples are given the all-clear by almost everyone.

As might be expected, risk is assessed rather differently by various subgroups within the population. Detailed figures are shown in **Table 5.3**. The differences

between those with degrees and those without are especially interesting, as the following data show:

Greatly or quite a lot at risk from AIDS	Degree	No degree
Gays	95%	98%
Promiscuous heterosexuals	88%	95%
Lesbians	32%	63%
Occasionally unfaithful couples	48%	66%
People who have a blood transfusion	20%	37%
Doctors and nurses with AIDS patients	14%	23%

People with degrees appear to be better informed than average about the 'real' risk groups, and they are rather more sanguine than average about the vulnerability of 'high-risk groups' to infection. Perhaps they are more likely to believe, correctly, that sexual orientation or amount of sexual activity is less relevant than the extent to which people take precautions. This possibility is indirectly supported by the answers (discussed later) to our questions on the likely spread of AIDS. The views of men and women are broadly similar, although there is a tendency for women to see greater dangers in heterosexual promiscuity or occasional infidelity. People over 54 of both sexes are most likely to assess the risks as highest, while younger men in particular tend to see heterosexual activity as being less risky. The health education messages may be getting through, but on the whole less clearly, it seems, to those who most need to receive them.

Predictions about the spread of AIDS

We asked respondents for their reactions to two statements, the first designed to elicit beliefs about the potential of a major epidemic, the second about the likelihood of discovering a cure. The two statements, with the response categories offered, are shown in the table below:

Within the next five years	%
... AIDS will cause more deaths in Britain than any other single disease	
Highly exaggerated	11
Slightly exaggerated	27
More or less true	60

...doctors will discover a vaccine against AIDS	%
Agree strongly	4
Agree	30
Neither	45
Disagree	16
Disagree strongly	3

The responses show a substantial majority of the British population to be deeply pessimistic in their prognosis for the disease. Only one-third are even mildly optimistic that its course will be halted by the discovery of a vaccine (with nearly half not even prepared to hazard a guess) and nearly two-thirds believe it will develop into a scourge.

Unless all informed forecasts of future rates of HIV infection and AIDS prove to be seriously wrong, it is inconceivable that by 1992 there will be

more deaths in Britain from AIDS than from, say, heart disease or lung cancer.[2] The most pessimistic predictions would put the number of fatalities in tens rather than hundreds of thousands (Anderson *et al*, 1987). But of course it was not the actual relative *numbers* of deaths that our question was designed to elicit, but the *mood* within the population, which is decidedly gloomy.

This pessimism is shared by all but a few subgroups in our sample, with women, older people (aged 55 +) and the less well educated more likely than average to display it. Noticeably more optimistic than the rest are younger men (not confined to the youngest age groups), those in Social Classes I and II and – conspicuously – graduates, who are only around half as likely as the sample as a whole to endorse the deliberately extreme prediction that we postulated. Their optimistic – and, dare we say, realistic – view of the future is not based on the belief (improbable, we understand) that a cure will be found for AIDS in the next five years. On the contrary, those with degrees are rather *less* likely than average to be optimistic on this count, and the majority of them are unwilling to give any prediction at all. Just under half of those who think that our dire prediction about AIDS is highly exaggerated are optimistic about the imminence of a vaccine. There is also the expected association between optimism about the spread and the assessment of risk to various groups. The more optimistic people are about the spread, the less likely they are to believe that *any* group is at risk.

Sympathy for AIDS sufferers

Fears about the spread of AIDS might well be accompanied by a lack of sympathy for the rising numbers of sufferers from the disease, especially in a society which believes that the risk is omnipresent. We asked a number of questions to try to gauge how attitudes stood in spring 1987 – and as a benchmark by which to monitor future trends.

First, two questions, one on the interview questionnaire and one on the self-completion supplement, were designed broadly to assess the level of general sympathy for those suffering from the disease. The responses indicate an element of ambivalence. A majority (60%) agrees that "people who have AIDS get much less sympathy from society than they ought to get"; and a very similar proportion (57%) believes that "most people with AIDS have only themselves to blame".

For many people, then, disapproval of the lifestyle of the 'typical' sufferers (at present, young homosexual men and abusers of intravenous drugs) does not preclude a degree of sympathy for them. By the same token, sympathy for sufferers is not necessarily accompanied by tolerance of the lifestyle that led to their plight. Nevertheless it is perhaps encouraging to those most concerned with the problem – doctors, nurses, relatives and, of course, the sufferers themselves – that a high proportion of a rather censorious population express broad sympathy towards those who have become infected. Responses to similar questions asked on a survey carried out in Wales in September 1987 indicate that attitudes towards AIDS sufferers had softened over the previous six months or so (Nutbeam *et al*, 1987). We shall see in *The 6th Report* whether or not our data show similar trends.[3]

Few striking differences emerged between the various population subgroups

on these questions, except that those who were most censorious of homosexuality tended to be the least sympathetic towards people with the disease. The association might, however, be rather more indirect than at first sight. Our preliminary analyses suggest that a far more effective discriminator of the respondent's attitudes towards these issues is the person's general value structure on an authoritarian–libertarian dimension. The index we have used here (similar to that used in Chapter 3) is constructed from responses to six questions, only one of which (on censoring of films and magazines) touches upon sexual issues; none deals specifically with attitudes towards homosexuality. Yet it serves as a good predictor of who will feel sympathy towards AIDS sufferers. So although attitudes to homosexuality *per se* do have a bearing on attitudes to and beliefs about AIDS, it appears that one's more *general* authoritarian or libertarian stance is more powerful in shaping one's attitudes. A brief note on how this scale was constructed appears at the end of this chapter.[4]

As the table below shows, authoritarians are much more ready than libertarians to assign blame to people with AIDS, and much less ready to express sympathy.

	% agreeing that AIDS sufferers . . .	
	. . . get much less sympathy than they ought	. . . have only themselves to blame
Strongly authoritarian	54%	80%
Authoritarian	57%	63%
Neither	71%	42%
Libertarian/strongly libertarian*	75%	20%
Total	60%	57%

*There are too few strong libertarians to show their responses separately.

The differences above are striking. For instance, four times the proportion of strong authoritarians as libertarians believe AIDS to be a disease for which sufferers from it have only themsleves to blame. We shall see later how this dimension also influences other attitudes towards the disease and those who have contracted it.

A better measure, perhaps, of public sympathy towards sufferers from the disease than general expressions of concern or otherwise, is the way in which society treats AIDS sufferers. Since the realisation by governments worldwide of the possibility of an epidemic spread of the disease, many countries have introduced measures which in one way or another discriminate against AIDS sufferers (and even against those regarded as in high-risk groups). Connor and Kingman (1988, pp.6–11) review some of these measures, taken in countries as disparate as South Africa and Cuba, Switzerland and the Soviet Union. In the USA and Western Europe, the traditions of civil libertarianism – linked, perhaps, with a realisation that most of the draconian steps proposed would be largely ineffectual – have so far resisted moves that would seriously impinge upon the rights of sufferers. In the USA, an influential turning point was the rejection by Californian voters of a new law, known as 'Proposition 64', under which compulsory reporting of HIV carriers and AIDS sufferers would have been introduced, and in turn led to a prohibition on these groups attending, or being employed by, all state institutions. Mass screening for the HIV infection through blood tests is, however, still supported by the Reagan administration,

and travel and other restrictions are likely to be adopted by an increasing number of countries in all continents (Boateng, 1988).

In Britain, the only legislative move taken so far against AIDS sufferers is a regulation under the Public Health (Control of Diseases) Act to give reserve powers to authorities to "allow for the medical inspection, removal to hospital and detention there of patients in a dangerously infected state".* These powers have to date hardly been used. Moreover, fears that some members of the medical profession would refuse to treat AIDS patients have been unfounded, even though concern has been expressed (particularly by dentists) that the NHS is failing to meet the high extra costs of protection. There have been isolated cases of parents withdrawing their children from school for fear of infection, but no calls from educationists for measures which would, for instance, enable pupils or teachers with the HIV virus to be excluded. Three cases have so far been brought by employees with AIDS against unfair treatment by employers but "to require existing staff to take tests [for AIDS] would probably be a breach of contract, amounting to constructive dismissal" (Dyer, 1988).

Calls for blood screening, or testing without consent, seem to be more common nowadays – both from the media and from public and professional bodies. The Public Health Laboratory Service, for instance, has issued a report advocating 'prevalence screening' (random and anonymous blood tests) as a way of predicting the size of the epidemic. In July 1987, doctors attending the BMA general meeting passed a resolution (later revised) pressing for the right to test patients for AIDS without their agreement "for the patients' own protection" – but the Council of the BMA swiftly rejected this move as against both their own and DHSS policy. In general, then, the position in Britain remains rather *laissez faire*. No requirements as yet exist which serve to control or even measure the potential spread of the disease, and no protection exists – or is planned – to protect AIDS sufferers from discrimination.

As far as the treatment of AIDS victims was concerned, we wanted to test whether this *laissez faire* approach was shared by the public and, in large measure, it is. We chose three areas of possible discrimination,[5] asking whether . . .

> . . . *employers should or should not have the legal right to dismiss people who have AIDS.*

> . . . *doctors and nurses should or should not have the legal right to refuse to treat people who have AIDS.*

> . . . *schools should or should not have the legal right to expel children who have AIDS.*

The distributions (shown below) reveal that very few people are *firmly* for discrimination in any of the three situations, although a rather larger number are *inclined* towards these measures, each of which may be thought rather draconian in the context of a liberal democracy.

---

*Source: Hansard, 6th series, vol. 75, col. 591w, 21 March 1985.

| | Should there be a legal right to ... | | |
| | dismiss employees? | refuse treatment? | expel children? |
	%	%	%
Definitely	13	11	8
Probably	25	20	16
Probably not	29	26	30
Definitely not	28	41	40
Don't know/not stated	5	2	6

While civil libertarians may take comfort from the fact that a firm majority on all three questions supported the rights of AIDS sufferers, they may nonetheless feel uneasy about the size of the minority that contemplated such measures against those suffering from an already devastating illness.

There were no major variations among the various population subgroups on these questions. Men, especially older men, were somewhat more willing than average to give employers the legal right to dismiss people who have AIDS; women (particularly younger women) were somewhat less willing to allow doctors and nurses the right to refuse to treat patients. But on expelling children, men and women hardly differed. Those in non-manual jobs tended to be less discriminatory than those in manual jobs. But once again it was those with higher educational qualifications – especially graduates – who stood out as the most liberal:

		Degree	No degree
Employers should have legal right to dismiss			
Definitely	%	6	14
Probably	%	13	26
Doctors and nurses should have legal right to refuse to treat			
Definitely	%	3	11
Probably	%	16	21
Schools should have legal right to expel			
Definitely	%	1	9
Probably	%	11	17

Subgroup differences are shown in more detail in **Table 5.4.**

Respondents whom we classified as authoritarian might be thought to be particularly discriminatory on these issues, but the tendency – although present – was not quite as marked as we expected; and, as far as schools were concerned, authoritarians were only slightly more inclined than were libertarians to be severe on sufferers.

Resources for AIDS

We have already revealed broad public sympathy for AIDS sufferers, coupled with an almost equally strong feeling that most are to blame for their situation. We examine now how sympathy – or lack of it – translates itself into resources: should more money be devoted to care for sufferers and to the search for a 'cure'? Two questions in our module are relevant to this issue, and both will become increasingly pertinent as more information becomes available on the high costs of both patient care and experimental treatments to alleviate suffering and prolong life (see, for example, Cunningham and Griffiths, 1987).[6]

One question (on the self-completion supplement) asked respondents to agree or disagree with the statement.

The National Health Service should spend more of its resources on giving better care to people dying from AIDS.

Another question, asked during the interview, required people to weigh the importance of research into a cure against the competing demands of other kinds of medical research.

More money should be spent trying to find a cure for AIDS, even if it means that research into other serious diseases is delayed.

Again respondents were asked to agree or disagree "strongly or a little"; this time no middle option was offered.

We found majority support for extra resources for both care and research, but a smaller majority for the former: given the option of saying "neither" over a quarter of the sample took it, despite the deliberately stark wording of the question.

	More NHS resources on care for the dying %	More money for research into a cure %
Agree strongly	8	32
Agree (a little*)	34	26
Neither agree nor disagree	29	n/a
Disagree (a little*)	23	20
Disagree strongly	5	18

*Interview questionnaire

Perhaps the striking difference between these two sets of figures is the lack of strong feeling for or against more resources for patient care; only 13% are to be found at either extreme (*strongly* agree or *strongly* disagree), compared with 50% with strong views about more money for research into a cure.* The combination of answers here looks remarkably similar in its suggestion of ambivalence to the answers noted earlier on attitudes to those with AIDS. We have noted the broad measure of sympathy for sufferers, coupled with a widespread feeling that they were to blame for getting the disease. Now we find a lack of *strong* support for better care for people dying from the disease, alongside greater support for research which may help to eradicate it.

If this is indeed a *reprise* of the same sense of ambivalence, then we would expect to see the authoritarians among our sample reasonably supportive of money for research but much less in favour than libertarians of NHS resources being spent on patient care. And this is precisely how it turned out. They differ little from the average on the first issue, and greatly on the second.

	Authoritarians %	Libertarians %
More money for research into a cure		
Agree (strongly or a little)	54	61
Disagree (strongly or a little)	25	27
More NHS resources on care for the dying		
Agree (strongly or just agree)	39	63
Disagree (strongly or just disagree)	32	16

*As we have noted, responses to the two questions are not strictly comparable. Nevertheless, there can be no doubt that the search for a cure elicits stronger feelings (and stronger support).

In none of the various demographic subgroups do these differences emerge, although it is worth noting that party identification, almost never associated with attitudes towards AIDS, does have a bearing on this issue. Labour identifiers are especially likely to favour more NHS resources spent on care of AIDS patients while Conservatives are almost evenly divided for and against. It is probable, however, that more general political ideologies in relation to government spending on the NHS are at work here, rather than specific views about AIDS.

AIDS as a moral issue

AIDS has several characteristics which make it a particularly difficult challenge for health educationists. They have to overcome "prejudices and taboos, not just about sex, but about sexual preferences, lifestyles, drug addiction, race and nationality" (Connor and Kingman, 1988, p.3). The long period of latency between infection and the appearance of symptoms, and the absence of any vaccine or cure, make the disease seem uniquely threatening. To examine the wider moral dimensions associated with the disease would constitute a large-scale investigation in its own right. We limited ourselves to just three questions (all asked on the self-completion supplement) to serve as a benchmark, allowing us to track attitudes to AIDS as a moral, rather than a medical, issue in future years.

The first two statements, with which respondents were invited to agree or disagree (strongly or slightly), were:

Official warnings about AIDS should say that some sexual practices are morally wrong.

AIDS is a way of punishing the world for its decline in moral standards.

The balance of public opinion is, surprisingly perhaps, strongly in favour of the first statement and mildly against the second.

	Official warnings	Punishment for world
	%	%
Agree strongly	31	10
Agree	35	19
Neither agree nor disagree	13	25
Disagree	14	24
Disagree strongly	5	22

It will be recalled that our fieldwork coincided with the second wave of a government advertising campaign (larger than ever before in the field of health education). Its impact, according to the research available, was considerable, and there was widespread support for government expenditure on education about AIDS (DHSS, 1987). Yet according to our findings, a majority in almost all of the population subgroups (and an overwhelming majority in some) would – in theory at any rate – have approved of a campaign that did not just inform about the risk of certain kinds of sexual behaviour but also made judgements about their morality or otherwise. Only among graduates is there a (slight) majority who would have disapproved of such an approach. There were, however, other substantial (and predictable) subgroup differences in the extent of

approval and disapproval of moral exhortations in official advertising. Young people (men *and* women) are singularly unenthusiastic, and those in non-manual occupations are fairly unenthusiastic too (see **Table 5.5** for full details).

Very similar patterns were evident in answer to our question as to whether or not AIDS was a punishment for a decline in moral standards (except that social class divisions were not nearly so pronounced). Not surprisingly, an overwhelming majority of graduates (76%) reject this retributive notion of AIDS. More surprisingly, perhaps, religious affiliation – or lack of it – does not influence answers either to any marked degree (again full details are given in **Table 5.5**).

Once again the most powerful predictor of attitudes – on both these questions – is a person's position on the authoritarian-libertarian scale:

	% agreeing that ...	
	... official warnings should say some sexual practices morally wrong	... AIDS is way of punishing world for decline in moral standards
Strongly authoritarian	86%	49%
Authoritarian	74%	34%
Neither	52%	12%
Libertarian/strongly libertarian	18%	10%

Our final question, on the effects of AIDS on young people, provides an intriguing contrast to what we have seen as an increasing censoriousness of sexual behaviour generally. By a majority of over three to one (63% to 19%) our sample agrees that "AIDS is a tragedy for young people because it surrounds their sex lives with fear". Moreover, on this question, respondents of different ages and backgrounds were much more united, and even those who took a strongly authoritarian stance were not markedly less likely to disagree.* Curiously, however, attitudes are somewhat associated with class and – even more so – with education in a counter-intuitive direction: those in non-manual occupations and those with degrees are more likely than their counterparts to *disagree* that AIDS is a tragedy for young people. We can only guess at the reasons for this paradox, but it may have something to do with the finding (noted earlier) that these groups are less likely to believe that the spread of AIDS is inevitable: they are more likely to believe that 'safer sex' can and should control the spread of AIDS and that there is therefore no cause for the disease to assume the proportions of a tragedy.

Conclusions

Our evidence suggests that health educationists in Britain have an uphill task if their aim is to create an environment in which the epidemiological challenge of AIDS, and the problem of caring sympathetically for AIDS sufferers, are to be addressed simultaneously. There is, after all, a strong authoritarian streak in British society. We should not (and do not) use this phrase pejoratively,

---

*We have, however, to be a little sceptical about giving too much credence to the answers to this question – which seems, in retrospect, to have flaws. In particular the reason that the answers do not discriminate so much between authoritarians and libertarians is probably that the term 'young people' could refer to whatever reference group one chooses – young married people, teenagers and so on. We shall try to rectify this problem in future rounds.

since it relates to a deep-rooted sense of conformity and traditionalism, not necessarily to an aggressive or punitive stance on particular social issues. But it makes people resistant to change, especially on issues that are infused with moral overtones. Unlike most illnesses which may be as threatening in their effects, AIDS has certain characteristics which make sufferers peculiarly vulnerable to a sort of remote disapproval – a distancing of those viewing it from those suffering from it. This is especially the case for people who do not *themselves* feel threatened by the disease because their lifestyles are unlikely to permit it, which is why the elderly on almost all these questions are so much more censorious than others. Moreover, with increasing public awareness of how to avoid, or at least minimise the chances of getting the virus, there is a real possibility that future sufferers may be held to account as at least partly responsible for their predicament.

There is, nonetheless, broad public sympathy for AIDS sufferers. But there is also a somewhat chilling lack of strong concern for increasing the resources available for helping sufferers. Instead, it seems better treatment is regarded as much less pressing than more research. From a Benthamite point of view that is clearly a rational approach. From the point of view of the anticipated fast-growing number of sufferers during the next decade or so, it may seem like rather cold comfort.

Notes

1.　In January–February 1987, just before the start of fieldwork on our survey, a BMRB survey revealed that 43% believed that AIDS could definitely be caught from "sex between two women", precisely the proportion we found who thought that lesbians were greatly at risk (Orton and Samuels, 1988).
2.　As Eastwood and Maynard (1987) remark, with a commendable degree of understatement, "it is difficult to make accurate predictions of the future numbers of AIDS cases and HIV infection because of limitations of the data", (p.5) and "the predictions are very sensitive to changes in the parameters" (p.15). The parameters include alterations in patterns of sexual behaviour (leading to a fall in transmission rates) and assumptions about the mean incubation period of the AIDS virus. See also Doll (1988).
3.　Nutbeam *et al.* (1988) report a nine per cent fall in the proportion saying that they "didn't feel sorry for homosexuals who catch AIDS because it is their own fault", and a five per cent fall in the proportion saying the same of "drug abusers". Nonetheless nearly half of those interviewed were unsympathetic towards both groups. They conclude that there is "a need to prevent unwarranted prejudice against people with HIV infection or AIDS", but that "major progress is unlikely to occur unless there are wider changes in social attitudes" which they judge necessary both on humanitarian and public health grounds.
4.　The six items from which the authoritarian–libertarian scale was constructed were included in question A227 of the self-completion questionnaire. (The scale itself is derived from factor analyses carried out by Heath, Jowell, Curtice and Witherspoon (1986).)

> *Young people today don't have enough respect for traditional British values.*
> *People who break the law should be given stiffer sentences*
> *For some crimes, the death penalty is the most appropriate sentence*
> *Schools should teach children to obey authority*
> *The law should always be obeyed, even if a particular law is wrong*
> *Censorship of films and magazines is necessary to uphold moral standards*

Respondents were asked whether they agreed or disagreed with these statements on a simple five-point scale, ranging from "agree strongly" to "disagree strongly". Those who agreed strongly were given a score of 1, those who simply "agreed" a score of 2 and so on, to 5 for strong disagreement. The range of possible scores is thus between 5 (strong authoritarians) and 25 (strong libertarians). Each respondent's score was divided by 5 to give an average score.

5. We considered carefully, but rejected, asking questions about random blood screening, and testing with or without consent. Questions asked on these topics on other surveys seemed flawed and the complexity of the subject – in particular, what action should be taken following a HIV positive result – demanded, in our view, more questionnaire space than was available.

6. Cunningham and Griffiths (1987) have estimated the total lifetime cost for each AIDS patient to be around £21 000. If the drug zidovodine (Retrovir) is used, the cost per patient rises to around £27 000. Eastwood and Maynard (1987) conclude that "the cost of AIDS and HIV infection in the UK is clearly a significant burden on limited NHS resources. It is quite likely that new drugs will be introduced into the treatment of AIDS and such drugs may well be more expensive than Retrovir", (p.23).

References

AIREY, C., 'Social and moral values' in Jowell, R. and Airey, C. (eds), *British Social Attitudes: the 1984 Report*, Gower, Aldershot (1984).

AIREY, C. and BROOK, L., 'Interim report: Social and moral issues', in Jowell, R., Witherspoon, S. and Brook, L. (eds), *British Social Attitudes: the 1986 Report*, Gower, Aldershot (1986).

ANDERSON, R.M., MEDLEY, G.F., BLYTHE, S.P. and JOHNSON, A.M., 'Is it possible to predict the minimum size of the acquired immunodeficiency syndrome (AIDS) epidemic in the United Kingdom?', *The Lancet*, i, (1987), pp. 1073–75.

BOATENG, P., 'HIV tests defy boundaries and logic', *The Guardian* (11 May, 1988).

CONNOR, S. and KINGMAN, S., *The Search for the Virus*, Penguin Books, Harmondsworth (1988).

CUNNINGHAM, D.G. and GRIFFITHS, F.J., 'AIDS: counting the cost', [letter to] *British Medical Journal*, vol.295 (1987), pp. 921–22.

DHSS & THE WELSH OFFICE, *AIDS, Monitoring Response to the Public Education Campaign, February 1986–February 1987*, HMSO, London (1987).

DOLL, R., 'Major Epidemics of the 20th Century: from Coronary Thrombosis to AIDS', *Social Trends*, vol.18, HMSO, London (1988), pp.13–22.

DYER, C., 'Coming to Terms with AIDS in the Courts', *The Law Magazine* (4 March, 1988), p.18.

EASTWOOD, A., and MAYNARD, A., 'Treating AIDS Patients: is it Ethical to be Efficient?', *Paper presented to the IRISS Conference: Quality of life: perspectives and policies*, University of York (1987).

HEATH, A., JOWELL, R., CURTICE, J. and WITHERSPOON, S., *End of Award Report to the ESRC: Methodological Aspects of Attitude Research*, SCPR, London (1986).

NUTBEAM, D., SMAIL, S.A., CATFORD, J.C. and GRIFFITHS, C., 'Public Knowledge and Attitudes to AIDS in 1987' (1988, forthcoming).

ORTON, S. and SAMUELS, J., 'What we have Learned from Researching AIDS', *Journal of the Market Research Society*, vol. 30, no. 1 (1988), pp. 3–34.

TERRENCE HIGGINS TRUST, *AIDS and HIV: Medical Briefing*, 3rd edn, THT, (April 1987).

Acknowledgements

The author is grateful to the members of the staff of the Terrence Higgins Trust for their advice and for use of the Trust's library; and to Dr Don Nutbeam and his colleagues at the Institute for Health Promotion, University of Wales College of Medicine and of The Welsh AIDS Campaign for access to unpublished data on attitudes to AIDS.

5.1 ATTITUDES TO EXTRA-MARITAL AND HOMOSEXUAL RELATIONSHIPS, 1985 AND 1987 (1987: A88b,c)
by highest educational qualification obtained

1985

| | TOTAL | HIGHEST EDUCATIONAL QUALIFICATION | | | |
		Degree	Professional	'A' level/ 'O' level/ CSE	Foreign/ Other/ None
	%	%	%	%	%
SEXUAL RELATIONS OUTSIDE MARRIAGE:					
Always wrong	57	26	53	52	67
Mostly wrong	25	47	30	30	17
Sometimes wrong	11	18	10	14	8
Rarely wrong	1	1	2	*	1
Not wrong at all	2	2	2	2	3
Depends/varies	3	5	2	3	3
Don't know/not answered	1	2	1	1	2
SEXUAL RELATIONS BETWEEN TWO PERSONS OF THE SAME SEX:					
Always wrong	59	26	53	53	70
Mostly wrong	10	13	15	11	7
Sometimes wrong	7	20	8	9	3
Rarely wrong	4	7	5	4	3
Not wrong at all	12	23	12	16	8
Depends/varies	6	5	6	6	6
Don't know/not answered	1	7	2	1	3
Weighted	1769	123	199	625	822
Unweighted	1804	122	206	640	836

1987

| | TOTAL | HIGHEST EDUCATIONAL QUALIFICATION | | | |
		Degree	Professional	'A' level/ 'O' level/ CSE	Foreign/ Other/ None
	%	%	%	%	%
SEXUAL RELATIONS OUTSIDE MARRIAGE:					
Always wrong	63	41	66	57	71
Mostly wrong	25	45	23	30	18
Sometimes wrong	9	12	8	11	7
Rarely wrong	1	1	1	1	1
Not wrong at all	1	-	1	*	1
Depends/varies	1	-	1	1	2
Don't know/not answered	*	-	-	*	1
SEXUAL RELATIONS BETWEEN TWO PERSONS OF THE SAME SEX:					
Always wrong	64	39	62	55	76
Mostly wrong	11	12	9	12	10
Sometimes wrong	8	17	9	11	3
Rarely wrong	2	4	3	4	1
Not wrong at all	11	25	13	12	6
Depends/varies	4	3	4	5	3
Don't know/not answered	1	-	*	1	2
Weighted	1391	110	182	510	587
Unweighted	1437	114	191	521	608

BASES: ALL RESPONDENTS, 1985;
A RESPONDENTS, 1987

5.2 DISCRIMINATION AGAINST HOMOSEXUALS, 1985 AND 1987 (1987:A89a) by age within sex, social class and highest educational qualification obtained

1985

IN YOUR OPINION, IS [IT] ACCEPTABLE FOR A HOMOSEXUAL PERSON

	TOTAL	MEN 18-34	MEN 35-54	MEN 55+	WOMEN 18-34	WOMEN 35-54	WOMEN 55+	SOCIAL CLASS I/II	III non-manual	III manual	IV/v	Degree	Profess-ional	'A' level/'O' level/CSE	Foreign/Other/None
	%	%	%	%	%	%	%	%	%	%	%	%	%	%	%
... to be a teacher in a school?															
Yes	36	49	32	16	54	45	17	45	43	30	27	65	43	43	25
No	54	44	55	75	37	48	68	45	47	62	62	28	47	47	64
... to be a teacher in a college or university?															
Yes	44	62	42	23	59	55	19	55	50	38	35	75	54	53	31
No	48	36	46	70	32	39	68	38	41	56	57	22	38	39	61
... to hold a responsible position in public life?															
Yes	50	62	48	25	71	60	29	59	60	44	42	79	59	59	37
No	41	31	41	67	22	33	58	33	32	50	48	17	32	32	54
BASE: ALL RESPONDENTS, 1985															
Weighted	1769	287	288	247	333	308	306	396	393	366	444	123	199	625	822
Unweighted	1804	284	295	241	340	329	310	403	411	362	448	122	206	640	836

1987

IN YOUR OPINION, IS [IT] ACCEPTABLE FOR A HOMOSEXUAL PERSON

	TOTAL	MEN 18-34	MEN 35-54	MEN 55+	WOMEN 18-34	WOMEN 35-54	WOMEN 55+	SOCIAL CLASS I/II	III non-manual	III manual	IV/v	Degree	Profess-ional	'A' level/'O' level/CSE	Foreign/Other/None
	%	%	%	%	%	%	%	%	%	%	%	%	%	%	%
... to be a teacher in a school?															
Yes	43	51	43	24	64	49	24	51	48	36	39	69	50	49	31
No	50	44	54	69	31	42	65	40	45	58	57	25	40	45	63
... to be a teacher in a college or university?															
Yes	51	62	54	30	70	56	31	61	55	43	44	83	59	58	36
No	44	35	44	66	26	37	62	34	40	53	52	14	34	37	60
... to hold a responsible position in public life?															
Yes	54	64	55	34	75	60	36	62	60	45	52	79	62	60	43
No	39	33	40	62	19	30	55	30	34	49	42	16	31	34	50
BASE: A RESPONDENTS, 1987															
Weighted	1391	214	233	201	238	272	230	352	323	286	330	110	182	510	587
Unweighted	1437	204	247	214	236	285	249	368	344	298	327	114	191	521	608

5.3 GROUPS PERCEIVED TO BE AT RISK FROM AIDS (A107) by sex, age within sex and highest educational qualification obtained

	TOTAL	SEX		AGE WITHIN SEX						HIGHEST EDUCATIONAL QUALIFICATION			
				MEN			WOMEN						
		Men	Women	18-34	35-54	55+	18-34	35-54	55+	Degree	Professional	'A' level/ 'O' level/ CSE	Foreign/ Other/ None
	%	%	%	%	%	%	%	%	%	%	%	%	%
HOW MUCH AT RISK [IS] EACH OF THESE GROUPS FROM AIDS?													
People who have sex with many different partners of the opposite sex													
- greatly/quite a lot at risk	95	92	98	91	91	94	98	99	97	88	96	95	96
- not very much/not at all at risk	4	7	1	8	8	4	2	*	-	10	4	5	2
Married couples who have sex only with each other													
- greatly/quite a lot at risk	*	*	-	-	*	*	-	*	-	-	-	-	*
- not very much/not at all at risk	99	99	99	100	100	97	100	99	97	100	100	100	98
Married couples who occasionally have sex with someone other than their regular partner													
- greatly/quite a lot at risk	65	60	68	56	56	70	66	64	75	48	66	59	71
- not very much/not at all at risk	34	38	30	43	43	27	34	35	20	50	32	40	26
People who have a blood transfusion													
- greatly/quite a lot at risk	35	33	37	32	31	37	32	35	45	19	25	33	43
- not very much/not at all at risk	62	64	60	68	67	56	68	63	50	79	73	66	52
Doctors and nurses who treat people who have AIDS													
- greatly/quite a lot at risk	23	23	23	21	19	30	16	24	27	13	16	21	28
- not very much/not at all at risk	75	75	74	78	80	66	83	74	67	85	84	77	68
Male homosexuals - that is, gays													
- greatly/quite a lot at risk	98	97	98	96	98	97	98	98	98	96	98	97	98
- not very much/not at all at risk	1	2	1	3	1	2	2	1	-	4	1	2	1
Female homosexuals - that is, lesbians													
- greatly/quite a lot at risk	60	60	61	49	60	70	57	57	69	32	59	56	69
- not very much/not at all at risk	32	34	30	47	34	20	39	32	18	58	33	37	22
People who inject themselves with drugs using shared needles													
- greatly/quite a lot at risk	99	99	99	99	100	99	100	100	98	99	100	100	98
- not very much/not at all at risk	*	*	*	1	-	-	-	-	*	-	-	*	*
BASE: A RESPONDENTS													
Weighted	1391	648	742	214	233	201	238	272	230	110	182	510	587
Unweighted	1437	665	772	204	247	214	236	285	249	114	191	521	608

5.4 DISCRIMINATION AGAINST AIDS SUFFERERS (A108)
by age within sex, social class and highest educational qualification obtained

	TOTAL	MEN 18-34	MEN 35-54	MEN 55+	WOMEN 18-34	WOMEN 35-54	WOMEN 55+	I/II	III non-manual	III manual	IV/V	Degree	Profess-ional	'A' level/'O' level/CSE	Foreign/Other/None
		AGE WITHIN SEX						**SOCIAL CLASS**				**HIGHEST EDUCATIONAL QUALIFICATION**			
SHOULD OR SHOULD NOT EMPLOYERS HAVE THE LEGAL RIGHT TO DISMISS PEOPLE WHO HAVE AIDS?	%	%	%	%	%	%	%	%	%	%	%	%	%	%	%
Definitely should	13	14	16	21	8	11	10	12	10	18	14	6	14	11	16
Probably should	25	25	23	27	23	23	27	19	25	28	28	13	19	27	26
Probably should not	29	30	25	27	33	29	28	31	31	25	26	40	29	28	28
Definitely should not	28	30	31	17	34	32	22	34	31	22	25	34	36	30	22
Don't know/not answered	5	1	4	7	2	6	13	4	4	7	7	6	2	4	8
SHOULD OR SHOULD NOT DOCTORS AND NURSES HAVE THE LEGAL RIGHT TO REFUSE TO TREAT PEOPLE WHO HAVE AIDS?															
Definitely should	11	11	11	11	12	11	8	9	12	12	10	3	11	10	12
Probably should	20	21	17	20	24	20	21	16	20	23	25	16	17	21	22
Probably should not	26	23	21	23	30	30	27	26	29	24	24	27	26	28	25
Definitely should not	41	43	50	44	33	37	37	48	37	38	37	54	45	40	37
Don't know/not answered	2	1	1	2	1	1	7	1	2	3	3	1	1	2	4
SHOULD OR SHOULD NOT SCHOOLS HAVE THE LEGAL RIGHT TO EXPEL CHILDREN WHO HAVE AIDS?															
Definitely should	8	12	11	11	5	7	4	6	7	10	8	1	8	9	9
Probably should	16	18	15	18	16	14	16	14	17	18	16	11	14	17	17
Probably should not	30	28	31	27	35	34	25	31	33	31	27	39	32	30	28
Definitely should not	40	40	40	37	43	40	42	46	39	33	41	44	46	41	37
Don't know/not answered	6	3	4	6	1	5	13	3	3	8	8	4	2	3	9
BASE: A RESPONDENTS															
Weighted	1391	214	233	201	238	272	230	352	323	286	330	110	182	510	587
Unweighted	1437	204	247	214	236	285	249	368	344	298	337	114	191	521	608

5.5 AIDS AS A MORAL ISSUE (A225c,e)
by age within sex, social class, highest educational qualification obtained and religion

	TOTAL	AGE WITHIN SEX — MEN 18-34	MEN 35-54	MEN 55+	WOMEN 18-34	WOMEN 35-54	WOMEN 55+	SOCIAL CLASS I/II	III non-manual	III manual	IV/V	EDUC. QUAL. Degree	Professional	'A' level/'O' level/CSE	Foreign/Other/None	RELIGION Roman Catholic	C of E/Anglican	Other Christian	(No religion)
	%	%	%	%	%	%	%	%	%	%	%	%	%	%	%	%	%	%	%
OFFICIAL WARNINGS ABOUT AIDS SHOULD SAY THAT SOME SEXUAL PRACTICES ARE MORALLY WRONG																			
Agree strongly	31	19	31	55	15	27	44	27	25	34	38	18	29	24	41	37	34	33	26
Agree	35	30	38	34	34	37	39	30	37	42	33	24	37	34	38	32	37	39	32
Neither agree nor disagree	13	19	11	4	22	12	10	14	17	10	12	14	14	15	11	9	12	12	15
Disagree	14	22	15	4	20	18	4	19	16	10	12	26	15	20	7	18	12	12	17
Disagree strongly	5	10	5	2	9	5	-	10	3	3	5	18	5	6	2	3	2	3	9
Don't know/not answered	1	-	*	*	*	1	3	-	1	2	1	-	-	*	2	-	2	1	*
AIDS IS A WAY OF PUNISHING THE WORLD FOR ITS DECLINE IN MORAL STANDARDS																			
Agree strongly	10	6	9	17	3	7	18	8	5	12	11	-	9	7	14	8	11	12	7
Agree	19	12	15	25	13	22	26	14	22	21	18	8	21	17	22	21	21	17	15
Neither agree nor disagree	25	17	25	28	28	24	28	23	28	26	25	17	24	23	29	21	27	26	23
Disagree	24	23	25	18	30	27	20	24	25	24	25	30	25	25	22	25	24	26	23
Disagree strongly	22	42	26	12	24	18	7	31	18	16	21	46	22	27	12	24	14	18	31
Don't know/not answered	1	-	-	-	1	2	2	-	2	1	*	-	-	1	1	-	1	1	1
BASE: A RESPONDENTS																			
Weighted	1243	195	213	179	217	241	196	326	292	254	286	98	169	476	499	124	441	220	441
Unweighted	1281	184	225	191	215	252	211	339	309	264	291	102	177	485	514	124	463	228	445

6 An ailing state of National Health

*Nick Bosanquet**

Looking back to 1983 when this series began, public confidence in, and satisfaction with, the National Health Service were both at a high level, almost irrespective of people's party identities or other characteristics, such as age and class. Between then and now there has been a number of crises within the NHS, culminating in 1988 in a fundamental review of options for change. Our data suggest that the broad consensus evident in 1983 was by 1987 showing signs of fracture, resulting in an increased politicisation of the whole issue of health care.

In the arguments about future policy, choices have often been presented in terms of increased private – as against public – health care, but our surveys show that respondents do not on the whole see the debate in these terms: there was little change in perceptions of the private sector. Rather, support for the *principle* of state health care, and for increased government expenditure to provide it, has grown stronger over the period. At the same time levels of general dissatisfaction with the NHS have been rising – from 25% in 1983 to almost 40% in 1987. Dissatisfaction with some *specific* NHS services, notably hospital services, has also grown, but not nearly as much.

To understand these changes in attitudes, we trace first a brief background to the policy debates that have been taking place in recent years.

First there has been continued controversy over funding, in particular over the minimum rate of increase in real terms required to meet changes in demography, in technology and in policy aims (such as the extension of community care). Organisations representing health professionals commissioned reports which argued that a two per cent increase in funding in real terms was needed to meet these demands, about half of which was required simply to cater for the growing numbers of people aged over 75 in the population (Bosanquet,

* Senior Research Fellow, Centre for Health Economics, University of York.

1985; Maynard and Bosanquet, 1986).* In addition, there was continuing disagreement about how increases in real terms should be measured. One way of calculating expenditure – using the GDP deflator – showed an increase in NHS spending of 21.6% between 1980 and 1987; another method – using the NHS specific index of pay and prices, which takes into account changes in the prices of goods and services used by the service – showed an increase of only 10.4%. But regardless of measurement methods, the increase was distributed unevenly: the hospital services in particular came off badly, with an increase of only 4.8 per cent, apart from any effect of cost improvements (House of Commons Social Services Committee, 1988).

During 1987 the debate swung towards the more urgent issue of closures of beds and restrictions of services and, by the end of the year, the government had announced a special allocation of £90m "to meet the immediate problem". However, even this failed to assuage concerns about underfunding (House of Commons Social Services Committee, 1988).

The management and efficiency of the NHS also came in for close scrutiny. A report commissioned from Sir Roy Griffiths criticised the lack of clear management responsibility for setting aims and achieving targets (DHSS, 1983). Following the report, a new system of management was introduced with clearer executive responsibility under District and Unit General Managers. A new Management Board was set up, with responsibility for setting targets, and an information system was developed to monitor the performance of local health districts. These changes did not end the debate about whether the NHS was adapting fast enough to change; but assessed by conventional measures, such as the numbers of cases treated, the productivity of the NHS did rise. On the other hand waiting lists also rose. In fact, since the mid-1970s, the number of people on waiting lists for non-emergency operations has continued to rise gradually; by September 1986, the figure for England and Wales was around 682,000.

One solution offered for increasing NHS efficiency was the introduction of "internal markets" (Enthoven, 1985); these would give each health district freedom to sell its services to others, possibly affording a wider choice for patients who could then select which districts they wanted for their treatment. Meanwhile, stories about anguished patients waiting in pain or distress for treatment began to get increasing publicity in the media. For instance, the case of a Birmingham baby whose heart operation had been long delayed because of a shortage of specialist nurses became the centre of attention during the 1987 general election campaign and after.

Manpower problems in the NHS had already begun to command attention in 1983 when health authorities began to introduce ceilings to limit staff levels. Then, over the next four years, in sharp distinction to earlier periods, NHS staffing levels showed little growth. By 1987 attention was focused not so much on manpower ceilings as on the difficulty of recruiting and retaining even minimum numbers of nursing staff. Research commissioned by the Royal College of Nursing suggested that the service might be losing as many as 30,000 nurses a year (Waite and Hutt, 1986). There was also continued publicity about nurses' pay and the repeated suggestion that industrial action might be imminent. Such

---

* The health services spend about eight times more on this group than on adults aged between 16 and 64. Between 1979 and 1986 their numbers have increased from 3.11m to 3.68m (Central Statistical Office, 1988).

action, consisting of sporadic and short-lived strikes by some nurses, came early in 1988, well after the end of our fieldwork period, as did the decision to introduce a new grading structure which led to substantial pay increases for some nurses.

Finally *private* health care in Britain was growing steadily; expenditure on it rose from around £450m in 1983 to an estimated £733m in 1986 (Laing, 1987). Patronised largely by the upper and middle classes – although even among these groups only 12–13% of in-patient stays are private (OPCS, 1987) – the number of private sector beds had risen by 50% between 1979 and 1986, accompanied by a steady reduction in the number of the private beds in NHS hospitals (Laing, 1987). Even so, the main expenditure in the private sector continued to be on nursing home care of the elderly and chronically ill.

With all these developments taking place, and amidst claims and counterclaims about levels of expenditure in the NHS, the extent of political controversy surrounding the NHS was, by 1987, very high – certainly much higher than in 1983. For instance, during the first six months of the 1987 parliament, there were 26 Early Day Motions drawing attention to cuts, ward closures and financial crises in health authorities; there were nine parliamentary debates on the subject, three of which were full-scale. It was probably the sheer weight of parliamentary and press attention that drove the NHS up the list of issues rated as important by the public in opinion polls at the time. Indeed, by the end of 1987 it had overtaken unemployment in Gallup polls as the issue nominated as most important in helping people to decide which party to support (Gallup, 1988).

Priorities for public spending

Our fieldwork took place in the weeks preceding the 1987 general election, when the debate over the 'crisis' in the NHS was at its most acute. However, most of the trends we uncovered were already clearly in evidence a year earlier, and indeed a year before that (Taylor-Gooby in *The 1987 Report* and Bosanquet in *The 1986 Report*).

We turn first to those questions which are most likely to have been influenced in the short term by the political climate. Each year we have asked:

Here are some items of government spending. Which of them, if any, would be your highest priority for extra spending? And which next?

Responses for 1983 and 1987 are shown below:*

	First priority		First or second priority	
	1983	1987	1983	1987
	%	%	%	%
Health	37	52	63	79
Education	24	24	50	55
Help for industry	16	5	29	11
Housing	7	8	20	24
Social security benefits	6	4	12	12

* Five other items of possible government expenditure are in the list given to respondents (see Appendix III, Q.57, p.227). None of them received more than eight per cent support in either year and they are all remote from health service interests. So they are omitted from the list here.

The NHS stands out in this list as the only one of the five shown to have had a sharp rise over the period. Over half our respondents now put health as their first priority for extra spending, and nearly 80% would give it first or second priority. A rise in support for NHS spending has now taken place in 1984, 1986 and 1987. Whereas in earlier years there were noticeable subgroup differences in the programmes favoured for extra expenditure, by 1987 health spending had become the first priority for all main subgroups (except graduates who, by a small margin, favour education over health).

Despite the different views expressed in the political debates, there has been an increase in support for extra health spending among those identifying with all the main political parties.

	Conservative		Alliance		Labour	
	1983	1987	1983	1987	1983	1987
	%	%	%	%	%	%
First priority to:						
Health	34	47	43	55	39	55
Education	24	27	24	26	24	22
Help for industry	20	6	16	3	13	4
Housing	5	6	6	8	10	10
Social security benefits	3	3	4	3	9	6

Notably, nearly half of Conservative identifiers – and more than half of people identifying with both other parties – now name health as the main priority for extra spending. Such common cause between the different party identifiers is rather rare. Moreover, attitudes to the NHS may also have influenced other attitudes. A more general and even more dramatic change has taken place in relation to public expenditure and taxation. We have asked in each of the five years:

Suppose the government had to choose between the three options on this card. Which do you think it should choose?

	1983	1984	1985	1986	1987
	%	%	%	%	%
Reduce taxes and spend less on health, education and social benefits	9	6	6	5	3
Keep taxes and spending on these services at the same level as now	54	50	43	44	42
Increase taxes and spend more on health, education and social benefits	32	39	45	46	50

While in 1983 just under a third of respondents favoured extra public expenditure, this proportion had risen to one half in 1987; and the rise was steady.

As noted above, however, there has been no real shift in preferences towards spending on education and social security benefits. So it seems likely that the preference for higher general expenditure stems *mainly* from concern about the health service. On this question, however, party political differences feature more strongly. Only about a third (35%) of Conservative identifiers would prefer more expenditure and taxation – compared with almost two-thirds of Labour (64%) and Alliance (63%) identifiers. On the one hand then, Conservatives are strong supporters of extra spending on the NHS, but on the other, a substantial majority seems to have ideological objections to the public expenditure implications of more resources for the NHS – or to the rise in taxation that would be needed.

A universal or two-tier NHS?

As we shall show, there has been an increase in dissatisfaction with the NHS and some of its services over the period. Nonetheless support for the underlying principle of free health care at the point of delivery has, if anything, risen since 1983 and remains at a high level. Around two-thirds of respondents consistently oppose the notion of a 'two-tier' health service.

It has been suggested that the National Health Service should be available only to those with lower incomes. This would mean that contributions and taxes could be lower and most people would then take out medical insurance or pay for health care. Do you support or oppose this idea?

	1983	1987
	%	%
Support	29	26
Oppose	64	68
Don't know	7	5

Recent research has shown that support for universally provided services within the welfare system is in general strongest among the middle classes. Le Grand (1987) has suggested that the political clout of the middle classes has led policy-makers to favour services used and supported by these classes. We too found in 1983 that the principle of a universal NHS commanded strongest support from people in high income groups, and in Social Classes I and II. As we noted then, the opposition to a two-tier NHS "is greatest from those who would be most likely to be excluded from its selective coverage" (*The 1984 Report*, p.84). Now, however, our data suggest a considerable rise in support for a universal health care system among the least well-off, with support from the middle classes and those in higher income groups remaining fairly stable.

Support for universal NHS, 1983–87

		1983	1987
Social Class:	I/II	70%	72%
	III Non-manual	67%	70%
	III Manual	60%	68%
	IV/V	60%	65%
Household income:	Highest 25%	72%	68%
	Middle 50%	64%	72%
	Lowest 25%	57%	66%

So the different class interests are becoming less discernible than they used to be. A corresponding merging of interests between identifiers with the different parties has also taken place over the period.

Attitudes to private health care

What effects have these changes had on demand for private health care and on its perceived impact on the NHS? The private sector has traditionally been a distinct system with its own special mix of services. By 1981, it accounted for 13% of the total case-load of in-patient elective surgery (Williams *et al*, 1984). A marked increase and diversification in activity then took place in the

first half of the 1980s. For instance, the number of places in private nursing homes in England has more than doubled since 1979. Even so, private care is still not providing a comprehensive range of services for the bulk of the population, and it too has faced some sobering experiences in internal management and cost control (Bosanquet, 1987).

In 1983 about 11% of our respondents were covered by a private health insurance scheme, just over half of which were paid for by the employer. By 1987, 14% were covered. These data support others which show that the increase in demand over the last five years or so has been steady rather than precipitous, the sharpest increase having already taken place between 1979–1983, during the first term of the present government. Our surveys show no evidence then that private health care is extending out of its fairly narrow income and class base (see **Table 6.1**). It is still the higher income groups who are both more dissatisfied with the NHS *and* more likely to be covered by private medical insurance.

As for *attitudes* to private medicine, there have been few significant changes. Hostility to private treatment in NHS hospitals remains at a high level, with 44% of respondents thinking it as a "bad thing" for the NHS. But only 20% think private treatment is, a "bad thing" if carried out in private hospitals (see **Table 6.2**). Similarly, although there has been a small drop over the last three years in the proportion who think NHS doctors (and dentists) should be free to take on private patients, the majority still supports such a right. It is in attitudes towards the NHS itself that the more marked changes have occurred.

General satisfaction with the NHS

We ask in each module a general question about satisfaction with the NHS. Such questions are useful only as monitoring devices, since they measure mood and orientation rather than specific attitudes:

All in all, how satisfied or dissatisfied would you say you are with the way in which the National Health Service runs nowadays?

	1983		1987	
	%		%	
Very satisfied	11	55	7	41
Quite satisfied	44		34	
Neither satisfied nor dissatisfied	20		20	
Quite dissatisfied	18	25	24	39
Very dissatisfied	7		15	

The change in mood since 1983 has been striking. Only six per cent of the population now claim to be very satisfied with the NHS. The rise in the proportion expressing dissatisfaction cannot be dismissed as an artefact of question wording; the *same* question has been used on each occasion and the proportion has been going up steadily year on year. Moreover, it is clearly the *general* performance of the NHS that is causing concern.[1] As we shall see, dissatisfaction with particular aspects of the health service is not nearly as high.

The sharpest rise in general dissatisfaction with the NHS occurred among those age groups within the population who were already the most likely to

complain in 1983. The differences between them and others has thus been accentuated:

	Dissatisfied ('very' or 'quite')		
	1983	1987	% rise
Men:	%	%	
18–34	30	43	+13
35–54	33	50	+17
55+	22	32	+10
Women:			
18–34	23	40	+17
35–54	28	44	+16
55+	19	27	+8

The steepest rise in dissatisfaction has been among younger women, and among 35–54-year-old men and women (which were in 1983 the most discontented groups anyway). The trend is least marked among the over 55s who in 1983 were the least critical of the NHS. It should be remembered, however, that older people tend to be less critical of other aspects of state provision too.

In 1983, Conservative and Labour identifiers had almost identical views about the performance of the NHS; only Alliance supporters stood out as less satisfied than average. By 1987, the position had entirely changed:

	Conservative		Alliance		Labour	
	%		%		%	
Very satisfied	10	} −8	4	} −13	5	} −21
Quite satisfied	39		27		30	
Neither satisfied nor dissatisfied	22		22		16	
Quite dissatisfied	21	} +6	32	} +13	24	} +23
Very dissatisfied	8		15		25	

Discontent among Conservatives has risen but it has risen by almost four times as much among Labour identifiers. Now almost half of Labour and Alliance identifiers are dissatisfied, as are nearly a third of Conservative identifiers. The sharp rise in Labour dissatisfaction is not paralleled by a similar rise among the working class. Those in Social Classes I and II are still expressing more dissatisfaction than are those in Social Classes IV and V (see **Table 6.3** for further details). So the main message conveyed by these changes is that general attitudes towards the NHS have clearly been affected by the very strong rise in the NHS's political saliency since 1983. Identifiers with the opposition parties are more persuaded than they used to be that something is wrong, but so to a lesser extent are Conservative identifiers.

Attitudes to particular aspects of the NHS

Satisfaction and dissatisfaction

Respondents were then asked to perform the less 'political' task of judging particular aspects of the health service on the basis of their own knowledge. Our survey is able to accommodate these sorts of specific questions to only a limited extent: for a much fuller treatment, see Prescott-Clarke *et al* (1988).

The question we ask about six aspects of the NHS is:

> From your own experience, or from what you have heard, please say how satisfied or dissatisfied you are with the way in which each of these parts of the National Health Service runs nowadays.

As we have noted, people tend to express considerably more favourable views about specific services than about the NHS as a whole. The exception is the hospital out-patient service which attracts a level of criticism similar to that expressed about the NHS as a whole.

		Satisfied ('very'/'quite')	Neither/don't know	Dissatisfied ('very'/'quite')
Local doctors/GPs	%	79	8	13
National Health Service dentists	%	74	17	9
Health visitors	%	46	45	8
District nurses	%	55	41	3
Being in hospital as an in-patient	%	67	19	13
Attending hospital as an out-patient	%	54	18	29

Whereas only six percent of respondents express themselves as being very satisfied with the NHS as a whole, around one in four are very satisfied with, for instance, the local GP service and in-patient services. So distinctions *are* made.*

As we have shown, levels of dissatisfaction with the NHS as a whole have gone up sharply, but this has not happened to any marked degree as far as most of the specific services are concerned. In general, those services providing primary health care have escaped criticism during four years of general controversy about the NHS. The rise in dissatisfaction with particular services was confined to hospitals, though even here the increase was not as great as the rise in negative sentiment about the NHS as a whole.

	% dissatisfied ('very' or 'quite')		
	1983	1987	% increase
Being in hospital as an in-patient	7%	13%	+6
Attending hospital as an out-patient	21%	29%	+8

Dissatisfaction expressed by subgroups seems to have changed somewhat since 1983. Women have become more dissatisfied and are now more or less indistinguishable in their attitudes from men. In 1983 there was no marked relationship between specific dissatisfactions and occupational background, but in 1987 this has changed. Now, for instance, 40% of respondents from Social Classes I and II are dissatisfied with out-patient treatment compared with only 21% of respondents from Social Classes IV and V. These differences are much greater than in relation to the NHS as a whole. In contrast, the differences according to party identification remain slight, indicating that the specific services provided by the NHS are not seen in the same politic context as is the institution as a whole.

---

* It is reassuring also, from a survey practitioner's point of view, that the level of 'don't knows' is highest on those services which are least used, suggesting that people are not giving ratings capriciously.

Where improvement is needed

We asked some new questions (on the self-completion questionnaire) in 1987, covering such matters as waiting times, appointments systems, the state of hospital buildings and perceptions of the adequacy of staffing. For each of twelve aspects of the NHS, respondents were asked if they thought it needed "a lot of improvement", "some improvement", whether it was "satisfactory", or "very good". For simplicity here we combine the first two answer categories – in need of "a lot" or "some" improvement. For full details, refer to Q.A201 in Appendix III, p.248.

	In need of improvement ('A lot' or 'Some')
Hospital waiting lists for *non*-emergency operations	87%
Waiting time before getting appointments with hospital consultants	83%
Staffing level of nurses in hospitals	75%
Staffing level of doctors in hospitals	70%
Hospital casualty departments	54%
General condition of hospital buildings	53%
GPs' appointment systems	47%
Amount of time GP gives to each patient	33%
Quality of medical treatment in hospitals	30%
Being able to choose which GP to see	29%
Quality of medical treatment by GPs	26%
Quality of nursing care in hospitals	21%

Direct questions about these sorts of issues elicit much more strongly critical answers – particularly about aspects of the hospital service – than did our previous questions about the services generally. Although there is some dissatisfaction with the appointments systems of family doctors, on the important issue of the medical treatment the provide, nearly three-quarters think it is satisfactory or very good. Similarly within the hospital service, there is still confidence in the actual quality of medical and nursing care, but against a background of substantial dissatisfaction with hospital buildings, organisation and staffing. Notably of the eight items that dealt with the hospital service, six were seen by the majority as needing improvement. Hospital care is seen to be good, but it is also seen to be rationed by queuing and delivered under great strain. A strong appreciation of the efforts of health professionals, particularly nurses, coexists with a high level of concern about the day-to-day functioning of hospitals. Only a minority – and among younger and better educated respondents, a very small minority – sees the hospital service as even satisfactory in respect of most aspects of staffing and organisation. The substantial public affection for the NHS will surely be eroded in the longer term if confidence in how hospital care is organised continues to fall.

In the early part of 1988, the government committed itself to carrying out a review of the long-term future of the NHS, which would involve assessing options for different models of services. It seems from our data that any new model would need to deal convincingly with the day-to-day functioning of the hospital service, if public concerns are to be addressed. These concerns are equally great among recent in- and out-patients; indeed, on the problem of

waiting lists the criticisms of recent 'consumers' are rather stronger.

The inconsistency of standards in general practice has come in for some criticism (Royal College of General Practitioners, 1985), and some 33% of our respondents regarded as inadequate the amount of time that GPs give to their patients. If this is a rather higher proportion than might have been expected, the level of concern about aspects of the hospital service (reaching over 70% on four different features) is astonishing. Worry about shortages of nurses and doctors is even greater among the small number of health professionals in our sample (those who work for a health authority) than among the population as a whole (see **Table 6.4**). Concern about the quality of medical treatment and nursing care offered by NHS hospitals was also higher among health workers. They are, on the other hand, rather *less* worried about waiting times, waiting lists and hospital casualty departments than were the 'consumers' of their services. Nonetheless the oft-repeated claim that morale in the health service is low is certainly given support by these findings. Over 80% of the health professionals in our sample are concerned about staffing levels of doctors and nurses, and a sizeable minority is worried about the quality of treatment they are able to give (again see **Table 6.4**). Our findings cannot be conclusive since the subsample of health workers is small, but these figures do suggest a substantial degree of frustration with their own or their colleagues' ability to cope.

Conclusions

Despite all the political exhortations in recent years which stress the desirability of cutting state spending, the public still wants government expenditure on the NHS to be increased; this is not so for, say, housing and unemployment. Moreover, at a time when the principle of comprehensive state health care is being widely challenged, there remains persistent – and indeed increasing – support for the idea of a universal service. In the past, however, public affection for the NHS has been based firmly on both support for the principle it embodied *and* on a high level of satisfaction with the service it provided. The latter is now beginning to decline, and discontent with the NHS is starting to approach the levels expressed for education and local authority housing. Any reform of health care – from whatever perspective – would now need to address the problem of restoring public confidence. One hopeful sign is that people's respect for health workers – doctors, nurses and community health-care workers – remains high. Satisfaction with their performance is widespread, and the dissatisfied minority has not increased in size over the years. But it must be doubtful that such support both for the principle of the NHS, and for the professionals who are attempting to deliver the services, can continue indefinitely in the face of increasing criticism of the services themselves. Increasingly visible are problems of staffing, organisation and the ability to deliver treatment at acceptable speed. Stresses and strains, in the hospital service particularly, are beginning to show all too clearly.

Our data also persuasively show a different perception of the NHS as a whole from that of its component parts. Greatest concern is directed towards the NHS at a general, 'political' level, less at the day-to-day functioning of most services. But at a detailed level, establishing a more positive perception of each of these services might paradoxically be more difficult to achieve because

the criticisms are based on more intimate accounts – either personally or from friends and relatives. Thus, whereas the mounting public disillusion suggested by our data might still be reversible, the worsening perceptions of specific services will take a great deal to shift. The NHS is not just a welfare state service; it is also a political institution. As such, it depends ultimately for its legitimacy on public confidence. Our results over the last five years show that public confidence is declining. People are beginning to demand improvements, and patience is starting to run out. It is not yet a crisis of confidence but it is moving in that direction.

Note

1. The same question was asked by Prescott-Clarke *et al*, also in the spring of 1987, in a survey of the public in four health districts in England. Interestingly, the percentages expressing dissatisfaction were much lower, ranging between 9% and 21% in each district. Clearly "attitude questions of this kind can be sensitive to differences in context, and it would be unsafe to conclude that the higher levels of satisfaction expressed in the four districts... really reflect a major divergence from the national picture" (Prescott-Clarke *et al*, 1988, p.29). The *British Social Attitudes* question has always been asked after questions on government expenditure options and so is likely to be seen in a political context; respondents in the four health districts were asked immediately after a series of questions on their recent experience (or their family's) of the NHS, placing the question firmly in the context of patient care.

References

BOSANQUET, N., *Public expenditure on the NHS: Recent Trends and the Outlook*, Institute of Health Services Management, London (1985).

BOSANQUET, N., 'Interim Report: Public Spending and the Welfare State', in Jowell, R., Witherspoon, S. and Brook, L. (eds), *British Social Attitudes: the 1986 Report*, Gower, Aldershot (1986).

BOSANQUET, N., 'Private Health Insurance in Britain and the National Health Service', *The Geneva Papers on Risk and Insurance*, vol.12, no.45, (Oct. 1987), pp.350–57.

CENTRAL STATISTICAL OFFICE, *Annual Abstract of Statistics*, HMSO, London (1988).

DHSS, *NHS Management Inquiry: Report to the Secretary of State for Social Services* ['the Griffiths Report'], HMSO, London (1983).

ENTHOVEN, A., *Reflections on the Management of the National Health Service*, Nuffield Provincial Hospitals Trust, London (1985).

GALLUP, *Gallup Political Index*, Report no. 328, London (1988).

HOUSE OF COMMONS SOCIAL SERVICES COMMITTEE 1987–88, *Resourcing the National Health Service: Short-term Issues*, HMSO, London (1988).

LAING, W., *Laing's Guide to Private Health Care*, Laing and Buisson, London (1987).

LE GRAND, J., 'Mrs Thatcher, the Welfare State and the Middle Classes', *LSE Quarterly*, vol.1, no.3 (1987), pp.255–271.

MAYNARD, A. and BOSANQUET, N., *Public Expenditure on the NHS: Recent Trends and Future Problems*, Institute of Health Services Management, London (1986).

OPCS, SOCIAL SURVEY DIVISION, *General Household Survey 1985*, Series GHS, no.15, HMSO, London (1987).

PRESCOTT-CLARKE, P., BROOKS, T., and MACHRAY, C., *Focus on Health Care: Surveying the Public in Four Health Districts (Vol.1)*, SCPR & RIPA, London (1988).

ROYAL COLLEGE OF GENERAL PRACTITIONERS, *Towards Quality in General Practice*, RCGP, London (1985).

TAYLOR-GOOBY, P., 'Citizenship and Welfare', in Jowell, R., Witherspoon, S. and Brook, L. (eds), *British Social Attitudes: the 1987 Report*, Gower, Aldershot (1987).

WAITE, R.K. and HUTT, R., *Attitudes, Jobs and Mobility of Qualified Nurses*, Institute of Manpower Services, University of Sussex (1986).

WILLIAMS, B.T., NICHOLL, J.P., THOMAS, K.J. and KNOWELDEN, J., 'Contribution of the Private Sector to Elective Surgery in England and Wales', *The Lancet*, vol. ii, no. 8394 (1984) pp. 89–92.

6.1 PRIVATE HEALTH INSURANCE (Q64a,b)
by age, social class and party identification

	TOTAL	AGE						SOCIAL CLASS				PARTY IDENTIFICATION			
		18-24	25-34	35-44	45-54	55-64	65+	I/II	III non-manual	III manual	IV/V	Conservative	Alliance	Labour	Non-aligned
	%	%	%	%	%	%	%	%	%	%	%	%	%	%	%
ARE YOU COVERED BY A PRIVATE HEALTH INSURANCE SCHEME, THAT IS AN INSURANCE SCHEME THAT ALLOWS YOU TO GET PRIVATE MEDICAL TREATMENT?															
Yes	14	9	15	22	17	13	9	23	16	9	7	23	14	6	9
No	86	91	85	78	83	87	91	76	84	91	93	77	86	94	90
Don't know/not answered	*	-	-	1	*	-	*	*	*	*	*	*	-	*	*
(IF YES)															
MAJORITY OF COST OF MEMBERSHIP															
- paid for by employer	8	4	8	15	10	5	2	14	9	5	3	12	7	3	5
- paid for respondent	6	5	6	7	5	7	6	9	6	4	3	9	6	2	4
Don't know/not answered	1	*	1	1	1	*	1	1	1	1	1	1	1	1	1
BASE: ALL RESPONDENTS															
Weighted	2766	371	532	556	424	425	454	725	634	570	649	1051	517	804	208
Unweighted	2847	347	538	564	460	457	482	749	667	588	658	1095	533	824	205

6.2 ATTITUDES TO PRIVATE MEDICINE (Q65a, b; 66; 67a) by age, social class and party identification

	TOTAL	AGE 18-24	25-34	35-44	45-54	55-64	65+	SOCIAL CLASS I/II	III non-manual	III manual	IV/V	PARTY IDENTIFICATION Conservative	Alliance	Labour	Non-aligned
	%	%	%	%	%	%	%	%	%	%	%	%	%	%	%
EXISTENCE OF PRIVATE MEDICAL TREATMENT IN NHS HOSPITALS IS ...															
... a good thing for the NHS	23	19	24	24	22	22	27	26	28	20	18	37	20	10	19
... a bad thing for the NHS	44	37	47	45	50	46	37	46	41	45	44	29	51	63	29
It makes no difference	29	40	25	29	25	28	28	24	27	32	32	30	27	24	44
Don't know/not stated	4	4	4	2	4	4	7	3	4	4	6	4	2	3	8
EXISTENCE OF PRIVATE MEDICAL TREATMENT IN PRIVATE HOSPITALS IS ...															
... a good thing for the NHS	39	29	38	44	40	40	41	47	42	37	30	55	39	21	27
... a bad thing for the NHS	20	22	23	18	18	18	19	19	16	21	21	8	21	35	17
It makes no difference	37	45	35	36	38	37	32	31	38	38	41	33	37	39	44
Don't know/not stated	4	4	4	1	4	4	8	3	3	4	8	3	3	4	11
PRIVATE MEDICAL TREATMENT ...															
... should be abolished in all hospitals	10	11	12	7	10	10	11	10	7	12	10	3	7	22	9
... should be allowed in private hospitals but <u>not</u> in NHS hospitals	51	47	52	52	55	56	56	51	51	52	54	45	58	55	43
... should be allowed in <u>both</u> private and NHS hospitals	37	42	36	39	33	32	31	39	40	34	32	50	33	21	38
Don't know/not stated	2	1	1	2	2	2	2	1	2	2	4	1	2	2	10
NHS GPs SHOULD ...															
... be free to take on private patients	54	50	47	60	54	58	55	58	59	48	52	66	53	39	57
... should not be free	41	46	49	38	42	38	35	39	37	47	42	30	43	56	33
Don't know/not stated	5	4	4	2	4	5	10	3	4	5	6	4	4	5	10
BASE: ALL RESPONDENTS															
Weighted	*2766*	*371*	*532*	*556*	*424*	*425*	*454*	*725*	*634*	*570*	*649*	*1051*	*517*	*804*	*208*
Unweighted	*2847*	*347*	*538*	*564*	*460*	*457*	*482*	*749*	*667*	*588*	*668*	*1095*	*533*	*824*	*205*

6.3 SATISFACTION WITH THE NHS (Q62)
by age within sex, social class and party identification

	TOTAL	AGE WITHIN SEX						SOCIAL CLASS				PARTY IDENTIFICATION			
		MEN			WOMEN			I/II	III non-manual	III manual	IV/V	Conservative	Alliance	Labour	Non-aligned
		18-34	35-54	55+	18-34	35-54	55+								
HOW SATISFIED OR DISSATISFIED .... ARE [YOU] WITH THE WAY IN WHICH THE NATIONAL HEALTH SERVICE RUNS NOWADAYS?	%	%	%	%	%	%	%	%	%	%	%	%	%	%	%
Very satisfied	7	3	5	10	4	6	12	5	8	6	8	10	4	5	6
Quite satisfied	34	35	26	33	36	33	38	28	36	35	35	39	27	30	39
Neither satisfied nor dissatisfied	20	19	18	25	20	17	22	20	20	20	21	22	22	16	24
Quite dissatisfied	24	26	30	18	26	27	17	31	22	23	20	21	32	24	16
Very dissatisfied	15	17	20	14	14	17	10	15	14	16	16	8	15	25	15
Don't know/not answered	*	*	*	-	*	-	*	*	*	*	-	*	-	-	-
BASE: ALL RESPONDENTS															
Weighted	2766	439	460	400	464	520	479	725	634	570	649	1051	517	804	208
Unweighted	2847	422	477	427	463	547	506	749	667	588	668	1095	533	824	205

6.4 ATTITUDES TOWARDS HOSPITAL SERVICES (A201e–l)
by age, highest educational qualification obtained and whether or not health professional

FROM WHAT YOU KNOW OR HAVE HEARD ... [IS] THE NATIONAL HEALTH SERVICE IN YOUR AREA, ON THE WHOLE, SATISFACTORY OR IN NEED OF IMPROVEMENT?	TOTAL	AGE						HIGHEST EDUCATIONAL QUALIFICATION				HEALTH PROFESSIONAL	
		18-24	25-34	35-44	45-54	55-64	65+	Degree	Professional	'A' level/ 'O' level/ CSE	Foreign/ Other/ None	Yes	No
	%	%	%	%	%	%	%	%	%	%	%	%	%
f. Waiting time before getting appointments with hospital consultants													
– in need of a lot of/some improvement	83	87	87	83	86	85	72	88	86	83	82	76	84
– satisfactory/very good	14	8	11	15	14	12	22	9	11	13	15	19	13
e. Hospital waiting lists for <u>non-emergency</u> operations													
– in need of a lot of/some improvement	87	90	91	87	90	83	78	93	89	87	83	84	87
– satisfactory/very good	10	7	7	11	10	13	14	3	9	10	13	14	10
i. Staffing levels of nurses in hospitals													
– in need of a lot of/some improvement	75	69	83	78	80	75	61	81	82	74	72	84	74
– satisfactory/very good	22	27	16	19	19	23	31	16	15	23	25	15	23
j. Staffing levels of doctors in hospitals													
– in need of a lot of/some improvement	70	65	77	74	74	69	60	78	78	71	66	81	70
– satisfactory/very good	27	32	22	23	25	28	31	20	19	26	31	18	27
h. Hospital casualty departments													
– in need of a lot of/some improvement	54	57	60	60	54	52	37	74	61	52	49	49	54
– satisfactory/very good	43	39	38	38	45	45	53	23	37	44	47	50	42
g. General condition of hospital buildings													
– in need of a lot of/some improvement	53	55	58	59	54	49	39	70	64	53	46	56	53
– satisfactory/very good	44	41	40	39	46	48	52	30	33	44	50	43	44
k. Quality of medical treatment in hospitals													
– in need of a lot of/some improvement	30	30	39	31	35	22	19	40	34	30	26	37	30
– satisfactory/very good	67	67	59	67	64	75	74	58	63	67	71	65	68
l. Quality of nursing care in hospitals													
– in need of a lot of/some improvement	21	20	27	24	25	18	12	30	30	19	19	29	21
– satisfactory/very good	76	77	71	74	74	80	83	70	67	78	79	69	78
BASE: A RESPONDENTS *Weighted*	1243	174	238	252	202	181	195	98	169	476	500	68	1175
Unweighted	1281	158	241	254	223	195	207	102	177	485	514	71	1209

7 Trust in the establishment

Roger Jowell and Richard Topf *

Britain's powerful public institutions – the monarchy, parliament, the judiciary, the police and so on – have long been said to be objects of national pride, enjoying great public confidence. Whether one regards this as a good thing or a bad thing in a democracy depends on one's point of view. It certainly contributes to a stable society. But, taken too far, it may also encourage the worship of idols, the granting of too much importance to the symbolic role of these institutions and too little to their present utility.

Until recently, reverence or otherwise for these pillars of the establishment was thought to be associated with party politics. Conservatives – particularly working-class Conservatives – were seen as the traditionalists, with Labour identifiers and Liberals as the radicals seeking to change the established order. But the last decade or so has altered all that, partly because Mrs Thatcher herself has always adopted a sceptical, almost iconoclastic, stance towards many cherished public institutions. Her preference for individualism, self-reliance and an 'enterprise culture' leads her to be an outright critic of what she sees as the suffocating blanket of too much government, the inappropriate respect in Britain for state institutions that have outlived their purpose. Anti-establishment attitudes are no longer party-specific, if they ever were: different parts of the establishment attract different sorts of critics.

We thought this series would be a good vehicle for exploring these issues and for monitoring changes over the years. Last year Heath and Topf (*The 1987 Report*) began with an examination of some aspects of British political culture, particularly attitudes towards government and politicians. They concluded that far from being deferential or respectful, most British people were

* Roger Jowell is the Director of SCPR, and Co-director of this survey series; Richard Topf is Senior Lecturer in Politics, City of London Polytechnic and Member of Nuffield College, Oxford.

rather distrustful of, and cynical about, their elected representatives. On the other hand, only a minority expressed a wish to see the present political system changed, and hardly anyone was inclined to engage in political protest. This sense of ambivalence highlights the difficulty of trying to define and measure such large abstractions as deference towards state institutions, or confidence in the *status quo*, or trust in the establishment. One problem is distinguishing between diffuse and specific support (Easton, 1975), that is between people's belief in, say, the political system as such, and their attitudes to the government of the day. Another problem is that people's feelings about parliament, or the judiciary, or the police, or trade unions, are complex and mixed. They will be proud *and* ashamed, respectful *and* contemptuous, affectionate *and* despairing, in varying measures. (Most people's feelings about their friends or families are probably similarly ambivalent, differing only in degree.)

So, in trying to monitor people's attitudes towards such large issues, especially when limited to just a few questions about a range of institutions, we are forced to focus on a minute aspect of the subject in the hope that it represents something of the essence, but in the fear that we may end up with only the anodyne and the predictable.

For instance, we could no doubt have confirmed what Marsh (1977) established, that people do not much trust politicians to tell either the whole truth or nothing but the truth. That is not meant to be disparaging to politicians. The point is that people the world over surely do not expect from politicians the same qualities of straightforwardness that they expect from, say, their neighbours or the local vicar. Machiavelli, despite his rather bad press, was stating what now seems only the obvious when he proposed that political leaders are not *supposed* to act like private citizens, that they do things routinely and justifiably which would be considered morally wrong if done by individuals in their daily transactions.

Although politicians are generally wise enough not to expose their more questionable methods to too much scrutiny – for they would condemned if they did – their perceived role is nonetheless to try to be effective rather than meticulously or innocently straightforward. Politicians are much more likely to be judged on their commitment to achieving results on behalf of their constituents, or on behalf of the nation – the ends or the motives, at least to an extent, justifying the means. If there is a moral imperative for politicians, it is that they ought not to be self-serving but nation-serving. Questionable methods are probably acceptable only so long as they are prompted by honourable motives to achieve a worthwhile result for, say, the nation or the constituency.

Here is something we can begin to measure in this series: whose interests are different groups in the establishment seen to be serving? This is a much smaller, more manageable question than the ones about, say, deference or respect and, as such, the more capable of being asked and answered in a series of this sort, whose purpose is to measure change over the years, not to try to capture the whole of a subject in a single, heroic sweep. Our aim here is therefore to cast a cursory glance at some of the data, in the expectation that we will return to the subject periodically for a closer and longer look.

We should admit first to an important but deliberate omission from our coverage. We decided not to include questions this time about the very institution that most people would regard as the epitome of the British establishment, the monarchy. We took this decision because, having included such questions

in the 1983 survey, we found that the monarchy is regarded as so special as to be more or less above criticism. We did not have space for the more detailed treatment the subject would demand. Moreover, we are involved in a binational study with colleagues in West Germany which covers not only the monarchy itself, but also some wider questions on the subject of patriotism.*

The public interest

Confidence and trust

Although people holding public office in a democracy are presumably expected to try to serve the public good, the ethical requirements of different institutions are different. As we have noted, politicians, for instance, are unlikely to be judged by their straightforwardness and openness alone. In their case the more likely requirement is that, when faced with a conflict, they should subordinate their own interests to the public good. So our particular question about politicians in this context was along these lines: how far do respondents generally trust governments *of any party* to place the interests of the nation above those of the party? Marsh (1977) asked an almost identical question of a national sample in 1974. We added an analogous question this time about local councillors.

In other organisations, however, the institutional ethic certainly does demand truthfulness and a strict adherence to high standards of probity. An example is the legal system which depends *par excellence* on the whole truth, given under oath. So we added a question about the police, exploring how far people trust them not to bend the rules in trying to get a conviction.

Institutions such as the civil service and the national press presumably come somewhere between politicians and the police in the character of their ethical codes. One of the age-old ethical conflicts for British civil servants is between their duties to ministers and to citizens – whether, when faced with a conflict, they act principally like *government* servants or like *public* servants. We posited such a conflict – involving a proposed deception by a Minister – and asked respondents, in effect, what line they thought a top civil servant would take in those circumstances.† Similarly, journalists work partly within the traditional ethic of the fourth estate and partly within a commercial ethic. How far, we asked, would respondents generally trust journalists on national newspapers to pursue the truth even when doing so might ruin a good story? (For the actual wording of these items, see Appendix III, Q. B 88a–d, p.243.)

As shown in the table below, our respondents display less than full-hearted confidence that any of these five pillars of the establishment would act in the broadest *public* interest. Only the police command the confidence of even a bare majority of our sample, hardly signifying unqualified trust or esteem. On the other hand the public does regard the police and the civil service as easily the most likely of the five institutions to do 'the proper thing', with the national

---

* This work is being supported by the Anglo-German Foundation, and is being carried out as part of the SCPR/Oxford 1987 *British General Election* study.
† The item about civil servants was included in the British/West German comparative study, not in the *British Social Attitudes* series. We have included it here for purposes of comparison.

press as by far the least likely to do so: journalists command less than half of the (low) level of confidence that politicians achieve.

	Can be trusted 'just about always' or 'most of the time' to serve the public interest
The police	51%
Civil servants	46%
Governments of any party	37%
Local councillors of any party	31%
Journalists on national newspapers	15%

As might be expected, not all groups in society are of one mind. Conservatives (50%) are far more likely than Labour (29%) or Alliance identifiers (32%) to say that they trust governments to put the national interest first (see **Table 7.1** for full details). A likely explanation is that, despite the careful phrasing of the question, some respondents found it difficult to distinguish governments in general from the present government (nor must we forget that many respondents have known no other government since reaching voting age).

As **Table 7.1** reveals, older people and Conservative identifiers are predictably more likely than younger people and Labour identifiers to have confidence in the police. But apart from these variations, there are remarkably few subgroup differences on these questions. Even education, usually an important variable on this sort of issue, has little relationship to people's answers.

Last year, when we looked at attitudes towards national politicians, we employed two indices, one of political cynicism and one of egalitarianism (see Heath and Topf in *The 1987 Report*). The two indices were associated, egalitarians tending to be more 'cynical' about politics. Having reconstructed the same indices, we find now that cynicism about national politicians is related to distrust of local councillors and the police too. However, although egalitarianism also goes with distrust of national politicians and the police, it does *not* go with distrust of local councillors (again, see **Table 7.1**). Surprisingly, perhaps, in the light of the antipathy between central and local government during the 1980s, the people who support the present government (Conservative identifiers) and those who share its general philosophy (people on the right of the egalitarian scale) are just about as likely as their counterparts to trust local councils to do the 'proper' thing. In any event, our data on this subject reveal a society that seems at least to be sceptical about, and at worst highly critical of, these central pillars of the establishment.

Doing the 'right thing'

Trust in the institutions of democratic government (including the press) is only one part of the story. There are other prominent and powerful institutions to reckon with too, such as big business and the trade unions. Are we more likely to trust them to do the 'right thing' when faced with a conflict of interest? The difficulty here is that the 'right thing' is not nearly as easy to define in this context as it was in the case of, say, government. For instance, whose interests *ought* to prevail in a clash of priorities between shareholders and employees (or, for that matter, customers) in a public company? We cannot assume now, as we did implicitly before, that one set of interests has a 'morally superior' claim to that of another.

So in trying to devise suitable questions about public interest in relation to these different branches of the establishment, we had to approach the problem in a different way. Now we needed to establish not only how respondents think the institution itself would react when faced with a hypothetical conflict, but also which course respondents themselves would choose were they in a position to decide. The difference between these two judgements would then represent the extent to which these institutions were thought likely to take the 'wrong' decision, amounting to a sort of confidence gap (see Lipset and Schneider, 1983).

In a highly deferential society this gap would be small, approaching zero. People would have confidence in their leaders and in their institutions to act irreproachably and to make 'wise' judgements, or at any rate judgements in line with their own assessments of what is appropriate or inappropriate. The opposite would be true in a highly sceptical or critical population, whose leaders would be expected to take the 'wrong' decisions; then the gap would be large.

We presented respondents to the self-completion questionnaire with two hypothetical strategic conflicts, one faced by a 'large company', the other by a 'large trade union'.* Each involved a clash of institutional priorities:

> *Suppose a large company **had** to choose between:*
> *doing something that improves pay and conditions for its staff; OR*
> *doing something that increases profits.*
>
> *Suppose a large trade union **had** to choose between:*
> *doing something that improves an industry's long-term chances of survival, OR*
> *doing something that improves the present pay and condition of . . . members.*

In both cases we posed two questions: first, which choice did respondents think the *institution* would generally make; and second, which choice would *respondents* make if it were up to them to decide. The figures themselves and the gap between them are shown below. The bigger the gap, the lower is the public's expectation of, or trust in, that institution to take appropriate action. The size of the gap depends partly, of course, on people's expectations of the institution and partly on their own preferences, in resolving the clash of priorities.

	Institution would	Respondent would	Gap between preference and expectation*
	%	%	
Large company			
Improve pay and conditions of staff	18	69	52%
Increase profits	80	28	
Large trade union	%	%	
Improve industry's long-term chances of survival	41	79	39%
Improve present pay and conditions of members	57	18	

*Because of the small numbers of 'don't knows', the difference between the proportions in each of the two rows for each institution is slightly different. We have taken the average difference as the gap.

---

* We also included a third institutional conflict – between the convenience of doctors and the interests of patients in a 'large hospital' – but it is not reported here.

It must be stressed that the hypothetical example selected in each case is likely to have a large effect on responses to this sort of question. In any event, on the dimensions we chose, large companies – surprisingly perhaps – are seen to be more out of tune with public priorities than are large trade unions. We may vary the hypothetical examples in future rounds to see the extent to which it is the institution or the actual dilemma that makes most difference to people's judgements.

In the summary table below we show some of the subgroup differences on these judgements (for full details see **Table 7.2**). We present here only the size of the gap between preference and expectation for each subgroup. The expected differences emerge according to party identification and class, but so do large variations according to education and 'egalitarianism'. It should be remembered that the higher the percentage gap, the lower is the level of confidence in that institution to take the 'appropriate' decision when faced with a conflict of interest.

	Company: gap between preference and expectation	Trade union: gap between preference and expectation
Party identification:		
Conservative	41%	52%
Alliance	58%	52%
Labour	65%	15%
Class (Goldthorpe schema):		
Salariat	49%	58%
Working class	55%	22%
Education:		
Degree	67%	50%
No qualification	46%	26%
Egalitarianism scale:		
Left	70%	24%
Centre	56%	39%
Right	38%	55%

The gaps have arisen in different ways. In the case of large companies there is little variation among subgroups in what they believe *would* happen: a near consensus exists that large companies would go for larger profits, given the conflict posed. So the different sizes of the gaps here are largely an indication of different subgroup's *preferences*. In the case of large unions, however, there is little variation between subgroups as to what they believe *ought* to happen, so the different gaps are indicative of different *expectations*.

Commercial interests

Business, industry and profits

Given the near-consensus among all groups about how companies would choose to act when faced with a clash of priorities, it is worth focusing briefly on the public's general attitudes towards business and industry. As Collins said in *The 1987 Report* (p.34), nearly two-thirds of the British public sees a link between the profitability of industry and the money available for public expenditure; more than half believe we would all be better off if industry made higher

profits; only around one person in six believes that profits are already too high.

So it is certainly not the case that public opinion is against profits, *per se.* But there is a striking disparity between how people think profits *should* be used and how they think they *would* be used. The extent is underlined by the answers to a question we have asked for two years running about what a company would be 'most likely' to do with a large profit in a particular year and what respondents thought it 'ought' to do. The distribution of answers in each of the two years has been much the same, so we show only the latest figures below:

	Where *would* the profit go?	Where *should* the profit go?
Investment	%	%
New machinery	20	29
Training the workforce	?	11
Researching new products	10	12
Workforce benefits		
Pay rise	4	22
Conditions	2	8
Customer benefit		
Lower prices	3	13
Shareholders/managers		
Increase in dividends	34	3
Bonus to top management	21	*

The story is consistent: British industry is seen as being too partial towards its shareholders and top managers at the expense of investment, its workforce and its customers. As if further confirmation were needed, however, here are the answers to yet another question in a different form which we asked in the self-completion supplement:

Who do you think benefits most from the profits made by British firms?

	%
Mainly the owners or shareholders	68
Mainly the directors and managers	21
Mainly the employees	3
The public generally	6

The picture here is even starker. There seems to be an insistent public feeling that customer and employee interests are subordinated too much to those of shareholders and directors in British industry. A glance at the answers to another series of questions about business (included in Appendix III of this Report but not dealt with separately in the text) shows that British industry is thought generally to be rather efficient, and likely to become more so. It also enjoys considerable public support. Almost four in five people believe, for instance, that the economy cannot flourish without manufacturing industry, over 60% believe British people should buy British goods even if they are a bit more expensive, and large majorities support various schemes for extra government help to industry.

As a powerful pillar of the establishment, therefore, industry commands a great deal of public sympathy. Criticism seems to be focused narrowly – even obsessively – on industry's apparent undue favouritism towards its owners and top managers at the expense of more or less everyone and everything else, including implicitly the national interest.

The City of London

But what of the City's image nowadays, especially after it has experienced so much public attention in recent years? During much of the postwar period, awareness of the City has mostly been limited to references to invisible earnings which improved Britain's balance of payments. The present government has, however, explicitly promoted an 'enterprise culture', encouraged a share-owning, as well as a property-owning, democracy, brought in prominent City figures to advise on policy, and presided over major changes such as the 'big bang' in the Stock Exchange. There have also been a number of well-publicised financial scandals in recent years, serving to keep the City prominently in the public eye. As we will show later, a probable result of all this is that the City is now firmly perceived as being at the centre of the nation's *political* stage. Of several large institutions we asked about, the City of London is regarded as the most influential over governments, even Labour governments.

The City's importance to the British economy is also more or less undisputed. Fewer than one in ten disagree with the statement that *the success of 'The City' is essential to the success of Britain's economy*. Even among those on the left of the egalitarian scale, only 15% disagree with this sentiment. On the other hand, the City too is seen by nearly two-thirds of respondents as out for quick profits at the expense of long-term investment.

Once again, a key national institution is not seen to be acting in what is perceived as the broad public interest. The public's view, by a margin of ten to one, is that long-term investment does not have sufficient priority.

We asked also whether the City could be relied on to uncover dishonest deals without government intervention. Respondents, not surprisingly perhaps, split three ways, with around one-third wanting to leave it to the City, one-third wanting the government involved, and one-third holding neither view. The City does not yet seem to have established itself in the public mind as an institution possessing well-embedded regulatory mechanisms. Surprisingly, however, it is people with degrees (64%) who stand out as the most insistent that the City cannot be trusted to uncover dishonest deals; this compares with 24% of people with no qualifications who thought this. Even Labour identifiers, who are hardly likely to be among the City's most ardent admirers, trust the City more than graduates do in this respect. And people on the left and right of the egalitarian scale differ surprisingly little on this issue.

The image of the City as a nationally important institution, but also as a place where large fortunes are made and lost, creates obvious difficulties for people in making judgements. On the other hand, as we have noted, the culture of 'quick profits' is widely frowned upon, and the City more or less epitomises that culture. On the other hand, the City has a recognisably vital role in investment, in creating the resources which British industry *and* the welfare state are thought to need for the wider economic and social good. Thus it is not too surprising that even convinced egalitarians seem not to begrudge the City its economic successes, despite the fact that they feel the fruits are improperly used.

Power brokers

Who has the most influence over British governments, the greatest lobbying

power to get their own way? We asked only one question on this subject as a way of preparing the ground for more detailed future scrutiny if the results proved promising. We introduced the question like this:

> *Different institutions or groups have a lot of influence over governments: others have less.*

We then asked:

> *From what you know or have heard, how much say do you think each of these groups generally has in what a Conservative government does?*

We then repeated the question for "what a Labour government does", and "what an Alliance government might do."* Respondents were given four choices for each institution, from "a lot of say" to "no say at all".

For the sake of simplicity we confine our attention here to the grouped answers of those saying "a lot of say" or "quite a lot of say". The figures are shown below:

	Has a lot or quite a bit of influence over:		
	... Conservative governments	... Alliance governments	... Labour governments
The City of London	78%	64%	52%
Manufacturing industry	54%	64%	61%
The police	51%	50%	35%
Farmers	32%	39%	30%
The trade unions	20%	40%	87%
School-teachers	17%	46%	48%

It is instructive to see that Conservative governments (although, as we noted earlier, it is probably *this* Conservative government that many people are referring to) are seen primarily as creatures of the City rather than of manufacturing industry. Indeed manufacturers are thought to have somewhat more sway with Labour governments, while the City is thought to have much more influence over the Conservatives. Still, what is striking about these answers is how much influence the business community in general is seen to have over *all* governments. The variation in the influence people feel manufacturing industry, or even the City, has over governments of different parties is actually rather small, when compared with the yawning gap between the perceived influence of trade unions over Labour governments as opposed to other governments.

This finding also emphasises the difficulty that the Labour Party is likely to have if it wishes to throw off its image of being a creature of the unions. Eighty-seven per cent believe that trade unions have at least quite a bit of say in what a Labour government does, and this is higher than any other figure in the table. Given that around half of the population believes that trade unions have too much power anyway, the influence they are thought to have on Labour governments may well be an electoral liability. In contrast, the strong perceived link between the City and the Conservatives does not seem to be nearly so embarrassing to the Conservative Party. With the Labour Party also concentrating harder than ever on the priority it gives to law and order issues, it may need to tackle the problem that the police – who enjoy a lot of public

---

* Fieldwork preceded the final split between the Liberals and the SDP.

confidence – are still seen to have comparatively little sway with Labour governments. Some, however, would regard this as a healthy state of affairs.

It would be interesting in time to compare these results with those from
other countries. For instance, the powerlessness attributed to British farmers
by our respondents surely contrasts starkly with how, say, the French public
would view things.

See how they run

We have dealt briefly with conflicts of interest and conflicts of influence. Now
we turn finally to the rather more prosaic question of how well various large
British institutions are seen to run. We have asked much the same question
(although not of all items) in 1983, 1986 and 1987:

> *From what you know or have heard about each (of these institutions),*
> *can you say whether, on the whole, it is well run or not well run?*

This rather rudimentary measure is designed only to plot the changing relative
images of each of a number of organisations or institutions. As the table below
shows, there are clearly some large changes, made all the more surprising by
the contrast between them and the other obstinately stable trend lines that
also appear in the list. As before, for reasons of simplicity, we confine our
attention here to the answer "well run" ("very" or "quite").

		Well run		Difference
	1983	**1986**	**1987***	**between**
				1983 & 1987
The public sector				
The police	77%	74%	66%	− 11
The civil service	42%	47%	46%	+ 4
The NHS	52%	36%	35%	− 17
Local government	35%	35%	29%	− 6
The industrial sector				
Manufacturing industry	43%	41%	48%	+ 5
Trade unions	29%	27%	27%	− 2
Nationalised industries	21%	31%	33%	+ 12
The financial sector				
Banks	90%	92%	91%	+ 1
The Stock Exchange	–	–	75%	n/a
The City	–	–	62%	n/a
The media				
Independent TV/radio	74%	84%	83%	+ 9
The BBC	72%	70%	67%	− 5
The press	53%	48%	39%	− 14
The educational sector				
Universities	–	–	65%	n/a
State schools	–	–	30%	n/a

*In 1987 the question was the same but we extended the scale from a two-point
(well run/not well run) to a four-point scale.

Some of these results are surprising indeed, while some – in retrospect at any

rate – might have been anticipated. The precipitous fall in the image of the NHS is entirely in line with the findings in Chapter 6. But why should the image of nationalised industries have enjoyed a sharp improvement over the period? Has the spate of privatisations since 1983 got anything to do with it, creating confusion as to what a nationalised industry is (assuming there was clarity in the past)? Perhaps people took the question as referring to the *privatised,* formerly nationalised, industries which they regard as better run nowadays? Or perhaps the results of privatisation have been so disappointing that people now feel more affectionate towards the *remaining* nationalised industries? We cannot tell from these figures. Perhaps, after all, they represent only what they seem to represent – an improvement in the image of organisations, such as the National Coal Board, the Post Office and the major utilities, between 1983 and 1987, although this was not the period in which many of their finances improved so dramatically; that came later.

The conduct of the police has also come under scrutiny in recent years, ranging from the residual debate about the miners' strike, to whether they should be armed, to questions of racial discrimination. A generation ago, Almond and Verba (1963) were struck by the high standing of the British police. They reported that some 89% of the British public expected equal treatment by the police. More recently Rose (1985) noted that 83% of people expressed a great deal or quite a lot of confidence in the British police, admiring them more than parliamentarians, the civil service and the courts. When Johnston and Wood (*The 1985 Report*) examined situations which people thought were morally wrong, the most serious transaction they nominated was that of a policeman soliciting a bribe. Eighty-one per cent of respondents judged this to be seriously wrong, with little variation between classes, age groups, or party identifiers. Against those findings, the significant decline we find between 1986 and 1987 in the proportion believing the police are well run is particularly striking. It suggests that the long-standing image of the British police as being more or less above criticism may be somewhat in danger.

Local government started low down the list in 1983 and has now slumped further; and state schools are held in very low public esteem, possible reasons for which are discussed in Chapter 2. Both have attracted much media and parliamentary attention since 1983, but no more than have nationalised industries. The image of trade unions remains very low but stable, while the image of the press seems to have suffered a severe blow in the twelve months between the 1986 and the 1987 readings. We wonder whether events at Wapping during this period might have had anything to do with it. If so, the press's image in future years should recover somewhat once memories have faded.

We looked, of course, for subgroup differences in people's evaluations. By and large, they are predictable and not overwhelming. For instance, the police are regarded in a more critical light by Labour supporters, by people with degrees, and by the young. Conservatives are more likely to feel that manufacturing industry is well run and that nationalised industries are not. But, interestingly, people with degrees emerge as very critical of the way in which manufacturing industry is run, just as they had been of some aspects of the City.

All subgroups have almost the same high levels of praise for the way banks are run, but reactions differ towards the City and the Stock Exchange. In particular, Labour identifiers are less convinced that these institutions are well run. Opinions about trade unions also divide in expected directions, but not even

one half (45%) of Labour identifiers feel they are well run. Still, this proportion compares favourably with the 16% of Conservatives who take this view. Details may be found in **Tables 7.3** and **7.4**.

Such subgroup differences as there are suggest that people's judgements are based on several different criteria of a 'well run' institution. Some seem to take the view that it means efficiency, others that it means fairness or evenhandedness, others that it means fulfilling an important role. We wish to pursue these shadings in future rounds: perhaps we can find out whether different subgroups judge the *same* institutions according to different criteria, or whether, as seems more likely, the same people judge *different* institutions in different ways.

Conclusions

Britain's unusually long period of social and political stability is attributed partly to the existence of an enduring public affection for, and pride in, its national political institutions. These institutions, including *par excellence* the monarchy, are said to symbolise a collective identity which promotes social cohesion. As Heath and Topf noted in *The 1987 Report* however, another feature of the British character, also perhaps an important element in the nation's stability, seems to be a healthy cynicism towards its powerful institutions (always excepting the monarchy) and their leaders. In contrast with the USA, for instance, Britain does not treat its flag or its anthem as an object of reverence. Similarly, the British do not, and perhaps never did, hold their leaders in any awe. Public figures and the institutions they run are regarded realistically as fallible and flawed.

Britain may be said to be pro-establishment in some ways. Its class system, for instance, remains largely intact where others have been eroded; the British people remain improbable revolutionaries; governments of any party can rely on a generally rather compliant electorate when it comes to implementing unpopular policies. But the essential sense of deference which makes for a truly pro-establishment society is missing, and may always have been. People's feelings towards the pillars of the establishment are rather like those of the world-weary theatre critic towards actors and directors, incorporating little respect for reputations or efforts, a slight air of superiority (suggesting they could do a lot better if only they could be bothered), and a constant vigilance lest the stars should begin to get too self-important for their own good. These feelings co-exist comfortably, though somewhat reticently, with affection and pride.

We cannot tell yet how much these feelings or instincts change over the years, let alone whether they tend to go in one direction or another. But the American experience is instructive. Lipset and Schneider (1983) chart what they call the increasing 'confidence gap' in the USA, a loss of public faith over the years in various pillars of the American establishment – the government, big business, unions, education, medicine, the military, the church and the press. They believe that a series of traumatic events during the last three decades, from racial conflict and social protest, to Vietnam and Watergate (including *en route* energy crises, inflation and recession), have combined to undermine the American public's confidence in the nation's institutions and leaders. They make a distinction, however (as we have done here), between what people regard as admirable institutions and the not-so-admirable behaviour of the people who

run them. It is not the 'system' itself that is blamed for deficiencies in its operation, though it must be said that the American public seems increasingly to
believe that some of its national institutions have become too powerful and
exploitative, and occasionally too corrupt, to be effective.

We wonder whether the British 'confidence gap' has been growing at a similar
pace. Unlike the Americans, we have not been taking measures systematically
year by year, decade by decade; and impressions about these matters are no
substitute for data. So we have to remain open-minded about whether the
irreverence we have found is part of some growing malaise, or just an assertion
of an enduring British national trait. We strongly suspect it is the latter, but
we may be proved wrong by the data in future rounds.

Peter Jenkins (1987) claims that Mrs Thatcher has achieved a 'revolution'.
But on the evidence we have this claim is exaggerated. True, the present government has made sweeping changes since 1979. But it has so far failed to achieve
the revolutionary task that Mrs Thatcher set for herself and her administration,
which involved not only the radical reform of many state institutions and their
practices, but of British culture itself. The over-riding aim was to replace the
'dependency culture' of the postwar years by a new 'enterprise culture',
embodying rewards for individual effort, entrepreneurship and the assumption
of responsibility, and disapproval of reliance on the state.

What might the expected values of such an 'enterprise culture' be? For one
thing, the public would surely regard the fruits of business investment and
entrepreneurship as a legitimate reward for shareholders and top managers,
not (only) for workers and customers. For another, they would support the
progressive privatisation of health and of education, as well as cuts in social
expenditure generally. They would frown on Keynesian solutions to unemployment, such as job creation. Yet, on the evidence of this series, only a minority
of the public embraces these ideas, despite all the exhortations over the last
eight years, and despite what even many of Mrs Thatcher's critics would concede
are her formidable qualities of leadership. Since 1983 at any rate, when this
series began, British public opinion has actually become more alienated from
many of the goals of an 'enterprise culture'. To the extent that attitudes have
moved, they have become less sympathetic to these central tenets of the 'Thatcher
Revolution'. As we noted earlier, the British are improbable revolutionaries,
even in support of this kind of revolution.

Of course it takes time to change a political culture, especially when the
change proposed is so radical. It may still happen. But another serious obstacle
to change is that the very people who ought to be in the vanguard on such
issues – those on the right of the egalitarianism scale – are themselves faint-
hearted. They are unconvinced, for instance, that industrial profits should go
primarily to entrepreneurs or shareholders or top managers, being generally
sympathetic to the claims of workers and customers. They are, in short, too
ambivalent about many of the issues to be effective crusaders (see Topf, 1988).

In summary then, our data show once again that the British electorate is
far from being compliant or deferential. For all Britain's political and social
stability over the years, and despite the obvious pride its people have in the
system of government, the British reveal an uncompromisingly irreverent and
critical streak which runs too deep to be dismissed as a mannerism. The public's
trust in the pillars of the British establishment is at best highly qualified.

Perhaps because of this, disenchantment does not seem to have set in. The

British public seems intuitively to have discovered that the surest protection against disillusionment with public figures and powerful institutions is to avoid developing illusions about them in the first place.

References

ALMOND, G. A. and VERBA, S., *The Civic Culture: Political Attitudes and Democracy in Five Nations*, Princeton University Press, Princeton (1963).

COLLINS, M., 'Business and Industry' in Jowell, R., Witherspoon, S. and Brook, L. (eds), *British Social Attitudes: the 1987 Report*, Gower, Aldershot (1987).

EASTON, D., 'A Reassessment of the Concept of Political Support', *British Journal of Political Science*, vol. 5 (1975), pp. 435–57.

HEATH, A. and TOPF, R., 'Political Culture' in Jowell, R., Witherspoon, S. and Brook, L. (eds), *British Social Attitudes: the 1987 Report*, Gower, Aldershot (1987).

JENKINS, P., *Mrs Thatcher's Revolution: The Ending of the Socialist Era*, Cape, London (1987)

JOHNSTON, M. and WOOD, D., 'Right and Wrong in Public and Private Life', in Jowell, R. and Witherspoon, S. (eds), *British Social Attitudes: the 1985 Report*, Gower, Aldershot (1985).

LIPSET, S. M. and SCHNEIDER, W., *The Confidence Gap: Business, Labor and Government in the Public Mind*, The Free Press, New York (1983).

MARSH, A., *Protest and Political Consciousness*, Sage, London (1977).

ROSE, R., *Politics in England* (4th ed.), Faber and Faber, London (1985).

TOPF, R., 'Political Culture and Political Change in Britain, 1959–1987', in Gibbons, J. (ed.), *Politics and Culture*, Sage, London (1988).

7.1 CONFIDENCE THAT BRITISH INSTITUTIONS WOULD ACT IN THE PUBLIC INTEREST (B88)
by age, party identification, egalitarian scale and cynicism scale

	TOTAL	AGE			PARTY IDENTIFICATION				EGALITARIAN SCALE			CYNICISM SCALE		
		18-34	35-54	55+	Conservative	Alliance	Labour	Non-aligned	Left	Centre	Right	High	Medium	Low
	%	%	%	%	%	%	%	%	%	%	%	%	%	%
TRUST BRITISH GOVERNMENTS OF ANY PARTY TO PLACE NEEDS OF THE NATION ABOVE INTERESTS OF OWN POLITICAL PARTY														
Just about always	5	4	4	7	6	3	5	1	3	5	7	-	4	10
Most of the time	32	31	31	34	43	28	25	13	24	30	48	6	27	60
Only some of the time	49	48	51	48	43	56	53	49	53	52	40	54	60	24
Almost never	11	15	11	7	5	11	14	23	19	10	4	39	5	1
Other answer/don't know	3	3	3	5	3	1	3	14	1	3	1	1	4	5
TRUST LOCAL COUNCILLORS OF ANY PARTY TO PLACE NEEDS OF THEIR AREA ABOVE INTERESTS OF OWN POLITICAL PARTY														
Just about always	4	4	3	4	5	2	4	4	4	4	5	2	4	5
Most of the time	27	28	25	27	26	33	27	15	25	26	32	13	26	37
Only some of the time	52	54	55	47	53	49	53	48	51	56	50	52	56	44
Almost never	13	10	14	15	14	14	11	15	18	12	11	30	9	9
Other answer/don't know	4	4	3	5	2	3	5	18	3	2	2	3	4	5
TRUST BRITISH JOURNALISTS ON NATIONAL NEWSPAPERS TO PURSUE TRUTH ABOVE GETTING A GOOD STORY														
Just about always	2	2	2	3	1	3	3	5	5	2	1	3	3	2
Most of the time	13	15	11	13	12	12	14	12	11	15	8	11	13	13
Only some of the time	42	38	45	44	48	41	39	34	37	43	50	37	40	51
Almost never	39	42	39	35	37	42	40	41	44	38	38	47	40	30
Other answer/don't know	4	2	3	5	3	2	4	8	3	3	3	1	4	5
TRUST BRITISH POLICE NOT TO BEND RULES IN TRYING TO GET A CONVICTION														
Just about always	11	10	6	17	14	12	6	9	7	9	16	9	9	15
Most of the time	41	40	44	38	48	42	35	27	32	43	52	32	40	49
Only some of the time	33	33	36	30	27	33	38	44	37	35	24	36	36	25
Almost never	11	16	9	9	8	12	16	12	21	9	5	20	11	6
Other answer/don't know	4	2	4	6	3	2	5	8	3	3	3	3	4	5
BASE: B RESPONDENTS														
Weighted	*1375*	*450*	*475*	*448*	*526*	*257*	*421*	*88*	*268*	*563*	*250*	*285*	*708*	*382*
Unweighted	*1410*	*445*	*492*	*470*	*543*	*259*	*432*	*93*	*290*	*653*	*269*	*294*	*726*	*390*

7.2 TRUST IN LARGE INSTITUTIONS TO MAKE THE 'RIGHT' DECISION (B221, B222) by compressed Goldthorpe class schema, highest educational qualification obtained and party identification

	TOTAL	COMPRESSED GOLDTHORPE CLASS SCHEMA					HIGHEST EDUCATIONAL QUALIFICATION				PARTY IDENTIFICATION			
		Salariat	Routine non-manual	Petty bourg-eoisie	Foremen and technicians	Working class	Degree	Pro-fessional	'A' level/ 'O' level/ CSE	Foreign/ Other/ None	Con-servative	Alliance	Labour	Non-aligned
	%	%	%	%	%	%	%	%	%	%	%	%	%	%
LARGE COMPANY														
If a large company had to choose between doing something that improves pay and conditions for its staff, and doing something that increases profits ...														
... company would improve staff pay and conditions	18	13	13	14	38	24	7	9	11	29	16	17	21	24
... respondent would improve staff pay and conditions	69	60	71	59	55	76	71	62	66	73	55	72	82	78
(Difference)	*51*	*47*	*58*	*45*	*17*	*52*	*64*	*53*	*55*	*44*	*39*	*55*	*61*	*54*
... company would increase profits	80	85	84	83	56	75	91	88	88	68	82	82	76	76
... respondent would increase profits	28	37	26	36	36	21	25	35	31	23	42	24	13	22
(Difference)	*52*	*48*	*58*	*47*	*20*	*54*	*66*	*53*	*57*	*45*	*40*	*58*	*63*	*54*
LARGE TRADE UNION														
If a large trade union had to choose between doing something that improves an industry's long-term chances of survival, and doing something that improves the present pay and conditions of the union's members ...														
... trade union would improve industry's chances of survival	41	33	40	32	33	49	37	29	38	48	35	34	52	46
... respondent would improve industry's chances of survival	79	90	80	87	84	70	87	87	81	72	85	85	66	79
(Difference)	*38*	*57*	*40*	*55*	*51*	*21*	*50*	*58*	*43*	*24*	*50*	*51*	*14*	*33*
... trade union would improve present pay and conditions	57	66	58	64	62	48	63	68	60	49	63	65	44	54
... respondent would improve present pay and conditions	18	9	17	8	13	26	13	10	16	24	12	14	29	20
(Difference)	*39*	*57*	*41*	*56*	*49*	*22*	*50*	*58*	*44*	*25*	*51*	*51*	*15*	*34*
BASE: B RESPONDENTS *Weighted*	1181	269	269	83	55	418	100	160	437	482	465	225	352	68
Unweighted	1212	282	282	86	58	426	96	164	446	504	480	225	362	72

N.B. In this table, the differences between what the institution and respondent would do are simply the differences between the two percentages. In the text, the 'gap' has been calculated from averaging the raw figures, so there are (very small) discrepancies between the two sets of figures.

7.3 HOW WELL VARIOUS INSTITUTIONS ARE THOUGHT TO BE RUN – 1 (B220) by age, highest educational qualification obtained and party identification

		TOTAL	AGE 18-34	AGE 35-54	AGE 55+	Degree	Professional	'A' level/'O' level/CSE	Foreign/Other/None	Conservative	Alliance	Labour	Non-aligned
		%	%	%	%	%	%	%	%	%	%	%	%
THE PUBLIC SECTOR													
THE POLICE	Very well run/well run	66	62	66	71	55	69	70	64	79	63	54	53
	Not very well run/not at all well run	31	37	31	25	44	28	29	31	19	35	42	40
THE CIVIL SERVICE	Very well run/well run	46	51	41	45	44	38	53	42	47	48	44	45
	Not very well run/not at all well run	50	46	55	48	54	57	46	50	51	48	50	48
THE NATIONAL HEALTH SERVICE	Very well run/well run	35	38	27	42	34	24	39	36	43	28	31	32
	Not very well run/not at all well run	64	60	72	57	66	75	60	62	56	71	66	65
LOCAL GOVERNMENT	Very well run/well run	29	32	25	31	33	19	31	30	28	28	32	29
	Not very well run/not at all well run	67	65	72	62	66	76	67	64	68	69	62	69
THE INDUSTRIAL SECTOR													
MANUFACTURING INDUSTRY	Very well run/well run	48	47	45	52	31	46	48	51	55	47	40	38
	Not very well run/not at all well run	47	51	52	39	68	49	50	40	41	49	52	55
THE TRADE UNIONS	Very well run/well run	27	35	25	21	34	22	27	28	16	22	45	26
	Not very well run/not at all well run	68	62	71	72	62	74	72	65	80	76	50	66
NATIONALISED INDUSTRIES	Very well run/well run	33	42	30	26	36	24	35	33	27	34	39	37
	Not very well run/not at all well run	61	53	66	65	62	70	63	57	68	62	53	53
THE FINANCIAL SECTOR													
BANKS	Very well run/well run	91	91	92	90	97	92	93	88	93	94	88	81
	Not very well run/not at all well run	6	6	4	6	2	5	5	7	5	3	8	10
THE 'CITY OF LONDON' STOCK EXCHANGE	Very well run/well run	75	78	78	69	67	72	82	72	82	75	69	75
	Not very well run/not at all well run	18	17	18	18	31	22	14	17	12	19	22	16
THE 'CITY OF LONDON' GENERALLY	Very well run/well run	62	68	62	55	63	62	65	58	66	63	57	60
	Not very well run/not at all well run	31	29	33	31	34	31	31	30	28	31	34	31
BASE: B RESPONDENTS	Weighted	1181	387	420	374	100	160	437	482	465	225	352	68
	Unweighted	1212	382	439	390	96	164	446	504	480	225	362	72

7.4 HOW WELL VARIOUS INSTITUTIONS ARE THOUGHT TO BE RUN – 2 (B220)
by age, highest educational qualification obtained and party identification

	TOTAL	AGE			HIGHEST EDUCATIONAL QUALIFICATION				PARTY IDENTIFICATION			
		18-34	35-54	55+	Degree	Professional	'A' level/ 'O' level/ CSE	Foreign/ Other/ None	Conservative	Alliance	Labour	Non- aligned
	%	%	%	%	%	%	%	%	%	%	%	%
THE MEDIA												
INDEPENDENT TV AND RADIO Very well run/well run	83	89	85	74	86	84	89	77	85	87	79	78
Not very well run/not at all well run	14	9	13	21	13	13	10	18	13	11	16	17
THE BBC Very well run/well run	67	75	68	57	80	69	74	58	65	71	65	68
Not very well run/not at all well run	30	23	29	38	20	28	25	38	32	27	30	28
THE PRESS Very well run/well run	39	42	39	37	31	37	41	40	44	34	36	45
Not very well run/not at all well run	57	56	58	56	65	59	58	54	53	64	59	51
THE EDUCATION SECTOR												
UNIVERSITIES Very well run/well run	65	68	65	61	68	67	66	68	66	64	65	58
Not very well run/not at all well run	31	30	32	31	31	28	33	30	30	32	29	33
STATE SCHOOLS Very well run/well run	30	31	29	31	38	24	29	32	29	31	33	20
Not very well run/not at all well run	67	67	69	64	61	73	70	63	68	67	63	72
BASE: B RESPONDENTS												
Weighted	*1181*	*387*	*420*	*374*	*100*	*160*	*437*	*482*	*465*	*235*	*352*	*68*
Unweighted	*1212*	*382*	*439*	*390*	*96*	*164*	*446*	*504*	*480*	*225*	*362*	*72*

8 One nation?

*John Curtice**

So much attention has been focused in recent years on the apparent existence of a North/South divide in Britain that the phrase has fast become a cliché. This interest has come about not only because the results of recent general elections have been different in the two parts of the country, but also because the already considerable discrepancies between the economic health of the North and the South of Britain have grown even larger in recent times.

There has always been some regional variation in the level of support for Britain's two main political parties, but since 1955 this has gradually increased (Curtice and Steed, 1982; 1986; 1988). Labour's support has become more concentrated in the North of England and Scotland, while the Conservatives have prospered in the South and the Midlands. Only in Wales has there been no systematic long-term trend. In the last three general elections the divergence between North and South has been particularly dramatic. Between 1983 and 1987, for instance, there was a small swing to the Conservatives in the South of England, while in Scotland and the North of England there was a substantial swing to Labour. As a result, the two halves of the country look more and more different politically. This can be seen too in the distribution of party identification in the five *British Social Attitudes* surveys:

	Scotland	North	Wales	Midlands	Greater London	South
	%	%	%	%	%	%
Party identification:						
Conservative	23	30	22	42	36	44
Labour	41	42	48	30	35	22
Alliance	15	16	13	14	15	21

The regions are as defined by OPCS, or amalgamations of them. 'North' comprises the Northern region, North-West and Yorkshire & Humberside; 'Midlands' comprises the East and West Midlands; 'South' comprises the South East (excluding Greater London), South-West and East Anglia.

* Lecturer in the Department of Politics, University of Strathclyde.

Labour is clearly the most popular party in Scotland, the North of England and Wales. The Conservatives dominate in the Midlands and the South. Only in London is there no clear advantage for either party. Politically, Britain appears to be divided along a line from the Humber to just south of the Mersey and from there, along Offa's Dyke.

As with the political divide, regional variation in Britain's economic perform-ance is nothing new. The difficulties caused by the decline in the heavy industries of Scotland, Wales and the North of England have attracted the attention of governments since the 1930s. But the 1980s have seen an accentuation of the regional differences in economic performance (Champion and Green, 1987). Manufacturing industry, which is disproportionately concentrated in the North, was badly affected by the recession at the beginning of the decade. The subse-quent recovery has been led by financial and service industries concentrated in London and the South-East. Thus on a number of indicators – personal disposable income, unemployment, population growth and house prices – the differences between North and South are now distinctly sharper than they were at the beginning of the decade (CSO, 1988; Champion and Green, 1987). More-over, this has occurred at a time when government expenditure on the regions has been cut. The amount of money allocated to regional development grants between 1984 and 1987 was approximately half the level it was between 1976 and 1979, the final three years of the last Labour government (Barclay, 1987).

There is however one qualification to this simple picture of a matching political and economic divide. Among the regions hit hardest by the recession of the early 1980s was the West Midlands. In 1974, the personal disposable income in the West Midlands was second only to that of Londoners and those living in the South-East, but by 1983 it was higher only than in Wales and the Northern region. Economically, then, Britain became divided along a line from the Severn to the Wash rather than from the Mersey to the Humber. More recently, however, the latter line has begun to reassert itself economically because of the fast pace of the recovery in the West Midlands; but the region is still nowhere near its 1974 level of economic strength.

Theory and data

The aim of this chapter is to examine the geographical variation in social attitudes in the wake of the political and economic polarisation of the country, which has gathered pace in recent years. In particular we attempt to answer four principal questions.

First, is Britain divided not only politically and economically but also ideologically? Are the social attitudes of Northerners very different from those of Southerners?

Second, insofar as there are any attitudinal differences between the North and South, how do we account for them? Do they simply reflect differences in the social composition of the regions, or does where people live affect their views?

Third, if where people live does affect their views, how does the process occur? Do people respond to the character of their immediate neighbourhood (as suggested by theories about the 'neighbourhood effect'), or are they influenced by something larger – their region?

Fourth, can our data help to explain the political polarisation of Britain? Has it been caused by the differences in the economic health of the regions? Can we now say that there is a regional political divide in Britain?

But before we examine the evidence, it may be useful to speculate briefly about some of the possible mechanisms by which where people live might influence their attitudes and political identification. We need to consider in particular two concepts, the *neighbourhood effect* and a *regional divide*. We also mention briefly how we have derived the data for this chapter.

The neighbourhood effect

A popular thesis, widely discussed in the literature on voting behaviour, suggests that the way people vote is influenced not only by their individual social and economic circumstances, but also by those of their neighbours. It has been shown that a person living in a working-class neighbourhood is more likely to vote Labour than someone living in a middle-class neighbourhood, *irrespective* of his or her own class position (Butler and Stokes, 1974; Cox, 1968; Fitton, 1973; Heath, Jowell and Curtice, 1985; Taylor and Johnston, 1979). But precisely why this happens has been the subject of some debate. Some have argued that people who live in a working-class neighbourhood are more likely to talk to working-class people than those living in a middle-class neighbourhood; they are therefore more likely to hear views favouring the Labour Party which leads them in turn to be more likely to vote Labour.

But other plausible explanations have also been put forward (see also Puttnam, 1966; Rumley, 1981). The effect might result from a neighbourhood's economic climate. People living in an economically depressed area might be more likely to believe that the area needs more public sector investment and that Labour would be the more likely party to provide it.

The problem is that little work has been undertaken so far to demonstrate how the neighbourhood effect might in practice work (but see Huckfeldt and Sprague, 1987). The social interaction thesis has come under fire from Dunleavy (1979): since voting is a secret act, he argues, it is shielded from social pressure; moreover, since people do not discuss party politics much, conversations between neighbours are hardly likely to have a strong influence on voting. Dunleavy also argues that in many neighbourhoods one particular form of tenure tends to dominate, and that voters may be more influenced by their tenure than by their neighbourhood; the association of voting with neighbourhood may thus be a statistical artefact, not a real effect.

Other writers have made a similar claim. Tate (1974) and Kelley and McAllister (1985) have argued that if sufficient account is taken of all the factors likely to influence voting behaviour, such as an individual's subjective social class identity or parents' voting patterns, the neighbourhood effect can be shown to be spurious. So in examining the evidence in our data for a neighbourhood effect, we will have to take account of these criticisms.

A regional cleavage

A regional political cleavage (or divide) is different from a neighbourhood effect in more respects than just the size of the geographical unit to which it refers.* The neighbourhood effect transmits and modifies a social division, such as class or religion, which is not geographical in origin. A regional divide, in contrast, exists where different parts of a country have conflicts of interest and ideological disagreements, and where these are championed by different political parties (Lipset and Rokkan, 1967). The USA, for instance, has long been said to have a regional political divide, with Southern attitudes and voting patterns differing from Northern ones over the years. Bavarian attitudes and politics in West Germany are similarly distinctive. At their most intense such conflicts produce nationalistic demands for self-government over a particular area of territory (such as, for example, the Basque region of Spain) and threaten the integrity of the state. This tends to happen when several sources of territorial conflict – nationality, language and standard of living – coincide.

So, in countries where there is a regional divide, people are influenced in their social and political attitudes by the interests and identities of a much larger area than that of their own immediate neighbourhood. But to demonstrate the existence of a regional divide in Britain, we would clearly have to show more than that social or political attitudes vary from region to region. After all, regions differ in their social and economic composition – in, for example, the number of middle-class persons or council tenants they contain – and these factors are associated with social attitudes.† So our analysis will have to take account of such differences to ensure that any regional variations discovered are real.

Concentrating on the possibility of a North/South regional divide in Britain makes the analysis particularly interesting. If instead we had been considering differences between England and Scotland or between England and Wales, we would have been able to call on traditional sources of division such as differences of national identity and, to some extent, of language, which provide a foundation for Scottish and Welsh nationalism. But a North/South divide crosses the heart of England, and only economic differences could be at work here. Are these differences in economic prosperity sufficient to produce a regional divide on their own? If so, they would unite the North of England with Scotland and Wales against the Midlands and the South of England.

The data

The literature on regional variation in popular attitudes is sparse. Although separate studies of Scotland and less commonly, Wales, have been undertaken, little is known about the geographical variation in attitudes within England.

---

* In the political science literature, this divide is often termed a 'regional cleavage'. In this Chapter, we use the term only when people in different regions hold different attitudes *and* when they vote for different parties. Otherwise we refer to 'divisions', 'gaps' or 'splits'.

† This can be seen in **Table 8.10** which shows the percentage of respondents in each region with particular characteristics. Five years of *British Social Attitudes* data have been amalgamated. Respondents who could not be classified into a particular group are excluded.

The reason is that a survey of the typical size of 1,000–1,500 respondents is too small to permit detailed regional analyses, let alone possible differences in the behaviour of subgroups in different parts of the country. To overcome this problem we have combined responses from different years to a number of the questions repeatedly asked in the five *British Social Attitudes* surveys conducted to date.* The bulk of the analysis in this chapter is based on this combined dataset.

But to look at the neighbourhood effect, we need data not only about individual respondents but also about the character of the neighbourhood they live in. For this we have relied on the decennial census. We identified the enumeration districts in which our 1985 and 1986 respondents lived, and used information from the census to ascertain the social and economic character of these neighbourhoods.[1] Although we are confined to the rather limited range of information collected by a census conducted some five years previously,[2] we are nonetheless able to begin the complicated process of examining the relationship between neighbourhood and social attitudes.

We start with an examination of a possible regional division – notably that between the North and South – and work down to the possibility of a neighbourhood effect later in the chapter.

A North/South division

We begin by assembling evidence which allows us to judge the existence and extent of a discrepancy between the perceptions, attitudes and values of people in the North and the South. For these purposes we include in the North people living in Scotland, Northern England and Wales. The South includes people living in the Midlands, East Anglia, London and Southern England.

Economic evaluations

Given the differences in regional economic health, we would anticipate that those living in the North would be less optimistic about the country's economic future, and more concerned about unemployment, than those living in the South. This is indeed what we find.

Economic evaluations by region

	Scotland	North	Wales	Midlands	Greater London	South
Expect prices to go up a lot in next year	31%	34%	33%	25%	28%	25%
Expect unemployment to go up a lot in next year	33%	31%	30%	22%	27%	21%
Unemployment of greater concern to me and my family than inflation	50%	50%	41%	41%	39%	39%
Expect household income to fall behind prices in next year	49%	49%	51%	44%	36%	37%
Living on household income difficult or very difficult	28%	29%	30%	27%	27%	20%

* For those questions asked in all five years, this gives us a dataset of 10,942 (weighted) respondents. Even for those questions asked rather less frequently, we have a large enough number of cases for our purposes.

Here then is a clean split in attitudes. Those living in the North, Scotland and Wales are consistently more pessimistic about the economic situation than those living elsewhere. The division is clearest on expectations about household income and unemployment. Interestingly it is least marked on the question of how difficult respondents find it to live on their household income. But despite the consistency of the results overall, the differences are not very large. For instance, the difference between the proportions of Scots and Southerners expecting unemployment to go up a lot is just 12%. This is, perhaps, not surprising, for although the speed of economic recovery in the mid-1980s varied from one part of the country to another, the trend was in the same direction virtually everywhere.

Finer analysis does confirm the importance of a Mersey/Humber rather than a Severn/Wash line in people's perceptions. For instance on all items bar one – difficulty of living on current income – those living in the West Midlands are more optimistic than those living in Scotland or the North of England (see **Table 8.1**). Evaluations in the West Midlands may have been influenced by the region's relatively fast recovery in the mid-1980s (rather than by its even more sudden earlier crash) or by its previous economic strength. Whatever the reason, these findings may help to explain why the West Midlands maintained its long-term drift to the Conservatives in the 1980s, despite its economic misfortunes.

But can the North/South division on economic evaluations be accounted for simply by differences in the individual economic circumstances of those who live in the different regions? Evaluations of inflation and household income are, after all, associated with other characteristics such as income: the rich tend to be more optimistic than the poor, and there are more rich people in the South. Evaluations can also be shown to vary according to class, or whether a person is unemployed, retired or in work. Might such differences account for the regional variations?

As the following tables illustrate, the general answer to that question is no. For example, if we look just at those in the lowest income quintile, the Scots are more likely to anticipate that their income will fall behind prices than are those living in the South of England (difference = 19%); similarly, if we look just at the working class, the Scots are more likely to expect unemployment to go up a lot in the next year than are their counterparts in the South of England (difference = 14%).

% expecting income to fall behind prices

	Scotland	North	Wales	Midlands	Greater London	South
Income quintile						
Lowest	76%	68%	69%	72%	60%	57%
Highest	36%	24%	31%	15%	19%	19%

% expecting unemployment to go up a lot

	Scotland	North	Wales	Midlands	Greater London	South
Class*						
Salariat	20%	21%	18%	14%	18%	14%
Working class	41%	38%	38%	28%	31%	27%

* Respondents have been classified according to their own current or last occupation unless they are economically inactive (excluding those who are retired) and are married to respondents who are economically active or retired, in which case they have been classified according to the *spouse's* occupation.

These differences in perceptions are clearcut. Respondents certainly appear to be influenced by the health of the economy in their region as well as by their own individual circumstances.

Perceptions of a North/South division

We have discovered so far that the relative prosperity of the South is reflected in people's economic evaluations. But do people in the North and South actually believe that their circumstances differ? Do they recognise a gap? If they do not, this regional division is unlikely to be salient enough to have much effect on, for instance, their voting behaviour.

In the 1987 survey, we asked respondents for the first time what differences they thought there were between the North and the South. We asked about five aspects of life. The responses were:

		Better in North	Better in South	No real difference
Chance of young people buying their first home	%	51	20	27
Education standards	%	7	21	70
National Health Service	%	5	17	75
Opportunities to set up own business	%	5	54	39
Employment prospects	%	1	84	14

There is thus a widespread feeling that things are different in the North and the South, but it does not apply equally to all matters. On aspects of life which depend on market forces, North and South are thought to be very unequal. But on state-provided services, such as education and the NHS, the differences are generally felt to be smaller. Whatever arguments there may be about the efficiency of state-provided services, they are certainly seen as being distributed more equitably across the country than are the resources provided by the market economy. Not that the North is always thought to come off the worst. A large majority of the population recognises that cheaper house prices in the North make it easier for young people to buy their own home there, though for nearly half our respondents this was evidently at least counterbalanced by the North's bleaker employment prospects. Housing was, in fact, the one issue on which there was substantial disagreement between people living in the two halves of the country. Whereas two-thirds of people in the North of England thought it was easier for young Northerners to buy their first home, only around half of those in the South of England and fewer than 40% in the Midlands thought this. The higher house prices in the South are, not surprisingly, even more daunting to those not living there than they are to those who witness them daily, many of whom of course have a personal stake in the buoyant housing market.

Ideological differences

On the evidence we have assembled so far, we have found that economic evaluations vary somewhat between North and South and that there is a widespread recognition of a North/South division, especially in areas where the

market economy operates. Now we turn to the more telling test as to whether people living in the various regions differ in what they believe on more fundamental issues – such as in attitudes towards the role of the state in society. If such an ideological schism were to exist, independently of demographic and socio-economic differences between the regions, then we would find it hard to deny the existence of a regional division. We would still not know whether any divide was important politically, but to establish its existence would be a useful first step.

To examine this we looked at the variation in attitudes towards a wide range of subjects, including how the economy should be run, moral issues and the welfare state, to see on which issues people in the various regions differed. These were the items which produced the largest variations:

	Scotland	North	Wales	Midlands	Greater London	South
Agreeing that:						
Unemployment benefit is too low and causes hardship	65%	55%	50%	43%	45%	36%
Income should be redistributed from better-off to less well-off	54%	50%	55%	42%	41%	37%
Ordinary people don't get fair share of nation's wealth	73%	70%	72%	64%	65%	57%
Differences between high and low incomes should be reduced	62%	63%	67%	55%	48%	46%
Big business benefits owners at expense of workers	59%	55%	60%	50%	45%	45%
There is one law for rich and one for poor	68%	68%	74%	62%	64%	58%
Unemployment should be higher priority than inflation	78%	77%	75%	69%	72%	68%

A clear theme dominates this table. Those items which most sharply divide the North from the South are all ones which stress the need for greater economic equality in society and on what ought to be done about one of the major sources of economic inequality, unemployment. Notably we find included in the list here four of the five items we introduced into the survey explicitly to measure attitudes towards equality (see Curtice in *The 1987 Report*). The sharpest division between North and South is on attitudes towards unemployment benefit, an issue which appears to reflect both the higher levels of egalitarianism in the North and the greater degree of pessimism there about future trends in unemployment.

Moreover, this ideological division is between North and South (as we have defined it), providing striking confirmation of the importance of the Humber/Mersey dividing line in favour of any other.

But three other points about the table are also important. First, although the differences between the regions on these ideological items are generally greater than the differences on economic evaluations, they are still not very large. With the exception of attitudes towards unemployment benefit, the largest difference is 21%. And remember these are the items which produced the *greatest* variations between the regions. So, while it is true to say that Northerners and Southerners differ in their attitudes, we cannot go on to say that the North and the South are polarised ideologically.

Second, those living in the North are more likely to favour action by government to reduce inequality. It appears that the differing economic circumstances of the North and the South have influenced their inhabitants' perceptions of the respective roles of state and free market. The individualistic philosophy of the market has a firmer hold in the South, where the market is believed to have delivered opportunities more effectively.[3]

Third, all of the items here have been identified in earlier Reports as among those which most divide Conservative and Labour identifiers (Curtice in *The 1986* and *1987 Reports*). So the issues on which the regions are most divided are the very ones which are central to the ideological debate between Britain's main political parties. Moreover, when we look at some of the other issues on which there are differences – but less strong ones – between the North and the South, we again find a number of the items which divide partisans. Northerners are, for example, less keen on nuclear weapons than are Southerners, while they also differ in their views on certain aspects of the welfare state. But once we move away from those items on which there is a strong partisan divide, the regional differences largely disappear.

But is the North/South ideological division a real one? Can we not account for it, for instance, by differences in the social and economic composition of the regions? After all, the items in question are amongst those which not only sharply divide partisans, but also divide people in different social classes and housing tenures (see **Table 8.3**). And since the working classes are better represented in the North of England than in the South, and council tenants are most common in Scotland, might it be these differences which explain such regional variation as we have seen?

Tables 8.4 and **8.5** at the end of this chapter illustrate why differences in the distribution of the social classes cannot be responsible. We summarise these tables below, giving figures for the salariat and working class only. This shows that the differences between the regions *within* each social class are generally almost as great as across the population as a whole.

Agree that unemployment benefit is too low

	Scotland	North	Wales	Midlands	Greater London	South
Salariat	60%	48%	41%	33%	41%	33%
Working class	73%	60%	57%	52%	48%	44%

Agree government should redistribute income

	Scotland	North	Wales	Midlands	Greater London	South
Salariat	58%	43%	40%	26%	41%	31%
Working class	65%	59%	74%	53%	52%	46%

The trouble with tables like these, however, is that they control for only one aspect of regional composition at a time. Yet we know attitudes towards the equality items are associated with class *and* housing tenure. So if we want to make sure that region really is an independent influence on attitudes towards egalitarianism, we should control for the impact of both class and tenure simultaneously. Similarly, we might wish to control simultaneously for class *and* for whether or not someone is unemployed.

The best answer is to construct a logit model, which uses a statistical technique

known as log-linear analysis (see Gilbert, 1981). This enables us to see whether or not there is a statistically significant relationship between region and attitudes *controlling* for the association between attitudes and a number of other variables.

In the table below are the results of such an analysis for six items (egalitarian and economic evaluation items) on which we found the largest regional differences. In short, the table contains estimates of the *independent* effect of region on attitudes, having controlled (simultaneously) for differences in class, tenure and employment status between regions.[4] A plus sign indicates that people living in that region are more likely to adopt a 'left-wing' attitude; a minus sign shows that they are less likely to do so. An asterisked number (*) is one in which the effect of region is statistically significant at the five per cent level.

The independent impact of region

	Scotland	North	Wales	Midlands	Greater London	South
Expect unemployment to go up a lot in next year	+.08*	+.07*	+.09	−.10*	−.01	−.13*
Expect household income to fall behind prices in next year	+.05	+.07*	+.15*	+.00	−.17	−.10*
Unemployment benefit is too low and causes hardship	+.30*	+.11*	+.05	−.12*	−.10	−.24*
Income should be redistributed from better-off to less well-off	+.17*	+.03	+.18*	−.07	−.12	−.19*
Ordinary people don't get fair share of nation's wealth	+.20*	+.02	+.10	−.08	−.01	−.21*
Differences between high and low incomes should be reduced	+.09	+.14*	+.18*	−.01	−.21	−.20*

Each entry is the estimate of the size of the difference for the region having included the impact of class, housing tenure and work status on the item. In each case the original response item was dichotomised to ease interpretation of the results.

We find that, even after this more rigorous test, there are still clear signs of a North/South split. The plus signs dominate the three columns on the left, while the minus signs dominate the three on the right. So Northerners by our definition are more likely to be egalitarian or to have negative expectations about the economy than people in rest of the country, even after we have taken into account their different class, tenure and work status. People living in the South of England are less egalitarian and more optimistic than the country as a whole. True, not all of the entries are statistically significant, but for each item at least one of the regions in the North and one in the South does depart significantly from the national average. We must conclude therefore that on those values which form the core of the division between North and South, the regional differences cannot be explained away by differences in the kinds of people who live in the two parts of the country.

Moral issues

We have shown that attitudes to equality and the economy lie at the heart of the North/South division. But when we turn to moral issues we refer to

ones which in Britain at least are usually considered to be ones of personal conscience rather than the subject of debate between the political parties. We do not therefore necessarily anticipate that any regional variation will be on North/South lines. Rather, our interest is in ascertaining whether challenges to traditional social mores and attitudes are stronger in London, as the nation's media and cultural centre, than they are elsewhere.

We look in this section at attitudes towards four moral issues which have been the subject of considerable controversy and of a change in attitudes over the last twenty years. Three of these – homosexuality, divorce, abortion – are to do with sexual matters; the fourth is the death penalty. Although, as we show in Chapter 3, there has recently been a shift towards censoriousness in sexual matters, attitudes towards all four issues have over the past two or three decades became more liberal.

As the table below shows, on these moral issues, the gap between North and South disappears and is replaced by one between London and the rest of Britain – although Scottish attitudes also vary from the rest (particularly on divorce, where the law itself is much less liberal than in England and Wales).

% taking libertarian view

	Scotland	North	Wales	Midlands	South	Greater London
Homosexuality not at all wrong	10%	14%	10%	12%	16%	21%
Gays should be allowed to teach in schools	44%	40%	28%	34%	41%	49%
Divorce should be made easier	17%	11%	10%	11%	9%	13%
Allow abortion if woman does not want the child	36%	41%	43%	42%	43%	49%
Against death penalty	35%	28%	33%	27%	33%	40%

But once more we need to check that our regional difference is a real one and not associated, for example, with age, religious attendance or educational attainment – characteristics which previous Reports have shown to be relevant to attitudes on these issues. Yet the proportion of young people in London is only slightly higher than in the country as a whole, and the capital has the second highest level of religious attendance of any of the regions. So these characteristics cannot account for London's relative liberalism. But London does have the highest proportion of graduates in the country. However, if we control for education, we still find that Londoners tend to be more liberal on these sorts of issues than people in the rest of the country. But apart from issues such as these – all subject to recent controversy – the dominant impression we gain from our data is that the nation is fairly uniform in its moral views (see **Table 8.6**).

Londoners also appear to be more worried than people elsewhere in Britain about some aspects of environmental pollution, such as aircraft and traffic noise, industrial fumes and lead from petrol. It may be that Londoners are again in the vanguard, this time on 'green' issues, or they may see the capital's environment as being uniquely less congenial, or perhaps both.

The influence of neighbourhood

Our evidence so far indicates three things. First, the biggest division is between North and South, and it centres on the need or otherwise for greater economic equality in society; it is accompanied by divergences in people's economic evaluations, and appears to arise out of the differences in the economic health of the two halves of the country. Moreover, those issues which most divide North and South are also at the centre of party political debate. Second, there is a split – but a smaller one – between London and the rest of the country on a number of moral issues which have been the subject of increased public attention and controversy in the recent past. Third, although the North is more egalitarian than the South, and London more liberal than the rest of the country, Britain looks more like one nation than two. On only a handful of issues is the regional variation in attitudes very large and on virtually none can the country be said to be polarised.

So far we have concentrated on *regional* variations in attitudes. As we indicated at the beginning of the chapter, however, these are not necessarily the sole source of geographical differences in attitudes. Now we turn to the question of whether people are influenced by a much smaller unit, their residential community or neighbourhood, and if so, how.

Neighbourhood and attitudes

Confining ourselves still to those issues which we have shown to be central to the division between North and South, *and* which we know also divide the classes, we shall examine whether or not there is any relationship between neighbourhood and attitudes to accompany the demonstrable link between neighbourhood and voting behaviour. In doing so, we shall also see how far the regional division between North and South might in fact be a consequence of a 'neighbourhood effect'.

To test for the existence of a neighbourhood effect we again used a logit model, but this time we looked only at those (1985 and 1986) respondents about whose neighbourhoods we had collected details from the 1981 census. So, as in our earlier analysis, we control for the respondent's own social class, housing tenure and employment status, but instead of then measuring the independent effect of *region* on people's attitudes, we now look at the effect of *neighbourhood*.

As the table below shows, there is indeed an association between neighbourhood and attitudes. Each of the items is associated with either the class make-up of the neighbourhood or its unemployment level, and in most cases one or other, if not both, is statistically significant at the five per cent level (marked with a *).[5]

Influence of neighbourhood

	Working-class neighbourhood	High unemployment neighbourhood
Expect unemployment to go up a lot in next year	+ .06*	+ .15*
Expect household income to fall behind prices in next year	+ .02	+ .11*
Unemployment benefit is too low and causes hardship	+ .04*	+ .17*
Income should be redistributed from better-off to less well-off	+ .06	+ .11
Ordinary people don't get fair share of nation's wealth	+ .12*	+ .00
Differences between high and low incomes should be reduced	+ .07*	− .06

'Working-class neighbourhood': less than 20% of residents aged 16 + and economically active, engaged in professional and managerial occupations, i.e. socio-economic groups 1, 2, 3, 4 and 13 (1981 Census enumeration district-level data).
'High unemployment neighbourhood': over 17% of residents, aged 16 + and economically active, seeking work.

Moreover, the significant associations above are all in the expected direction. Thus, for example, those living in working-class neighbourhoods, or in neighbourhoods where a large number of people are out of work, are more likely to take a pessimistic view about the future trend in unemployment and to adopt an egalitatian position on income redistribution.

This is an important finding, because it suggests strongly that neighbourhood is not an influence just on voting behaviour. It seems instead to act as part of the social process by which ideas are passed from one person to another. If this is so, some of the doubts about the existence of a neighbourhood effect have been misplaced. It may well be true, for instance, that conversations between neighbours are rarely *explicitly* about party politics. Nonetheless, they may still have an effect on voting behaviour if they repeatedly embrace values or evaluations to do with 'the state of the world', which conversations in pubs or over the garden fence often do. Someone living in a working-class area is probably less likely to be persuaded to vote Labour because neighbours exhort him to do so than because, say, through discussions or conversations, he or she discovers that local unemployment is taking a severe toll on the area, or that the government is reducing public expenditure in a way that affects the area adversely.

Our analysis also undermines the frequent assertion that the association between neighbourhood and attitudes is just a statistical artefact.[6] Our logit model shows, for example, that the neighbourhood effect remains, even after we have taken account of people's tenure.

Still, this does not actually demonstrate that the neighbourhood effect operates through social interaction or any other mechanism. But the data do produce some clues. For instance, a neighbourhood's level of *unemployment*, rather than its class composition, appears to be the more important factor in predicting people's economic evaluations, but on items tapping people's egalitarianism the *class composition* of the neighbourhood becomes relatively more important. This suggests that the social process behind the neighbourhood effect varies somewhat from one set of attitudes to another. Evaluations of unemployment and the state of the economy may well be influenced by the existence of deprivation which people see around them: people do not necessarily have to

talk to their jobless neighbours for the impact of unemployment to be felt. In contrast, conversations may be more influential on matters to do with more basic values such as egalitarianism, for which class provides the social basis of support.

There is one other important finding. It has been argued (see, for example, Heath *et al*, 1985) that the neighbourhood effect might be expected to be stronger for members of the working class than for members of the salariat, because the former were less likely to have friends from outside their neighbourhood. Members of the salariat, they argued, were generally the more geographically mobile and more likely to form social networks across large distances. But, this is not what we find. Only on attitudes towards unemployment benefit do we find a significant difference in the influence of the neighbourhood effect upon the working class and the salariat. On other issues, there are no significant differences between the classes in the strength of the neighbourhood effect on their attitudes.

Neighbourhood and region

So we find that neighbourhood does matter. But the question remains: once we take into account neighbourhood effects, does the North/South division disappear?

As a first step, let us look at the distribution of neighbourhood characteristics by region. If the neighbourhood effect is to account for the North/South division, then we should find that people in the North are more likely to live in working-class or high unemployment neighbourhoods, irrespective of their own individual social position, than people in the South.

Regional variation in neighbourhood characteristics

	Scotland	North	Wales	Midlands	Greater London	South
Salariat living in middle-class neighbourhood	58%	44%	43%	47%	51%	49%
Working class living in working-class neighbourhood	67%	53%	50%	53%	42%	39%
Salariat living in low unemployment neighbourhood	56%	40%	12%	38%	46%	56%
Working class living in high unemployment neighbourhood	24%	22%	22%	13%	4%	5%

N.B. 'Middle-class neighbourhood': enumeration district with over 20% of residents, aged 16+ and in employment, in professional and managerial occupations (1981 Census).
'Working-class neighbourhood': enumeration district with less than 10% of residents, aged 16+ and in employment, in professional and managerial occupations.
'Low unemployment neighbourhood': enumeration district with less than 5% of residents, aged 16+, seeking work.
'High unemployment neighbourhood': enumeration district with over 17% of residents, aged 16+, seeking work.

And, as the table above shows, this is largely the case. Working-class Northerners are indeed more likely than their counterparts in the South to live in a working-

class neighbourhood, and in a neighbourhood with high unemployment, though the pattern is not straightforward. But for the salariat the required pattern does not hold. For instance, Scottish members of the salariat are most likely to live in a middle-class neighbourhood. Indeed, the different classes in Scotland tend to live in distinct neighbourhoods to a far greater extent than they do in England and Wales. So it seems unlikely that the neighbourhood effect by itself can account for the North/South divide. A logit model incorporating *both* neighbourhood *and* region confirms that this is so. The estimated effects on attitudes to economic equality of living in a particular region are still very similar to those we reported on p.134. We can conclude that the North/South division is indeed real.

Politics and place

If we are to argue that the North/South division has political implications, there is one final piece of jigsaw yet to be fitted. We need to be able to show not only that there is an ideological division between the regions, but also a regional *political* divide – that is, the difference in party identification between North and South is independent of the regional distribution of individual social characteristics and of neighbourhoods.

If we first examine whether or not there is a neighbourhood effect on party identification, we find that both the class composition of a neighbourhood and its level of unemployment have an impact on party. Indeed, the association between party identification and living in a working-class neighbourhood, and between party identification and living in an area of high unemployment, is in both cases noticeably stronger than for any of the attitudinal items we analysed above.[7] Labour identification is significantly higher in working-class and high unemployment neighbourhoods. Only Alliance identification, with its weaker ties to any particular social group, fails to display a strong neighbourhood effect.

When we add region into the model, together with individual and neighbourhood characteristics, we also find an independent association between region and party identification. Thus the level of Labour identification is significantly higher for Northerners and significantly lower for Southerners. As with the neighbourhood effect, the impact of region on party identification is greater than it is on attitudes.[8] So we find there is a North/South party political divide, in addition to a neighbourhood effect. From the Humber to the Mersey and along Offa's Dyke lies an imaginary boundary delineating two different political characters. However, this regional divide largely expresses itself through two traditionally class-based parties, rather than specifically regional ones. Why is this so?

We have already provided clues to the answer, which it may be useful to rehearse. Differences in the long-term health of Britain's regional economies seem to have had an impact upon people's attitudes. Northerners are less optimistic about the future of the economy, have less faith in the ability of the market economy to deliver solutions, and are more likely to favour state intervention as a way of creating a more equal society. But these are precisely the issues, as we have noted, which divide Conservative and Labour identifiers and which are central to the ideological debate between those parties.

It appears then that economic differences alone have been sufficient to produce a regional divide in Britain. They are not new ones, however, but those that have traditionally divided the classes. The Conservative and Labour parties have therefore been able to act as vehicles for the political expression of these regional differences of interest. As a consequence, it is Labour which is the dominant party in Scotland and Wales and not, despite their advances in the 1970s, the nationalist parties with their appeals to distinctive national and linguistic identities.

Of course, this argument rests on the important assumption that regional differences in attitudes have resulted in the differences in voting behaviour, and not the other way around. This may not be so. After all, political parties not only react to public opinion, but also mould it – especially in the case of their own supporters. So the regional divide in voting behaviour may have occurred first for some entirely different reason. Having gained Labour adherents in the North and Conservative adherents in the South, the two parties might then have moulded the views of followers to their own views on economics and other matters. Far from being fanciful, it is actually likely that this process has occurred, to an extent at least, on some issues such as defence. It is difficult to see otherwise why the regions should differ on the issue of nuclear weapons. This is more plausibly the result of the parties leading and their supporters following. As **Table 8.8** illustrates, once we control for respondents' party, the North/South divide on nuclear weapons largely disappears.

In the case of egalitarianism, however, the causal link is more likely to have been the other way around. Our data argue persuasively that the regional divide on this issue is not simply a consequence of party identification. Again, referring to **Table 8.8**, having controlled for respondents' party, the regional divide on economic equality items largely survives. Thus the egalitarian preference of the North cannot simply be explained away by its higher level of Labour identification.

Conclusion

'Class is the basis of British politics; all else is embellishment and detail' (Pulzer, 1967). This chapter suggests otherwise. Region now accompanies class as a basis of voting behaviour and as an influence upon social attitudes. But it has not replaced it. For as **Table 8.9** shows, even on those issues which are central to the North/South divide, the effect of region is in general clearly weaker than that of class.

So where we live does influence our social attitudes and choice of party. But attitudes still vary more between people of different classes living in the same part of the country than they do between those in the same class living in a different part of the country. Region is not the dominant dividing line in Britain. Even so it is clear that there is a North/South divide. Where we live is no longer a 'detail', but an important influence upon how we think and vote.

Notes

1. The identification was made by ascertaining the postcode of each respondent's

address and then using a computer program which assigns postcodes to enumeration districts by identifying the district whose centroid is closest to the grid reference of each postcode. This procedure produces some misidentification, but this is unlikely to invalidate our conclusions. Every step has been taken to ensure that the detailed geographical coding that this work has required cannot be used to identify the individual respondents to the surveys. In particular it should be noted that it will not be possible to release the full details of either the postcodes or the enumeration district data to potential secondary analysts of the data.

2. We are also at this stage limited to the range of census variables supplied by CACI. In particular we could only use the standard collapses of the socio-economic groups into professional and managerial workers, lower non-manual workers, etc. to measure the class composition of each neighbourhood. In future work we intend to use a collapse which more closely approximates to the Goldthorpe class schema used in this chapter in the analysis of individual class position, and which previous work suggests would demonstrate a stronger neighbourhood effect.

3. This point might seem to be contradicted by a strong North/South divide which exists on the issue of the power of the government. Those living in Wales (59%), Scotland (57%) and the North of England (53%) are *more* likely to agree that the government has too much power than people living in London (48%), the Midlands (43%) or the South of England (39%). But we find that answers to this question are strongly associated with partisanship, with Labour partisans much more likely to agree with the statement (see **Table 8.2**). Rather than making a comment about the power of the government in general, many respondents are undoubtedly saying that the current *Conservative* government has too much power. And indeed if we control for partisanship, the North/South divide on this question almost entirely disappears.

The regional variation in attitudes towards government power might alternatively have been evidence that the regions on the periphery of the nation questioned the legitimacy of the central state power. But if this were so we should also find a clear regional division on whether or not the government has too much control over local councils. We would anticipate that people living in the North are much more likely to think that the government has too much control. Yet we find virtually no North/South pattern (again see **Table 8.2**). In contrast to most regional cleavages, the North/South divide in Britain does not appear to threaten the sovereignty of the central state or the continued unity of the nation.

4. Level of household income has not been included in the model, despite the fact that it correlates with some of the economic evaluation items, including in particular expectations about household income. This has been done to simplify the analysis. In fact, if we do include the level of household income in the model for *expectations* about household income, we are still left with positive parameter estimates for the three regions in the north and negative ones for those in the south, while those for both the North of England and the South of England are still statistically significant.

Readers might also ask whether or not there are other variables, such as union membership or whether a respondent works in the public or private sector, which are correlated with attitudes towards economic equality and which might account for the regional variation. One of the difficulties here is that, even with a dataset of the size we are using, there is a limit to the number of variables we can sensibly include in our model. But we find in fact that the regional variation in both union membership and sectoral location, like that in social class, fails to conform to a clear North/South pattern and is thus unable to account for the ideological divide.

5. In contrast, neighbourhood housing tenure proved to be unimportant. Despite the claims of some proponents of the *embourgeoisement* thesis, the attitudes of working-class people are not influenced by whether they live on a council estate or not. While their own individual tenure position is important, it is their neighbours'

class composition which matters, not their tenure position.

6. Our analysis also undermines the claims by Tate (1974) and Kelley and McAllister (1985), among others, that the neighbourhood effect on voting disappears when additional variables measuring attitudes or identities are added to the model. This argument is circular. If an individual's attitudes and identities are influenced by his or her neighbourhood, items which measure these attitudes may already incorporate some of the neighbourhood effect – in other words, they are not truly *individual-level* variables. Thus, for example, we can show that respondent's self-rated class varies with the class character of his neighbourhood (see **Table 8.7**) Yet this is one of the 'individual-level' variables included in Tate's model. That the neighbourhood effect should disappear when such a variable is included in a model is not an indication that the effect is spurious, but rather that the impact of neighbourhood on class identity is one of the mechanisms through which the neighbourhood effect operates.

7. The parameter estimate for living for a working-class neighbourhood was $+0.13$, and for living in an area of high unemployment, $+0.25$. In all of the analyses of party identification reported here, only Conservative and Labour partisans have been included. This simplifies the analysis considerably, and in any case Alliance support does not display a clear North/South pattern of variation.

8. The parameter estimates were: Scotland $+0.19$; North of England $+0.09$; Wales $+0.32$; Midlands -0.26; London $+0.02$; South of England -0.37. All the estimates were statistically significant at the five per cent level except that for London.

References

BARCLAY, C. R., *Regional Policy and the North-South Divide*, Background Paper no. 198, House of Commons Library, London (1987).

BUTLER, D. and STOKES, D., *Political Change in Britain*, Macmillan, London (1974).

CENTRAL STATISTICAL OFFICE, *Regional Trends*, no.23, HMSO, London (1988).

CHAMPION, A. G. and GREEN, A., *Local Prosperity and the Northern-South Divide: Winners and Losers in 1980s Britain,* Institute for Employment Research, University of Warwick, Coventry (1988).

COX, K. R., 'Suburbia and voting behaviour in the London Metropolitan area', *Annals, Association of American Geographers*, vol.58 (1968), pp.111–27.

CURTICE, J., 'Political Partisanship', in Jowell, R., Witherspoon, S. and Brook, L. (eds), *British Social Attitudes: the 1986 Report*, Gower, Aldershot (1986).

CURTICE, J., 'Interim report: Party politics', in Jowell, R., Witherspoon, S. and Brook, L. (eds), *British Social Attitudes: the 1987 Report*, Gower, Aldershot (1987).

CURTICE, J. and STEED, M., 'Electoral Choice and the Production of Government: The Changing Operation of the Electoral System in the United Kingdom since 1955', *British Journal of Political Science*, vol.12 (1982), pp.249–98.

CURTICE, J. and STEED, M., 'Proportionality and Exaggeration in the British Electoral System', *Electoral Studies*, vol.5 (1986), pp.209–28.

CURTICE, J. and STEED, M., 'Analysis', in Butler, D. and Kavanagh, D., *The British General Election of 1987*, Macmillan, London (1988).

DUNLEAVY, P., 'The Urban Basis of Political Alignment: Social Class, Domestic Property Ownership, and State Intervention in Consumption Processes', *British Journal of Political Science*, vol.9 (1979), pp.409–43.

FITTON, M., 'Neighbourhood and Voting: A Sociometric Explanation', *British Journal of Political Science*, vol.3 (1973), pp.445–72.

GILBERT, N., *Modelling Society*, Allen & Unwin, London (1981).

HEATH, A., JOWELL, R. and CURTICE, J., *How Britain Votes*, Pergamon, Oxford (1985).

HUCKFELDT, R. and SPRAGUE, J., 'Networks in Context: The Social Flow of Political Information', *American Political Science Review*, vol.81 (1987), pp.1197–1216.

KELLEY, J. and McALLISTER, I., 'Social Context and Electoral Behaviour in Britain', *American Journal of Political Science,* vol.29 (1985), pp.565–86.

LIPSET, S. M. and ROKKAN, S., 'Cleavage Structures, Party Systems, and Voter Alignments: An Introduction', in Lipset, S. M. and Rokkan, S. (eds), *Party Systems and Voter Alignments*, Free Press, New York (1967).

PULZER, P., *Political Representation and Elections in Britain*, Allen and Unwin, London (1967).

PUTTNAM, R., 'Political Attitudes and the Local Community', *American Political Science Review*, vol.60 (1966), pp.640–54.

RUMLEY, D., 'Spatial Structural Effects in Voting Behaviour: Description and Explanation', *Tijdschrift voor Economische en Sociale Geografie*, vol. 72 (1981), pp.214–23.

TATE, C. N., 'Individual and Contextual Variables in British Voting Behaviour: an Exploratory Note', *American Political Science Review*, vol.68, (1974), pp.1656–62.

TAYLOR, P. J. and JOHNSTON, R. J., *Geography of Elections*, Penguin, Harmondsworth (1979).

Acknowledgements

This chapter was written while the author was on paid study leave granted by the University of Liverpool and supported by a Nuffield Foundation Social Science Research Fellowship. The creation of a combined dataset of a selection of the variables from the 1983–7 *British Social Attitudes* series was undertaken in collaboration with Martin Harrop and Stan Openshaw of the University of Newcastle, and was supported by a grant from that university's research fund. Research assistance was provided by Andrew Shaw of the Department of Politics, University of Liverpool. The identification of the census enumeration district of respondents to the 1985 and 1986 surveys was undertaken by CACI Analysis Ltd who also provided a selection of 1981 census variables for the enumeration districts they identified. Some of the analysis in this chapter was first presented at the Annual Joint Workshops of the European Consortium for Political Research held in Rimini, Italy, in April 1988, and benefited from participants' comments. Valuable assistance was also given by Sharon Witherspoon, Kevin McGrath and Denise Lievesley of SCPR.

8.1 ECONOMIC EVALUATIONS (1987: Qs 11, 12, 13b, 21a, 20b) by region

	TOTAL		Scotland	North	North West	Yorks and Humber	Wales	West Midlands	East Midlands	East Anglia	Greater London	South West	South East
	%		%	%	%	%	%	%	%	%	%	%	%
+INFLATION													
Expect prices generally to have gone up a lot in a year from now	29		31	39	35	30	33	26	25	30	28	22	26
+UNEMPLOYMENT													
Expect unemployment to have gone up a lot in a year from now	26		33	34	33	27	30	23	22	21	27	17	23
*INFLATION V. UNEMPLOYMENT													
Unemployment of greater concern than inflation to respondent and his/her family	43		50	51	51	48	41	41	40	46	39	38	38
*HOUSEHOLD INCOME V. PRICES													
Expect household's income to fall behind prices in the year ahead	43		49	54	47	48	51	44	43	37	36	38	36
*LIVING STANDARDS													
Find it difficult or very difficult [to live] on present household income	26		28	28	32	27	30	29	25	22	27	22	19
+BASE : ALL RESPONDENTS, 1983-1987 Weighted	10965		1112	646	1252	1055	609	1050	768	451	1141	918	1962
Unweighted	11187		1098	676	1287	1061	625	1076	790	452	1167	932	2023
*BASE : ALL RESPONDENTS, 1984-1987 Weighted	9246		928	552	1056	891	523	893	637	379	950	769	1668
Unweighted	9426		918	577	1078	896	538	915	659	382	972	780	1711

8.2 ATTITUDES TOWARDS POWER OF GOVERNMENT AND GOVERNMENT CONTROL OF LOCAL COUNCILS (1987: A213, Q3a) by compressed region and party identification

+THE GOVERNMENT HAS:

	TOTAL	COMPRESSED REGION						PARTY IDENTIFICATION			
		Scotland	North	Wales	Midlands	London	South	Conservative	Alliance	Labour	Non-aligned
	%	%	%	%	%	%	%	%	%	%	%
Far too much power	18	20	23	25	17	16	12	4	16	32	21
Too much power	30	37	30	34	26	32	27	15	38	38	30
About the right amount of power	42	36	37	31	45	38	45	67	39	21	30
Too little power	4	2	4	4	4	5	5	7	3	2	5
Far too little power	1	-	1	1	1	-	1	1	*	*	1
(Can't choose/don't know)	6	4	6	5	8	9	6	5	5	6	13

*SHOULD LOCAL COUNCILS BE CONTROLLED BY CENTRAL GOVERNMENT MORE, LESS OR ABOUT THE SAME AMOUNT AS NOW?

	TOTAL										
More	15	15	16	16	17	19	13	22	12	11	13
Less	35	43	36	33	33	29	35	24	46	43	26
About the same	39	32	37	41	41	40	42	46	34	36	36
Don't know/not answered	10	10	10	10	9	13	10	8	8	9	24

+ BASE : ALL RESPONDENTS, 1985; B RESPONDENTS, 1986; A RESPONDENTS, 1987.

Weighted	4061	402	1142	203	689	379	1245	1406	742	1349	299
Unweighted	4132	381	1167	213	712	379	1273	1453	760	1358	291

* BASE : ALL RESPONDENTS, 1983-1987

Weighted	10965	1112	2953	609	1817	1141	3332	3930	1834	3661	832
Unweighted	11187	1098	3024	625	1866	1167	3407	4029	1870	3732	834

8.3 ATTITUDES TO ECONOMIC EQUALITY (1987: Q60, A227a/B238a, A227c/B238c, B207b, A227b/B238b, A227d/B238d, Q13a) by compressed Goldthorpe class schema, housing tenure and party identification

	TOTAL	COMPRESSED GOLDTHORPE CLASS SCHEMA					HOUSING TENURE				PARTY IDENTIFICATION			
		Salariat	Routine non-manual	Petty bourgeoisie	Foremen and technicians	Working class	Owner occupier	Rented from Council/ New Town D.C.	Rented from Housing Association	Other rented	Con- servative	Alliance	Labour	Non- aligned
	%	%	%	%	%	%	%	%	%	%	%	%	%	%
AGREE THAT														
+-benefits for the unemployed are too low and cause hardship	47	40	44	33	46	54	42	59	55	51	28	50	66	46
AGREE STRONGLY OR AGREE THAT														
*-government should redistribute income from the better-off to those who are less well-off	44	38	37	34	42	55	39	59	55	47	21	49	67	55
*-ordinary working people do not get their fair share of the nation's wealth	65	52	60	54	68	78	60	80	69	65	42	69	87	76
++-it is the responsibility of the government to reduce the differences between people with high income and those with low income	55	42	53	44	52	67	49	68	80	60	37	56	71	55
*-big business benefits owners at the expense of workers	52	43	46	45	57	62	48	64	60	54	33	56	71	59
*-there is one law for the rich and one for the poor	64	50	60	54	67	77	60	77	68	60	43	69	83	74
AGREE THAT														
+-government should give highest priority to keeping down unemployment	72	64	77	62	71	78	70	78	74	72	56	81	85	72
+BASE: ALL RESPONDENTS, 1983-1987														
Weighted	10965	2661	1775	876	765	3836	7251	2756	159	768	3930	1834	3661	832
Unweighted	11187	2730	1833	888	778	3910	7435	2817	164	737	4029	1870	3732	334
*BASE: B RESPONDENTS, 1986; ALL RESPONDENTS, 1987														
Weighted	3740	978	678	330	221	1339	2580	797	47	308	1398	691	1151	258
Unweighted	3814	1007	708	336	225	1348	2655	815	50	286	1438	706	1170	253
++BASE: ALL RESPONDENTS, 1985; B RESPONDENTS, 1986														
Weighted	2817	693	500	229	188	1017	1825	709	55	224	923	500	1018	199
Unweighted	2851	707	518	228	188	1030	1867	707	60	213	947	506	1021	198

8.4 ATTITUDES TO LEVEL OF UNEMPLOYMENT BENEFIT (Q60) AND REDISTRIBUTION (A227a/B238a) – 1
by compressed region within compressed Goldthorpe class schema

	TOTAL	SALARIAT						ROUTINE NON-MANUAL WORKERS						PETTY BOURGEOISIE					
		Scot-land	North	Wales	Midlands	Greater London	South	Scot-land	North	Wales	Midlands	Greater London	South	Scot-land	North	Wales	Midlands	Greater London	South
	%	%	%	%	%	%	%	%	%	%	%	%	%	%	%	%	%	%	%
+WHICH OF THESE TWO STATEMENTS COMES CLOSEST TO YOUR OWN OPINION ABOUT BENEFITS FOR THE UNEMPLOYED?																			
Too low and cause hardship	47	60	48	41	33	41	33	62	55	51	38	42	34	48	40	26	27	47	26
Too high and discourage people from finding jobs	32	26	32	35	40	37	39	20	25	19	39	32	41	34	39	43	50	35	53
(Neither)	7	7	8	15	12	9	11	8	5	13	6	7	9	7	7	22	10	4	7
Both/varies/about right /other answer/don't know /not stated	14	7	12	9	15	13	17	11	16	17	20	20	17	10	15	10	13	13	15
+GOVERNMENT SHOULD RE-DISTRIBUTE INCOME FROM THE BETTER-OFF TO THOSE WHO ARE LESS WELL-OFF																			
Agree strongly/agree	44	58	43	(40)	26	41	31	40	41	(n/c)	44	27	30	(33)	38	(n/c)	39	(n/c)	27
Neither agree nor disagree	22	15	14	(21)	21	23	17	16	27	(n/c)	22	21	24	(36)	15	(n/c)	19	(n/c)	27
Disagree/disagree strongly	32	28	42	(34)	52	36	51	43	30	(n/c)	33	50	44	(33)	45	(n/c)	43	(n/c)	42
(Don't know/not answered)	2	1	1	(5)	-	-	1	1	2	(n/c)	3	2	2	(-)	2	(n/c)	-	(n/c)	3
+BASE: ALL RESPONDENTS, 1983-1987 Weighted	10965	273	576	119	415	358	920	170	471	64	276	219	575	79	198	73	155	67	304
Unweighted	11187	274	604	125	430	353	944	176	474	67	284	231	601	72	208	74	157	70	307
+BASE: B RESPONDENTS, 1986; ALL RESPONDENTS, 1987 Weighted	3740	114	197	(43)	154	127	344	72	198	(21)	119	70	197	(23)	89	(20)	46	(23)	119
Unweighted	3814	114	205	(46)	157	128	357	75	204	(23)	126	77	209	(29)	92	(23)	50	(25)	117

n/c = not calculated (base too small)

8.5 ATTITUDES TO LEVEL OF UNEMPLOYMENT BENEFIT (Q60) AND REDISTRIBUTION (A227a/B238a) – 2
by compressed region within compressed Goldthorpe class schema

	TOTAL	FOREMEN AND TECHNICIANS						WORKING CLASS					
		Scot-land	North	Wales	Midlands	Greater London	South	Scot-land	North	Wales	Midlands	Greater London	South
	%	%	%	%	%	%	%	%	%	%	%	%	%
+WHICH OF THESE TWO STATEMENTS COMES CLOSEST TO YOUR OWN OPINION ABOUT BENEFITS FOR THE UNEMPLOYED?													
Too low and cause hardship	47	61	52	(69)	44	44	34	73	60	57	52	48	44
Too high and discourage people from finding jobs	32	20	32	(14)	31	38	43	1b	23	28	30	26	34
(Neither)	7	10	7	(8)	9	3	10	3	4	8	4	4	7
Both/varies/about right/other answer/don't know/not stated	14	9	9	(10)	16	16	13	9	12	7	13	22	15
*GOVERNMENT SHOULD REDISTRIBUTE INCOME FROM THE BETTER-OFF TO THOSE WHO ARE LESS WELL-OFF													
Agree strongly/agree	44	(n/c)	41	(n/c)	(53)	(n/c)	39	65	59	74	53	52	46
Neither agree nor disagree	22	(n/c)	33	(n/c)	(26)	(n/c)	31	16	22	20	22	25	26
Disagree/disagree strongly	32	(n/c)	23	(n/c)	(21)	(n/c)	28	17	18	5	23	22	25
(Don't know/not answered)	2	(n/c)	4	(n/c)	(-)	(n/c)	2	1	2	1	1	1	2
+BASE: ALL RESPONDENTS, 1983–1987 Weighted	10965	64	224	(39)	133	64	241	386	1160	230	682	340	1039
Unweighted	11187	67	227	(39)	135	64	246	381	1195	235	700	346	3910
*BASE: B RESPONDENTS, 1986; ALL RESPONDENTS, 1987 Weighted	3740	(16)	79	(14)	(38)	(11)	52	98	411	86	228	103	403
Unweighted	3814	(18)	79	(13)	(40)	(11)	64	99	421	87	229	105	407

n/c = not calculated (base too small)

8.6 ATTITUDES TO MORAL ISSUES (1987: A88a, b; A215d, e, f) by compressed region

	TOTAL	COMPRESSED REGION					
		Scotland	North	Wales	Midlands	London	South
SEXUAL RELATIONS	%	%	%	%	%	%	%
+Sexual relations between a man and a woman before marriage are not wrong at all	42	41	45	36	40	41	43
*A married person having sexual relations with someone other than partner is rarely wrong/not wrong at all	2	2	2	3	2	3	2
ABORTION							
**The law should allow abortion if the couple cannot afford any more children	50	45	48	47	51	53	51
**the law should allow abortion if there is a strong chance of a defect in the baby	85	80	83	84	85	84	88
**The law should allow abortion if the woman's health is seriously endangered by the pregnancy	91	89	90	93	91	89	93
+BASE: ALL RESPONDENTS, 1983-1985; A RESPONDENTS, 1987							
Weighted	6524	678	1768	355	1109	673	1942
Unweighted	6677	667	1814	363	1137	690	2006
*BASE: ALL RESPONDENTS, 1984-1985; A RESPONDENTS, 1987							
Weighted	4805	494	1313	268	821	482	1426
Unweighted	4916	487	1341	276	845	495	1472
**BASE: ALL RESPONDENTS, 1983-1985; A RESPONDENTS, 1986-1987							
Weighted	7265	731	1982	373	1223	714	2242
Unweighted	7439	724	2046	382	1253	727	2307

8.7 SELF-RATED SOCIAL CLASS (1987: Q76a)
by class of neighbourhood lived in* within tenure within compressed Goldthorpe class schema

WHICH SOCIAL CLASS WOULD YOU SAY YOU BELONG TO?	TOTAL	SALARIAT						INTERMEDIATE						WORKING CLASS					
		Owner occupier Neighbourhood:			Rented from council/New Town Neighbourhood:			Owner occupier Neighbourhood:			Rented from council/New Town Neighbourhood:			Owner occupier Neighbourhood:			Rented from council/New Town Neighbourhood:		
		Working class	Mixed	Middle class	Working class	Mixed	Middle class	Working class	Mixed	Middle class	Working class	Mixed	Middle class	Working class	Mixed	Middle class	Working class	Mixed	Middle class
	%	%	%	%	%	%	%	%	%	%	%	%	%	%	%	%	%	%	%
Upper middle	1	1	1	4	(-)	(-)	(n/c)	2	1	2	-	-	(-)	*	1	1	*	-	-
Middle	25	40	45	54	(7)	(26)	(n/c)	18	27	35	11	8	(10)	15	11	16	10	9	11
Upper working	20	26	24	26	(20)	(23)	(n/c)	23	29	29	12	18	(36)	16	16	25	8	10	5
Working	48	30	28	13	(65)	(46)	(n/c)	54	42	29	71	66	(48)	64	68	53	70	63	77
Poor	3	-	-	-	(-)	(3)	(n/c)	1	1	*	5	8	(-)	3	2	1	10	15	6
Refused/don't know/not answered	3	3	2	4	(9)	(3)	(n/c)	2	1	5	1	1	(6)	1	2	3	1	3	1
BASE: ALL RESPONDENTS 1985 AND 1986																			
Weighted	4835	199	273	510	(40)	(38)	(21)	324	351	406	186	102	(34)	356	325	212	444	179	95
Unweighted	4904	203	281	525	(41)	(39)	(22)	328	364	413	180	103	(36)	361	329	215	454	180	93

* Working class neighbourhood: 0-10% professional and managerial
Mixed neighbourhood: over 10%-20% professional and managerial
Middle class neighbourhood: over 20% professional and managerial

n/c = not calculated (base too small)

8.8 ATTITUDES TO LEVEL OF UNEMPLOYMENT BENEFIT (1987: Q60), REDISTRIBUTION (1987: A227a/B238a) AND US NUCLEAR MISSILES IN BRITAIN (1987: Q6a) by compressed region within party identification

	TOTAL	CONSERVATIVE Scotland	North	Wales	Midlands	London	South	ALLIANCE Scotland	North	Wales	Midlands	London	South	LABOUR Scotland	North	Wales	Midlands	London	South
	%	%	%	%	%	%	%	%	%	%	%	%	%	%	%	%	%	%	%
+WHICH OF THESE TWO STATEMENTS COMES CLOSEST TO YOUR OWN [OPINION]?																			
Benefits for the unemployed are too low and cause hardship	47	41	33	28	27	27	24	64	59	51	47	46	43	78	70	66	61	62	56
Benefits for the unemployed are too high and discourage people from finding jobs	32	39	45	44	48	47	50	21	24	27	31	24	32	12	16	19	24	21	25
(Neither)	7	9	8	15	10	9	9	7	6	11	10	9	10	3	4	6	5	3	7
Both/varies/about right/other answer/don't know/not answered	14	11	14	13	15	16	17	8	12	11	12	21	15	7	9	10	11	13	12
*GOVERNMENT SHOULD REDISTRIBUTE INCOME FROM THE BETTER-OFF TO THOSE WHO ARE LESS WELL-OFF																			
Agree strongly/agree	44	30	25	(26)	22	22	17	66	55	(42)	50	47	42	62	69	72	67	57	70
Neither agree nor disagree	22	24	20	(28)	19	18	24	17	21	(32)	25	25	28	21	19	19	21	27	18
Disagree/disagree strongly	32	44	54	(45)	58	59	56	19	19	(21)	24	27	29	17	10	8	10	13	11
(Don't know/not answered)	2	1	1	(2)	*	*	2	*	4	(6)	2	2	1	1	2	1	2	2	1
+THINKS THAT THE SITING OF AMERICAN NUCLEAR MISSILES IN BRITAIN MAKES BRITAIN A ..																			
... safer place to live	35	46	58	55	52	52	55	28	27	32	33	23	28	18	23	22	24	16	23
... less safe place to live	53	40	31	35	35	31	32	59	62	62	60	58	58	76	69	69	66	73	70
(No difference)	2	2	3	2	2	2	4	4	3	-	2	2	4	1	1	1	1	1	1
(Don't know/not answered)	10	12	8	8	11	15	10	10	9	6	6	15	11	6	7	9	9	9	5
+BASE: ALL RESPONDENTS, 1983-1987 Weighted	10965	258	890	136	757	407	1482	163	463	80	252	165	712	461	1234	293	550	402	722
Unweighted	11187	263	907	144	780	409	1526	163	470	79	259	171	728	438	1278	300	569	416	731
*BASE: B RESPONDENTS, 1986; ALL RESPONDENTS 1987 Weighted	3740	86	338	(42)	255	138	539	70	170	(33)	101	58	259	128	415	100	158	110	240
Unweighted	3814	85	342	(47)	266	140	558	71	178	(31)	106	60	260	124	430	102	159	113	242

8.9 RELATIVE IMPORTANCE OF REGION AND CLASS (parameter estimates)

% AGREEING ...	'North' (ie Scotland, North of England and Wales)	Salariat	Owner occupier	Unemployed	BASES Weighted	Unweighted
- expect unemployment to go up a lot in next year (Q.12)	+.07	-.18	-.07	+.19	4424	4502
- expect household income to fall behind prices in next year (Q.21b)	+.08	-.15	-.11	+.07	4414	4490
- unemployment benefit is too low and causes hardship (Q.60)	+.15	-.07	-.13	+.37	4423	4502
- government should redistribute income from the better-off to those who are less well-off (A227a/B238a)	+.11	-.12	-.15	+.19	1199	1212
- ordinary people do not get their fair share of the nation's wealth (A227c/B238c)	+.10	-.18	-.14	+.16	1201	1214
- it is the responsibility of government to reduce the difference in income between people with high incomes and those with low incomes (B207b)	+.14	-.18	-.18	+.16	2567	2610
LABOUR PARTISANSHIP	+.20	-.29	-.22	+.22	3024	3084

This table reports the parameter estimates for region, being a member of the salariat, being an owner occupier and being unemployed from a logit model which also contains neighbourhood class and unemployment level. Region was dichotomised into North (Scotland, North of England and Wales) and South. All the estimates are statistically significant at the 5% level except for the impact of being unemployed on attitudes towards whether or not people get their fair share of the nation's wealth, and on expectations about household income.

8.10 SELECTED DEMOGRAPHIC AND OTHER CHARACTERISTICS by compressed region

	TOTAL	COMPRESSED REGION Scotland	North	Wales	Midlands	Greater London	South
	%	%	%	%	%	%	%
+ AGE: 18-34	33	36	35	30	31	35	31
+ CLASS: Salariat	24	25	20	20	23	31	28
Working class	35	35	39	38	38	30	31
++ HIGHEST EDUCATIONAL QUALIFICATION: Degree	7	8	6	7	5	12	8
@ + INCOME: Top quintile	20	18	14	13	17	32	25
+ RELIGIOUS ATTENDANCE: Attends service/meeting at least once a week	12	19	12	13	11	14	10
* WORK STATUS: Respondent or spouse unemployed	10	11	14	10	9	10	6
+ TENURE: Owner occupier	66	49	65	72	69	58	73
+ BASE: ALL RESPONDENTS 1983-87 Weighted	10965	1112	2953	609	1817	1141	3334
Unweighted	11187	1098	3024	625	1866	1167	3407
* BASE: ALL RESPONDENTS 1984-87 Weighted	9346	928	2499	523	1530	960	2816
Unweighted	9426	918	2551	538	1574	972	2873
++ BASE: ALL RESPONDENTS 1986-87 Weighted	7601	751	2059	429	1247	793	2321
Unweighted	7751	743	2110	445	1283	811	2359

@ Base excludes 1392 cases missing income information

9 Interim report: Rural prospects

*Ken Young**

For three successive years we have asked a series of questions about the country-side and its future – an issue of increasing importance as Britain, in line with EEC policy, is attempting to limit agricultural production and encourage new economic activities and land uses in rural areas. The debate so far has focused largely on the views of those with a direct interest in the countryside: farmers, developers, conservationists and so on. But the future of rural Britain is also, or should be, a matter of concern to "people at large" (Countryside Commission, 1987). If public opinion is strong enough, and if it extends beyond the rural population, then it is more likely to play a part in shaping policies.

So we wanted to find out how much people feel they own the countryside, and how significant it is in their lives. To assess these issues in the context of a countryside under severe pressure for change, we felt it was not enough just to find out how much use people make of the countryside for relaxation and enjoyment. Rather, we wanted to gauge how far underlying beliefs, values and predispositions might operate in creating political pressures for or against change. Such an approach distinguishes between the visibility or salience of an issue, whether people approve or disapprove of what is happening, and how much they feel *involved*. A gulf between what people would like to see happening and what is actually happening might either reconcile them to accept unwelcome changes, or spur them to political action, such as vote-switching or even protest action of one sort or another.[1]

Even when people recognise, deplore *and* feel a sense of involvement in an issue, they will not necessarily translate it into a political issue. Indeed, the *political* significance of changes to the countryside may well turn upon who feels what, since people vary in their dispositions to act politically. Paradoxically perhaps, as Marris (1974) and Schon (1971) have argued, those most likely

---

* Professor of Local Government Studies, University of Birmingham.

to assert themselves are often the most *conservative*, driven by an unwillingness to accept the loss of the past. And the countryside does evoke the past, as *The 1986* and *1987 Reports* confirmed: "an image of bucolic rurality that in reality has been steadily vanishing over the past two decades" (Newby, 1979). How long can these images survive in the face of such visible changes in the landscape and in the quality of country life? Moreover, the new policy debates – about housing development, the industrialisation of the countryside and non-agricultural activity on farms – must surely serve to sharpen perceptions and for the first time bring the future of the countryside into the broader political arena.

As we turn to the 1987 data, we examine first the extent to which changes to the countryside are *recognised* and by whom. We then examine in turn how people *feel* about such changes, and the extent to which they feel *concerned* or personally affected by them. We then move on to look at the extent to which the countryside matters politically, and the choices respondents make when faced with a series of policy options. Finally, we draw together these strands and assess their significance.

Recognition of change in the countryside

As in 1985 and 1986, we asked respondents to say *whether or not* and, if so, *how far* the countryside had changed in the past 20 years. Around a half believe that it has changed a lot and, as the table below shows, the proportion holding this view seems to be increasing:

	1985	1986	1987
	%	%	%
The countryside:			
is much the same	20	22	20
has changed a bit	23	25	21
has changed a lot	49	48	55
don't know/not answered	7	5	3

The form of the question assumes that respondents can grasp a time-span of two decades. The younger age groups are, of course, less able to base their views on experience, so we would expect older respondents to have a more acute sense of countryside change. To some extent this is the case, although the association with age is not as clearcut as we expected. Indeed, those in the middle age groups – generally the most environmentally conscious – seem to be the most evenly divided in their responses.

		The countryside ...		
		... is much the same	... has changed a bit	... has changed a lot
Age				
18–24	%	15	25	51
25–34	%	17	27	52
35–44	%	24	21	53
45–54	%	27	16	56
55–64	%	19	21	59
65 +	%	19	19	61

We also expected to find a relationship between place of residence and perceptions of change. Those who live in or close by the countryside are, perhaps,
more likely to recognise the extent of the changes that are undoubtedly occurring.
Again, this is the case, but it is only the two (relatively small) groups of
respondents who either live in the big cities or in the countryside itself, who
have views that mark them out from the majority. As the next table shows,
city dwellers are the least, and country people the most, aware of substantial
change.

	The countryside has changed a lot
Current residence:	
big city	43%
suburbs	57%
small city or town	53%
country town or village	59%
countryside	74%

However, it is also among country dwellers and city dwellers that the increase
in consciousness of change has been greatest – around an 11% to 12% rise
in each case since 1985 in the proportion saying the countryside has changed
"a lot".

Another relationship which might be expected to affect perceptions of change
is the use people make of the countryside: those who go there most for recreational purposes are most likely to have a heightened consciousness of change.
For this analysis we used respondents' answers to a question about participation
in a number of countryside leisure activities during the four weeks prior to
interview.[2] We do not suggest, of course, that a day recently spent in the country
provides a perspective on change there over two decades. But direct and recent
experience provides us with at least a measure to relate leisure activities in
the countryside with appreciation of the extent it was believed to have changed.
What we found, however, is that *use* of the countryside, whether recent or
distant, does very little to raise consciousness of change (for details see **Table
9.1**).*

Similarly, we expected but did not find large differences according to
respondents' level of education. Indeed, to the extent that educational qualifications bear upon awareness, it is in the opposite direction from that expected.
Graduates seem to have the *least* sense of the countryside having changed "a
lot", while those with no educational qualifications have the greatest awareness
of substantial change (again see **Table 9.1**).

But this finding may reflect little more than a general tendency (noted in
previous Reports) for people in the higher educational and occupational groupings to be more tentative in their agreement or disagreement, avoiding poles
of opinion. In other words, the differences here might be concerned less with
attitudes *per se* than with ways of expressing them.

---

* Possibly *frequency* of use might have discriminated better, but we did not ask about frequency.

The unwelcome impact of change

We have reported that a majority of most social groups recognise that the countryside *has* changed over the last 20 years, but this does not in itself demonstrate that these changes are thought to be bad. On the whole, however, they are felt to be so: as many as 74% of those who thought there had been change (56% of all respondents) believe that the British countryside has changed for the worse.

Taking the findings from earlier rounds of this series as a guide, we would expect this overall picture to conceal marked differences among the subgroups. But this no longer seems to be the case. On the contrary, there is now a remarkable degree of consensus, with few differences emerging even between groups which might have been expected to differ. For example, **Table 9.2** at the end of this chapter shows that, apart from the small group of respondents who live in the countryside itself, there is scant relationship between place of residence and evaluations of changes in the countryside. Similarly, recent use of the countryside for recreation has little impact. Nor do people's characteristics such as age and education make much difference to attitudes.

As the table below shows, however, the extent of the consensus is new. By and large, those groups who, in 1985, were out of line with the majority are now coming closer to it. The result is that the overall proportion thinking that the countryside has changed for the worse has risen from 49% to 56% in two years.

	The countryside has changed for the worse...		
	1985	**1987**	**% change**
Total	49%	56%	+ 7
Current residence:			
big city	37%	52%	+15
suburbs	56%	56%	0
small city or town	48%	58%	+10
country	49%	56%	+ 7
Men:			
18–34	44%	62%	+18
35–54	59%	57%	− 2
55+	47%	57%	+10
Women:			
18–34	48%	57%	+ 9
35–54	51%	52%	+ 1
55+	47%	54%	+ 7

Particularly striking are the increases in negative views registered by town and city dwellers. The attitudes of the urban population, formerly more sanguine about the countryside, are now barely different from those who live in suburban and rural Britain. And while there has been virtually no change in the views of the middle age group, fairly marked shifts have occurred in those held by older people and – especially – by younger men. The point is that *changes* in attitude have been both substantial and in the direction of consensus.

Should this trend persist, it is potentially of great importance. It may well owe something to a general popularisation of environmental issues and to

INTERIM REPORT: RURAL PROSPECTS

changes in the portrayal of the countryside by the mass media. In any event, support for the view that the countryside is deteriorating seems to be broadening its base. But do people register *concern* about the change?

Concern about the countryside

Whether shifts in the pattern of opinion are of potential *political* significance depends to a large extent on whether or not the feeling that things are getting worse translates itself into real concern. In other words, do changes in the environment intrude upon people's personal domain? We asked: *Are you person-ally concerned about things that may happen to the countryside, or does it not concern you particularly?* [and if concerned] *Are you very concerned, or just a bit concerned?* Overall, 77% of respondents express concern, 44% being "very concerned" about the countryside.

In assessing how seriously to take such answers, we plotted them against others. Encouragingly, direct experience of the countryside relates directly to concern, suggesting that this question taps something more immediate than the more general 'attitude to change' question reported earlier:

		Very concerned	Just a bit concerned	Not particularly concerned
Current/past residence:				
living in country now	%	56	27	17
lived sometime in the country	%	50	33	17
never lived in the country	%	34	37	29
Last did countryside activity:				
within last 4 weeks	%	52	33	14
within last year	%	34	34	32
not within last year	%	29	27	44

This relationship suggests not only that direct recent experience of the countryside is within the 'personal domain' of respondents, but that there is what we might term a distinct 'user base' in concern for the countryside.

On this question too we found some of the more marked changes in patterns of response over the years. The proportion saying that they were "very con-cerned" has increased by 13% in two years, with a more or less corresponding fall in the proportion expressing no particular concern:

Concern about countryside changes 1985–1987			
	1985	1986	1987
Respondent is:	%	%	%
very concerned	31	40	44
a bit concerned	37	35	33
not particularly concerned	32	25	22

This trend is dramatic: in only two years the proportion expressing strong concern has risen to twice that of the unconcerned. And as the next table shows, the size and direction of this shift is similar to the pattern we have already seen in people's recognition of adverse change:

	Change since 1985 in % saying that...	
	...the countryside has changed for the worse	...they are "very concerned" about countryside change
Current residence:		
big city	+15	+11
suburbs	0	+12
small city or town	+10	+13
country	+ 7	+18
Men:		
18–34	+18	+14
35–54	− 2	+12
55+	+10	+18
Women:		
18–34	+ 9	+ 6
35–54	+ 1	+15
55+	+ 7	+14
Highest qualification:		
degree	+ 1	+ 5
professional	+ 5	+19
GCE or CSE	+10	+11
Foreign/other/none	+ 5	+14

Full data for 1987 are given in **Table 9.3**. Also, while those in Social Classes I and II still register much higher levels of concern than others, rises in concern are universal and of much the same magnitude in all social classes.

So the results again suggest a 'filtering down' of what, on past evidence, were attitudes held mainly by the more highly educated. No longer then are perceptions of adverse change, or of concern about their effect, the particular preserve of the group whom we described in *The 1987 Report* as "most likely to use the countryside as its playground" (Young, 1987, p.161). Now they are everybody's concerns, at least to a greater degree than before.

Is the countryside a political issue?

We turn now to the possible political ramifications of this broad-based movement in opinion. In general, it would be a mistake to overemphasise the political significance of the growing awareness that something unwelcome is happening to the countryside. Despite the shifts in people's perceptions of change, in the negative evaluation of that change, and in the levels of concern about it, the issue does not emerge as a highly political one.

In the first place, people's disapproval does not in every case translate itself into the far more potent quality of *concern*. Without such individual identification, people are unlikely to do much about it. Even among those who are very concerned, the extent to which they will actually do something about it will be conditioned partly by their own sense of political efficacy, that is, their expectation of being able to wield effective political influence. And efficacy, as past Reports (Young, 1984, pp. 20–27; Young, 1985, pp.11–17) have illustrated, is related to a complex of factors which have more to do with people's

own personalities and characteristics than with the issue at stake. But efficacy is nonetheless likely to be greatest in issues which are clearly focused in particular groups. This is not one of them.

Second, even when high levels of concern *and* of political efficacy surround an issue, this will tend to have little political impact when voters do not see the parties as distinctively different on the issue. And on countryside matters, voters *do* find it hard to distinguish between the parties. Asked *Which political party's views on the environment come closest to your own?*, as many as 53% of those who responded were unable to say. Generally, among those who could make a choice, they overwhelmingly identified the party which they were disposed to support anyway.

	Conservative	Alliance	Labour
	%	%	%
Party closest to respondent's own views on the environment:			
Conservative	36	2	2
Alliance	7	30	4
Labour	1	3	33
Ecology/Green	4	7	8
Don't know	52	55	48

The third obstacle to the politicisation of countryside issues is that we have been dealing so far with generalities, and it is rare for a generalised sense of concern about an issue to shape the outcome of political contests. While we have found substantial shifts in attitudes to the countryside, and a high level of concern, such forces are not likely to lead to political action except in relation to *specific* issues. It is on just such specifics – in particular, the intensiveness and extensiveness of farming and the realisation of different rural land uses – that the debate is likely to centre in the coming decade.

Expectations and policy options

Threats to the countryside

Perceived threats to the countryside take many forms: changes in agricultural practice, the removal of the landscape in the interests of greater yield, the development of employment and homes in rural areas and the opening up of the countryside as a leisure resource. This latter issue raises a paradox: as the countryside is opened up for leisure, the very qualities of tranquillity and beauty sought by the visitor are themselves put at risk.

As in previous years, we asked the respondents to say which was the greatest, and which the next greatest, among a list of threats to the countryside. In the table below, the responses are grouped together in a rough rank ordering.

Sources of threat to the countryside

	Greatest threat %	Next greatest threat %
Urbanisation:		
industrial pollution	32	21
urban growth	16	12
motorways and roads	11	11
Agriculture:		
chemicals and pesticides	18	26
removal of the landscape	11	12
Recreation:		
litter	9	12
tourism and visitors	1	2

There has been little change in the pattern visible since the question was first asked in 1985. The most striking finding is that tourism and more visitors are seen by hardly anyone as a possible threat. So it seems that the interwar concern with protecting the countryside *from* people has now given way to what might be termed a 'socialisation' of leisure, a concern to open up the countryside *to* more people.

These findings differ little from those presented in *The 1986 Report*. We showed then that popular preoccupations with changes to the countryside focused on traditional sources of danger to the rural idyll – those of an urban-industrial society. Then, as now, there was little perception that changing methods of farming were a source of threat. Indeed, there has been little change since 1985 in the extent to which specific developments are seen to be threatening. Yet, as we have seen, overall concern has grown.

On the widely perceived threat of industrial pollution, those who live in country towns or villages are almost indistinguishable in their views from urban and suburban dwellers; those who live in the countryside itself are the least likely to register concern. On the other hand, country dwellers as a whole tend to be rather more concerned than average about the use of chemicals and pesticides in agriculture, with just over half (51%) naming it as the greatest or next greatest threat. This finding may reflect mounting concern over the contamination of water supplies by nitrates and other chemicals.

It is noticeable, however, that urban growth into the countryside is seen as a greater threat by urban dwellers than by those living in country towns or villages – although not by those living in the countryside itself; the latter see changes to the traditional landscape as a particular threat. Concern about urban growth also varies by region, with those in the Midlands and South – understandably perhaps – particularly likely to see it as a threat. These and other differences can be seen in **Tables 9.4** and **9.5**.

Prices, jobs and the countryside

What priority do respondents give to protecting the countryside against demands for lower prices and higher employment? Each year since 1984 we have asked respondents to say which of two statements came closest to their own views:

Industry should be prevented from causing damage to the countryside, even if this sometimes leads to higher prices;
OR
Industry should keep prices down, even if this sometimes causes damage to the countryside.

In 1984, 77% of our respondents chose the first statement. Three years later, the already large 'conservationist' majority has risen to 83%. This is further – and perhaps more tangible – evidence of a solid increase in concern for the countryside.

This year we added a further question, asking respondents to choose between:

The countryside should be protected from development, even if this sometimes leads to fewer jobs;
OR
New jobs should be created, even if this sometimes causes damage to the countryside.

In this case the 'conservationist' majority is rather lower, although 60% of respondents do give higher priority to the countryside than to job creation. But here there were very marked regional differences, more striking than those which emerged from the analysis of price *versus* countryside priorities, with almost twice as many Scots opting for new jobs as those living in the more prosperous South:

		Countryside should be protected	New jobs should be created
Total	%	60	35
Region:			
Scotland	%	45	51
Wales	%	51	42
North	%	54	40
Midlands	%	63	32
Greater London	%	65	28
South	%	68	26

Similar sharp (and unsurprising) divisions emerged according to whether people lived in the countryside or a town. The general concern that city dwellers expressed about the countryside was put to the test when pitted against, say, unemployment, and it did not stand up very well. Their support for the countryside, however real, seems rather 'soft' – not robust enough to withstand other important counterclaims. Notably, despite the fact that rural unemployment is also of concern, those who live in the countryside proper are especially steadfast in their determination to protect their environment against other claims.

		Countryside should be protected	New jobs should be created
Current residence:			
big city	%	50	46
suburbs	%	60	33
small city or town	%	61	34
country town/village	%	61	34
countryside	%	74	24

The role of the farmer

One of the most pressing policy issues facing the countryside is that of agricultural production. Changes in policy are designed to reduce surpluses and control the EEC Common Agricultural Policy budget. These measures threaten the economic interests of farmers, but they may also lead to improvements in the countryside through less intensive farming, so freeing land for recreational uses.

Since 1985, we have asked respondents to express the strength of their agreement or disagreement with a series of statements about modern farming methods and the roles and responsibilities of farmers.

The following table compares the responses to this question over time.

	% agreeing strongly or agreeing	
	1985	**1987**
Modern methods of farming have caused damage to the countryside	63%	68%
If farmers have to choose between producing more food and looking after the countryside, they should produce more food	53%	35%
All things considered, farmers do a good job in looking after the countryside	75%	74%
Government should withhold some subsidies from farmers and use them to protect the countryside, even if this leads to higher prices	47%	51%

So the popularity of the farmer remains substantially intact. However, perceptions of the policy issues appear to have sharpened over the two-year period, with a surge of support for the proposition that food production should be limited in the interests of the countryside. Within this overall pattern, we find the expected associations with education and social class, with graduates in particular favouring countryside protection. We shall monitor with interest whether or not policy choices at this level of sophistication are also susceptible to the filtering down process, evident already in respect of more generalised issues.

We also asked which of two views came closest to the respondents' own:

> *Looking after the countryside is too important to be left to the farmers – government authorities should have more control over what's done and built on farms;*
> *OR*
> *Farmers know how important it is to look after the countryside – there are enough controls, and farmers should be left to decide what's done on farms.*

Here opinion was fairly evenly divided: 38% favour further intervention, while 44% are prepared to trust the farmer. But once again, the shift since 1985 is against the farmer's autonomy. Some seven per cent fewer people in 1987 than in 1985 were prepared to support the second proposition. The view that the farmer knows best may be starting to wane.

Alternative land uses

We also attempted to tap respondents' attitudes towards a range of future policy options (such as afforestation, housing, jobs and tourism) at a time when, uniquely in modern British history, clear choices are being posed for rural areas.

For instance, an obvious consequence of freeing former agricultural land is that many farmers will need to face up to change if they are to maintain

their economic base. This might lead to a greater mix of agricultural activities (with perhaps a shift towards less intensivity and greater use of organic methods); more involvement in small-scale industry, or providing holiday lets or bed and breakfast accommodation; perhaps producing more farmhouse foods for sale or opening up nature trails. These are just some of the ways of 'on-farm diversification' currently being promoted by the Ministry of Agriculture.

Another option is that land released from agriculture might be used for residential or industrial purposes, so easing the shortages of sites suitable for development outside the conurbations (although such a policy would immediately highlight the need for more decisive management of the urban fringe). Another possibility is a direct shift from agriculture to amenity uses, securing as a matter of policy the public enjoyment of the countryside as a claim equal to that of production. This might be answered through the medium of the Agriculture Improvement Scheme and the designation of further Environmentally Sensitive Areas (ESAs). These choices do not represent bald options; rather, future policy is likely to involve attempts to find locally acceptable balances between production and recreation, conservation and development.

Our questions are intended to contribute to an assessment of public views on the possible conflicts of interest between farmer, tourist, and resident which arise in any consideration of the future of the countryside. They all pose real and immediate choices.

		Agree (strongly or just disagree)	Neither agree nor disagree	Disagree (strongly or just disagree)
New housing should be built in cities, towns and villages rather than in the countryside	%	82	11	4
It is more important to keep green belt areas than to build new homes there	%	78	12	8
Planning laws should be relaxed so that people who want to live in the countryside may do so	%	34	23	41
Compared with other users of the countryside, farmers have too much say	%	30	39	28
The beauty of the countryside depends on stopping too many people from visiting it	%	14	21	63

There is little support for the notion that casual visitors to the countryside spoil it; the paradox of tourism has lost its sharpness. On the other hand, the desire to protect the countryside from urban development is remarkably strong. There are clear signals for future policy discussion here, for these responses are strongly 'conservationist' in respect of the green belt and rural areas generally. If farming land is to be freed, in the public's view it should not be made over for housing.

Responses to each of the questions are shaped to degree by where respondents live, demonstrating the obvious point that resolution of alternatives for the future of the countryside will entail at least some conflict between the various

interests involved. For example, those living in the countryside are more likely than their urban and suburban counterparts to favour restrictions on casual visitors, and noticeably less likely than average to favour relaxation of the planning laws. Midlanders and Southerners are particularly protective of the green belt, with 87% of people in the South East agreeing that its preservation was more important than new homes (see **Table 9.6**). We shall discover in future rounds of this series whether or not these differences widen as pressures mount to release more land for housing.

Finally, we come to the most specific of all our questions on the future of the countryside. They covered, for example, the issue of afforestation and what should be grown – the ubiquitous evergreen or broadleaf trees – and where further cultivation should take place. Perhaps because these questions *were* so specific, a large proportion of respondents opted to give neutral answers, preferring to say "don't know" rather than guessing.

We began by reminding respondents that *modern farming methods have meant that it now takes less land to produce the same amount of food*, and went on to ask them which of a series of options would be the "best", the "next best" and the "worst" ways *that land no longer needed for farming might be used:*

	Best or next best
Create national parks and wildlife reserves	64%
Plant forests of oak and beech for timber and woodlands	44%
Plant forests of pine and conifers for timber and woodlands	22%
Provide places for countryside recreation, such as riding and golf	19%
Pay farmers to return to methods of farming which need more land	17%
Develop new areas for rural industries	15%
Develop new housing areas	12%

So it appears that, while the demand for recreation and amenity uses of the countryside is high, there is little wish to see a diversification of rural Britain in anything more than a visual sense. Industry – even rural industry – and new housing remain the *least* popular alternative uses. Strong opposition such as this, alongside the real difficulties encountered in pressing forward farm diversification on existing policies, suggests that the real debate on the future of the British countryside has yet to take place, and that it may be both protracted and bitter.

Conclusion: how important is the countryside?

Placing the various responses in the context of our opening discussion makes it clear that most, but not all, of the conditions for the countryside becoming a 'cause' have been met. People are largely aware of the changes of the past two decades, regard these changes as being for the worse, and register their concern. To that extent, the countryside has become an important issue in modern Britain. At the same time, however, much of the concern is not robust enough to stand up to larger national issues such as unemployment. Particularly among people living in the North of England and Scotland, there is rather

more concern about jobs, for instance, than about countryside conservation. Moreover as yet only a minority of respondents can distinguish between the various parties' policies on environmental issues.

Nonetheless there is a substantial – and growing – bedrock of concern about the future of the countryside. The extent to which this awareness and concern have become general throughout the various social groups suggests that increasing use of the countryside for recreation, coupled with the media attention of recent years, has brought about a popularisation of an issue which was once a rather exclusive concern. The public in general is more aware of what is happening to the countryside and increasingly willing to pay the price of protecting what is left of it.

Accompanying this growth in concern, and apparently not at odds with it, is a demand for the greater *socialisation* of the countryside, that is a demand for greater access to rural Britain. Conservation today seems to imply opening up the countryside to people rather than protecting it from them. And this vision of the preferred future for the countryside places heavy emphasis on the visual, rather than on the economic, environment. The pressing questions about the economic base of rural Britain, and of farm income maintenance in particular, seem as yet to have attracted little recognition.

Any government which seeks to alleviate housing pressures in the southern half of England by releasing swathes of land for development would, on the evidence of this survey, be taking a considerable political risk. The overall conclusion from our findings is that the countryside is a latent political issue which has not yet quite arrived. It does not, however, appear to need much of a push to become a cause and, as other countries have discovered, it is an awkward cause for established political parties to contend with. Notably, the issue of countryside protection increasingly unites British middle-class and working-class interests, as well as urban and rural interests, in an unfamiliar and refreshing way.

Notes

1. This framework was first put forward as a way of exploring the *assumptive worlds* of people who are already politically active (Young, 1979), but it may help us to determine whether wider public attitudes (in this case, towards countryside issues) are of potential political importance. It is based on the premise that the importance of these sorts of issues cannot be taken for granted, and that each component must be considered separately. At its simplest, if people have no sense that the world is changing, then change itself, however extensive, cannot become an issue. Further, even those who do notice some change may nevertheless be either indifferent, or at least ambivalent, towards it. Again, this would have little or no political significance. Others may recognise the extent of change and indeed deplore it, but still stop short of feeling that the issue actually *touches* them, feeling that it lies in some remote domain. Only when people both deplore and feel *connected* to the changes they see are they likely to act politically, either as individuals or collectively.
2. As **Table 9.7** shows, those who live close to or in the countryside are especially likely to have engaged in some recent countryside leisure activity (listed at Q.B96 in Appendix III, p.245). Of particular interest is that almost two-thirds of dwellers in big cities also claim to have engaged in one of the listed activities during the month prior to interview. It is even more remarkable that no less than 90% of

respondents claimed to have taken part in one of these activities during the past 12 months. These figures on the extent to which people have recourse to the country-side for recreation show little change from when we first asked the question in the spring of 1985.

References

COUNTRYSIDE COMMISSION, *Policies for Enjoying the Countryside*, Countryside Commission, Cheltenham (1987).

MARRIS, P., *Loss and Change*, Routledge & Kegan Paul, London (1974).

NEWBY, H., *Green and Pleasant Land: Social Change in Rural England*, Temple Smith, London (1979).

SCHON, D., *Beyond the Stable State*, Temple Smith, London (1971).

YOUNG, K., 'Values in the Policy Process', in Pollitt, C. *et al* (eds) *Public Policy in Theory and Practice*, Hodder and Stoughton, Sevenoaks (1979).

YOUNG, K., 'Political attitudes' in Jowell, R. and Airey, C. (eds), *British Social Attitudes: the 1985 Report*, Gower, Aldershot (1984).

YOUNG, K., 'Shades of opinion' in Jowell, R. and Witherspoon, S. (eds), *British Social Attitudes: the 1985 Report*, Gower, Aldershot (1985).

YOUNG, K., 'Interim report: the countryside' in Jowell, R., Witherspoon, S. and Brook, L. (eds), *British Social Attitudes: the 1987 Report*, Gower, Aldershot (1987).

Acknowledgement

We are grateful to the Countryside Commission both for its financial support, which has allowed us to include questions on countryside issues since 1985, and for its advice and help in designing the questionnaire modules. However, the final responsibility for question topics and wording, and for the interpretation of the results, must lie with SCPR and the author.

9.1 PERCEPTION OF COUNTRYSIDE CHANGE (B96a)
by current residence, use made of the countryside and highest educational qualification obtained

	TOTAL	CURRENT RESIDENCE					LAST DID COUNTRYSIDE ACTIVITY				HIGHEST EDUCATIONAL QUALIFICATION			
		Big city	Suburbs	Small city or town	Country village or town	Country-side	Within last 4 weeks	Within last 3 months	Within last year	More than a year ago	Degree	Profess-ional	'A' level/'O' level/CSE	Foreign/Other/None
	%	%	%	%	%	%	%	%	%	%	%	%	%	%
COMPARED WITH TWENTY YEARS AGO, THE COUNTRYSIDE ...														
... is much the same	20	23	20	20	23	12	19	28	22	20	20	22	21	20
... has changed a bit	21	27	20	24	18	14	22	24	21	18	35	19	23	19
... has changed a lot	55	43	57	53	59	74	57	47	55	56	43	57	53	59
Don't know/not answered	3	7	3	3	1	-	2	1	2	5	3	3	4	3
BASE: B RESPONDENTS Weighted	1375	186	400	499	280	60	818	77	340	89	109	181	490	590
Unweighted	1410	122	411	521	281	66	828	84	347	97	104	183	499	620

9.2 EVALUATION OF COUNTRYSIDE CHANGES (B96b)
by current residence, use made of the countryside and highest educational qualification obtained

	TOTAL	CURRENT RESIDENCE					LAST DID COUNTRYSIDE ACTIVITY				HIGHEST EDUCATIONAL QUALIFICATION			
		Big city	Suburbs	Small city or town	Country village or town	Country-side	Within last 4 weeks	Within last 3 months	Within last year	More than a year ago	Degree	Profess-ional	'A' level/'O' level/CSE	Foreign/Other/None
	%	%	%	%	%	%	%	%	%	%	%	%	%	%
COMPARED WITH TWENTY YEARS AGO, THE COUNTRYSIDE ...														
... has not changed	20	23	20	20	23	12	19	28	22	20	20	22	21	20
... has changed for the better	12	9	14	11	7	7	13	8	11	15	7	9	9	17
... has changed for the worse	56	52	56	58	52	75	58	53	56	50	62	55	60	52
... is better in some ways/worse in others	8	9	8	8	9	7	7	10	9	10	8	11	7	8
Don't know/not answered	3	7	3	3	1	-	3	1	2	5	3	3	4	3
BASE: B RESPONDENTS Weighted	1375	186	400	499	280	60	818	77	340	89	109	181	490	590
Unweighted	1410	122	411	521	281	66	828	84	347	97	104	183	499	620

9.3 CONCERN ABOUT THE COUNTRYSIDE (B97)
by current residence, use made of the countryside and age within sex

CONCERN ABOUT THINGS THAT MAY HAPPEN TO THE COUNTRYSIDE	TOTAL	CURRENT RESIDENCE					LAST DID COUNTRYSIDE ACTIVITY				AGE WITHIN SEX					
											MEN			WOMEN		
		Big city	Suburbs	Small city or town	Country village or town	Country-side	Within last 4 weeks	Within last 3 months	Within last year	More than a year ago	18-34	35-54	55+	18-34	35-54	55+
	%	%	%	%	%	%	%	%	%	%	%	%	%	%	%	%
Very concerned	44	38	40	42	53	68	52	33	34	29	43	50	51	29	46	48
A bit concerned	33	38	36	33	30	16	33	46	31	27	36	31	30	38	27	34
Does not concern me personally	22	24	24	24	18	13	14	22	34	44	22	19	18	31	26	19
Don't know/not answered	1	-	*	*	-	3	*	-	-	1	-	-	1	1	1	-
BASE: B RESPONDENTS																
Weighted	1375	126	400	499	280	60	818	77	340	89	225	227	199	226	248	248
Unweighted	1410	122	411	521	281	66	828	84	347	97	218	230	213	227	262	257

9.4 SOURCES OF THREAT TO THE COUNTRYSIDE – 1 (B98a, b)
by current residence and age within sex

	TOTAL	CURRENT RESIDENCE					AGE WITHIN SEX					
							MEN			WOMEN		
		Big city	Suburbs	Small city or town	Country village or town	Country-side	18-34	35-54	55+	18-34	35-54	55+
	%	%	%	%	%	%	%	%	%	%	%	%
URBANISATION:												
Industrial pollution - greatest threat	32	32	33	34	30	23	42	30	36	32	31	25
- next greatest threat	21	20	20	21	24	18	20	24	22	24	17	20
Urban growth and housing development - greatest threat	15	15	17	17	11	18	21	15	11	22	14	10
- next greatest threat	12	15	12	12	12	16	15	14	9	18	13	7
Motorways and road building - greatest threat	11	6	12	13	10	7	10	7	8	18	13	11
- next greatest threat	11	10	12	12	10	8	12	8	6	19	10	11
AGRICULTURE:												
Use of chemicals and pesticides in farming - greatest threat	18	20	16	16	25	20	12	23	21	15	17	21
- next greatest threat	26	25	28	24	27	25	26	27	29	25	23	27
Removal by farmers of the traditional landscape - greatest threat	11	18	9	8	11	21	10	17	11	4	10	12
- next greatest threat	12	9	11	13	13	14	12	14	13	7	15	11
RECREATION:												
Litter - greatest threat	9	3	9	9	10	10	3	7	10	4	9	19
- next greatest threat	12	10	12	13	11	12	9	9	16	4	13	19
Tourism and visitors - greatest threat	1	2	1	1	1	1	1	1	-	3	1	*
- next greatest threat	2	4	1	2	2	5	4	2	1	1	1	2
NONE OF THESE:												
- greatest threat	1	2	2	1	-	-	*	1	2	1	1	1
- next greatest threat	2	3	2	1	-	2	2	2	1	1	3	1
BASE: B RESPONDENTS Weighted	*1375*	*126*	*400*	*499*	*280*	*60*	*225*	*227*	*199*	*226*	*248*	*248*
Unweighted	*1410*	*122*	*411*	*521*	*281*	*66*	*218*	*230*	*213*	*227*	*262*	*257*

9.5 SOURCES OF THREAT TO THE COUNTRYSIDE – 2 (B98a, b) by highest educational qualification obtained and compressed region

	TOTAL	HIGHEST EDUCATIONAL QUALIFICATION				COMPRESSED REGION					
		Degree	Professional	'A' level/'O' level/ CSE	Foreign/ Other/ None	Scotland	North	Midlands	Wales	South	Greater London
	%	%	%	%	%	%	%	%	%	%	%
URBANISATION:											
Industrial pollution - greatest threat	32	33	29	34	32	35	35	32	38	28	35
- next greatest threat	21	23	24	19	21	18	18	20	26	25	16
Urban growth and housing development - greatest threat	15	20	19	20	9	14	13	17	6	19	15
- next greatest threat	12	18	13	14	10	9	13	13	14	10	17
Motorways and road building - greatest threat	11	3	9	11	13	6	12	13	11	9	15
- next greatest threat	11	7	11	13	10	13	11	9	9	11	11
AGRICULTURE:											
Use of chemicals and pesticides in farming - greatest threat	18	25	27	14	17	25	16	16	23	20	10
- next greatest threat	26	23	23	28	26	21	27	29	27	25	24
Removal by farmers of the traditional landscape - greatest threat	11	14	10	11	10	8	11	10	6	12	11
- next greatest threat	12	17	18	12	10	15	12	14	8	13	9
RECREATION:											
Litter - greatest threat	9	4	6	6	13	6	10	9	13	9	4
- next greatest threat	12	7	7	10	16	15	12	10	12	11	13
Tourism and visitors - greatest threat	1	1	1	1	1	1	1	1	1	1	2
- next greatest threat	2	5	2	2	1	1	2	1	2	3	1
NONE OF THESE: - greatest threat	1	-	1	1	2	3	1	1	-	1	2
- next greatest threat	2	-	1	2	2	3	1	3	1	1	4
BASE: B RESPONDENTS *Weighted*	*1375*	*109*	*181*	*490*	*590*	*122*	*379*	*208*	*85*	*439*	*143*
Unweighted	*1410*	*104*	*183*	*499*	*620*	*129*	*389*	*212*	*87*	*448*	*145*

9.6 ALTERNATIVE LAND USES FOR THE COUNTRYSIDE (B234) by current residence and region

| | TOTAL | CURRENT RESIDENCE | | | | | REGION | | | | | | | | | | |
		Big city	Suburbs	Small city or town	Country village or town	Country-side	Scotland	North	North West	Yorks and Humber	West Midlands	East Midlands	East Anglia	South West	South East	Greater London	Wales
	%	%	%	%	%	%	%	%	%	%	%	%	%	%	%	%	%
A. NEW HOUSING SHOULD BE BUILT IN CITIES, TOWNS AND VILLAGES RATHER THAN IN THE COUNTRYSIDE																	
- agree strongly/agree	82	80	83	83	80	84	80	77	81	79	89	81	84	82	85	84	75
- neither agree nor disagree	11	16	11	10	12	10	14	11	11	12	6	19	9	11	10	12	13
- disagree/disagree strongly	4	3	5	4	5	6	4	5	5	5	3	-	6	7	2	4	9
B. IT IS MORE IMPORTANT TO KEEP GREEN-BELT AREAS THAN TO BUILD NEW HOMES THERE																	
- agree strongly/agree	78	67	79	77	80	76	74	73	63	74	84	84	77	83	87	80	68
- neither agree nor disagree	12	19	11	13	10	14	19	16	15	14	9	10	14	9	7	11	19
- disagree/disagree strongly	8	13	8	7	6	9	7	6	18	9	6	4	9	8	3	7	10
C. PLANNING LAWS SHOULD BE RELAXED SO THAT PEOPLE WHO WANT TO LIVE IN THE COUNTRY-SIDE MAY DO SO																	
- agree strongly/agree	34	30	35	33	37	24	39	38	41	36	24	34	39	35	24	33	47
- neither agree nor disagree	23	29	22	24	20	18	25	27	26	22	25	24	15	22	21	19	23
- disagree/disagree strongly	41	41	41	40	39	55	35	25	29	38	49	40	46	45	53	45	29
D. COMPARED WITH OTHER USERS OF THE COUNTRYSIDE, FARMERS HAVE TOO MUCH SAY																	
- agree strongly/agree	30	32	28	30	30	31	28	34	31	27	29	31	35	26	28	32	33
- neither agree nor disagree	39	46	42	41	33	25	48	36	38	39	39	40	31	44	40	38	31
- disagree/disagree strongly	28	21	29	26	34	41	24	23	26	30	31	25	33	30	29	29	34
E. THE BEAUTY OF THE COUNTRYSIDE DEPENDS ON STOPPING TOO MANY PEOPLE FROM VISITING IT																	
- agree strongly/agree	14	20	12	11	17	22	11	16	8	19	11	4	16	15	15	21	15
- neither agree nor disagree	21	20	20	21	20	22	25	13	23	18	19	21	21	19	23	19	22
- disagree/disagree strongly	63	60	66	65	60	55	62	63	65	60	68	72	61	66	60	58	60
BASE: B RESPONDENTS Weighted	1181	104	345	437	241	49	106	79	131	117	114	67	57	110	217	110	73
Unweighted	1212	102	355	455	242	53	111	84	134	124	115	67	59	109	223	113	73

9.7 COUNTRYSIDE LEISURE ACTIVITIES (B95a, b)
by current residence, age within sex and highest educational qualification obtained

COUNTRYSIDE LEISURE ACTIVITY ...	TOTAL	CURRENT RESIDENCE					AGE WITHIN SEX						HIGHEST EDUCATIONAL QUALIFICATION			
							MEN			WOMEN						
		Big city	Suburbs	Small city or town	Country village or town	Country side	18-34	35-54	55+	18-34	35-54	55+	Degree	Profess-ional	'A' level/'O' level/CSE	Foreign/Other/None
	%	%	%	%	%	%	%	%	%	%	%	%	%	%	%	%
... not taken part in over previous four weeks	41	34	47	42	32	28	39	37	47	29	42	48	24	27	35	52
... taken part in over previous four weeks	59	66	53	58	68	72	61	63	52	71	58	52	76	73	65	48
- one to three months ago	6	6	5	7	2	11	7	5	6	6	4	5	9	5	7	4
- four to six months ago	10	4	14	9	10	4	14	10	11	6	11	8	4	11	10	11
- seven to twelve months ago	15	13	16	15	15	7	9	13	16	11	19	20	7	9	13	20
- more than one year ago	6	9	9	6	3	4	7	6	7	3	5	10	3	2	4	11
- can't remember/don't know	3	3	4	3	2	2	2	2	6	2	3	3	1	*	1	5
BASE: B RESPONDENTS																
Weighted	1375	126	400	499	280	60	225	227	199	226	248	248	109	181	490	590
Unweighted	1410	122	411	521	281	66	218	230	213	227	262	257	104	183	499	620

10 Interim report: A woman's work

Sharon Witherspoon [*]

This chapter is about women's work – not just paid work, but unpaid work in the home as well. It examines the kinds of work women do inside and outside the home and how it compares with the work men do in either place. It looks at the attitudes of men and women towards sexual discrimination. It also explores how women feel about the conflicts caused by juggling work inside and outside the home, especially when they also care for children. The very content of this chapter reflects the fact that it is impossible to describe women's participation in paid employment without also examining how men and women share the job of looking after the home.

The dramatic rise in the number of British women who are economically active outside the home is well documented. The 1951 Census showed that 43% of women aged 15–59 (and only 26% of married women) were economically active (Hakim, 1979); by 1986, 66% of all women (and 61% of married women) were working or looking for work (CSO, 1988; OPCS, 1988). The rise in *married* women's participation in the labour market has been especially marked. Sociologists, economists and other social scientists vie with each other in trying to explain why there is still sexual inequality in employment when there are now so many more women in the labour market (Becker, 1985; Breugel, 1983; Dex, 1985). We now know quite a lot about the work that women do outside the home, and even a bit about why they do it.

But we know less about changes in the domestic division of labour and still less about how women and men feel about all these changes. Perhaps the most widely cited findings from the *British Social Attitudes* series are responses to a series of questions on the domestic division of labour for various household tasks – who does the dishes, organises the household money, looks after the children when they are unwell, and so on. We last asked questions on women's

---

* Senior researcher at SCPR and Co-director of this survey series.

issues in the 1984 survey, covering issues such as sexual equality at work and at home, childcare roles, attitudes to work and choice of work (see Witherspoon in *The 1985 Report*). We have now repeated the questions with some additions, many of which are again drawn from the Women and Employment Survey – WES. (See Martin and Roberts, 1984.)

Work outside the home

Alongside the increase in the number of women at work has been a marked rise in the number of part-time women workers, particularly married women. Since 1951 the number of part-time women workers has risen five-fold; since 1971, the increase has been greater than 50% (Robinson and Wallace, 1984; CSO, 1988). This trend is expected to continue for the foreseeable future (EOC, 1988). Women part-timers now comprise about 44% of the female labourforce and about one in five of all employees (EOC, 1988).

This increase in part-time working cannot simply be explained away as a by-product of the growth in the number of working women. Part-time working is not as common in other European countries (EOC, 1988; Beechey and Perkins, 1987), or in the USA (Dex and Shaw, 1986) as it is in Britain. British women are more than twice as likely as their American counterparts to work part-time, and those who do work part-time here work shorter hours on average (Dex and Shaw, 1986).

This in itself might not matter if all other factors were equal. But, as usual, they are not. Part-time workers are known to be disadvantaged in a number of ways. Hourly rates of pay for part-time women workers are worse than those of men or full-time women workers. According to Joshi's estimates (1987), women part-timers suffer a 10% reduction in hourly pay for otherwise identical work. Job security and job protection are worse for part-timers, as are entitlements to pensions and other benefits. Part-time working also often entails downward mobility. Many women who turn from full-time to part-time work after having children find themselves going from better-paid and higher-status jobs to lower-paid and lower-status ones (Dex, 1985). Finally, the jobs that part-time women have tend to be those that nobody else will do, and so some jobs become identified or stereotyped as being suitable only for part-time working women.

Occupational segregation

Hakim (1979) defined occupational segregation by sex as the condition under which "men and women do different kinds of work, so that one can speak of two separate labour forces, one male and one female, which are not in competition with each other for the same jobs". She then went on to make a further distinction between *vertical* segregation (when women are employed in *less highly-graded* occupations than men) and *horizontal* segregation (where women are employed in *different* occupations from men). The table below shows the occupations of full-time male employees in our sample, compared with those of full-time and part-time women employees.*

---

* We excluded from these questions women working less than 10 hours per week. Had we included them, the contrasts between full-time and part-time employees would have been even greater.

Condensed occupational order	Full-time male employees %	Full-time female employees %	Part-time female employees %
Senior management and professional	9	5	*
Professionals in health, education and welfare	7	21	12
Other professionals	11	4	2
Managers	11	4	1
Clerical	6	40	27
Sales	4	4	13
Manual	43	14	6
Personal service	4	9	39
Other	5	*	*

Although full-time men and women workers work in very different occupations,
part-time women workers seem to be distinctively disadvantaged. Full-time working women are clustered in typically female fields such as health, education
and welfare, and clerical work. But part-time working women are especially
crowded into clerical working and personal service sector jobs like catering,
cleaning, hairdressing, sales and so on; with the exception of clerical work,
these all tend to be very low-paying jobs with little job security. Moreover,
there has been little change in the amount of occupational segregation during
this century (Hakim, 1979), even though some occupations (such as clerical
work) were formerly more likely to be done by men (Cohn, 1985). Changes
in *which* occupations are predominantly 'male' or 'female' have not affected
the *level* of occupational segregation. Men too are concentrated in certain kinds
of jobs, with a high proportion in skilled manual work.

But these figures are likely to understate the extent to which men and women
actually work in separate environments *within* the same workplace. This may
preclude the sort of close comparison of men's and women's jobs which is
a precondition of claims for equal pay under the amended Equal Pay Act.
So we asked employees, both in 1984 and in 1987, whether at their workplace
there were any people of the opposite sex doing the same sort of work.

	1984		1987	
	Men	Women	Men	Women
Respondent	%	%	%	%
Works with own sex only	72	51	66	49
Works with both sexes	27	47	32	49
Works alone/only person doing that job	*	2	2	1

Half of all women employees in our sampleand two-thirds of all men employees,
work exclusively with people of their own sex. Men, particularly, are likely
to work in same-sex enclaves, giving them little experience of women as workers
– and their enclaves are relatively privileged ones. Our figures suggest there
has been a small decrease in men's workplace job segregation, but this may
well be due to the decline in the number of manual jobs. This change is, however,
a small one; and there seems to have been no corresponding change in the
experience of working women.

This question was also included in the 1980 Women and Employment Survey,
but as their definition of part-time work included women working under 10
hours a week (who are particularly likely to work only with other women),

it is possible only to compare the job segregation experienced by full-time working women. For them, at least, there may have been some improvement in workplace job segregation since 1980. But on our figures, between 1984 and 1987 there has not been a similar improvement in the job segregation of part-time working women.*

	1980	Women 1984		1987	
	Full-time	Full-time	Part-time	Full-time	Part-time
	%	%	%	%	%
Works only with women	58	46	65	43	62
Works with women and men	42	55	34	57	36

There are, of course, differences in occupational segregation by class[†] (see **Table 10.1**). Whereas half of all men in the salariat work with women, fewer than one in five of working-class men do so; conversely, nearly two-thirds of women in the salariat work with men, while only one-third of working-class women do so.

In 1987 we decided to add follow-up questions on people's images of, or sex stereotypes about, their own jobs. Again we had exemplars on hand from WES. We asked all employees:

Do you think of your work as mainly men's work, mainly women's work or work that either men or women do?

Those who thought of their work as being mainly for their own sex were asked whether they thought this was because members of the opposite sex *could not* do the work or because they *would not be willing* to do it. These were the results:

	Men	Women	
		Full-time	Part-time
	All		
	%	%	%
Work is:			
Mainly men's work	47	2	1
Mainly women's work	1	24	37
Work that either men or women do	53	74	61
[If work is 'mainly for own sex']	%	%	%
Opposite sex:			
Could not do the work	41	9	7
Would not do the work	26	51	51
Could and would do the work	29	34	37

Men are nearly twice as likely as full-time working women to think of their work as exclusively for their own sex; even so, just over half of men say their work *could* be done by either sex. Part-time working women are more likely than full-time working women to claim sex exclusivity for their jobs, but they

---

* We excluded the answers of those women who said they do not work with *anyone* else who does the same job, in order to make comparisons with WES.

† We have used the (compressed) Goldthorpe class schema – see Appendix I, p.207.

are not as likely as men to do so. And when we confine attention to those who say their job is *in fact* sex-exclusive, men are much more likely (62%) than women (40%) to say they *think* of it as being so.

While men do not seem to have changed their views much since 1984, women are less likely nowadays than they were in 1980 or in 1984 to say they think of their work as women's work. In 1984 we reported that around one-third of full-time working women and nearly a half of part-timers (much the same proportions as in 1980) thought of their work as mainly women's work. Now the proportions have fallen to nearer one-quarter and one-third respectively.

When asked the reasons why they think their work is mainly done by one sex or the other, men and women seem to arrive at their conclusions by different routes. Men are much more likely to feel that women are *unable* to do their work, while women are more likely to think that men are *unwilling* to do their work. Surprisingly (in view of the different work they do), there are no differences in the reasons given by full-time and part-time working women. The last line of figures in the table above may represent the extent to which the sex stereo-typing is based simply on custom and practice, rather than on physical or social reasons – and again this has shown little change.

To the extent that we can compare these results with WES, there seems to have been only a slight weakening in the sex stereotyping of jobs by women since 1980, and no change at all in the reasons they give (Martin and Roberts, 1984, pp. 29–31). An open-ended question exploring why people thought of their jobs as sex-exclusive reveals the same pattern. Men mention physical strength (68%), dirty or unpleasant working conditions (29%) and say that women just don't do, or aren't trained for, the sort of work (20%) men do. Women are more likely to say that their work is traditionally done by women (55%), that the work is too low paid to attract men (22%), or that men do not have the right sorts of personal skills to do the work (16%). Again there seems to have been little change since 1980.

In sum then, workplace sex segregation of full-time working men and women seems to have diminished only slightly since 1980; it has not changed at all for part-time working women. As Joshi *et al* (1985) suggest, however, occupa-tional segregation may have been useful to women in one respect: increases in women's pay, such as those brought about by the Equal Pay Act in the mid-1970s, do not necessarily lead to a lower demand for female labour, because women occupy jobs to which it is not customary to recruit men. On the other hand, occupational segregation makes it harder to prove that women are under-paid relative to their (non-existant) male counterparts. Even though equal pay for similar (rather than identical) work is increasingly likely to be the subject of legal dispute (and to have a profound influence on women in some jobs), it is unlikely that the amended Equal Pay Act will have a significant effect on women's earnings as long as sex segregation at the workplace is so widespread.

Job stereotyping

As in 1984, we asked respondents to the self-completion supplement to look at a list of 11 occupations and to categorise them as being *particularly suitable for men, particularly suitable for women, or suitable for both equally*. We selected the jobs so that a 'principled egalitarian' would probably answer that all the

jobs were suitable for both sexes. In these terms, we have found an increase in the number of principled egalitarians compared with three years ago. But traditional distinctions between men's and women's jobs are still common. The table below shows the 1987 responses and the percentage change since 1984 in the proportion answering "suitable for both equally".

		Particularly suitable for men	Particularly suitable for women	Suitable for both equally	% change since 1984 saying "equally"
Traditionally male jobs					
Car mechanic	%	67	1	31	+6
Bus driver	%	40	1	59	+10
Police officer	%	37	*	62	+13
Bank manager	%	28	1	70	+12
Traditionally female jobs					
Secretary	%	1	54	44	+6
Nurse	%	*	31	67	+10
Political and 'professional' jobs					
Member of parliament	%	10	*	89	+7
Local councillor	%	7	1	91	+6
Family doctor/GP	%	6	1	93	+6
Computer programmer	%	4	2	93	+4
Social worker	%	1	15	83	−4

It is heartening that less than one per cent of the sample seem to have given tongue-in-cheek answers to any of these questions. More important, it is tempting to speculate as to why some of the jobs have changed their image so much. All occupations except social work have now become less sex-exclusive in image. Being a police officer, for instance, is now thought to be much less sex-exclusive; almost two-thirds of respondents think of it as being equally suitable for both sexes. Is this a result of the increasing visibility of women bobbies on the beat, or is it the Juliet Bravo effect? Somewhat remarkably, although Mrs Thatcher had been Prime Minister for eight years at the time of our survey, one-tenth of our sample still think that being an MP is particularly suitable for men. In general, the older respondents are, the more likely they are to take a traditionalist line, and younger women tend to be much more egalitarian than their male counterparts. Women with degrees are particularly likely not to engage in job stereotyping, with 53% saying that 10 or all 11 of the jobs were suitable for both sexes, compared with 42% of male graduates.

Still, the message of the table above is likely to vary according to the standpoint of the observer. Although egalitarianism in general is apparently increasing, traditionalism is still strong in respect of just those occupations that are in fact the most segregated. Cultural images like these may take a long time to fade.

Returning to paid work

But what of the women* who described themselves as "looking after the home",

---

* Of over 2800 respondents, only three men said their full-time activity was caring for the home and children. They are excluded from the discussion in this section, as are women aged over 59. 'Paid work' in our definition is 10 or more hours per week.

and who were not in paid work according to our definition? Do they expect to return to the labour market, and would they prefer full-time or part-time work? Each year we ask these women why they are not in paid employment, what experience of paid work they have had over the past five years, and their plans over the next five.

First, it should be noted that 15% of these women do in fact have a paid job, though one of less than 10 hours a week.* And most women of working age mentioned family responsibilities as their main reason for not having a job (of 10 hours a week or more), although whether they viewed this as a constraint or a preference differed according to their age and the age of their youngest child. Other reasons were also given, including mentions that no suitable jobs were available (five per cent), that benefit rules meant that her earnings would reduce overall family income (four per cent), that she did unpaid work in a family business (four per cent), that she had a dependent relative requiring care (four per cent), and that her husband did not want her to work (three per cent).

Omitting these other reasons, the table below shows that younger women, and women with younger children, are more likely to mention children as their main reason for not working, while older women, and those whose youngest child is at least of secondary school age, are more likely to say it is their preference not to work.

| | | Main reason for not having a paid job | | |
		Raising children	Prefer to look after home & family	Pregnancy or ill-health
Women aged 18–59:				
Aged 18–34	%	81	8	7
35–44	%	45	31	7
45–59	%	11	38	21
Whose youngest child is aged:				
4 or younger	%	88	7	7
5 to 10	%	62	17	4
11 to 15	%	19	46	7
Older/no child	%	5	41	22

Our respondents then seem to distinguish between an unconstrained and a constrained choice. Proponents of the 'new home economics' ought not, perhaps, to infer that women 'prefer' childcare to jobs or careers simply because they choose to look after their young children. Indeed, over half of the women in our sample who were currently looking after the home planned to look for a job in the next five years, 11% wanting a full-time and 40% wanting a part-time job. Overall, women's expectations of returning to paid work have not changed much since 1983. Younger women, and mothers of younger children, are especially likely to expect to go back to a paid job outside the home.

When mothers of young children *do* return to paid work, they are more

---

* Including these women in our definition would raise our estimate of the proportion of economically active women of working age from 57% to 61%, in line with current government estimates (CSO, 1988).

likely to work part-time. Of those mothers in our survey who said they did not have a paid job because of their children, 58% planned to get a part-time job within five years, while only nine per cent planned to seek a full-time job. In contrast, among those mothers who claimed not to work out of *preference*, around two-thirds underlined that fact, saying they did not plan to seek work in the next five years.

Yet for women the cost of choosing to care for home and children is high and is likely to increase. A government White Paper of 1986 proposes to raise the number of hours part-timers need to work in order to quality for main employment rights; current thresholds of 8 and 16 hours would be raised to 10 and 20 hours respectively (EOC, 1988). Moreover, as more marriages break up and the number of single mothers rise, choices for women tend to diminish as work increasingly becomes an economic necessity. The need to leave work altogether to look after young children, and the subsequent need to work part-time rather than full-time for a period, add up to a bad economic bargain for women, the sizeable lifetime costs of which have been elegantly documented by Joshi (1987).

Work in the home

The domestic division of labour

Our findings in previous rounds of this series on the domestic division of labour have been widely quoted. Who does what in the home is obviously a subject of much fascination, offering people the chance, perhaps, to compare other households with their own. Joshi (1987) has shown how the presence of a husband in a household, independently of children, has a major effect on a woman's disposable time. Our 1987 data re-confirm that, even for couples with no children at home, the bulk of household work is still done by women and, overall, the position has hardly changed in the last few years. We asked all respondents who were married or living as married who did various tasks within the home, including – for couples with children – two childcare tasks. Male respondents tended to report slightly higher participation levels for themselves than female respondents did about their male partners (see **Table 10.2**). The table below is confined to the aggregate data.

	1983	1984	1987
Who:			
does household shopping?	%	%	%
mainly man	5	6	7
mainly woman	51	54	50
shared equally	44	39	43
makes evening meal?	%	%	%
mainly man	5	5	6
mainly woman	77	77	77
shared equally	17	16	17

Who:	1983	1984	1987
does evening dishes?	%	%	%
mainly man	17	18	22
mainly woman	40	37	39
shared equally	40	41	36
does household cleaning?	%	%	%
mainly man	3	3	4
mainly woman	72	72	72
shared equally	24	23	23
does washing and ironing?	%	%	%
mainly man	1	1	2
mainly woman	89	88	88
shared equally	10	9	9
repairs household equipment?	%	%	%
mainly man	82	83	82
mainly woman	6	6	6
shared equally	10	8	8
organises household money/bills?	%	%	%
mainly man	29	32	32
mainly woman	39	38	38
shared equally	32	28	30
looks after sick children?		%	%
mainly man		1	2
mainly woman	n/a	63	67
shared equally		35	30
teaches children discipline?		%	%
mainly man		10	13
mainly woman	n/a	12	19
shared equally		77	67

There have been almost no changes in the extent to which women perform the household tasks we asked about: they still do the bulk of all household work. But, as **Table 10.2** also shows, in households where the woman works *full-time* outside the home, tasks are more likely to be shared. Part-time women workers are less lucky, though there are different patterns for different tasks (see **Table 10.2** again). For most items – household shopping, cooking the evening meal, household cleaning, washing and ironing – households where the woman works part-time divide these tasks more like households where the woman is not in paid work. On tasks like doing the evening dishes, however, households with part-time women workers are similar to those with full-time working women. On this evidence, part-time working women may have the worst of both worlds: extra responsibilities outside the home, but only limited sharing of activities within it. We cannot tell, of course, whether they work only part-time *because* these household chores preclude full-time work, or whether the causal link is the other way around. Still, it is clearly part of the 'bargain' that in households with part-time women workers and in those with no paid jobs, men do very little household work.

Later in the questionnaire we asked all respondents who were married (or living as married) which partner was "mainly responsible for general domestic duties" in the household. Eighty-two per cent of respondents nominated the woman, and 12% said the duties were shared equally between spouses. As before, men are more likely to say duties are shared equally (16% compared with nine per cent of women). Here too households with part-time working women are virtually identical to households where the women did not have a paid job; those living in households with full-time working women are more likely to say domestic duties are shared (22%), though the discrepancy between men's and women's answers is also greatest in these households. Still, there is no disagreement that even in those households where the woman partner has a full-time job, she also (overwhelmingly) has the main responsibility for household chores. The next most 'egalitarian' households are those in which neither partner works, many of which are made up of retired couples.

	Respondents living in households where ...			
	...man works, woman works full-time	... man works, woman works part-time	... man works, woman does not work	other arrange-ment
	%	%	%	%
Who is responsible for general domestic duties?				
Mainly woman	72	88	91	76
Shared equally	22	7	5	15

Similarly, we asked who was mainly responsible for the general care of children and 82% said the woman was, with almost all the rest saying responsibility was shared.

It is one thing to ask people how domestic tasks *are* shared in their households and another to find out how they think such tasks *should* be shared. As in 1984, we asked all respondents – married, cohabiting, separated, widowed, divorced and not married – who they thought *ought* to do the household tasks on our lists. As might be expected, over the three years all items have shown a modest increase (ranging from two per cent to eight per cent) in the proportion answering that chores should be shared equally. Even so, there is still a gap between the prescriptive views of the never-married and of the 'married' (including those living as married); ideals are still tempered by experience. As the table below shows, respondents who have never married are almost always more likely to prescribe an egalitarian division of labour.

	'Married' do share equally	'Married' should share equally	Never 'married' should share equally
Proportion answering 'shared equally'			
Household shopping	43%	65%	77%
Evening meal	17%	42%	55%
Evening dishes	36%	69%	74%
Household cleaning	23%	52%	62%
Washing and ironing	9%	27%	41%
Household repairs	8%	23%	34%
Organising household money	30%	62%	59%
Caring for sick children	30%	51%	58%
Teaching children discipline	67%	83%	80%

But the difference between the last two columns in the table above should not obscure the yawning gulf between the first two – the difference between what 'married' respondents say actually happens and what they think ought to. Control of household money is reported separately below; looking at the other items on the list there is a gap of between 15% and 33% in what is and what ought to be according to married people themselves. Apart from any obvious charge of hypocrisy, why should this gap be so large?

On first examination, the difference between the ideals and reality of 'married' men and 'married' women are similar. But when we distinguish responses according to whether the woman in the household has a full-time job, a part-time job, or no job outside the home, a different pattern emerges. On the question of who should do most of the household chores, full-time working women are much more egalitarian than are their male partners. The gap between part-time working women and their spouses is much less marked, and in households in which the woman does not work, women are sometimes *less* egalitarian than their spouses (see **Table 10.3**). Of course, women with full-time jobs are younger on average than other women, which may also contribute to their greater sense of egalitarianism. On the other hand, an equally plausible explanation is that full-time women workers simply feel that the burden they carry is unfairly heavy.

This explanation is supported by the answers to our questions on childcare, where women in all types of household are readier to nominate the woman as the primary carer. (Though it should be noted that households where the woman has a full-time job are much less likely than others to contain young children.) On these items, women working full-time are no more egalitarian than their spouses, and women working part-time or without a paid job are actually *less* egalitarian than their partners. While 61% of men whose partners either worked part-time or did not have a job said that caring for a sick child should be shared equally, only 46% of these women gave this response.

Clearly, then, women are more likely than men to feel they ought to be primary carers in the home – at any rate they are more likely to admit that they hold this view. But they are less likely than men to feel they ought to do everything else around the home too, particularly when they are working similar hours to those of their well-serviced partners.

Descriptively then, most women are likely to be mainly responsible for household work and childcare. Moreover, prescriptively, although the majority view is that men should help out more than they do, most of the chores – such as washing and ironing (69%), making the evening meal (52%), looking after sick children (46%) and general household cleaning (44%) – are still viewed widely as mainly women's work. The list is a telling one, for the items constitute a large part of the service work within the household and are all likely to place limits on women's availability for work outside the home.

The domestic division of money

We return to the subject of family finances raised by Ashford (in *The 1987 Report*). We asked all respondents who were married or living as married:

> *How do you and your partner organise the money that comes into your household?*

The options we gave, and the percentages choosing them, are shown below.

Family finance arrangements

	%
I manage all the money and give my partner his or her share	12
My partner manages all the money and gives me my share	14
We pool all the money and each take out what we need	57
We pool some of the money and keep the rest separate	12
We each keep our own money separate	6

The proportion claiming to pool all their money (called the 'common pot' system) has increased slightly since last year, but this may well be an artefact of questionnaire order. This time the question came after the items on household chores with their strong normative bias towards sharing; it is probable that use of the common pot system has been slightly exaggerated this time.

We followed this question with another looking at how allocations actually take place when one partner is responsible for money management: does the other partner ask for money when it is needed, or is there a regular allowance? Are there different patterns according to whether a man or a woman is in control of the household finances? Overall, we found the following:

	%
Man manages money, woman gets a regular allowance	9
Man manages money, woman asks whenever she needs money	2
Woman manages money, man gets a regular allowance	5
Woman manages money, man asks whenever he needs money	5

Women are more likely to be receiving an allowance, probably a housekeeping allowance, whereas men are as likely to ask for money as to receive an allowance.

This goes only some way towards helping us to understand financial decision-making. As Pahl (1984) says, family finances have always been a sort of 'black box', and our question only touches on the complicated processes of income dynamics within the family. Nonetheless, looking at households in which the respondent is aged under 59 (in most of which wives are eligible to work), we find a number of differences, as the table below shows.

	Respondents aged under 59 living in households where . . .			
	. . . man works, woman works full-time	. . . man works, woman works part-time	. . . man works, woman does not work	Other arrangements
	%	%	%	%
Common pot	62	61	54	58
Partial pool or full independence	24	18	12	13
Man manages, woman asks	2	1	4	5
Man manages, woman gets allowance	3	7	15	5
Woman manages finances	9	12	13	13

For instance, household money is less likely to be managed by just one partner

when the woman works full-time, and women are much more likely to be limited to an allowance (rather than having discretionary access to the household money) if they do not work outside the home (or work only part-time). Respondents living in households where the woman works full-time are much more likely to report that both partners have access to some independent money. Looking back to people's preferences on the earlier item about who *should* have responsibility for household money and bills, we find that single men are particularly likely to say that the man should have control, and that men generally are less likely than women to say that control of money should be shared. Learning to share financial control may be one of the more difficult negotiations in marriage.

But control is only part of the story. As Pahl (1984) notes further, what matters too is what items of expenditure are under whose control. Our questions are not refined enough to distinguish cases where a woman has an allowance for personal spending money from those where she has one which must cover all household spending. When this module comes up again, we hope to ask further questions to improve our understanding of household money management. But even on the data we have, it is clear that having a full-time job increases a woman's access to household money. Tax and benefit laws assume equal access to funds within the family; they may therefore be less helpful to women without jobs than is, say, child benefit, which ends up in the purse rather than the wallet (Land, 1983).

Attitudes towards women's work

Up to this point we have focused on attitudes related to people's own working lives. But what about general attitudes towards women and work? Has the increase in women's participation in paid work meant that views towards traditionally male and female roles have also changed? What are people's views about the 'proper' role for women in the late 1980s? In particular, are there any trends in people's attitudes? Although this series only goes back to 1984, we have some measures from the WES in 1980, and a few from the 1965 OPCS survey of women's employment (Hunt, 1968).

Equal opportunities outside the home

Before examining views on the special roles attributed to women, we touch on attitudes towards women's rights and the extent to which respondents support laws against sex discrimination.

*There is a law in Britain against sex discrimination, that is, against giving unfair preference to men – or to women – in employment, pay and so on. Do you generally support or oppose the idea of a law for this purpose?**

	1983	1984	1987
	%	%	%
Support	76	80	75
Oppose	22	17	22

* As noted in *The 1985 Report* (p.73) there is some evidence that the wording of this question may lead to an *under*estimate of the extent of support for sex discrimination laws. But this should not affect trend measurements.

There are slight fluctuations but nothing suggests there has been any real change in attitudes since 1983. Around one in every four or five people continue to question the desirability of laws against sex discrimination.

But the perception that sex discrimination does in fact take place has *not* diminished. Indeed, on some issues, there has even been a slight increase in the proportions who think women are treated worse than their male counterparts. Perhaps the safest assumption is that little has changed, with a clear majority of the population believing that various inequalities of treatment still exist. We asked about opportunities for promotion in 1984 and again in 1987.

	1984	1987
Women are generally less likely than men to be promoted at work even when their qualifications and experience are the same: does this happen . . .	%	%
a lot	40	44
a little	42	37
hardly at all	10	12

We also asked three further questions about discrimination in 1985 and repeated them in 1987.

	1985	1987
Opportunities for university education are:	%	%
Better for women	3	2
No different for men and women	68	76
Worse for women	16	11
Job opportunities are:*	%	%
Better for women	7	6
No different for men and women	37	34
Worse for women	51	54
Income and wages are*:	%	%
Better for women	2	1
No different for men and women	31	27
Worse for women	61	66

*These questions were asked about men and women with similar "education and experience" or "education and jobs" respectively.

The small minority saying that job opportunities are actually better for women may in fact be right. Labour market growth in Britain has been highly concentrated in the area of part-time work and in the service sector, both of which are more likely to provide jobs for women than for men. But on two of these three issues respondents are more likely now than in 1985 to feel that opportunities are worse for women.

A woman's place

However, support for egalitarian treatment in the workplace can co-exist comfortably with 'traditional' views about a woman's role in the home. Indeed,

since a majority of respondents believes that women should remain responsible for housework and childcare, the view that women's role is 'separate but equal' is likely to be popular. We have repeated items from the 1980 Women and Employment Survey before, and have now added a few more.

Betwen 1984 and 1987 there has been no real change in attitudes on the four questions common to both years; for simplicity, therefore, the table below shows only 1987 results for all items included.[1] Following Martin and Roberts (1984), we divide the statements into three groups. First we look at attitudes towards women's traditional role as homemaker.

		Agree ('strongly' or 'slightly')	Neither agree nor disagree	Disagree ('strongly' or 'slightly')
A husband's job is to earn the money; a wife's job is to look after the home and family	%	48	19	33
Most married women work only to earn money for extras, rather than because they need the money	%	45	16	39
A job is all right, but what most women really want is a home and children	%	36	22	42
In times of high unemployment married women should stay at home	%	32	19	48
Women shouldn't try to combine a career and children	%	32	22	45

We then looked at attitudes towards benefits to women of going out to work.

		Agree ('strongly' or 'slightly')	Neither agree nor disagree	Disagree ('strongly' or 'slightly')
Having a job is the best way for a woman to be an independent person	%	60	25	15
If the children are well looked after, it's good for a woman to work	%	56	28	16
A woman and her family will all be happier if she goes out to work	%	14	40	46

And finally we asked two other questions on women's rights and duties.

		Agree ('strongly' or 'slightly')	Neither agree nor disagree	Disagree ('strongly' or 'slightly')
Married women have a right to work if they want to, whatever their family situation	%	63	15	22
If a woman takes several years off to look after her children, it's only fair her career should suffer	%	29	25	44

These figures show just how divided our respondents are about the appropriate role for women, and about how to balance women's rights with family responsibilities. Substantial minorities of beween one-third and just under a half disagree with the statements asserting traditional attitudes towards the primacy of women's role in the home. While majorities believe it is beneficial for *women* if they have a job, only 14% agree it is better for a woman *and her family* if she has a job. Similarly, although 63% feel women should have the right to work regardless of family circumstances, only 44% believe it is unfair if their careers suffer as a result of time off for child-rearing.

Not surprisingly, the views of women of working age are less 'traditional' than those of the population as a whole. And though we can find little change in women's views since 1984, the overall picture suggests a slight liberalisation since 1980. On the other hand there seems to have been a decline over that period in the proportion who think working is beneficial to a woman *and* her family. Most of the movement in attitudes has been towards the neutral option rather than 'traditionalism', but on the item about the effect of women's work on the family, attitudes have shifted decisively towards 'traditionalism'. Since traditional views on women's roles have not generally increased, this movement may well result from women's greater awareness of, or their greater honesty about, the real conflicts involved between the respective claims of paid work and bringing up children.

| | | Women only* | | |
		Agree ('strongly' or 'slightly')	Neither agree nor disagree	Disagree ('strongly' or 'slightly')
Traditionalist attitudes				
Wife's job to look after home				
1980	%	46	21	33
1987	%	38	17	44
Job all right, but most women really want home and children				
1980	%	41	25	34
1987	%	24	19	57
In high unemployment, married women should stay home				
1980	%	35	16	49
1987	%	21	18	60
Benefits of women working				
If children looked after, it's good for women to work				
1980	%	71	17	12
1987	%	62	25	12
Job is best way for woman to be independent				
1980	%	67	17	16
1987	%	65	21	14

		Agree ('strongly' or 'slightly')	Women only* Neither agree nor disagree	Disagree ('strongly' or 'slightly')
Woman and family both happier if she goes out to work				
1980	%	29	32	39
1987	%	13	40	47
Other				
Married women have a right to work whatever their family situation				
1980	%	71	12	17
1987	%	72	15	13

*WES data (1980) refer to women aged 16–59; our data (1987) refer to women aged 18–59.

Following a strategy similar to that in WES, we devised a scale using the 'traditionalism' items, scoring each strong agreement as 5, slight agreement as 4, and so on, so as to examine the groups most likely to have strongly traditionalist views. **Table 10.4** gives full details. As will be seen, women are only slightly more likely than men to have highly egalitarian views and people with degrees are more egalitarian than those without. But the effect of education is particularly noticeable in women; 59% of women graduates are 'strong egalitarians', disagreeing with all five traditionalist statements, compared with only 28% of men graduates. Similarly, nearly two in five women working full-time are strongly egalitarian, possibly because many of them have not yet reached the life-stage when hard choices between domestic work, childcare and paid work have to be made. Their spouses are less likely to share their optimism, with only one in five being strong egalitarians.

Paid work versus childcare

We reported last year that three in four respondents felt it was best for mothers of children aged under five to stay at home, while one in five said the same of mothers of teenage children.

But despite people's views on the ideal, how strongly do they feel that women in various circumstances should positively *not* work? We included a question from the Women and Employment Survey, which had also been asked in the 1965 OPCS study of working-age women (Hunt, 1968). For each of five specified family circumstances, respondents were asked to choose one of these options for the woman:

> *She ought to go out to work if she's fit.*
> *It's up to her whether to go out to work or not*
> *She should only go out to work if she really needs the money*
> *She ought to stay at home*

First we show overall results from 1987. As the table below shows, people's views about a woman's right to work are influenced by at least two factors: the age of her children and her financial needs. Whatever the woman's circum-

stances, people are more reluctant to disapprove of her working if she "really needs the money".

		Ought to work	Up to her	Only if really needs money	Ought to stay at home
Single woman with:					
no family responsibilities	%	70	28	2	*
Married woman with:					
no children	%	23	70	6	*
children under school age	%	1	19	22	57
children at school	%	2	50	32	15
children but all left school	%	8	82	9	1

Respondents clearly believe that women without children have the right or the duty to work; the only distinction they make between a married woman with no children and a single woman is that the latter is seen to have a duty to work, and the former the right. But where she has children under school age, a majority of respondents feel that the mother should stay at home, though the proportion making a categorical judgement does decrease somewhat in circumstances where money is said to be short. So in 1986, 76% of respondents said it was best for mothers of young children to stay at home; in 1987, when offered the chance to qualify their views, just under a quarter would make an exception where money was scarce. In any case by the time children are at school, only a minority feels the woman should stay at home whatever the circumstances.

But let us look briefly at changes in attitudes since 1965. Three of the hypothetical circumstances we asked about have been more or less constant since 1965.* How have the views of working-age women changed in the 22 years since then?

	Working-age women		
	1965	**1980**	**1987**
Married woman with no children	%	%	%
Ought to work	13	33	27
Up to her	75	62	69
Only if she needs money	9	4	3
Ought to stay at home	1	1	–
Married woman with children under school age	%	%	%
Ought to work	–	–	*
Up to her	5	15	26
Only if she needs money	15	25	29
Ought to stay at home	78	62	45
Married woman with children at school.	%	%	%
Ought to work	3	3	3
Up to her	35	50	61
Only if she needs money	39	36	29
Ought to stay at home	20	11	7

* There was a wording change to one response option in 1980, which we have followed: "She has a right to work if she wants to" (1965); "It's up to her whether to go out to work or not" (1980 and 1987).

Even in 1965 the vast majority of women felt that being married was not in itself a disqualification from working. But there has been an enormous change since then in beliefs about women with children. In 1965, 78% of women felt that mothers of under-fives should stay at home; by 1980 that proportion had fallen to 62%, and by 1987 it had dropped further to 45%. Attitudes towards working mothers with school-age children have also changed, though not quite as dramatically. What we find here, however, is tantamount to a sea-change.

Conclusions

Part-time working is often an ideal arrangement for women, especially in the case of mothers who wish to spend time with their young children, as many do. But it has dangers. In particular, it tends to trap women in sex-stereotyped jobs which pay less well (even on an hourly basis) than full-time jobs. This is a serious problem, since most part-time workers are women and a majority of women are likely to work part-time after having children. The lack of employment protection and prospects for part-time workers thus affects women disproportionately. Lack of provision of childcare or nursery schools for the under-fives also prevents women from entering, or staying in, the workforce. Overall, then, women suffer various disadvantages in the labour market which rarely affect men.

In the home too, women feel at a disadvantage. They are generally responsible for the domestic servicing of both husband and children, and feel that household tasks should be shared more equally. Moreover, at a time when one in three marriages is predicted to end in divorce, women are particularly vulnerable if their domestic role is not recognised by the market. Nearly half of our respondents think that where a wife's earnings are much lower than her husband's at the time of a divorce, the man should make maintenance payments; and more than three-quarters think this should happen if the women has never had a paid job (see Appendix III, Q.A80, p.231). Yet the 1984 Matrimonial and Family Proceedings Act encourages the economic independence of women from their former spouses. As we have noted, however, economic independence at a reasonable level of income may be extremely difficult for many women to achieve while the sexual division of labour, inside and outside the home, remains so unequal, and while public policy does so little to remedy this problem. American women, for instance, are more likely than their British counterparts to work full-time perhaps because – as Dex and Shaw (1986) suggest – childcare expenses in the USA are deductible for income tax purposes, and American employers have no tax incentive to take on part-timers. Despite the laws against sex discrimination in Britain, the ever-increasing numbers of women workers here continue to be at a disadvantage.

The rapid changes in women's participation in the labour market have been accompanied by less rapid changes in attitudes to women's work. Even so, Britain seems to be much more egalitarian now on women's issues than it was, say, twenty years ago. As on so many matters, circumstances tend to change first and attitudes lag behind. Put another way, such longstanding aspects of culture change only slowly and, it seems, reluctantly.

Note

1. The wording of some items has been changed, in order to make them normative rather than factual; wording used was suggested by Iain Noble of Sheffield University (personal communication).

References

ASHFORD, S., 'Family Matters', in Jowell, R., Witherspoon, S. and Brook, L. (eds), *British Social Attitudes: the 1987 Report*, Gower, Aldershot, (1987).
BECKER, G. S., 'Human Capital, Effort, and the Sexual Division of Labour', *Journal of Labor Economics*, vol.3, no.1, Part 2 (January 1985), pp. 33–58.
BEECHEY, V. and PERKINS, T., *A Matter of Hours: Women, Part-time Work and the Labour Market*, Polity Press, Cambridge (1987).
BREUGEL, I., 'Women's Employment, Legislation and the Labour Market', in Lewis, J. (ed.), *Women's Welfare, Women's Rights,* Croom Helm, London (1983).
CENTRAL STATISTICAL OFFICE, *Social Trends 18*, HMSO, London (1988).
COHN, S., *The Process of Occupational Sex-Typing*, Temple University Press, Philadelphia (1985).
DEX, S., *The Sexual Division of Work*, Wheatsheaf Books, London (1985).
DEX, S. and SHAW, L., *British and American Women at Work: do Equal Opportunities Policies Matter?* Macmillan, London (1986).
EQUAL OPPORTUNITIES COMMISSION, *Women and Men in Britain: a Research Profile*, HMSO, London (1988).
HAKIM, C., *Occupational Segregation: A Comparative Study of the Degree and Pattern of Differentiation between Men's and Women's Work in Britain, the United States and Other Countries*, Research Paper No. 9, Department of Employment (1979).
HUNT, A., *A Survey of Women's Employment*, Government Social Survey, London (1968).
JOSHI, H., 'The Cost of Caring', in Glendinning, C. and Millar, J. (eds), *Women and Poverty in Britain*, Wheatsheaf Books, London (1987).
JOSHI, H., LAYARD, R. and OWEN, S., 'Why are More Women Working in Britain?', *Journal of Labor Economics*, vol.3, no.1, Part 2 (January 1985), pp. 147–76.
LAND, H., 'Who Still Cares for the Family?', in Lewis, J. (ed.), *Women's Welfare, Women's Rights*, Croom Helm, London (1983).
MARTIN, J. and ROBERTS, C., *Women and Employment: A Lifetime Perspective*, HMSO, London (1984).
OPCS, *General Household Survey 1986*, HMSO, London (1988).
PAHL, J., 'The Allocation of Money within the Household', in Freeman, M. (ed), *The State, the Law and the Family*, Tavistock Publications, London (1984).
ROBINSON, O. and WALLACE, J., *Part-time Employment and Sex Discrimination Legislation in Great Britain*, Research Paper No. 43, Department of Employment (1984).
WITHERSPOON, S., 'Sex Roles and Gender Issues', in Jowell, R. and Witherspoon, S. (eds), *British Social Attitudes: the 1985 Report*, Gower, Aldershot (1985).

10.1 OCCUPATIONAL SEGREGATION AND STEREOTYPING (Q27–Q30)
by compressed Goldthorpe class schema within sex

	MEN					WOMEN				
	All men	Salariat	Routine non-manual	Foremen and technicians	Working class	All women	Salariat	Routine non-manual	Foremen and technicians	Working class
	%	%	%	%	%	%	%	%	%	%
RESPONDENT										
works with men only	66	48	(43)	82	83	-	-	-	-	-
works with women only	-	-	-	-	-	49	36	51	(38)	57
works with both men and women	32	49	(57)	18	16	49	63	48	(62)	37
works alone, other	2	3	(-)	-	1	2	1	1	(-)	5
RESPONDENT THINKS OF WORK										
as mainly men's work	47	25	(13)	62	69	2	4	*	(4)	1
as mainly women's work	1	1	(-)	2	*	29	10	30	(34)	41
as work that either do	53	74	(87)	36	31	70	86	70	(62)	56
other or don't know	-	-	(-)	-	-	*	-	-	(-)	1
BASE: ALL EMPLOYEES *Weighted*	718	295	(43)	58	310	624	146	277	(12)	188
Unweighted	729	303	(47)	61	307	652	152	291	(12)	196

	MEN					WOMEN				
	All men	Salariat	Routine non-manual	Foremen and technicians	Working class	All women	Salariat	Routine non-manual	Foremen and technicians	Working class
	%	%	%	%	%	%	%	%	%	%
RESPONDENT BELIEVES										
opposite sex could not do the work	41	24	(9)	(38)	48	8	12	7	(-)	9
opposite sex would not be willing to do the work	26	26	(-)	(27)	28	51	40	51	(63)	53
opposite sex could and would do the work	30	48	(47)	(33)	22	36	48	39	(38)	29
other or don't know	3	2	(44)	(3)	3	5	-	2	(-)	9
BASE: [IF THINKS OF WORK AS MAINLY SUITABLE FOR OWN SEX ONLY] *Weighted*	334	74	(6)	(36)	213	178	(14)	82	(4)	78
Unweighted	335	72	(7)	(38)	213	188	(15)	87	(5)	81

N.B. Some of the bases are very small; results in brackets should be treated with particular caution

10.2 DOMESTIC DIVISION OF LABOUR (A84i–v)
by sex and working status of woman partner

WHO DOES EACH OF THE FOLLOWING TASKS IN YOUR HOUSEHOLD?	TOTAL	SEX		WORKING STATUS OF WOMAN PARTNER			
		Men	Women	Man works, woman works full-time	Man works, woman works part-time	Man works, woman does not work	Other, not answered
	%	%	%	%	%	%	%
HOUSEHOLD SHOPPING							
mainly man	7	7	7	8	1	6	12
mainly woman	50	48	52	43	64	62	34
shared equally	43	44	41	49	35	31	54
MAKES EVENING MEAL							
mainly man	6	6	6	7	4	1	10
mainly woman	77	74	79	63	83	89	71
shared equally	17	20	15	28	13	10	20
DOES EVENING DISHES							
mainly man	22	24	20	22	19	13	33
mainly woman	39	31	46	33	40	52	29
shared equally	36	43	30	41	36	33	36
DOES HOUSEHOLD CLEANING							
mainly man	4	4	3	4	1	1	7
mainly woman	72	71	73	60	84	86	58
shared equally	23	24	23	33	14	11	34
DOES WASHING AND IRONING							
mainly man	2	2	1	1	-	2	3
mainly woman	88	85	90	81	94	93	85
shared equally	9	11	8	18	5	5	11
Weighted	983	473	510	206	189	289	299
Unweighted	1005	489	516	211	198	295	301

BASE: A RESPONDENTS, MARRIED OR LIVING AS MARRIED

10.2 (continued) DOMESTIC DIVISION OF LABOUR (A84vi–ix; A906a) by sex and working status of woman partner

WHO DOES EACH OF THE FOLLOWING TASKS IN YOUR HOUSEHOLD?	TOTAL	SEX		WORKING STATUS OF WOMAN PARTNER			
		Men	Women	Man works, woman works full-time	Men works, woman works part-time	Man works, woman does not work	Other, not answered
	%	%	%	%	%	%	%
+REPAIRS HOUSEHOLD EQUIPMENT							
mainly man	82	87	78	86	87	79	80
mainly woman	6	5	7	3	4	9	7
shared equally	8	7	10	10	7	9	8
+ORGANISES HOUSEHOLD MONEY AND BILLS							
mainly man	32	32	32	36	32	34	28
mainly woman	38	37	38	31	42	38	40
shared equally	30	30	30	33	26	29	31
*LOOKS AFTER CHILDREN WHEN THEY ARE SICK							
mainly man	2	3	1	1	3	1	3
mainly woman	67	59	74	56	66	83	37
shared equally	30	37	23	40	31	15	57
*TEACHES CHILDREN DISCIPLINE							
mainly man	13	16	10	10	14	9	22
mainly woman	19	13	23	6	16	24	21
shared equally	67	70	65	81	69	66	54
+IS RESPONSIBLE FOR GENERAL DOMESTIC DUTIES (SUMMARY)							
mainly woman	82	77	86	70	91	91	75
shared equally	12	16	8	22	6	5	15
other	7	8	6	8	3	5	10
+BASE: A RESPONDENTS, MARRIED OR LIVING AS MARRIED — Weighted	983	473	510	206	189	289	299
Unweighted	1005	489	516	211	198	295	301
*BASE: A RESPONDENTS, MARRIED OR LIVING AS MARRIED, WITH CHILDREN AGED UNDER 16 — Weighted	422	201	221	65	114	177	66
Unweighted	417	202	215	67	115	173	62

10.3 PRESCRIPTIVE DOMESTIC DIVISION OF LABOUR (A85i–v)
by sex and working status within sex

WHO SHOULD DO EACH OF THE FOLLOWING TASKS?	TOTAL	Total	Men	MARRIED OR LIVING AS MARRIED								
				Working men whose spouse works full-time	Working men whose spouse works part-time	Working men whose spouse does not work	Other men	Women	Full-time working women whose spouse works	Part-time working women whose spouse works	Non-working women whose spouse works	Other women
	%	%	%	%	%	%	%	%	%	%	%	%
HOUSEHOLD SHOPPING												
mainly man	1	1	1	2	-	1	2	1	-	-	-	1
mainly woman	30	33	33	24	37	38	32	33	18	34	38	36
shared equally	68	65	65	74	62	60	65	65	82	64	58	61
MAKE EVENING MEAL												
mainly man	*	*	1	-	1	1	1	*	1	-	-	-
mainly woman	52	55	56	36	56	65	62	54	30	52	65	60
shared equally	45	42	40	61	37	33	37	43	68	43	30	38
DO EVENING DISHES												
mainly man	11	11	11	13	9	6	17	10	9	9	8	15
mainly woman	17	18	18	14	14	24	17	18	9	9	27	20
shared equally	70	69	69	72	74	68	66	69	81	77	63	63
DO HOUSEHOLD CLEANING												
mainly man	1	1	1	2	-	-	-	1	2	-	-	1
mainly woman	44	46	46	35	44	58	42	46	21	50	62	45
shared equally	54	52	52	61	54	41	56	52	77	47	37	53
DO WASHING AND IRONING												
mainly man	*	*	*	-	-	1	-	-	-	-	-	-
mainly woman	69	72	72	60	74	75	73	72	50	81	77	76
shared equally	30	27	27	39	23	23	25	27	50	17	21	24
BASE: A RESPONDENTS Weighted	1391	983	473	94	93	134	153	510	112	97	155	146
Unweighted	1437	1005	489	98	95	140	156	516	113	103	155	145

10.3 (continued) PRESCRIPTIVE DOMESTIC DIVISION OF LABOUR (A85vi–ix) by sex and working status within sex

WHO SHOULD DO EACH OF THE FOLLOWING TASKS?	TOTAL	Total	Men	MARRIED OR LIVING AS MARRIED								
				Working men whose spouse works full-time	Working men whose spouse works part-time	Working men whose spouse does not work	Other men	Women	Full-time working women whose spouse works	Part-time working women whose spouse works	Non-working women whose spouse works	Other women
	%	%	%	%	%	%	%	%	%	%	%	%
REPAIR HOUSEHOLD EQUIPMENT												
mainly man	73	74	79	70	88	75	83	69	51	79	71	76
mainly woman	1	1	1	-	-	4	*	1	-	-	-	3
shared equally	24	23	18	30	10	20	15	27	45	18	28	19
ORGANISE HOUSEHOLD MONEY AND BILLS												
mainly man	22	22	23	24	24	24	20	21	15	25	21	24
mainly woman	15	14	17	10	22	13	22	11	5	10	9	15
shared equally	61	62	58	63	54	62	55	65	75	65	66	58
LOOK AFTER CHILDREN WHEN THEY ARE SICK												
mainly man	*	*	*	-	1	1	-	*	1	-	-	1
mainly women	47	47	42	42	34	38	51	51	40	53	53	55
shared equally	51	51	55	57	63	60	46	47	58	45	45	41
TEACH CHILDREN DISCIPLINE												
mainly man	12	10	12	13	8	5	18	9	5	9	6	14
mainly women	5	6	6	2	7	8	6	5	2	4	5	8
shared equally	82	83	81	84	84	86	73	85	93	87	88	75
BASE: A RESPONDENTS Weighted	1391	983	473	94	93	134	153	510	112	97	155	146
Unweighted	1437	1005	489	98	95	140	156	516	112	103	155	145

10.4 TRADITIONAL ATTITUDES TOWARDS WOMEN'S ROLES (A222, A223)
by sex, education, education within sex and working status of woman (respondent or partner)

	TOTAL	SEX		EDUCATION		EDUCATION WITHIN SEX				WORKING STATUS OF WOMAN (respondent or partner)			
		Men	Women	Degree	Others	Women with degrees	Other women	Men with degrees	Other men	Women working full-time	Other women	Men whose spouse works full-time	Other men
	%	%	%	%	%	%	%	%	%	%	%	%	%
COMPOSITE TRADITIONALISM SCALE (A223a,c,d,e,g)													
Highly traditional views	5	6	4	2	5	(-)	5	3	6	1	6	1	7
Traditional views	26	30	22	10	27	(2)	23	16	32	9	27	16	33
Neither	37	38	36	34	37	(31)	36	36	38	28	39	41	37
Egalitarian views	21	18	24	17	22	(12)	25	21	18	33	20	23	17
Highly egalitarian views	11	8	14	37	9	(56)	11	24	7	28	7	20	7
SHOULD THE WOMAN WORK? (A222b,c)													
MARRIED WOMAN WITH CHILDREN AT SCHOOL:													
Ought to work	2	2	3	1	2	(-)	3	2	2	4	2	1	2
Up to her	50	47	53	69	49	(76)	51	65	45	64	48	67	44
Only if she really needs money	32	31	32	21	32	(13)	34	27	31	28	34	23	32
Ought to stay at home	15	20	11	8	16	(12)	11	6	21	3	14	9	22
MARRIED WOMAN WITH CHILDREN UNDER SCHOOL AGE:													
Ought to work	1	1	1	1	1	(-)	1	2	1	1	*	1	1
Up to her	20	18	21	38	18	(52)	19	30	16	34	16	30	16
Only if she really needs money	22	18	27	17	23	(12)	27	20	18	26	26	25	17
Ought to stay at home	57	63	51	44	58	(36)	52	48	64	39	56	45	66
BASE: A RESPONDENTS													
Weighted	*1243*	*587*	*656*	*98*	*1145*	*(39)*	*617*	*59*	*528*	*189*	*458*	*85*	*497*
Unweighted	*1266*	*595*	*671*	*102*	*1164*	*(38)*	*633*	*64*	*531*	*195*	*476*	*89*	*506*

Appendix I
Technical details of the survey

In the first three years of the *British Social Attitudes* survey, we interviewed between 1,700 and 1,800 respondents. In 1986, and again in 1987, the generosity of the Sainsbury Family Charitable Trusts enabled us to increase the sample size substantially, and so cover more topics in the questionnaire. Core questions were asked of all respondents, and the remaining questions were asked of a half sample of around 1,400 respondents each – version A of one half, version B of the other. (The structure of the questionnaire is shown diagrammatically in Appendix III.)

Sample design

The survey was designed to yield a representative sample of adults aged 18 or over living in private households in Great Britain.

For practical reasons, the sample was confined to those living in private households whose addresses were listed in the electoral registers. People living in institutions (though not in private households at such institutions) were excluded, as were households whose addresses were not on the electoral registers. Because fieldwork was timed to start in early March, we had to draw the sample from registers that were just reaching the end of their period of currency. In fact, we used the same registers, and the same constituencies, as those drawn for the 1986 *British Social Attitudes* survey.

The sampling method involved a multi-stage design, with four separate stages of selection.

Selection of parliamentary constituencies

One hundred and fifty one parliamentary constituencies were selected among

all those in England, Scotland and Wales. (In Scotland, constituencies north of the Caledonian Canal were omitted for reasons of cost.)

Before selection, the constituencies were stratified according to information held in SCPR's constituency datafile. This datafile is a compilation of information gathered from *OPCS Monitors*, and includes a variety of social indicators such as population density, percentage Labour vote at the 1983 general election, percentage of those holding professional qualifications, percentage of male unemployment and so on. The stratification factors used in this survey were:

1. Registrar General's Standard Region
2. Population density (persons per hectare): over 10
    5–10
    under 5
3. A ranking by percentage of homes that were owner-occupied. (This factor was likely to give more equal strata than, for instance, the percentage of those voting Labour at the 1983 election.)

Constituencies were then selected systematically with probability of selection proportionate to size of electorate.

After the selection of constituencies, alternate constituencies were allotted to the A or B half of the sample. In 75 areas interviewers were allocated version A of the questionnaire, and in 75 areas they were given version B. In the remaining constituency, half the addresses were allocated version A, and half were allocated version B.

Selection of polling districts

Within each of the selected constituencies, a single polling district was selected, again with probability proportionate to size of electorate.

Selection of addresses

Twenty-nine addresses were selected in each of the 151 polling districts, using electoral registers. The sample issued to interviewers was therefore 151 × 29 = 4,379 addresses. The selection was made from a random starting point and, treating the list of electors as circular, a fixed interval was applied to generate the required number of addresses for each polling district. By this means, addresses were chosen with probability proportionate to their number of listed electors. At each sampled address the names of all electors given on the register were listed, and the name of the individual on which the sampling interval had landed was marked with an asterisk (we called this person the 'starred elector').

Selection of individuals

The electoral register is an unsatisfactory sampling frame of *individuals*, although it is reasonably complete as a frame of *addresses*. So a further selection stage

is required to convert the listing of addresses into a sample of individuals.

Interviewers were instructed to call at the address of each 'starred elector', and to list all those eligible for inclusion in the sample, that is, all persons currently aged 18 or over and resident in the 'starred elector's' household. Where this listing revealed a difference between those household members named in the register and those eligible to take part in the survey (because there had been movement in or out since the register was compiled, or because some people were not registered) the interviewer selected one respondent by a random selection procedure (using a 'Kish grid').

In households where there had been no change, the interviewer was instructed to interview the 'starred elector'. Where there were two or more households at the selected address, interviewers were required to identify the household of the 'starred elector' (or the household occupying that part of the address where he or she used to live) and then followed the procedure described above.

Before analysis, the data were weighted to take account of any differences between the number of people listed on the register and the number found at the address. There were differences in 27% of cases, in each of which the data were weighted by the number of persons aged 18 or over found living at the household divided by the number of electors listed on the register for the address. Almost all of the weights fell within a range between 0.2 and 2.0. In only 14 cases weights greater than 2.0 were applied; these ranged between 2.5 and 5.0.

In the remaining 73% of cases, the number of persons listed on the register matched those found at the address, so the effective weight was one. The unweighted sample (the number of persons interviewed) was 2,847 and the weighted sample was 2,766.

Fieldwork

Interviewing was carried out mainly during March and April 1987; about 11% of interviews were conducted in May and June.

Fieldwork was conducted by 146 interviewers drawn from SCPR's regular panel. All attended a one-day briefing conference to familiarise themselves with the questionnaires and selection procedures. The interview, on both versions of the questionnaire, took on average 64 minutes to administer. Overall response achieved was:

	No.	%
Addresses issued	4,379	
Vacant, derelict, out of scope	139	
In scope	4,240	100
Interview achieved	2,847	67
Interview not achieved	1,393	33
Refused	1,000	24
Non-contact	255	6
Other non-response	138	3

Response rates achieved with the A and B versions of the questionnaires were similar – 68% with the A version and 66% with the B version. They ranged between 80% in the North of England and 55% in Greater London. Regional variations in response to the two different versions of the questionnaire were sometimes more marked, but in general they differed by only one to six per cent. Full details are given in the Technical Report (Brook and Witherspoon, 1988). As in earlier rounds of the series, respondents were asked to fill in a self-completion questionnaire which was, whenever possible, collected by the interviewer. Otherwise, the respondent was asked to post it to SCPR. If necessary, up to two postal reminders were sent to obtain the self-completion supplement: questionnaires were accepted until early July.

Three hundred and fifty-four respondents, 12% of those interviewed, failed to return the supplement. Eighty-nine per cent of respondents returned version A of the self-completion questionnaire, and 86% returned version B. Non-respondents to the self-completion questionnaire included a higher proportion of those aged 65 or over, those who worked in unskilled manual occupations, those with no educational qualifications and those with no party allegiance. However, the overall proportion returning the supplement was high (88%), and so we decided against additional weighting to correct for non-response.

Analysis variables

A number of standard analyses have been used in the tables that appear both in the text and at the end of the chapters of this Report. The analysis groups requiring further definition are set out below.

Region

The Registrar General's 10 Standard Regions have been used, except that we have distinguished between Greater London and the remainder of the South-East. Sometimes these have been grouped into what we have termed 'compressed region': 'Northern' includes the North, North West and Yorkshire and Humberside. East Anglia is included in the 'South', as is the South West.

Social Class

Respondents are classified according to their own social class, not that of a putative 'head of household'. The main social class variable used in the analyses in this Report is the Registrar General's, although Socio-Economic Group (SEG) has also been coded, and so can be used by secondary analysts with access to the datatape.

Each respondent's social class is based on his or her current or last occupation. So all respondents in paid work at the time of the interview, or waiting to take up a paid job already offered, or retired, or seeking work, or looking after the home, have their occupation (present, future or last as appropriate) classified into Occupational Unit Groups, according to the *OPCS Classification of Occupations 1980*. This method has been adopted on each survey, except

for 1983 when we separately classified those looking after the home. The combination of occupational classification with employment status generates six social classes:

I	Professional	⎫
II	Intermediate	⎬ 'Non-manual'
III (Non-manual)	Skilled occupations	⎭
III (Manual)	Skilled occupations	⎫
IV	Semi-skilled occupations	⎬ 'Manual'
V	Unskilled occupations	⎭

In this report we have usually collapsed them into four groups: I & II, III Non-manual, III Manual, IV & V.

The remaining respondents are grouped as 'never worked/not classifiable', but not shown in the tables. For some analyses, it may be more appropriate to classify respondents according to their *current* social class, which takes into account only their present employment status. In this case, in addition to the six social classes listed above, the remaining respondents not currently in paid work fall into one of the following categories; 'not classified', 'retired', 'looking after the home', 'unemployed' or 'others not in paid occupations'.

In Chapters 4, 8 and 10, John Goldthorpe's schema is used. This system classifies occupations by their 'general comparability', considering such factors as sources and levels of income, economic security, promotion prospects, and level of job autonomy and authority. We have developed a programme which derives the Goldthorpe classification from the five-digit Occupational Unit Groups combined with employment status. The full Goldthorpe schema has 11 categories but the version used in this Report (the 'compressed schema') combines these into five classes:

1. Salariat (professional and managerial)
2. Routine non-manual workers (office and sales)
3. Petty bourgeoisie (the self-employed including farmers, with and without employees)
4. Manual foremen and supervisors
5. Working class (skilled, semi-skilled and unskilled manual workers, personal service and agricultural workers)

In some analyses in Chapter 8 classes 2, 3 and 4 are further combined into a grouping we have termed 'intermediate'. There is a residual category of those who have never had a job or who have given insufficient information, but this is not shown in any of the analyses in this Report.

Industry

All respondents whose occupation could be coded were allocated a Standard Industrial Classification (SIC, 1980). Two-digit class codes were applied. Respondents were also classified as working in public-sector services, public-sector manufacturing and transport, private-sector manufacturing, or private-sector non-manufacturing, by cross-analysing SIC categories with responses to a question about the type of employer for whom they worked. As with social

class, SIC may be generated on the basis of the respondent's current occupation only, or on his or her most recently-classifiable occupation.

Party identification

Respondents can be classified as identified with a particular political party, or party grouping, on one of three counts: if they consider themselves supporters of the party (Q.2a, b), or as closer to it than to others (Q.2c, d), or as more likely to support it in the event of a general election (Q.2e). The three groups are generally described respectively as *partisans, sympathisers* and *residual identifiers*. The three groups combined are referred to in both text and tables as 'identifiers'.

Alliance identifiers (in spring 1987) included those nominating the Social Democratic Party or the Liberal Party or the Alliance. Those who indicated no party preference were classified as 'non-aligned'.

Other analysis variables

These are taken directly from the questionnaire, and to that extent are self-explanatory.

Sex (Q.901)
Age (Q.902)
Household income (Q.914a)   Highest educational qualification obtained (Q.905)
Religion (Q.77a)
Religious attendance (Q.77b)   Current residence (B101a)
Housing tenure (A98/B103)   Self-rated social class (Q.76a)
Marital status (A83a/B102)   Last did countryside activity (B95a, b)
Private schooling (Q.903a,c)   Schoolchildren in household (Q.901c)
Employment Sector (Health Authority/
    hospital) (Q.907f)

Sampling errors

No sample precisely reflects the characteristics of the population it represents because of both sampling and non-sampling errors. If a sample were designed as random sample (i.e. if every adult had an equal and independent chance of inclusion in the sample) then we could calculate the sampling error of any percentage, p, using the formula:

$$\text{s.e. (p)} = \sqrt{\frac{p(100-p)}{n}}$$

where n is the number of respondents on which the percentage is based. Once the sampling error had been obtained, it would be a straightforward exercise to calculate a confidence interval for the true population percentage. For example, a 95% confidence interval would be given by the formula:

$$p \pm 1.96 \times \text{s.e. (p)}$$

Clearly, for a simple random sample (srs), the sampling error depends only on the values of p and n. However, simple random sampling is almost never used in practice because of its inefficiency in terms of time and cost.

As noted above, the *British Social Attitudes* sample, like that drawn for most large-scale surveys, was clustered according to a stratified multi-stage design into 151 polling districts. With a complex design like this, the sampling error of a percentage giving a particular response is not simply a function of the number of respondents in the sample and the size of the percentage; it also depends on how that percentage response is spread within and between polling districts. The complex design may be assessed relative to simple random sampling by calculating a range of design factors (DEFTs) associated with it, where

$$\text{DEFT} = \sqrt{\frac{\text{Variance of estimator with complex design, sample size n}}{\text{Variance of estimator with srs design, sample size n}}}$$

and represents the multiplying factor to be applied to the simple random sampling error to produce its complex equivalent. A design factor of one means that the complex sample has achieved the same precision as a simple random sample of the same size. A design factor greater than one means the complex sample is less precise than a simple random sample of equivalent size.

If the DEFT for a particular characteristic is known, a 95% confidence interval for a percentage may be calculated using the formula:

$$p \pm 1.96 \times \text{complex samping error (p)}$$

$$= p \pm 1.96 \times \text{DEFT} \times \sqrt{\frac{p(100 - p)}{n}}$$

Estimates of sampling error for the 1987 survey were made using a different procedure from that followed previously. Instead of using the World Fertility Survey 'Clusters' program and computing sampling errors for a single year, we used estimates from previous years' calculations in order to compute sampling error estimates for this year's data. Averaging previous estimates of the degree of clustering of a variable (roh), and taking account of the increased number of sampling points, 1987 sampling errors were computed clerically. The use of two or three previous estimates of the degree of clustering, instead of an estimate from a single year, may actually lead to more precise estimates of sampling error.

The table overleaf gives examples of the DEFTs and confidence intervals calculated. The majority of DEFTs lie in the range 1.2–1.8 – with the important exception of housing tenure, which has a high DEFT because tenure is strongly related to area. For many attitudinal variables, the DEFTs are at the lower end of the range and the fact that they are close to 1.0 means that the use of standard statistical tests of significance (based on the assumption of simple random sampling) is unlikely to be seriously misleading. For certain variables, however, particularly those strongly associated with area, care needs to be taken in the interpretation of test statistics and the estimation of parameter values.*

---

* These estimates do not apply to data presented in Chapter 8 which are estimates based on larger samples derived from combining several rounds of *British Social Attitudes* survey data.

	%(p)	Complex standard error of p(%)	DEFT	95% confidence interval
Classification variables				
Q.2 Party identification				
Conservative	38.0	1.43	1.54	35.21–40.79
Alliance	18.7	0.95	1.29	16.83–20.57
Labour	29.1	1.49	1.73	26.17–32.03
Q.23 Proportion of people who are				
self employed	**12.3**	**0.76**	**1.22**	**10.81–13.79**
Q.98/Housing tenure				
B103 Owns	68.2	2.15	2.43	63.98–72.42
Rents from local authority	22.5	2.11	2.65	18.37–26.63
Rents from housing association	1.1	0.35	1.77	0.41– 1.79
Other renting	8.0	0.85	1.65	6.33– 9.67
Q904 Age of completing continuous				
full-time education				
16 or under	71.5	1.43	1.66	68.70–74.30
17 or 18	15.3	0.85	1.25	13.63–16.97
19 or over	11.6	0.94	1.54	9.76–13.44
Attitudinal variables				
Q.7 Britain should rid itself of				
nuclear weapons	24.6	0.93	1.13	22.78–26.42
Q.11 Expect inflation to go up	78.7	0.84	1.08	77.06–80.34
Q.12 Expect unemployment to go up	40.2	1.22	1.30	37.82–42.58
Q.61 Government should increase				
taxes and spend more on health,				
education and social benefits	50.1	1.12	1.18	47.90–52.30

It should be noted that these calculations are based on the total sample from the 1987 survey (2,766 weighted. 2,847 unweighted); sampling errors for proportions administered only the A or B version of the questionnaire, or for subgroups within the total sample, would be larger.

Reference

BROOK, L. and WITHERSPOON, S., *British Social Attitudes, 1987 Survey: Technical Report*, SCPR, London (1988).

Appendix II
Notes on the tabulations

1. Tables at the end of chapters are percentaged vertically; tables within the text are percentaged as indicated.
2. In all the tables, whether in the text or at the end of chapters, a percentage of less than 0.5 is indicated by '*', and '–' is used to denote zero.
3. When findings based on the responses of fewer than 50 respondents are reported in the text, reference is made to the small base size. Percentages based on fewer than 50 unweighted respondents are bracketed in the end-of-chapter tables, as are the bases.
4. Percentages equal to or greater than 0.5 have been rounded up in all tables (e.g. 57.5% = 58%).
5. Weighted bases shown in the tables may be rounded up or down, and thus they may not always add to the expected figure.
6. As reported in Appendix I, 12% of respondents who completed the interview did not return a self-completion questionnaire. Percentage responses to the self-completion questionnaire are based on all those who completed it, not (as in Appendix III of *The 1984 Report*) on all respondents.

Appendix III
The questionnaires

As explained in Appendix I, two different versions of the questionnaire were used. The diagram below shows the questionnaire structure and the topics covered (not all of which are reported in this volume).

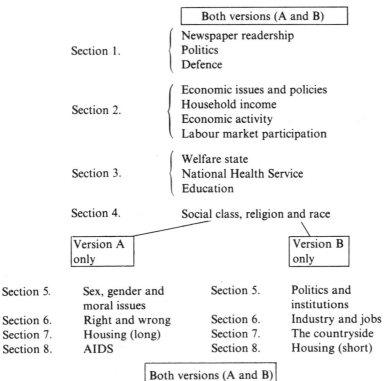

Both versions (A and B)

Section 1.
- Newspaper readership
- Politics
- Defence

Section 2.
- Economic issues and policies
- Household income
- Economic activity
- Labour market participation

Section 3.
- Welfare state
- National Health Service
- Education

Section 4.   Social class, religion and race

Version A only

Section 5.	Sex, gender and moral issues
Section 6.	Right and wrong
Section 7.	Housing (long)
Section 8.	AIDS

Version B only

Section 5.	Politics and institutions
Section 6.	Industry and jobs
Section 7.	The countryside
Section 8.	Housing (short)

Both versions (A and B)

Section 9. Classification items

There were also two versions of the self-completion supplement, reflecting the different topics covered in the main questionnaire. The module developed as part of SCPR's participation in the *International Social Survey Programme* (ISSP) – in 1987 on the subject of equality – is in version A (pages 1–10) of the supplement. Publication of the results is planned, in collaboration with Programme members, at some future date.

The questionnaires (interview and self-completion) are reproduced on the following pages. We have removed the punching codes and inserted instead the percentage distribution of answers to each question. Percentages for the core questions are based on the total sample (2,766 weighted), while those for questions in versions A and B are based on the appropriate subsamples (1,391 and 1,375 weighted). The pages that follow thus mirror the diagram above. Figures do not necessarily add up to 100% because of weighting and rounding, or for one or more of the following reasons:

(i)   We have not always included percentages for those not answering (which are usually very small). They are, of course, included on the datatape.

(ii)   Some subquestions are filtered, that is they are asked of only a proportion of respondents. In these cases the percentages add up (approximately) to the proportions who were asked them. Where, however, a *series* of questions is filtered (for instance in Section 2 of the interview questionnaire), we have indicated the weighted base at the beginning of that series, and throughout derived percentages from that base. Medians which could have been derived from unweighted bases of less than 50 have not been given.

(iii) At a few questions respondents were invited to give more than one answer and so percentages may add to well over 100%. These are clearly marked by interviewer instructions on the questionnaire.

(iv)   As reported in Appendix I, the self-completion questionnaire was not completed by 12% of respondents who were successfully interviewed. To allow for comparisons over time, the answers in the supplement have been re-percentaged on the base of those respondents who returned it (for version A: 1,243 weighted; for version B: 1,181 weighted.) This means that the figures are comparable with those given in *The 1985, 1986* and *1987 Reports*, but not with those given in *The 1984 Report*, where re-percentaging is necessary if comparisons are to be made.

A

SCPR

SOCIAL AND COMMUNITY PLANNING RESEARCH

Head Office: 35 Northampton Square London EC1V 0AX. Tel: 01-250 1866
Northern Fied Office: Charazel House Gainford Darlington Co. Durham DL2 3EG. Tel: 0325 730 888

P.905

March/April 1987

BRITISH SOCIAL ATTITUDES:

1987 SURVEY

NOTE:

In the self-completion questionnaire actually used, boxes were ticked by respondents to show their answers to the questions. In the questionnaire reproduced here, the boxes have been redrawn.

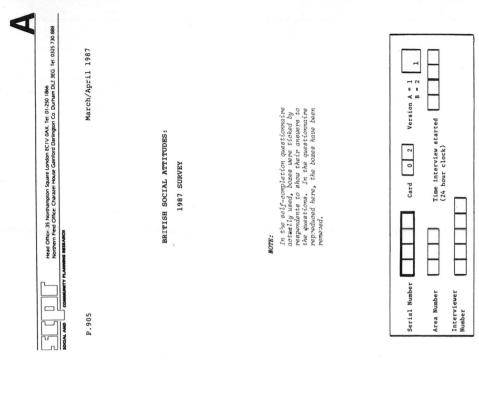

Serial Number

Card   0   2   Version A = 1
                       B = 2

Area Number

Time interview started
(24 hour clock)

Interviewer
Number

- 1 -

N = 2847

SECTION ONE

1.a) Do you normally read any daily morning newspaper at least 3 times a week?

		Skip to
Yes	70.7	b)
No	29.3	Q.2

IF YES

b) Which one do you normally read? IF MORE THAN ONE ASK: Which one do you read most frequently?

ONE CODE ONLY

(Scottish) Daily Express	7.7
Daily Mail	7.5
Daily Mirror/Record	15.5
Daily Star	3.7
The Sun	15.7
Today	0.9
Daily Telegraph	4.9
Financial Times	0.4
The Guardian	3.2
The Independent	1.4
The Times	1.8
Morning Star	0.1
Other Scottish/Welsh/regional or local daily morning paper (SPECIFY)	5.4
Other (SPECIFY)	0.3
More than one	2.2

ASK ALL

2.a) Generally speaking, do you think of yourself as a supporter of any one political party?

		Skip to
Yes	48.8	b)
No	51.1	c)

IF YES, ASK b). IF NO ASK c)

b) Which one? RECORD ANSWER BELOW AND GO TO f)

IF NO AT a)

c) Do you think of yourself as a little closer to one political party than to the others?

		Skip to
Yes	25.5	d)
No	24.8	e)

IF YES, ASK d). IF NO, ASK e)

d) Which one? RECORD ANSWER AND GO TO f)

IF NO AT a) AND c)

e) If there were a general election tomorrow which political party do you think you would be most likely to support?

CODE ONE ONLY

	b	d	e	Skip to
Conservative	25.5	9.2	3.6	
Labour	16.5	8.8	3.7	
Liberal				
SDP/Social Democrat	5.8	6.8	6.1	6.1
(Alliance)				
Scottish Nationalist				
Plaid Cymru			1.3	1.3
Other party (SPECIFY)				
Other answer (SPECIFY)			0.8	
None			7.5	
Don't know			3.6	3.6

IF ANY PARTY CODED AT a)-e), ASK f). OTHERS GO TO Q.3

f) Would you call yourself very strong ... (QUOTE PARTY NAMED)..fairly strong, or not very strong?

Very strong	11.2
Fairly strong	34.9
Not very strong	40.1
Don't know	0.3

- 2 -

N = 2847

ASK ALL

3.a) Do you think that local councils ought to be controlled by central government more, less or about the same amount as now?

		Skip to
More	18.8	
Less	34.1	
About the same	36.8	
Don't know	10.1	

b) And do you think the level of rates should be up to the local council to decide, or should central government have the final say? RECORD IN COL b)

	(b) Rates
Local council	67.7
Central government	23.5
Don't know	8.2

c) How about the level of council rents? Should that be up to the local council to decide or should central government have the final say? RECORD IN COL c)

	(c) Rents
	73.3
	18.0
	8.3

4. Now a few questions about Britain's relationships with other countries.

a) Do you think Britain should continue to be a member of the EEC - the Common Market - or should it withdraw?

	(a) EEC
Continue	62.6
Withdraw	31.5
Don't know	5.7

b) And do you think Britain should continue to be a member of NATO - the North Atlantic Treaty Organisation - or should it withdraw?

	(b) NATO
	78.9
	10.7
	10.2

5. On the whole, do you think that Britain's interests are better served by ... READ OUT ...

... closer links with Western Europe,	57.1
or - closer links with America?	18.4
(Both equally)	13.7
(Neither)	2.5
(Don't know)	8.2

6.a) Do you think that the siting of American nuclear missiles in Britain makes Britain a safer or a less safe place to live? RECORD IN COL a)

	(a) American nuclear missiles
Safer	38.6
Less safe	49.6
No difference	1.9
Don't know	9.6

b) And do you think that having our own independent nuclear missiles makes Britain a safer or a less safe place to live? RECORD IN COL b)

	(b) Own nuclear missiles
	58.1
	30.9
	1.7
	9.0

- 3 -

N = 2847

CARD A

7. Which, if either, of these two statements comes closest to your own opinion on British nuclear policy?

Britain should rid itself of nuclear weapons while persuading others to do the same	24.6
Britain should keep its nuclear weapons until we persuade others to reduce theirs	72.4
(Neither of these)	2.1
Don't know	0.8

8. Which political party's views on defence would you say comes closest to your own views?

Conservative	42.6
Labour	20.1
Liberal	4.1
SDP/Social Democrat	5.5
(Alliance)	3.1
Other (SPECIFY)	0.6
Don't know	21.3
None	2.4

CARD B

9. Which of the phrases on this card is closest to your opinion about threats to world peace?

America is a greater threat to world peace than Russia	18.3
Russia is a greater threat to world peace than America	17.3
Russia and America are equally great threats to world peace	53.6
Neither is a threat to world peace	7.9
(Don't know)	2.8

10.a) Do you think the long term policy for Northern Ireland should be for it ... READ OUT ...

... to remain part of the United Kingdom,	26.8
or - to reunify with the rest of Ireland?	57.0
Independent state	0.7
Let Irish decide	4.1
Other	1.4
Don't know	9.5

b) Some people think that government policy towards Northern Ireland should include a complete withdrawal of British troops. Would you personally support or oppose such a policy? Strongly or a little?

Support strongly	38.1
Support a little	23.2
Oppose strongly	15.6
Oppose a little	15.1
Withdraw in long term	0.8
Let Irish decide	0.4
Other	0.7
Don't know	5.7

- 4 -

N = 2847

SECTION TWO

Now I would like to ask you about two of Britain's economic problems - inflation and unemployment.

11. First, inflation: In a year from now, do you expect prices generally to have gone up, to have stayed the same, or to have gone down?

IF GONE UP OR GONE DOWN
By a lot or a little?

To have gone up by a lot	26.2
To have gone up by a little	52.4
To have stayed the same	16.5
To have gone down by a little	2.8
To have gone down by a lot	0.2
(Don't know)	1.8

12. Second, unemployment: In a year from now, do you expect unemployment to have gone up, or to have stayed the same, or to have gone down?

IF GONE UP OR GONE DOWN
By a lot or a little?

To have gone up by a lot	16.8
To have gone up by a little	23.4
To have stayed the same	31.8
To have gone down by a little	22.6
To have gone down by a lot	2.2
(Don't know)	3.1

13.a) If the government had to choose between keeping down inflation or keeping down unemployment, to which do you think it should give highest priority?

Keeping down inflation	23.2
Keeping down unemployment	72.6
Both equally	2.2
Other	0.1
Don't know	1.4

b) Which do you think is of most concern to you and your family ... READ OUT ...

... inflation,	54.5
or - unemployment?	41.4
Both equally	2.0
Neither	0.5
Other	0.1
Don't know	1.3

14. Looking ahead over the next year, do you think Britain's general industrial performance will improve, stay much the same, or decline?

IF IMPROVE OR DECLINE
By a lot or a little?

Improve a lot	6.8
Improve a little	28.7
Stay much the same	40.6
Decline a little	11.5
Decline a lot	5.6
(Don't know)	6.5

N = 2847

- 5 -

15. Here are a number of policies which might help Britain's economic problems. As I read them out, will you tell me whether you would support such a policy or oppose it? READ OUT ITEMS i)-ix) AND CODE IN GRID

	Support	Oppose	Don't know
i) Control of **wages** by legislation	34.2	60.1	5.5
ii) Control of **prices** by legislation	57.9	37.6	4.4
iii) Reducing the level of Government spending on health and education	7.1	91.5	1.0
iv) Introducing import controls	68.3	23.1	8.2
v) Increasing Government subsidies for private industry	59.7	31.0	8.9
vi) Devaluation of the pound	10.3	71.7	17.1
vii) Reducing Government spending on defence	51.5	44.3	3.8
viii) Government incentives to encourage job sharing or splitting	61.9	32.0	6.0
ix) Government to set up construction projects to create more jobs	90.1	7.8	1.8

16. On the whole, would you like to see more or less state ownership of industry, or about the same amount as now?

More: 16.5
Less: 30.2
About the same amount: 48.4
(Don't know): 4.9

17.a) It is said that many people manage to avoid paying their full income tax. Do you think that they should **not** be allowed to get away with it - or do you think good luck to them if they can get away with it?

Should not be allowed: 74.7 b)
Good luck if they can get away with it: 24.5 Q.18
Don't know: 0.6

IF 'SHOULD NOT BE ALLOWED' (CODE 1 AT a)

b) If you knew of somebody who wasn't paying their full income tax, would you be inclined to report him or her?

Yes: 9.5
No: 60.9
Other answer (SPECIFY): 2.0
Don't know: 2.0

ASK ALL

18. Thinking of income levels generally in Britain today, would you say that the **gap** between those with high incomes and those with low incomes is ... READ OUT ...

... too large, : 78.7
about right, : 16.6
or - too small? : 2.1
Don't know : 2.3

N = 2847

- 6 -

CARD C

19. Generally, how would you describe levels of taxation in Britain today?

a) Firstly for those with high incomes? Please choose a phrase from this card. RECORD ANSWER IN COL a) BELOW

b) Next for those with middle incomes? Please choose a phrase from this card. RECORD ANSWER IN COL b) BELOW

c) And lastly for those with low incomes? Please choose a phrase from this card. RECORD ANSWER IN COL c) BELOW

	(a) High incomes	(b) Middle incomes	(c) Low incomes
Taxes **are**: Much too high	4.8	3.7	30.2
Too high	15.9	32.5	51.3
About right	37.3	56.1	14.1
Too low	32.2	4.7	1.4
Much too low	6.5	0.1	0.5
Don't know	3.2	2.9	2.3

20.a) Among which group would you place yourself ... READ OUT ...

... high income, : 3.0
middle income, : 50.0
or - low income? : 46.4
Don't know? : 0.2

CARD D

b) Which of the phrases on this card would you say comes closest to your feelings about your household's income these days?

Living comfortably on present income : 25.3
Coping on present income : 50.2
Finding it difficult on present income : 18.2
Finding it very difficult on present income : 6.0
Other (SPECIFY) : 0.1
Don't know : 0.1

21.a) Looking back over the last year or so, would you say your household's income has ... READ OUT ...

... fallen behind prices, : 44.5
kept up with prices, : 44.2
or - gone up by more than prices? : 9.4
(Don't know) : 1.7

b) And looking forward to the year ahead, do you expect your household's income will ... READ OUT ...

... fall behind prices, : 39.2
keep up with prices, : 46.3
or - go up by more than prices? : 9.8
(Don't know) : 4.5

[N = 1381]

- 8 -

25.a) How would you describe the wages or salary you are paid for the job you do - on the low side, reasonable, or on the high side? IF 'on the low side': Very low or a bit low?

		Skip to
Very low	11.6	
A bit low	30.1	
Reasonable	53.6	
On the high side	4.5	
Don't know	0.1	

CARD F

b) Thinking of the highest and the lowest paid people at your place of work, how would you describe the gap between their pay, as far as you know? Please choose a phrase from this card.

Much too big a gap	15.2
Too big	25.4
About right	45.6
Too small	3.3
Much too small a gap	0.5
Other	0.2
Don't know	9.2

26.a) If you stay in this job would you expect your wages or salary over the coming year to ... READ OUT ...

... rise by more than the cost of living,	18.4
rise by the same as the cost of living,	51.8
rise by less than the cost of living,	19.0
or - not to rise at all?	7.8
(Will not stay in job)	1.3
(Don't know)	1.6

b) Over the coming year do you expect your workplace will be ... READ OUT ...

... increasing its number of employees,	23.4
reducing its number of employees,	21.9
or - will the number of employees stay about the same?	52.0
Other answer (SPECIFY)	0.4
Don't know	1.2

IF RESPONDENT IS MAN, ASK Q.27
IF RESPONDENT IS WOMAN, SKIP TO Q.29   [N = 729]

27. Where you work, are there any women doing the same sort of work as you?

Yes	32.4
No	65.6
Works alone	0.1
No-one else doing same job	1.4

[N = 2847]

- 7 -

CARD E

22. Which of these descriptions applies to what you were doing last week, that is, in the seven days ending last Sunday? Any others? CODE ALL THAT APPLY IN COLUMN I
IF ONLY ONE CODE AT I, TRANSFER IT TO COLUMN II
IF MORE THAN ONE AT I, TRANSFER HIGHEST ON LIST TO II

	COL I	COL II ECONOMIC POSITION	Skip to
In full-time education (not paid for by employer, including on vacation)		1.9	Q.57
On government training/employment scheme (e.g. Community Programme, Youth Training Scheme, etc)		0.4	Q.48
In paid work (or away temporarily) for at least 10 hours in the week		55.3	Q.23
Waiting to take up paid work already accepted		0.5	Q.48
Unemployed and registered at a benefit office		5.1	
Unemployed, not registered, but actively looking for a job		0.8	Q.49
Unemployed, wanting a job (of at least 10 hrs per week), but not actively looking for a job		0.9	
Permanently sick or disabled		2.8	Q.57
Wholly retired from work		15.5	Q.52
Looking after the home		16.5	Q.53
Doing something else (SPECIFY)		0.2	Q.57

FOLLOW SKIP INSTRUCTIONS TO GO
TO APPROPRIATE QUESTIONS

23. IF IN PAID WORK OR AWAY TEMPORARILY (CODE 03 AT Q.22)
In your (main) job are you ... READ OUT ...

		Skip to
... an employee,	87.7	Q.24
or self-employed?	12.3	Q.42

[N = 1576]

24. ALL EMPLOYEES (CODE 1 AT Q.23) ASK Qs.24-41   [N = 1381]
How many hours a week do you normally work in your (main) job?   MEDIAN [39] HOURS

(IF RESPONDENT CANNOT ANSWER, ASK ABOUT LAST WEEK)

AND CODE:		
10-15 hours a week	6.5	
16-23 hours a week	7.3	
24-29 hours a week	3.9	
30 or more hours a week	81.4	
Don't know	0.1	

- 9 -

28.a) [N = 729]

IF MALE EMPLOYEE

Do you think of your work as ... READ OUT ...

		Skip to
... mainly men's work,	46.5	b)
mainly women's work,	0.6	
or - work that either men or women do?	53.0	Q.31
Other (SPECIFY)	-	
(Don't know)	-	

IF MAINLY MEN'S WORK (CODE 1 AT a)

b) Do you think that women could do the same sort of work as you?

Yes	26.7	c)
No	19.0	d)
Don't know	0.8	c)

IF YES OR DON'T KNOW AT b)

c) Do you think that women would be willing to do the same sort of work as you?

Yes	13.8	
No	12.2	d)
Don't know	1.1	

IF MAINLY MEN'S WORK (CODE 1 AT a)

d) Why do you think your sort of work is mainly done by men? PROBE FULLY. RECORD VERBATIM

Women do not have physical strength	31.5
Conditions not suitable	13.4
Women would be uncomfortable/embarrassed in job	2.0
Women don't have right technical skills	2.9
Traditionally not a job for women	9.3
Shift work no good for women	4.5
Family reasons	0.1
Other answers	1.5
Don't know	0.1

GO TO Q.31

29. IF WOMAN EMPLOYEE [N = 652]

Where you work, are there any men doing the same sort of work as you?

Yes	48.6
No	49.1
Works alone	0.5
No-one else doing same job	0.6
Don't know	0.3

- 10 -

30.a) [N = 652]

IF WOMAN EMPLOYEE

Do you think of your work as ... READ OUT ...

		Skip to
... mainly women's work,	28.6	b)
mainly men's work,	1.5	
or - work that either men or women do?	69.6	Q.31
Other (SPECIFY)	-	
(Don't know)	-	

IF MAINLY WOMEN'S WORK (CODE 1 AT a)

b) Do you think that men could do the same sort of work as you?

Yes	25.4	c)
No	2.4	d)
Don't know	0.3	c)

IF YES OR DON'T KNOW AT b)

c) Do you think that men would be willing to do the same sort of work as you?

Yes	10.3	
No	14.7	d)
Don't know	0.8	

IF MAINLY WOMEN'S WORK (CODE 1 AT a)

d) Why do you think your sort of work is mainly done by women? PROBE FULLY. RECORD VERBATIM

Men don't have right personal skills	4.5
Men don't have right technical skills	1.4
Pay too low for men/part-time work	6.4
Work is boring/tedious/frustrating	2.9
The work would be embarrassing for men	1.6
Traditionally a women's job	15.5
Traditionally not a job for men	2.4
Other answers	0.2
Don't know	0.1

31.a) ASK ALL EMPLOYEES [N = 1381]

During the last five years (that is since March 1982) have you been unemployed and seeking work for any period?

Yes	21.5	b)
No	78.5	Q.32

IF YES

b) For how many months in total during the last five years?

MEDIAN [0][6] MONTHS OR [ ] YEARS

- 12 -

35.a) | N = 1381 |
ASK ALL EMPLOYEES

In the last two years, have you been on any courses or had other formal training, which was part of your work or helpful to your work?

INTERVIEWER: ANY TRAINING WHICH IS RELATED TO RESPONDENT'S PAST, PRESENT, OR FUTURE WORK MAY BE COUNTED, BUT DO NOT INCLUDE LEISURE COURSES OR HOBBIES WHICH ARE NOT JOB-RELATED

	Skip to
Yes, had training related to work 39.8	b)
No, had none 60.1	Q.36
Don't know -	

IF YES AT a)
b) In all, about how many full days have you spent in this kind of training over the last two years?

PROBE FOR TOTAL TIME SPENT IN JOB-RELATED TRAINING IN PAST OR PRESENT JOB; WRITE IN AS APPROPRIATE.

IF LESS THAN ½ DAY, WRITE IN "000"

DAYS [0] [1] [0]
OR
WEEKS [ ]
OR
MONTHS [ ]

36.a) ASK ALL EMPLOYEES

Over the next two years, would you like to have any (more) courses or formal training for your work, or are you not that bothered?

	Skip to
Yes, would like to 48.6	
No, not that bothered 48.3	
Don't know/depends 2.6	

b) And apart from what you would like, do you expect to have any (more) courses or training for your work in the next two years?

Yes, expect to 39.1	
No, don't expect to 55.2	
Don't know/depends 4.9	

Don't know   0.6

- 11 -

32.a) | N = 1381 |
ASK ALL EMPLOYEES

For any period during the last five years have you worked as a self-employed person as your main job?

	Skip to
Yes 4.4	b)
No 95.4	c)

IF YES, ASK b). IF NO, ASK c)
b) In total, for how many months during the last five years have you been self-employed?

MONTHS [1] [8] OR YEARS [ ]   Q.33

IF NO a)
c) How seriously in the last five years have you considered working as a self-employed person ... READ OUT ...

... very seriously,	4.7
quite seriously,	9.1
not very seriously,	13.3
or - not at all seriously?	67.9

33.a) ASK ALL EMPLOYEES

Suppose there was going to be some decision made at your place of work that changed the way you do your job. Do you think that you personally would have any say in the decision about the change, or not?

	Skip to
Yes 50.5	b)
No 45.1	c)
It depends/don't know 4.3	

IF YES AT a)
b) How much say or chance to influence the decision do you think you would have ... READ OUT ...

... a great deal,	10.6
quite a lot,	18.8
or - just a little?	19.9
(It depends/don't know)	1.1

ASK ALL EMPLOYEES
c) Do you think you should have more say in decisions affecting your work, or are you satisfied with the way things are?

Should have more say	46.1
Satisfied with the way things are	52.5
Don't know	0.8

34. CARD G

Some organisations have schemes which link pay or employee benefits to the financial performance of the organisation. As far as you know, does your organisation have any of the schemes on this card?
CODE ALL THAT APPLY IN COL a). IF NONE/DON'T KNOW, GO TO Q.35

FOR EACH MENTIONED AT a), ASK b)
b) Have you personally received any payments or benefits under the ... (ITEM MENTIONED AT a) ... in the last twelve months?

RECORD YES OR NO FOR EACH MENTIONED AT a)

	(a) Organisation has	(b) Received Yes	No
Productivity-linked bonus scheme	12.3	13.2	5.7
Annual bonus (at organisation's discretion)	16.5	13.0	3.5
Share ownership or share option scheme	12.3	5.2	6.9
Profit-sharing scheme	9.0	6.3	2.7
NONE OF THESE	55.8		
Don't know	1.8		

Q.35

- 13 -

N = 1381		Skip to

ASK ALL EMPLOYEES

37. In the last two years, have you done any of the following things in connection with your work? Please just answer yes or no.

    READ OUT AND CODE ITEMS a) TO g)

    a) Have you been asked to do anything just for <u>practice</u> in order to learn the work?

Yes	29.6	
No	70.3	
(Don't know)	-	

    b) Have you been given any special talks or lectures about the work?

Yes	41.2	
No	58.7	
(Don't know)	-	

    c) Have you been placed with more experienced people to see how the work should be done?

Yes	30.7	
No	69.2	
(Don't know)	0.1	

    d) Have you been sent round to different parts of the organisation to see what sort of work is done?

Yes	22.9	
No	77.1	
(Don't know)	0.1	

    e) Have you been asked to read things to help you learn about the work?

Yes	44.0	
No	56.0	
(Don't know)	-	

    f) Have you been taught or trained by anybody while you were actually doing the work?

Yes	35.7	
No	64.3	
(Don't know)	-	

    g) Have you been sent on any courses, to introduce you to new methods of working?

Yes	23.5	
No	76.5	
(Don't know)	-	

- 14 -

N = 1381				Skip to

Now I'd like to ask you about new technology at your workplace.

CARD H

38. a) Which, if any, of these kinds of new technology are installed at your place of work? It doesn't matter whether you work with them or not, just tell me all that you know of at your workplace. CODE ALL MENTIONED IN COL. a). IF NONE/DON'T KNOW GO TO Q.40

    FOR EACH MENTIONED AT a), ASK b)

    b) Do you yourself use, or does your own work involve the use of ... (ITEM MENTIONED AT a)?

    CODE YES OR NO FOR EACH MENTIONED AT a)

	(a) At work place	(b) Use/work with YES	NO
Computer:			
Main frame computer	32.9	13.3	18.2
Telephone link to computer at another place	27.9	9.7	16.9
Micro/mini computer	30.8	15.6	14.3
Type of computer unknown	21.9	3.7	17.5
Word processor	41.9	12.1	27.9
Electronic memory typewriter	33.3	7.1	24.4
Computer controlled plant, machinery or equipment (including robots) used for design, assembly, handling, production	19.2	6.6	11.3
Other new technology (SPECIFY)	7.7	4.6	2.9
NONE OF THESE	21.9		
Don't know	4.5		

Q.40

IF ANY NEW TECHNOLOGY AT WORKPLACE (CODES 01-95 AT Q.38a)

39. a) Would you say that the use of new technology at your place of work has affected <u>your own</u> job ...READ OUT ...

... for the better,	32.7
for the worse,	4.1
or - has it made no difference?	35.5

    b) Now thinking about all employees affected by new technology. Has new technology at your workplace generally meant ...

    READ OUT ITEMS i-iii AND CODE IN GRID

	More	Less	No Difference	(Don't Know)
i) ... that those affected by it have to work at a <u>more</u> or <u>less</u> skilled level, or has it made no difference?	29.1	4.5	33.4	5.7
ii) ... that those affected by it have <u>more</u> or less responsibility in their work, or has it made no difference?	25.1	3.6	38.4	5.6
iii) ... that those affected by it are paid <u>more</u> or less, or has it made no difference?	9.7	0.6	51.5	11.0

    c) And has the use of new technology at your workplace meant that ... READ OUT ...

... the organisation has increased the number of employees,	11.2
reduced the number of employees,	16.3
or - has it made no difference?	41.0
(Don't know)	4.3

- 15 -

		Skip to

N = 1381

ASK ALL EMPLOYEES

40.a) At your place of work are there unions, staff associations, or groups of unions recognised by the management for negotiating pay and conditions of employment?

Yes	62.5	b)
No	36.8	Q.41
Don't know	0.7	

IF YES

b) On the whole, do you think these unions or staff associations do their job well or not?

Yes	38.9
No	20.5
Don't know	3.0

ASK ALL EMPLOYEES

41.a) In general how would you describe relations between management and other employees at your workplace ... READ OUT ...

... very good,	34.3	
quite good,	47.5	
not very good,	14.0	
or - not at all good?	3.6	
Don't know	0.4	

b) And in general, would you say your workplace was ... READ OUT ...

... very well managed,	26.0	
quite well managed,	53.7	Q.57
or - not well managed?	19.6	
Don't know	0.1	

NOW GO TO SECTION 3 (p.23) - GREEN STRIPE

ALL SELF-EMPLOYED (CODE 2 AT Q.23): ASK Qs 42-47 | **N = 195**

42.a) How many hours a week do you normally work in your (main) job?

ROUND TO NEAREST HOUR

(IF RESPONDENT CANNOT ANSWER, ASK ABOUT LAST WEEK)

MEDIAN [5][0] HRS

AND CODE:

10-15 hours a week	4.3
16-23 hours a week	5.1
24-29 hours a week	1.6
30 or more hours a week	89.0

b) For about how many years have you been self-employed and doing the same sort of work as now?

PROBE FOR BEST ESTIMATE.
IF LESS THAN SIX MONTHS, CODE '00'.
IF 6 MONTHS OR MORE, ROUND UP TO NEAREST YEAR.

NO. OF YEARS
MEDIAN [0][6] YRS

c) During the last 5 years (that is since March 1982) have you been unemployed and seeking work for any period?

Yes	17.9	d)
No	81.6	Q.43

IF YES

d) For how many months in total during the last 5 years?

MEDIAN [0][9] MONTHS OR [ ] YEARS

- 16 -

		Skip to

N = 195

ASK ALL SELF-EMPLOYED

43.a) Have you, for any period in the last five years, worked as an employee as your main job rather than as self-employed?

Yes	31.8	b)
No	67.7	c)

IF YES, ASK b). IF NO, ASK c)

b) In total for how many months during the last five years have you been an employee?

MEDIAN [3][0] MONTHS OR [ ] YEARS

NOW SKIP TO Q.44

IF NO AT a)

c) How seriously in the last five years have you considered getting a job as an employee ... READ OUT ...

... very seriously,	4.8	
quite seriously,	5.8	
not very seriously,	6.4	
or - not at all seriously?	50.6	Q.44

ASK ALL SELF-EMPLOYED

44.a) Compared with a year ago, would you say (your work or) your business is doing ... READ OUT ...

... very well,	12.2
quite well,	21.0
about the same,	42.3
not very well,	10.7
or - not at all well?	1.4
(Business not in existence then)	11.9

b) And over the coming year, do you think (your work or) your business will do ... READ OUT ...

... better,	39.3
about the same,	48.1
or - worse than this year?	6.9
Other (SPECIFY) _____	0.5
(Don't know)	4.7

45.a) In your work or business, do you have any partners or other self-employed colleagues?

NOTE: DOES NOT INCLUDE EMPLOYEES

Yes, have partner(s)	47.0	b)
No	52.5	Q.46

IF HAS PARTNER(S) (CODE 1 AT a)

b) How many partners or self-employed colleagues do you work with?

MEDIAN [0][0][1]

N = 195

- 17 -

ASK ALL SELF-EMPLOYED

46a) And in your work or business do you have any employees, or not?
N.B. FAMILY MEMBERS MAY BE EMPLOYEES ONLY IF THEY RECEIVE A REGULAR WAGE OR SALARY

		Skip to
Yes, has employees	34.2	b)
No	65.2	f)

IF HAS EMPLOYEES (CODE 1 AT a)
b) How many full-time employees do you have now?
PROMPT IF NECESSARY: FULL-TIME IS 30+ HOURS PER WEEK

MEDIAN | 0 | 0 | 0 | 3 |

| CODE: Don't know: fewer than 25 | - |
| Don't know: 25 or more | - |

c) And how many part-time employees?

MEDIAN | 0 | 0 | 0 | 2 |

| CODE: Don't know: fewer than 25 | 0.5 |
| Don't know: 25 or more | - |

d) Over the coming year, do you expect to ... READ OUT ...

...take on (additional) full-time employees,	7.8
reduce the number of full-time employees,	-
or - keep about the same number as now?	21.6
(Don't know)	2.9

e) And over the coming year, do you expect to ... READ OUT ...

...take on (additional) part-time employees,	5.2
reduce the number of part-time employees,	1.9
or - keep about the same number as now?	23.5	Q.47
(Don't know)	2.4

IF NO EMPLOYEES (CODE 2 AT a)
f) Over the coming year, do you expect to take on any employees, or do you think this is unlikely?

| Expect to take on employees | 7.7 |
| Unlikely | 57.0 |

N = 195

- 18 -

ASK ALL SELF-EMPLOYED
CARD H
47a) Which, if any, of these kinds of new technology do you have or use in your work?
CODE ALL THAT APPLY

		Skip to
Computer: Main frame computer	0.9	
Micro/mini computer	1.1	
Telephone link to computer at another place	8.2	
Type of computer unknown	1.9	
Other: Word processor	10.0	b)
Electronic memory typewriter	4.2	
Computer-controlled plant, machinery, or equipment (including robots)	0.5	
Other new technology (SPECIFY)	2.5	c)
NONE OF THESE	82.4	*

IF ANY NEW TECHNOLOGY (CODES 01-95) AT a)
b) Would you say the use of new technology has affected your work ... READ OUT ...

... for the better,	13.3	
for the worse,	0.3	
or - has it made no difference?	4.0	d)

ASK ALL SELF-EMPLOYED
c) Do you think of your work as ... READ OUT ...

... mainly men's work,	36.3	
mainly women's work,	3.0	
or - work that either men or women do?	60.7	
(Don't know)	-	Q.57
	-	

IF MAINLY MEN'S OR WOMEN'S WORK (CODES 1 OR 2 AT c)
d) Why do you think your sort of work is mainly done by (men)/(women)?
PROBE FULLY. RECORD VERBATIM.

Why mainly men's work:

Women do not have physical strength	28.7
Conditions not suitable	9.0
Lack of technical skills	2.7
Traditionally not a job for women	6.9
Shift work no good for women	2.7

Why mainly women's work:

Men don't have right personal skills	1.0
Pay too low for men/part-time work	1.6
The work would be embarrassing for men	1.1
Traditionally not a job for men	1.1

NOW GO TO SECTION 3 (p.23) - GREEN STRIPE

- 19 -

N = 23

ALL ON GOVERNMENT SCHEMES OR WAITING TO TAKE UP PAID WORK (CODES 02 OR 04 AT Q.22): ASK Q.48

			Skip to
48.a) During the last five years (that is since March 1982) have you been unemployed and seeking work for any period?		Yes 87.8	b)
		No 12.2	Q.57
IF YES ASK b)			
b) For how many months in total during the last five years?	MEDIAN [1][2] MONTHS OR [__] YEARS		

NOW GO TO SECTION 3 (p.23) - GREEN STRIPE

ALL UNEMPLOYED (CODES 05, 06, 07 AT Q.22): ASK Qs49-51

N = 192

			Skip to
49.a) In total how many months in the last five years (that is, since March 1982) have you been unemployed and seeking work?	MEDIAN [2][0] MONTHS OR [__] YEARS		
b) How long has this present period of unemployment and seeking work lasted so far?	MEDIAN [1][2] MONTHS OR [__] YEARS		
c) How confident are you that you will find a job to match your qualifications ... READ OUT ...	... very confident,	13.5	
	quite confident,	26.9	
	not very confident,	26.5	
	or - not at all confident?	31.2	
d) Although it may be difficult to judge, how long from now do you think it will be before you find an acceptable job?	MEDIAN [0][6] MONTHS OR [__] YEARS		
	Don't know	39.1	
e) Have you ever considered moving to a different area - an area other than the one you live in now - to try to find work?	Yes	29.9	f)
	No	69.3	Q.50
IF YES AT e)			
f) Why did you not move to a different area? Any other reasons? PROBE FULLY. RECORD VERBATIM. (IF MOVED OUT OF THIS AREA AND HAS SINCE MOVED BACK - WRITE IN AND PROBE)	Other areas just as bad	4.0	
	Hoping/waiting/planning to move	5.3	
	Housing shortage/inflexibility of provision	7.4	
	Have already moved in past	6.7	
	Moving causes too much upheaval	6.9	
	Other answers	5.8	

- 20 -

N = 192

ASK ALL UNEMPLOYED

50a) Now thinking about the last 4 weeks, have you done any of the following? Please just answer yes or no.

READ OUT AND CODE a) to i)

Have you ...

			Skip to
a) ... had your name registered at a Jobcentre or Government Employment or Careers Office, or with Professional and Executive Recruitment?	Yes	53.6	
	No	45.6	
b) ... had your name registered at a private employment agency?	Yes	7.7	
	No	92.1	
c) ... studied situations vacant columns in newspapers or journals?	Yes	82.2	
	No	17.0	
d) ... advertised for jobs in newspapers or journals?	Yes	8.3	
	No	91.0	
And in the last 4 weeks, have you:			
e) ... answered advertisements for jobs in newspapers or journals?	Yes	30.8	
	No	69.0	
f) ... applied directly to employers?	Yes	38.8	
	No	61.0	
g) ... asked friends, relatives, colleagues or trade unions about jobs?	Yes	54.9	
	No	44.8	
And at any time in the last 4 weeks:			
h) ... were you waiting for the results of any job applications?	Yes	34.1	
	No	65.6	
i) ... did you do anything else to find work?	Yes	10.2	
	No	89.6	
(IF YES, SPECIFY)			

ALL UNEMPLOYED

			Skip to
51. Do you think that there is a real chance nowadays that you will get a job in this area, or is there no real chance nowadays?	Real chance	49.8	Q.57
	No real chance	49.5	
	Don't know	0.4	

NOW GO TO SECTION 3 (p.22) - GREEN STRIPE

- 21 -

N = 453

52.a) ALL WHOLLY RETIRED FROM WORK (CODE 09 AT Q.22): ASK Q.52

		Skip to
Do you (or does your husband/wife) receive a pension from any past employer?		
Yes	58.7	
No	40.8	c)

b) (Can I just check) are you (MEN) over 65? (WOMEN) over 60?

Yes	89.0	
No	11.0	e)

IF YES ASK c) AND d). IF NO GO TO e)

c) On the whole would you say the present state pension is on the low side, reasonable, or on the high side? IF 'On the low side': Very low or a bit low?

Very low	43.8
A bit low	29.2
Reasonable	14.2
On the high side	-
Don't know	0.9

d) Do you expect your state pension in a year's time to purchase more than it does now, less, or about the same?

More	3.7	
Less	50.9	Q.57
About the same	29.5	
Don't know	3.6	

IF NO AT b)

e) At what age did you retire from work?

MEDIAN 5 7 YEARS — Q.57

NOW GO TO SECTION 3 (p.23) - GREEN STRIPE

53.a) ALL LOOKING AFTER HOME (CODE 10 AT Q.22): ASK Qs 53-56

N = 470

Do you currently have a paid job of less than 10 hours a week?
INCLUDE THOSE TEMPORARILY AWAY FROM A PAID JOB OF LESS THAN 10 HOURS A WEEK

Yes	12.4	
No	85.6	

b) What are the main reasons you do not have a paid job (of more than 10 hours a week) outside the home? PROBE FULLY FOR MAIN REASONS AND RECORD VERBATIM

Raising children	34.3
Retired/too old	24.0
Prefer looking after home/family	21.9
No jobs available	4.8
Unsuitable for available jobs	1.5
Feel married women shouldn't work	0.7
Husband against working	3.1
Voluntary worker	1.3
Pregnant/ill health	11.4
Dependent relative	4.8
Poverty trap	3.1
Already works less than 10 hours per week	3.3
Childcare costs	0.9
Unpaid work/family business	2.4

- 22 -

N = 470

54.a) ASK ALL LOOKING AFTER THE HOME

		Skip to
Have you, during the last five years, ever had a full or part time job of 10 hours per week or more?		
Yes	29.9	b)
No	68.2	Q.55

IF YES

b) How long ago was it that you left that job?

NO. OF MONTHS AGO   OR   NO. OF YEARS AGO

MEDIAN 2 4   NOW SKIP TO Q.56

IF NO AT Q.54e)

55.a) How seriously in the past five years have you considered getting a full-time job? READ OUT ...

PROMPT, IF NECESSARY: FULL TIME IS 30 HRS+ PER WEEK

... very seriously,	2.3	
quite seriously,	5.0	Q.56
not very seriously,	5.4	
or - not at all seriously?	55.5	b)

IF NOT VERY OR NOT AT ALL SERIOUSLY, ASK b)

b) How seriously, in the past five years, have you considered getting a part-time job? ... READ OUT ...

... very seriously,	2.2
quite seriously,	5.1
not very seriously,	6.4
or - not at all seriously?	45.8

56. ASK ALL LOOKING AFTER THE HOME

Do you think you are likely to look for a paid job in the next 5 years?
IF YES: Full-time or part-time?

Yes - Full-time	7.7
Yes - Part-time	27.9
No	58.0
Other (SPECIFY) _____	1.0
Don't know	3.2

NOW GO TO SECTION 3 (p.23) - GREEN STRIPE

Section (page 23)

- 23 -

SECTION THREE

ASK ALL

CARD I

57. Here are some items of government spending. Which of them, if any, would be your highest priority for extra spending? And which next? Please read through the whole list before deciding.

ONE CODE ONLY IN EACH COL.

	1st Priority	2nd Priority
Education	24.1	31.4
Defence	1.2	2.3
Health	51.6	26.9
Housing	8.2	16.0
Public transport	0.4	0.7
Roads	1.1	2.1
Police and prisons	3.6	4.7
Social security benefits	4.4	7.2
Help for industry	4.6	6.8
Overseas aid	0.2	0.7
(NONE OF THESE)	0.2	0.3
(Don't know)	0.4	0.7

CARD J

58. Thinking now only of the government's spending on social benefits like those on the card. Which, if any, of these would be your highest priority for extra spending? And which next?

ONE CODE ONLY IN EACH COL.

	1st Priority	2nd Priority
Retirement pensions	47.2	21.0
Child benefits	9.0	14.5
Benefits for the unemployed	15.5	17.4
Benefits for disabled people	20.6	33.8
Benefits for single parents	6.0	10.4
(NONE OF THESE)	0.8	1.5
(Don't know)	0.8	1.3

59. I will read two statements. For each one please say whether you agree or disagree? Strongly or slightly?

	(a) Falsely claim	(b) Fail to claim
a) Large numbers of people these days falsely claim benefits. Agree strongly	38.9	48.1
Agree slightly	27.6	35.1
b) Large numbers of people who are eligible for benefits these days fail to claim them. Disagree slightly	13.4	7.4
Disagree strongly	11.7	3.4
(Don't know)	8.1	6.0

Section (page 24)

- 24 -

[N = 2847]

60. Opinions differ about the level of benefits for the unemployed. Which of these two statements comes closest to your own ... READ OUT ...

OR - ... benefits for the unemployed are too high and discourage people from finding jobs?

	Skip to
benefits for the unemployed are too low and cause hardship,	50.7
benefits for the unemployed are too high and discourage people from finding jobs?	29.4
Both because wages are low	6.0
Neither	0.8
Both, it varies	5.5
About right	1.2
Other answer	1.3
Don't know	5.1

CARD K

61. Suppose the government had to choose between the three options on this card. Which do you think it should choose?

Reduce taxes and spend less on health, education and social benefits	3.4
Keep taxes and spending on these services at the same level as now	42.2
Increase taxes and spend more on health, education and social benefits	50.1
(None)	2.6
(Don't know)	1.7

CARD L

62. All in all, how satisfied or dissatisfied would you say you are with the way in which the National Health Service runs nowadays? Choose a phrase from this card.

Very satisfied	6.5
Quite satisfied	33.7
Neither satisfied nor dissatisfied	20.1
Quite dissatisfied	24.1
Very dissatisfied	15.5
Don't know	0.1

CARD L AGAIN

63. From your own experience, or from what you have heard, please say how satisfied or dissatisfied you are with the way in which each of these parts of the National Health Service runs nowadays? READ OUT i-vi BELOW AND RING ONE CODE FOR EACH

	Very satisfied	Quite satisfied	Neither satisfied nor dis-satisfied	Quite dis-satisfied	Very dis-satisfied	Skip to
i) First, local doctors/ GPs?	27.2	52.1	7.7	9.1	3.5	0.4
ii) National Health Service dentists?	19.3	54.8	13.8	6.4	2.9	2.8
iii) Health visitors?	11.4	35.0	29.8	5.8	2.6	15.2
iv) District nurses?	17.1	38.2	26.9	2.6	0.7	14.3
v) Being in hospital as an inpatient?	24.0	43.2	15.5	9.7	3.6	3.9
vi) Attending hospital as an outpatient?	13.8	39.8	14.6	18.7	10.0	3.0

- 25 -

| N = 2847 | | Skip to |

64.a) Are you covered by a private health insurance scheme, that is an insurance scheme that allows you to get private medical treatment?

		Skip to
Yes	14.3	b)
No	85.6	Q.65
Don't know	0.1	

IF YES

b) Does your employer (or your husband's/wife's employer) pay the majority of the cost of membership of this scheme?

Yes	7.7
No	6.0
Don't know	0.4

ASK ALL

65.a) Do you think that the existence of private medical treatment in National Health Service hospitals is a good or bad thing for the National Health Service, or doesn't it make any difference to the NHS?

Good thing	23.1
Bad thing	44.0
No difference	28.9
Don't know	3.9

b) And do you think the existence of private medical treatment in private hospitals is a good thing or bad thing for the National Health Service, or doesn't it make any difference to the NHS?

Good thing	39.1
Bad thing	19.7
No difference	36.9
Don't know	4.0

CARD M

66. Which of the views on this card comes closest to your own views about private medical treatment in hospitals?

Private medical treatment in all hospitals should be abolished	10.0
Private medical treatment should be allowed in private hospitals, but not in National Health Service hospitals	51.1
Private medical treatment should be allowed in both private and National Health Service hospitals	36.6
(Don't know)	2.3

67.a) Now thinking of GPs and dentists.
Do you think that National Health Service GPs should or should not be free to take on private patients?

	Should	Should not	Don't know
	54.1	41.3	4.4

b) And do you think that National Health Service dentists should or should not be free to give private treatment?

	Should	Should not	Don't know
	60.3	34.7	4.7

68. Now thinking of GPs and dentists.
It has been suggested that the National Health Service should be available only to those with lower incomes. This would mean that contributions and taxes could be lower and most people would then take out medical insurance or pay for health care. Do you support or oppose this idea?

Support	25.7
Oppose	68.2
(Don't know)	5.2

- 26 -

| N = 2847 | |

ASK ALL

Now a few questions on education.

CARD N

69. First, which of the groups on this card, if any, would be your highest priority for extra government spending on education, and which next?

ONE CODE ONLY IN EACH COL.

	1st Priority	2nd Priority
Nursery/pre-school children	7.6	9.1
Primary school children	15.0	17.2
Secondary school children	36.9	25.6
Less able children with special needs	28.5	25.1
Students at colleges, universities or polytechnics	9.2	19.2
NONE OF THESE	0.4	0.7
Don't know	2.2	2.9

CARD O

70. Here are a number of factors that some people think would improve education in our schools.

a) Which do you think is the most important one for children in primary schools - aged 5-11 years? Please look at the whole list before deciding. ONE CODE ONLY

b) And which do you think is the most important one for children in secondary schools - aged 11-18 years? ONE CODE ONLY

	(a) PRIMARY	(b) SECONDARY
More resources for books and equipment	20.7	13.5
Better buildings	1.9	0.7
Better pay for teachers	3.5	4.2
More involvement of parents in governing bodies	2.5	1.0
More discussion between parents and teachers	7.5	2.9
Smaller classes	28.8	9.1
More emphasis on preparation for exams	1.6	8.9
More emphasis on developing the child's skills and interests	16.3	10.3
More training and preparation for jobs	1.7	25.4
More emphasis on arts subjects	0.1	0.1
More emphasis on mathematics	1.1	2.0
More emphasis on English	2.0	1.5
Stricter discipline	10.8	18.8
NONE OF THESE	0.7	0.6
Don't know	0.8	0.7

71. Do you think that what is taught in schools should be up to ... READ OUT ...

... the local education authority to decide,	47.8
or -- should central government have the final say?	46.5
Other	0.3
Don't know	4.9

Page 27

N = 2847		Skip to

72. Some people think it is best for secondary schoolchildren to be separated into grammar and secondary modern schools according to how well they have done when they leave primary school. Others think it is best for secondary schoolchildren not to be separated in this way, and to attend comprehensive schools.

On balance, which system do you think provides the best all-round education for secondary schoolchildren ... READ OUT ...

... a system of grammar and secondary modern schools,	52.3
or - a system of comprehensive schools?	41.1
Other (SPECIFY)	0.9
(Don't know)	5.5

73.a) Generally speaking, what is your opinion about private schools in Britain? Should there be ... READ OUT ...

... more private schools,	10.6
about the same number as now,	64.7
fewer private schools,	10.9
or - no private schools at all?	10.5
Other answer (SPECIFY)	0.8
Don't know	2.3

b) If there were fewer private schools in Britain today do you think, on the whole, that state schools would ... READ OUT ...

... benefit,	19.6
suffer,	15.7
or - would it make no difference?	59.8
(Don't know)	4.7

74.a) Do you feel that opportunities for young people in Britain to go on to higher education - to a university, college or polytechnic - should be increased or reduced, or are they at about the right level now?

IF INCREASED OR REDUCED: A lot or a little?

Increased a lot	29.2
Increased a little	23.5
About right	42.0
Reduced a little	1.9
Reduced a lot	0.8
Don't know	2.5

b) When British students go to university or college they generally get grants from the local authority. Do you think they should get grants as now, or loans which would have to be paid back when they start working?

Grants	64.7
Loans	31.3
Other	0.4
Don't know	3.3

Page 28

N = 2847		Col./Code	Skip to

SECTION FOUR

Now moving on to the subject of social class in Britain.

75.a) To what extent do you think a person's social class affects his or her opportunities in Britain today ... READ OUT ...

... a great deal,	28.1
quite a lot,	38.6
not very much,	26.5
or -not at all?	4.7
Don't know	0.4
Other answer (SPECIFY)	1.4

b) Do you think social class is more or less important now in affecting a person's opportunities than it was 10 years ago, or has there been no real change?

More important now	25.6
Less important now	28.5
No change	43.4
Don't know	2.4

c) Do you think that in 10 years time social class will be more or less important than it is now in affecting a person's opportunities, or will there be no real change?

More important in 10 years time	23.7
Less important in 10 years time	24.6
No change	48.0
Don't know	3.5

CARD P

76.a) Most people see themselves as belonging to a particular social class. Please look at this card and tell me which social class you would say you belong to? RECORD ANSWER IN COL (a)

b) And which social class would you say your parents belonged to when you started at primary school? RECORD ANSWER IN COL (b)

	(a) Self	(b) Parents
Upper middle	1.5	2.3
Middle	26.0	17.7
Upper working	21.3	12.1
Working	46.0	59.1
Poor	2.9	6.8
(Don't know)	1.4	1.2

- 29 -

N = 2847

		Skip to

77.a) Do you regard yourself as belonging to any particular religion?
IF YES: Which? IF 'Christian' PROBE FOR DENOMINATION
ONE CODE ONLY

	%	Skip to
No religion	34.3	Q.78
Christian – no denomination	3.4	
Roman Catholic	10.3	
Church of England/Anglican	36.6	
United Reform Church (URC)/Congregational	0.9	
Baptist	1.7	
Methodist	4.2	
CHRISTIAN DENOMINATIONS: Presbyterian/Church of Scotland	4.5	b)
Other Christian (SPECIFY)	1.6	
Hindu	0.4	
Jew	0.8	
OTHER RELIGIONS: Islam/Muslim	0.8	
Sikh	0.1	
Buddhist	0.1	
Other non-Christian (SPECIFY)	0.3	

IF RELIGION ENTERED AT a) ASK b). OTHERS SKIP TO Q.78

b) Apart from such special occasions as weddings, funerals and baptisms, how often nowadays do you attend services or meetings connected with your religion?
PROBE AS NECESSARY

	%
Once a week or more	11.9
Less often but at least once in two weeks	2.4
Less often but at least once a month	5.8
Less often but at least twice a year	11.7
Less often but at least once a year	4.9
Less often	3.8
Never or practically never	24.4
Varies	0.4

78. INTERVIEWER: CODE FROM OBSERVATION FOR ALL RESPONDENTS

	%
White/European	96.6
Indian/East African Asian/Pakistani/Bangladeshi/Sri Lankan	1.5
Black/African/West Indian	1.1
Other (inc. Chinese)	0.6

- 30 -

N = 2847

		Skip to

ASK ALL

Now I would like to ask you some questions about racial prejudice in Britain.

79.a) First, thinking of Asians - that is, people whose families were originally from India and Pakistan - who now live in Britain. Do you think there is a lot of prejudice against them in Britain nowadays, a little, or hardly any? RECORD IN COL (a)

b) And black people - that is people whose families were originally from the West Indies or Africa - who now live in Britain. Do you think there is a lot of prejudice against them in Britain nowadays, a little, or hardly any? RECORD IN COL (b)

	(a) Asians	(b) Blacks
A lot	62.0	57.0
A little	29.5	33.3
Hardly any	6.2	7.3
Don't know	2.1	2.0

c) Do you think there is generally more racial prejudice in Britain now than there was 5 years ago, less, or about the same amount?

	%
More now	50.0
Less now	12.6
About the same	35.1
Don't know	1.9
Other answer (SPECIFY)	0.1

d) Do you think there will be more, less or about the same amount of racial prejudice in Britain in 5 years time compared with now?

	%
More in 5 years	46.5
Less	12.4
About the same	37.0
Don't know	2.9
Other answer (SPECIFY)	1.1

e) How would you describe yourself:
... READ OUT ...
... as very prejudiced against people of other races, a little prejudiced, or - not prejudiced at all?

	%
very prejudiced	4.5
a little prejudiced	34.1
or - not prejudiced at all?	60.2
Don't know	0.7
Other answer (SPECIFY)	0.3

IF 'VERY' OR 'A LITTLE' PREJUDICED

f) Against any race in particular? PROBE FOR RACES AND RECORD. IF 'BLACK' OR COLOURED MENTIONED, PROBE FOR WHETHER WEST INDIAN, ASIAN, GENERAL, ETC. RECORD VERBATIM EVERYTHING MENTIONED.

- 31A -

SECTION FIVE

N = 1437

ASK ALL

80. Now I would like to ask you about the obligations that people who have been married have if they divorce.

		Skip to

a) Consider a married couple, both aged about 45, with no children at home. They are both working at the time of the divorce.

In your opinion should the man make maintenance payments to support the wife?

Yes	14.3
No	80.7
Depends whose fault/guilty	1.7
Depends on circumstances	1.1
Depends on income	0.9
Other answer	0.3
Don't know	0.9

b) Consider a similar couple, also aged about 45 with no children at home. They are both working at the time of the divorce, but the woman's earnings are much lower than the man's.

In your opinion should the man make maintenance payments to support the wife?

Yes	48.3
No	43.5
Depends whose fault/guilty	3.1
Depends on circumstances	2.1
Depends on income	1.4
Other answer	0.1
Don't know	1.6

c) Finally, consider another couple, also aged about 45 with no children at home. The man is working at the time of the divorce, but the woman has never worked in a paid job outside the home.

In your opinion, should the man make maintenance payments to support the wife?

Yes	77.1
No	17.4
Depends whose fault/guilty	2.5
Depends on circumstances	1.5
Depends on income	0.5
Other answer	-
Don't know	1.1

81. IF INTERVIEWING IN ENGLAND OR WALES, ASK ABOUT "BRITAIN".
IF INTERVIEWING IN SCOTLAND, ASK ABOUT "SCOTLAND".

Do you think that divorce in (Britain/Scotland) should be ... READ OUT ...

... easier to obtain than it is now,	9.8
more difficult,	37.6
or - should things remain as they are?	50.1
(Don't know)	2.4

82. There is a law in Britain against sex discrimination, that is against giving unfair preference to men - or to women - in employment, pay and so on. Do you generally support or oppose the idea of a law for this purpose?

Support	75.4
Oppose	22.2
Don't know	2.3

- 32A -

N = 2847

83.a) Can I just check your own marital status? At present are you ... READ OUT ...

... married,	66.9
living as married,	3.3
separated or divorced,	4.7
widowed,	7.2
or - not married?	17.9

N = 1437

b) And are there any children under 16 years old in this household?

Yes	35.9
No	63.8

84. IF MARRIED OR LIVING AS MARRIED (CODES 1 OR 2 AT Q.83a), ASK Q.84
OTHERS GO TO Q.85 N = 953

I would like to ask about how you and your (husband/wife/partner) generally share some family jobs. Who does the household shopping: mainly the man, mainly the woman or is the task shared equally?
RECORD ANSWER IN GRID BELOW AND CONTINUE WITH ii)-ix)

ONE CODE FOR EACH ITEM

	MAINLY MAN	MAINLY WOMAN	SHARED EQUALLY	OTHER
i) ... Household shopping?	7.0	50.0	42.8	0.1
ii) ... who makes the evening meal?	5.6	76.9	17.1	0.1
iii) ... who does the evening dishes?	22.0	38.9	36.1	2.0
iv) ... who does the household cleaning?	3.6	72.0	23.1	0.6
v) ... who does the washing and ironing?	1.7	88.0	9.4	0.3
vi) ... who repairs the household equipment?	82.3	6.1	8.4	0.8
vii) who organises the household money and payment of bills?	32.0	37.8	29.9	0.3

IF CHILD(REN) AT Q.83b) ASK viii-ix). OTHERS GO TO Q.85

	MAINLY MAN	MAINLY WOMAN	SHARED EQUALLY	OTHER
viii) ...who looks after the child(ren) when they are sick?	0.8	28.7	12.7	0.7
ix) ... who teaches the child(ren) discipline?	5.4	8.0	28.8	0.7

85. ASK ALL N = 1437

(Now) I would like to ask about how you think family jobs should generally be shared between men and women. For example, who do you think should do the household shopping: mainly the man, mainly the woman, or should the task be shared equally? RECORD ANSWER IN GRID BELOW AND CONTINUE WITH ii)-ix)

ONE CODE FOR EACH ITEM

	MAINLY MAN	MAINLY WOMAN	SHARED EQUALLY	DON'T KNOW
i) ... Household shopping?	0.8	30.1	67.8	0.1
ii) ... who should make the evening meal?	0.4	52.1	44.5	0.5
iii) ...who should do the evening dishes?	10.8	16.8	70.3	0.2
iv) ... who should do the household cleaning?	0.6	44.2	53.6	0.1
v) ...who should do the washing and ironing?	0.1	69.0	29.7	0.2
vi) ...who should repair the household equipment?	72.5	1.3	24.4	0.4
vii) ...organise the household money and payment of bills?	21.7	14.9	61.2	0.4
viii) ... look after the children when they are sick?	0.4	46.5	51.4	0.1
ix) ...who should teach the children discipline?	12.1	4.6	82.2	0.2

Skip to

86. Some people think that women are generally less likely than men to be promoted at work, even when their qualifications and experience are the same. Do you think this happens
... READ OUT ...

... a lot,	44.4
a little,	37.0
or - hardly at all?	12.1
(Don't know)	6.5

87. IF CURRENTLY MARRIED/LIVING AS MARRIED (CODES 1 OR 2 AT Q.83a),
ASK Q.87. OTHERS GO TO Q.88.
CARD Q

a) How do you and your partner organise the money that comes into your household? Please choose the phrase on this card that comes closest.

I manage all the money and give my partner his/her share	8.3	b)
My partner manages all the money and gives me my share	9.6	c)
We pool all the money and each take out what we need	40.0	
We pool some of the money and keep the rest separate	8.3	
We each keep our own money separate	4.4	Q.88
Other answer (SPECIFY)	0.1	
(Don't know)	-	

IF CODE 01 AT a)

b) Does your partner ask for his/her share of the household money whenever he/she needs it, or does he/she get a regular allowance?

Asks for when needed	2.9	
Gets regular allowance	4.1	
(Mixture of both)	1.2	Q.88

PROBE FOR BEST DESCRIPTION BEFORE ACCEPTING CODE 3

IF CODE 02 AT a)

c) Do you ask for your share of the household money whenever you need it, or do you get a regular allowance?

Ask for when needed	2.4
Gets regular allowance	6.2
(Mixture of both)	0.7

PROBE FOR BEST DESCRIPTION BEFORE ACCEPTING CODE 3

ASK ALL
CARD R

Now I would like to ask you some questions about sexual relationships

88.a) If a man and a woman have sexual relations before marriage, what would your general opinion be? Please choose a phrase from this card.
RECORD IN COL (a)

b) What about a married person having sexual relations with someone other than his or her partner? Please choose a phrase from this card.
RECORD IN COL (b)

c) What about sexual relations between two adults of the same sex? Please choose a phrase from this card. RECORD IN COL (c)

	(a) BEFORE MARRIAGE	(b) EXTRA MARITAL	(c) SAME SEX
Always wrong	13.4	63.0	63.6
Mostly wrong	11.5	25.3	10.8
Sometimes wrong	21.5	8.8	7.8
Rarely wrong	7.3	0.8	2.2
Not wrong at all	42.4	0.5	10.7
Depends/varies	3.3	1.3	4.0
Don't know	0.2	0.1	0.6

89.a) Now I would like you to tell me whether, in your opinion, it is acceptable for a homosexual person ...
READ OUT EACH ITEM AND CODE FOR EACH

	Yes	No	Other answers	
... to be a teacher in a school?	43.2	50.2	Depends on person/no proselytising	3.6
			Depends on age/sex of pupils	0.2
			As long as school knows	0.4
			Other	1.7
			Don't know	0.4
... to be a teacher in a college or university?	50.9	44.4	Depends on person/no proselytising	2.5
			As long as college knows	0.1
			Other	0.2
			Don't know	1.8
... to hold a responsible position in public life?	54.5	38.9	Depends on person/no proselytising	1.5
			Depends on person/as long as do job	1.3
			As long as not an MP	0.1
			As long as not working with children	0.3
			Other	0.5
			Don't know	2.3

b) What did you understand the phrase "homosexual" to mean at this question: ... READ OUT ...

men only - that is gays	32.5
women only - that is, lesbians	0.2
or - either	66.8
Don't know	0.2

c) Do you think female homosexual couples - that is, lesbians - should be allowed to adopt a baby under the same conditions as other couples?

Yes	10.6
No	86.4
Depends on person	0.3
Other answers	0.2
Don't know	2.4

d) And do you think male homosexual couples - that is, gays - should be allowed to adopt a baby under the same conditions as other couples?

Yes	5.4
No	92.6
Depends on person	0.2
Don't know	1.5

- 36A -

N = 1437

CARD S AGAIN

Still using this card to say what comes closest to what you think about the situation ...

		Nothing wrong	Bit wrong	Wrong	Seriously wrong	Very seriously wrong	(Don't know)	Skip to
91.a)	A householder is having a repair job done by a local plumber. He is told that if he pays cash he will not be charged VAT. So he pays cash.	26.1	29.3	35.7	6.3	1.9	0.8	
b)	Might you do this if the situation came up?				Yes		67.2	
					No		26.8	
					(Don't know)		5.0	
92.a)	A man gives a £5 note for goods he is buying in a big store. By mistake, he is given change for a £10 note. He notices but keeps the change.	7.6	20.0	58.1	9.6	4.7	-	
b)	Might you do this if the situation came up?				Yes		23.6	
					No		73.2	
					(Don't know)		2.6	
93.a)	A man gives a £5 note for goods he is buying in a corner shop. By mistake, he is given change for a £10 note. He notices but keeps the change.	4.0	11.8	63.3	14.7	5.9	-	
b)	Might you do this if the situation came up?				Yes		10.2	
					No		87.5	
					(Don't know)		1.0	
94.a)	In making an insurance claim, a man whose home has been burgled exaggerates the value of what was stolen by £100.	9.1	24.3	52.6	10.4	3.3	0.2	
b)	Might you do this if the situation came up?				Yes		26.5	
					No		68.7	
					(Don't know)		4.2	

- 35A -

SECTION SIX

N = 1437

CARD S

90.a) I am now going to read out some situations that might come up. As I read out each one, please say which of the phrases on this card comes closest to what you think of the situation.

READ OUT AND CODE a) TO i)

		Nothing wrong	Bit wrong	Wrong	Seriously wrong	Very seriously wrong	(Don't know)	Skip to
a)	A company employee exaggerates his claims for travel expenses over a period and makes £50.	5.2	20.3	51.7	14.7	7.8	0.2	
b)	A company employee exaggerates his claims for travel expenses over a period and makes £200.	1.6	6.7	38.0	35.9	17.3	0.2	
c)	A local plumber does some of his business for cash and does not declare it for tax. Over a period he avoids paying £500 to the Inland Revenue.	5.0	16.6	46.2	21.7	9.9	0.4	
d)	A milkman slightly over-charges customers over a period and makes £200.	0.2	3.9	38.5	36.7	20.5	0.1	
e)	A shop assistant sometimes rings up less on the till than the customer pays. He keeps the difference and over a period makes £200.	0.6	3.1	36.5	38.7	20.7	0.1	
f)	A man selling a piece of old furniture conceals the fact that it has woodworm. The price he can get increases by about £50.	3.5	11.1	49.2	26.2	9.8	0.2	
g)	A large firm of car dealers conceals the fact that a used car was in a serious accident. The price they can get increases by about £500.	0.4	1.4	14.1	29.9	54.1	0.1	
h)	In making an insurance claim, a man whose home has been flooded exaggerates the value of what was damaged by £500.	4.8	14.7	45.4	24.9	10.0	0.2	
i)	A man selling his car conceals the fact that it was in a serious accident. The price he can get increases by about £500.	1.7	2.2	19.4	30.0	46.5	0.1	

Left column

- 37A -

| N = 1437 | | Skip to |

95.a) Now, suppose you are alone in an empty street, no-one is likely to come by and see you. There is a £5 note lying on the pavement. Would you ... READ OUT ...

... leave it there,	1.4
pick it up and hand it in at the police station,	26.7
or - pick it up and pocket it?	68.6
Don't know	2.6

b) Suppose it was a £20 note lying there. What would you do? ... READ OUT ...

... leave it there,	0.7
pick it up and hand it in at the police station,	47.6
or - pick it up and pocket it?	48.1
Don't know	2.9

c) Suppose it was £100 in notes lying there. What would you do? ... READ OUT ...

... leave it there,	0.7
pick it up and hand it in at the police station,	75.2
or - pick it up and pocket it?	21.3
Don't know	2.4

Right column

- 38A -

SECTION SEVEN

| N = 1437 | | Skip to |

ASK ALL
CARD T

96. Now, a few questions on housing. First, in general how satisfied or dissatisfied are you with your own (house/flat?) Choose a phrase from the card.

Very satisfied	38.2
Quite satisfied	46.9
Neither satisfied nor dissatisfied	5.8
Quite dissatisfied	4.8
Very dissatisfied	4.2

97.a) How about the area you live in? Taking everything into account, would you say this area has got better, worse or remained about the same as a place to live during the last two years? RECORD IN COL a) BELOW

b) And what do you think will happen during the next two years: will this area get better, worse or remain about the same as a place to live? RECORD IN COL b)

	(a) Last 2 years	(b) Next 2 years
Better	9.8	12.1
Worse	22.4	18.0
About the same	64.2	67.9
Don't know	3.5	2.0

98. Does your household own or rent this accommodation? PROBE AS NECESSARY TO CLASSIFY

ONE CODE ONLY | N = 2847 |

		Skip to
OWN: Own leasehold or freehold outright	28.2	⎫ Q.102
Buying leasehold or freehold on mortgage	40.0	⎭
RENTED FROM: Local authority (inc. GLC)	22.5	Q.99
New Town Development Corporation	0.2	
Housing Association	1.1	
Property company	0.6	
Employer	2.0	⎫ Q.100
Other organisation	0.9	
Relative	0.3	
Other individual	3.9	
Don't know	0.1	⎭

99. IF ACCOMMODATION CURRENTLY RENTED FROM LOCAL AUTHORITY OR NEW TOWN DEVELOPMENT CORPORATION (CODES 03 OR 04 AT Q.98)
Is it likely or unlikely that you - or the person responsible for paying the rent - will buy this accommodation at some time in the future?

IF LIKELY OR UNLIKELY: Very or quite?

Very likely	1.8
Quite likely	1.9
Quite unlikely	1.7
Very unlikely	16.2
Not allowed to buy	0.6
Don't know	0.5

[N = 2847] – 40A –

104. And how long have you lived in your present home?
PROBE AS NECESSARY

	Skip to
Less than 1 year	9.4
1 year, less than 2 years	6.8
2 years, less than 5 years	19.4
5 years, less than 10 years	18.6
10 years, less than 20 years	22.8
20 years or more	22.8

105. May I check, is your home part of a housing estate? (SCOTLAND: or scheme)?
NOTE: MAY BE PUBLIC OR PRIVATE, BUT IT IS THE RESPONDENT'S VIEW WE WANT
[N = 1437]

Yes, part of estate	47.9
No	51.1

106(a) Thinking now just of council estates (SCOTLAND: or housing schemes.) What do you think are the good things about living on a council estate? (SCOTLAND: or housing scheme?) PROBE FULLY. RECORD VERBATIM.

Provide housing for people who need it	9.6
Good/quick/free repairs/maintenance	12.8
Cheap(ish) rents	7.8
Have (good) facilities/amenities	8.9
Friendly/neighbourly	26.0
Attractive	3.3
Quiet/peaceful	1.4
Estates have got worse	0.8
Nothing good	29.3
Other answers	6.5
Don't know	15.4

b) And what do you think are the bad things about living on a council estate? (SCOTLAND: or housing scheme?) PROBE FULLY. RECORD VERBATIM.

Neglected by tenants	16.5
Neglected by council/caretakers	7.9
Neglected by others	8.7
Get a bad name, reputation	9.3
Attacks on people	3.6
Attacks on property	6.0
Vandalism	19.6
Crime	2.9
Rowdiness/hooliganism	28.6
Racial tension/violence	0.3
Poorly designed/unattractive	12.1
Impersonal/unfriendly/isolated	2.7
No choice of type of property	2.4
Overcrowding	7.3
Lack of privacy	5.5
Lacking specific facilities/amenities	5.8
Estates have got worse	0.6
Nothing bad	11.3
Other answers	7.5
Don't know	9.4

[N = 1437] – 39A –

100.a) IF ACCOMMODATION CURRENTLY RENTED FROM ANY LANDLORD (CODES 03-10 at Q.98)
How would you describe the rent – not including rates – for this accommodation? Would you say it was ... READ OUT...

	Skip to
... on the high side,	16.3
reasonable,	13.7
or – on the low side?	1.7

b) If you had a free choice would you choose to rent accommodation, or would you choose to buy?

Would choose to rent	8.2
Would choose to buy	23.1
Don't know	1.0

c) And apart from what you would like, do you expect to buy a house or a flat in the next two years, or not?

Yes – expect to buy	5.7
No – do not expect to buy	25.7
Don't know	1.0

INCLUDES BUYING PRESENT ACCOMMODATION

101. IF ACCOMMODATION CURRENTLY RENTED FROM ANY LANDLORD (CODES 03 – 10 AT Q.98)
CARD T AGAIN
In general, how satisfied are you with the standard of repairs and maintenance your landlord provides? Please choose a phrase from this card.

	Skip to
Very satisfied	4.1
Quite satisfied	10.9
Neither satisfied nor dissatisfied	3.3
Quite dissatisfied	7.0
Very dissatisfied	6.7 → Q.103

102. IF CURRENTLY OWNS ACCOMMODATION (CODES 01 OR 02 AT Q.98) [N = 2847]
Did you or the person responsible for the mortgage buy your present home from the local authority as a tenant? 'LOCAL AUTHORITY' INCLUDES GLC AND NEW TOWN DEVELOPMENT CORPORATIONS.

Yes	7.8
No	60.1

103. ASK ALL
CODE FROM OBSERVATION AND CHECK WITH RESPONDENT
Would I be right in describing this accommodation as a –

Detached house or bungalow	21.9
Semi-detached house or bungalow	37.4
Terraced house	26.0
Self-contained, purpose-built flat/maisonette (inc. in tenement block)	10.4
Self-contained converted flat/maisonette	2.8
Room(s) – not self-contained	0.5
Other (SPECIFY) _____	0.7

- 41A -
SECTION EIGHT

N = 1437

107. ASK ALL

Now I'd like to ask you about the disease called AIDS. I'm going to read out a list of different kinds of people in Britain.

CARD V

Please choose a phrase from this card to tell me how much at risk you think each of these groups is from AIDS ...

READ OUT AND CODE ITEMS a)-h)

	Greatly at risk	Quite a lot at risk	Not very much at risk	Not at all at risk	(Don't know)
a) ... People who have sex with many different partners of the opposite sex.	70.9	24.4	3.4	0.2	0.8
b) ... Married couples who have sex only with each other.	0.1	0.1	15.5	83.3	0.7
c) ... Married couples who occasionally have sex with someone other than their regular partner.	12.3	52.3	32.7	1.2	1.1
d) ... People who have a blood transfusion.	11.5	23.8	48.6	13.5	2.3
e) ... Doctors and nurses who treat people who have AIDS.	4.8	17.9	44.9	29.7	2.4
f) ... Male homosexuals - that is, gays.	87.0	10.5	1.4	-	0.8
g) ... Female homosexuals - that is, lesbians.	43.2	17.0	17.4	14.5	7.7
h) ... People who inject themselves with drugs using shared needles.	92.7	6.4	0.2	-	0.4

108. CARD W

Please look at this card and tell me whether ...

READ OUT a)-c) BELOW AND CODE FOR EACH

	Definitely should	Probably should	Probably should not	Definitely should not	(Don't know)
a) ... employers should or should not have the legal right to dismiss people who have AIDS?	12.9	24.7	29.0	28.0	5.0
b) ... doctors and nurses should or should not have the legal right to refuse to treat people who have AIDS?	10.5	20.4	26.2	40.6	2.2
c) ... schools should or should not have the legal right to expel children who have AIDS?	8.1	16.1	30.1	40.2	5.3

109.

I am going to read out two statements. For each one, please say whether you agree or disagree.

	Sympathy	Research
a) People who have AIDS get much less sympathy from society then they ought to get.' Do you agree or disagree? Strongly or a little?		
b) 'More money should be spent trying to find a cure for AIDS, even if it means that research into other serious diseases is delayed.' Do you agree or disagree? Strongly or a little?		
Strongly agree	24.9	31.6
Agree a little	35.3	25.6
Disagree a little	21.4	20.4
Strongly disagree	12.0	17.8
(Don't know)	5.7	4.2

- 42 -
SECTION NINE

N = 2847

900. ASK ALL

Finally, a few questions about you and your household. Including yourself, how many people live here regularly as members of this household? INTERVIEWER: CHECK INTERVIEWER MANUAL FOR DEFINITION OF HOUSEHOLD IF NECESSARY.

Median | 0 3

901.

Now I'd like to ask for a few details about each person in your household. Starting with yourself, what was your age last birthday? WORK DOWN COLUMNS OF GRID FOR EACH HOUSEHOLD MEMBER.

Respondent

a) Sex:　　Male 47.0　　Female 53.0

b) Age last birthday:

c) Relationship to respondent:
Spouse/partner
Son/daughter
Parent/parent-in-law
Other relative
Not related

d) HOUSEHOLD MEMBERS WITH LEGAL RESPONSIBILITY FOR ACCOMMODATION (INC. JOINT AND SHARED)
Sole 25.5
Shared 53.1

* CHECK THAT NUMBER OF PEOPLE IN GRID EQUALS NUMBER GIVEN AT Q.900

902. ASK ALL

Apart from people you've just mentioned who live in your household, have you had any (other) children, including stepchildren, who grew up in your household?

NB: INCLUDES CHILDREN NO LONGER LIVING

Yes 37.3　　No 62.5

903.a) ASK ALL

Have you ever attended a private primary or secondary school in the United Kingdom? 'PRIVATE' INCLUDES PUBLIC AND DIRECT GRANT SCHOOLS, BUT EXCLUDES NURSERY SCHOOLS AND VOLUNTARY-AIDED SCHOOLS. CODE YES OR NO IN COL a) BELOW

IF MARRIED OR LIVING AS MARRIED ASK b). OTHERS GO TO c)
b) And has your(husband/wife/partner) ever attended a private primary or secondary school in the United Kingdom? CODE YES OR NO IN COL b) BELOW

IF SON OR DAUGHTER OVER 5 YRS IN HH. ASK c). OTHERS GO TO Q.904
c) And(have any of your children/has your child) ever attended a private primary or secondary school in the United Kingdom? CODE YES OR NO IN COL c)

	Self (a)	Partner (b)	Children (c)
Yes	13.0	7.8	4.1
No	86.6	61.7	34.7
Don't know	0.1	0.3	-

N = 2847

-43 -

ASK ALL

904. How old were you when you completed your continuous full-time education?

		%	Skip to
	15 or under	46.9	
	16	24.5	
	17	8.6	
	18	6.7	
	19 or over	11.6	
	Still at school	0.1	
	Still at college, polytechnic, or university	1.3	
Other answer (SPECIFY) ______		0.1	

ASK ALL
CARD X1

905.a) Have you passed any exams or got any of the qualifications on this card?

	Yes	58.0	b)
	No, none	41.8	Q.906

IF YES (CODE 1 AT a)
b) Which ones? Any others?
CODE ALL THAT APPLY

CSE Grades 2-5	13.1	
CSE Grade 1 / GCE 'O' level / School certificate / Scottish (SCE) Ordinary	37.8	
GCE 'A' level/'S' level / Higher certificate / Matriculation / Scottish (SCE) Higher	16.6	
Overseas School Leaving Exam/Certificate	1.1	
Recognised trade apprenticeship completed	6.1	
RSA/other clerical, commercial qualification	8.1	
City & Guilds Certificate - Craft/Intermediate/Ordinary/Part I	6.5	
City & Guilds Certificate - Advanced/Final/Part II or Part III	3.8	
City & Guilds Certificate - Full technological	1.7	
BEC/TEC General/Ordinary National Certificate (ONC) or Diploma (OND)	3.5	
BEC/TEC Higher/Higher National Certificate (HNC) or Diploma (HND)	2.7	
Teachers training qualification	3.6	
Nursing qualification	2.9	
Other technical or business qualification/certificate	6.0	
University or CNAA degree or diploma	7.9	
Other (SPECIFY) ______	0.7	

IS THIS A SINGLE PERSON HOUSEHOLD: Yes → SKIP TO Q.907
No → ASK a)

906.a) Who is the person mainly responsible for general domestic duties in this household?

Respondent mainly	37.8
Someone else mainly (SPECIFY RELATIONSHIP TO RESP.) ______	37.4
Duties shared equally (SPECIFY BY WHOM) ______	

IS THERE A CHILD UNDER 16 IN THE HOUSEHOLD? Yes → ASK b)
No → SKIP TO Q.907

b) Who is the person mainly responsible for the general care of the child(ren) here?

Respondent mainly	15.0
Someone else mainly (SPECIFY RELATIONSHIP TO RESP.) ______	13.4
Duties shared equally (SPECIFY BY WHOM) ______	5.9

N = 2847

- 44 -

REFER TO ECONOMIC POSITION OF RESPONDENT (Q.22) PAGE 7.
IF:

- IF PAID WORK (CODE 03) ASK a) TO h) ABOUT PRESENT MAIN JOB
- WAITING TO TAKE UP JOB OFFERED (CODE 04) ASK a) TO h) ABOUT FUTURE JOB
- ON GOV'T SCHEME (CODE 02), UNEMPLOYED (CODES 05, 06 OR 07) OR SICK/DISABLED (CODE 08) OR LOOKING AFTER HOME (CODE 10) OR SOMETHING ELSE (CODE 11) ASK a) TO h) ABOUT LAST JOB
- NEVER HAD A JOB, WRITE IN AT a), THEN GO TO Q.908
- OTHERS GO TO Q.908

Now I want to ask you about your (present/future/last) job.
CHANGE TENSES FOR (BRACKETED) WORDS AS APPROPRIATE

907.a) What (is) your job? PROBE AS NECESSARY:
What (is) the name or title of the job? ______

b) What kind of work (do) you do most of the time? IF RELEVANT: What materials/machinery (do) you use? ______

c) What training or qualifications do you have that (are) needed for that job? ______

d) (Do) you supervise or (are) you responsible for the work of any other people? IF YES: How many?
Yes: WRITE IN NO.: [ ][ ][ ][ ]
No: RING: 0000

e) Can I just check: (are) you ... READ OUT ...

			Skip to
	... an employee,	85.2	f)
	or - self-employed?	9.1	g)

IF EMPLOYEE (CODE 1)
CARD X2

f) Which of the types of organisation on this card (do) you work for?
PRIORITY CODE

Private firm or company	54.1
Nationalised industry/public corporation	6.2
Local Authority/Local Education Authority	11.8
Health Authority/hospital	5.4
Central Government/Civil Service	4.4
Charity or trust	0.9
Other (SPECIFY) ______	2.3

ASK ALL

g) What (does) your employer (IF SELF-EMPLOYED: you) make or do at the place where you usually (work)? IF FARM, GIVE NO. OF ACRES ______

h) Including yourself, how many people (are) employed at the place you usually (work) from?
IF SELF-EMPLOYED: (Do) you have any employees?
IF YES: How many?

(No employees)	5.2
Under 10	17.8
10-24	12.9
25-99	19.4
100-499	21.3
500 or more	15.7
Don't know	1.1

- 46 -

N = 2847

REFER TO ECONOMIC POSITION OF RESPONDENT'S SPOUSE/PARTNER (Q.909)

IF:
- SPOUSE IS IN PAID WORK (CODE 03) - ASK a) TO i) ABOUT PRESENT MAIN JOB
- SPOUSE IS WAITING TO TAKE UP JOB OFFERED (CODE 04) - ASK a) TO i) ABOUT FUTURE JOB
- SPOUSE IS UNEMPLOYED (CODES 05, 06 OR 07), OR RETIRED (CODE 09) OR LOOKING AFTER HOME (CODE 10), OR DOING SOMETHING ELSE (CODES 01-02, 08,11), ASK a) TO i) ABOUT LAST JOB

Now I want to ask you about your (husband's/wife's/partner's) job.

910.a) What (is the name or title of that job?

b) What kind of work (does) he/she do most of the time? IF RELEVANT: What materials/machinery (does) he/she use?

c) What training or qualifications does he/she have that (are) needed for the job?

d) (Does) he/she supervise or (is) he/she responsible for the work of any other people?
Yes: WRITE IN: No:(RING): 0000
IF YES: How many?

e) (Is) he/she .. READ OUT...
...an employee, 55.9
or - self-employed? 8.5

IF EMPLOYEE (CODE 1)
CARD X4

f) Which of the types of organisation on this card (does) he/she work for?
PRIORITY CODE

	f)
Private firm or company	35.4
Nationalised industry/public corporation	4.3
Local Authority/Local Education Authority	8.1
Health Authority/hospital	3.5
Central Government/Civil Service	2.6
Charity or trust	0.9
OTHER (SPECIFY)	0.8

ASK ALL

g) What (does) the employer (IF SELF-EMPLOYED: he/she) make or do at the place where he/she usually (works)? IF FARM GIVE NO. OF ACRES   g)

h) Including him/herself, roughly how many people (are) employed at the place where he/she usually (works) (from? IF SELF-EMPLOYED: Do you have any employees? IF YES: How many?

(No employees)	4.3
Under 10	13.1
10-24	7.5
25-99	12.4
100-499	12.8
500 or more	11.0
Don't know	2.8

i) (Is) the job ... READ OUT ...
...full-time (30 HOURS+) 50.4
or - part-time (10-29) hours)? 12.7

- 45 -

N = 2847

ASK ALL

900.a) Are you now a member of a trade union or staff association?

		Skip to
Yes: trade union	23.6	c)
Yes: staff association	3.5	b)
No	72.6	b)

IF NO AT a)

b) Have you ever been a member of a trade union or staff association?

		Skip to
Yes: trade union	27.1	c)
Yes: staff association	3.1	c)
No	42.4	Q.909

IF NOW OR EVER A MEMBER (CODES 1 OR 2 AT a) OR b)

c) Have you ever ... READ OUT ... (RING ONE CODE FOR EACH)

	YES	NO	DON'T KNOW
... attended a union or staff association meeting?	38.2	18.8	-
... voted in a union or staff association election or meeting?	34.9	21.9	-
... put forward a proposal or motion at a union or staff association meeting?	12.9	43.9	0.1
... gone on strike?	19.7	37.2	-
... stood in a picket line?	8.3	48.6	-
... served as a lay representative such as a shop steward or branch committee member?	7.4	49.4	-

IF RESPONDENT IS MARRIED OR LIVING AS MARRIED, ASK Q.909 ABOUT HUSBAND/WIFE/PARTNER. OTHERS GO TO Q.911
CARD X3

909.a) Which of these descriptions applied to what your (husband/wife/partner) was doing last week, that is the seven days ending last Sunday? PROBE: Any others? CODE ALL THAT APPLY IN COL. I

IF ONLY ONE CODE AT I, TRANSFER IT TO COL. II
IF MORE THAN ONE AT I, TRANSFER HIGHEST ON LIST TO II

	COL. I	COL. II ECONOMIC POSITION	Skip to
In full-time education (not paid for by employer, including on vacation)		0.4	b)
On government training/employment scheme (e.g. Community Programme, Youth Training Scheme etc.)		0.1	
In paid work (or away temporarily) for at least 10 hours in the week		42.1	
Waiting to take up paid work already accepted		0.1	
Unemployed and registered at a benefit office		2.5	Q.910
Unemployed, not registered, but actively looking for a job		0.2	
Unemployed, wanting a job (of at least 10 hrs per week), but not actively looking for a job		0.4	
Permanently sick or disabled		1.9	
Wholly retired from work		8.7	b)
Looking after the home		13.8	
Doing something else (SPECIFY)		0.1	

IF CODES 01-02, OR 08-11 AT a)

b) How long ago did your (husband/wife/partner) last have a paid job (other than the government scheme you mentioned) of at least 10 hours a week?

		Skip to
Within past 12 months	1.9	Q.910
Over 1-5 years ago	7.0	
Over 5-10 years ago	5.9	
Over 10-20 years ago	4.5	
Over 20 years ago	4.6	
Never had a paid job of 10+ hours a week	1.0	Q.911

N = 2847 — - 48 -

ASK ALL
CARD X6

914.a) Which of the letters on this card represents the total income of your household from all sources, before tax?

NB: INCLUDES INCOME FROM BENEFITS, SAVINGS, ETC.

ONE CODE IN COLUMN a)

IF IN PAID WORK (ECONOMIC POSITION CODE 03 AT Q.22) ASK b). OTHERS GO TO Q.915

b) Which of the letters on this card represents your own gross or total earnings, before deduction of income tax and national insurance? ONE CODE IN COLUMN b)

	a) Household Income	b) Own Earnings
Under £2,000	1.9	3.7
£2,000-£2,999	6.3	3.9
£3,000-£3,999	7.4	3.3
£4,000-£4,999	5.5	4.7
£5,000-£5,999	5.2	4.9
£6,000-£6,999	5.8	5.6
£7,000-£7,999	4.5	4.2
£8,000-£9,999	7.9	5.4
£10,000-£11,999	8.1	5.6
£12,000-£14,999	10.5	5.3
£15,000-£17,999	7.5	2.5
£18,000-£19,999	4.4	1.1
More than £20,000	12.1	2.1
Don't know	9.5	0.5

915. **ASK ALL**
Do you (or your husband/wife/partner) own any shares quoted on the Stock Exchange, including unit trusts?

		Skip to
Yes	25.1	
No	73.9	
Don't know	0.1	

916.a) **ASK ALL**
Is there a telephone in (your part of) this accommodation?

		Skip to
Yes	87.0	c)
No	12.9	b)

IF NO ASK b)

b) Do you have easy access to a 'phone where you can receive incoming calls? IF YES, ASK: Is this a home or a work number? IF BOTH, CODE HOME ONLY

		Skip to
Yes - home	0.4	
Yes - work	0.5	c)
No	11.4	Q.917

IF YES AT a) OR b)

c) A few interviews on any survey are checked by a supervisor to make sure that people are satisfied with the way the interview was carried out. In case my supervisor needs to contact you, it would be helpful if we could have your telephone number.

RECORD HOME OR WORK NUMBER ON ADDRESS SLIP ONLY - NOT HERE

Number given	81.8
Number refused	4.7

N = 2847 — - 47 -

ASK ALL

911.a) Talking to people, we have found that a lot of people don't manage to vote. How about you? Did you manage to vote in the last general election in June 1983?

		Skip to
Yes, voted	75.7	
No	23.8	b) Q.912
Don't know	0.3	

ASK ALL WHO VOTED (CODE 1 AT a)

b) Can you remember, which party did you vote for in the 1983 general election?

DO NOT PROMPT - RECORD EXACT ANSWER GIVEN

Conservative	32.8
Labour	25.9
(SDP/Lib) Alliance	4.6
Liberal	6.7
SDP/Social Democrat	1.0
Scottish Nationalist	0.5
Plaid Cymru	0.4
Other (SPECIFY)	0.3
Refused to disclose voting	1.6
Can't remember/Don't know	1.8

912. **ASK ALL**
Do you, or does anyone else in your household, own or have the regular use of a car or a van?

Yes	74.0
No	25.6

ASK ALL
CARD X5

913. Have you or anyone in this household been in receipt of any of the benefits on this card during the last five years?
IF YES: Which ones? Any others?
CODE ALL THAT APPLY

Child benefit (family allowance)	44.3
Maternity benefit or allowance	9.7
One-parent benefit	3.5
Family income supplement	2.1
State retirement or widow's pension	23.9
State supplementary pension	2.9
Invalidity or disabled pension or benefit	6.8
Attendance/invalid care/Mobility allowance	3.1
Sickness or injury benefit	12.0
Unemployment benefit	20.9
Supplementary benefit	16.3
Rate or rent rebate or allowance	18.1
Other benefit(s) volunteered (SPECIFY)	0.2
NO, NONE	15.8

N = 2847

- 49 -

		Col./Code	Ship to

917. ASK ALL

In a year's time we may be doing a similar interview and we may wish to include you again. Would this be all right?

	Col./Code
Yes	90.3
No	9.0

918.a) INTERVIEWER TO COMPLETE ABOUT SELF-COMPLETION QUESTIONNAIRE

Was it ... ... filled in immediately after interview

ONE CODE ONLY   in interviewer's presence,

or - left behind to be filled in after interview?

Other (SPECIFY) ___

	Col./Code
... filled in immediately after interview	4.5
in interviewer's presence,	90.2
Refused	3.7
Other (SPECIFY)	-

b) Was (is) it ... ... returned by interviewer with this questionnaire,

(planned to be) collected by interviewer,

or - (planned to be) posted back by respondent?

	Col./Code
returned by interviewer with this questionnaire,	14.9
(planned to be) collected by interviewer,	61.1
or - (planned to be) posted back by respondent?	18.2
No self-completion	3.8

Time interview completed [24 hour clock] [ ][ ]

Minutes

TOTAL DURATION OF INTERVIEW   [0][6][0]   MEDIAN

Name of interviewer _____ No: [ ][ ][ ]

DATE OF INTERVIEW: DAY [ ][ ] MONTH [0][ ] YEAR [8][7]

THANK RESPONDENT FOR HIS OR HER HELP - AND PLEASE REMEMBER TO WRITE THE NAME OF THE RESPONDENT ON THE BACK OF THE ARF SLIP!   Leg.

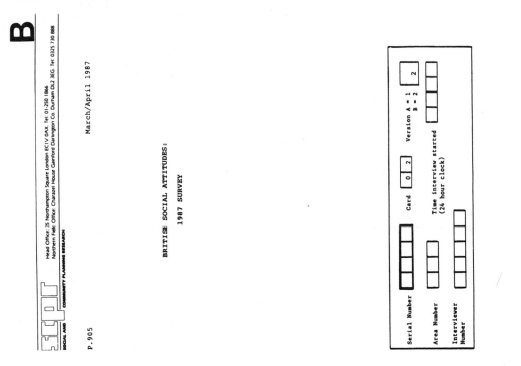

B

SOCIAL AND COMMUNITY PLANNING RESEARCH

Head Office: 35 Northampton Square London EC1V 0AX. Tel: 01-250 1866
Northern Field Office: Charazel House Gainford Darlington Co. Durham DL2 3EG. Tel: 0325 730 888

P.905

March/April 1987

BRITISH SOCIAL ATTITUDES:

1987 SURVEY

Serial Number

Card 0 2 Version A = 1
B = 2

Area Number

Interviewer
Number

Time interview started
(24 hour clock)

- 31B - SECTION FIVE

N = 1410

ASK ALL
CARD Q

80. Which of the four statements on this card comes closest to the way you vote in a general election?

ONE CODE ONLY

	%	Skip to
I vote for a Party, regardless of the candidate	58.7	
I vote for a party, only if I approve of the candidate	23.2	
I vote for a candidate, regardless of his or her party	5.1	
I do not generally vote at all	11.7	
Not yet voted	0.6	
Other answer (SPECIFY) _____	0.3	
Don't know	0.4	

81.a) How likely do you think you are to vote in the next General Election ... READ OUT ...

	%	Skip to
... very likely,	72.3	b)
quite likely,	15.5	b)
not very likely,	4.0	Q.82
or - not at all likely?	7.8	Q.82
Don't know	0.2	

IF VERY OR QUITE LIKELY

b) Suppose in the next General Election the party or candidate you prefer has no chance of winning in your constituency, do you think you would ... READ OUT ...

	%
... still vote for that party or candidate,	74.1
vote for another party or candidate,	8.9
or - not bother to vote at all?	3.5
Don't know	1.0

82.a) Which do you think is generally better for Britain ... READ OUT ...

	%	Skip to
... to have a government formed by one political party,	58.2	Q.83
or - for two or more parties to get together to form a government?	37.3	b)
Don't know	0.3	

IF TWO OR MORE PARTIES (CODE 2 AT a)

b) Which of these party groupings do you think would provide the best government for Britain ... READ OUT ...

	%
... Conservative and Alliance,	12.3
Labour and Alliance,	13.3
Conservative and Labour,	4.9
or - some other grouping?	4.3
(Don't know)	2.5

ASK ALL

83. Some people say that we should change the voting system to allow smaller political parties to get a fairer share of MPs. Others say that we should keep the voting system as it is, to produce more effective government. Which view comes closest to your own ... READ OUT ...

	%
... that we should change the voting system,	30.2
or - keep it as it is?	64.1
(Don't know)	5.3

IF ASKED, REFERS TO 'PROPORTIONAL REPRESENTATION'

- 32B -

N = 1410
CARD R

84. Please choose a phrase from this card to say how you feel about ... READ OUT ...

	Very strongly in favour	Strongly in favour	In favour	Neither in favour nor against	Against	Strongly against	Very strongly against	(DK/Can't say)
a) ..the Conservative Party?	7.2	9.9	22.4	21.1	15.1	8.8	13.0	1.7
b) ..the Labour Party?	6.1	7.3	18.0	20.6	23.2	12.2	9.9	1.9
c) ..The Social Democrat Party?	1.2	3.2	21.8	42.9	17.9	4.7	2.8	4.6
d) ..the Liberal Party?	1.9	3.7	24.0	44.0	16.3	4.0	1.7	3.5
SCOTLAND e) ..the Scottish Nationalist Party?	-	0.5	2.0	2.8	1.9	0.8	0.6	0.2
WALES f) ..Plaid Cymru?	0.2	0.1	1.1	2.4	1.5	0.3	0.4	-

ASK ALL

85.a) On the whole, would you describe the Conservative Party nowadays as extreme or moderate?

b) And the Labour Party nowadays, is it extreme or moderate?

c) And the SDP/Liberal Alliance nowadays, is it extreme or moderate?
RECORD IN APPROPRIATE COL.

	(a) Conservative	(b) Labour	(c) Alliance
Extreme	44.1	51.0	5.4
Moderate	44.5	36.9	75.2
(Neither or both)	2.7	3.2	5.5
(Don't know)	8.2	8.2	13.2

d) On the whole, would you describe the Conservative Party as good for one class, or good for all classes?

e) And the Labour Party, is it good for one class or good for all?

f) And the Alliance, is it good for one class or good for all?

	(d) Conservative	(e) Labour	(f) Alliance
Good for one class	57.0	52.6	11.0
Good for all classes	35.7	31.9	61.1
(Neither or both)	2.0	7.9	8.3
(Don't know)	4.6	6.7	18.9

g) And would you describe the Conservative Party nowadays as united or divided?

h) And the Labour Party, is it united or divided?

i) And the Alliance, is it united or divided?

	(g) Conservative	(h) Labour	(i) Alliance
United	61.7	15.7	50.0
Divided	28.8	76.0	31.1
(Neither or both)	0.9	0.9	2.8
(Don't know)	7.9	6.6	15.3

- 33B -

N = 1410

CARD S

86. Suppose your local council had to choose between the three options on this card. Which do you think it should choose?

	Skip to
Reduce rates and spend less on local services	12.5
Keep rates and spending on these local services at the same level as now	68.5
Increase rates and spend more on local services	14.5
(None)	1.7
(Don't know)	2.3

CARD T

87. Please choose a phrase from this card to say how much you agree or disagree with the following statements ...

READ OUT a)-c) BELOW AND CODE FOR EACH ...

	Agree strongly	Agree	Neither agree nor dis-agree	Dis-agree	Disagree strongly	(Don't know)
a) ... People like me have no say in what the government does.	19.5	49.8	9.5	18.1	1.4	1.2
b) ... Generally speaking, those we elect as MPs lose touch with people pretty quickly.	16.1	54.6	9.3	16.0	0.7	2.7
c) ... Parties are only interested in people's votes, not in their opinions.	15.1	49.3	9.7	22.8	0.6	1.9

CARD U

88.a) How much do you trust British governments of any party to place the needs of the nation above the interests of their own political party? Please choose a phrase from this card. RECORD IN COLUMN a) BELOW

b) And how much do you trust local councillors of any party to place the needs of their area above the interests of their own political party? Choose a phrase from the card. RECORD IN COLUMN b) BELOW

c) How much do you trust British journalists on national newspapers to pursue the truth above getting a good story? RECORD IN COLUMN c) BELOW

d) And how much do you trust British police not to bend the rules in trying to get a conviction? RECORD IN COLUMN d)

	(a) Governments	(b) Councillors	(c) Journalists	(d) Police
Just about always	4.8	3.9	2.3	10.8
Most of the time	32.0	26.7	12.8	40.7
Only some of the time	49.0	51.9	42.4	33.0
Almost never	10.8	13.4	38.8	11.4
(Don't know/Can't say)	2.8	3.5	3.1	3.5

- 34B -

SECTION SIX

N = 1410

ASK ALL

89. Now I'd like to ask a few questions about industry and jobs.

Suppose you were advising a young person who was looking for his or her first job.

CARD V

Which one of these would you say is the most important, and which next?

ONE CODE ONLY IN EACH COLUMN

	MOST IMPOR-TANT	NEXT MOST IMPOR-TANT	Skip to
Good starting pay	2.4	7.0	
A secure job for the future	50.6	20.0	
Opportunities for promotion	12.0	31.0	
Interesting work	29.9	24.7	
Good working conditions	4.1	16.4	
(Don't know)	0.6	0.7	

CARD W

90. Suppose this young person could choose between different kinds of jobs anywhere in Britain.

From what you know or have heard, which one of these kind of jobs is most likely to offer him or her ...

READ OUT AND RECORD UNDER a)-e) BELOW

a) ... good starting pay?

b) ... a secure job for the future? You may choose the same one again or a different one.

c) ... opportunities for promotion?

d) ... interesting work?

e) ... good working conditions?

ONE CODE ONLY IN EACH COLUMN

	(a) Good starting pay	(b) Secure job	(c) Promo-tion	(d) Inter-esting work	(e) Good working condi-tions
A building society	8.7	13.1	8.5	4.4	22.8
A large firm of accountants	14.6	13.0	16.6	9.9	13.0
A large engineering factory	11.0	3.9	7.2	17.6	4.4
A department store	1.1	1.2	4.6	8.7	4.1
The Civil Service	22.4	49.9	34.5	15.8	29.6
A large firm making computers	33.2	15.1	21.0	30.6	16.0
(None of these)	0.4	0.1	0.1	2.6	0.2
(Don't know)	8.2	3.3	7.1	9.9	9.2

- 36B -

| N = 1410 | | | | | Skip to |

CARD Y

93.a) Suppose a big British firm made a large profit in a particular year. Which one of these things do you think it would be most likely to do? RECORD IN COL a) BELOW

b) And which one would it be next most likely to do? RECORD IN COL b) BELOW

c) Now which one do you think should be its first priority? RECORD IN COL c) BELOW

d) And which should be its next priority? RECORD IN COL d) BELOW

CODE ONE ONLY IN EACH COLUMN	Likely to do		Should be	
	(a) Most	(b) Next	(c) First priority	(d) Next priority
Increase dividends to the shareholders	34.1	17.0	3.0	1.8
Give the employees a pay rise	4.2	3.6	22.5	11.9
Cut the prices of its products	2.5	3.3	12.5	10.5
Invest in new machinery or new technology	20.4	22.1	28.9	19.0
Improve the employees' working conditions	1.7	3.3	8.1	15.4
Research into new products	10.2	19.0	11.8	20.3
Invest in training for the employees	1.9	4.3	10.5	17.8
Give a bonus to top management	21.1	22.7	0.3	0.8
(None of these)	0.3	0.2	0.1	0.1
(Don't know)	3.0	3.8	1.7	1.7

94.a) Do you think that British industry is more efficient than it was five years ago, less efficient, or about the same? CODE UNDER a) BELOW

b) And do you think that, in five years' time, British industry will be more efficient or less efficient compared with now, or about the same? CODE UNDER b) BELOW

	(a) 5 years ago	(b) 5 years time
More	38.8	44.7
Less	18.4	8.3
About the same	37.4	39.9
(Don't know)	4.9	6.7

- 35B -

| N = 1410 | | | | Skip to |

CARD W AGAIN

91.a) Now taking everything together, which job would you be most likely to advise this young person to choose? RECORD UNDER a) BELOW

b) And which next? RECORD UNDER b) BELOW

c) And which would you be least likely to advise him or her to choose? RECORD UNDER c) BELOW

ONE CODE ONLY IN EACH COLUMN	(a) Most likely	(b) Next	(c) Least likely
A building society	10.0	16.2	3.8
A large firm of accountants	17.4	23.7	2.7
A large engineering factory	8.0	11.0	20.1
A department store	1.7	2.8	52.7
The Civil Service	30.9	19.4	7.3
A large firm making computers	24.6	17.6	4.3
(None of these)	1.1	1.3	0.8
(Don't know)	5.5	6.8	7.4

CARD X

92.a) How good do you think Britain is at selling its goods abroad, compared with other countries that compete with us? Please choose a phrase from this card. RECORD IN GRID BELOW

b) And inventing new products? RECORD IN GRID BELOW

REPEAT FOR EACH STATEMENT c)-i)

Britain is ...	better than most	worse than most	about the same	(Don't know/varies)
a) ... In selling its goods abroad?	9.4	48.0	37.5	4.7
b) ... In inventing new products?	48.8	16.0	29.9	4.7
c) ... In making well-designed products?	45.0	12.6	37.3	4.4
d) ... In investing in new machinery and technology?	9.8	48.2	35.5	5.9
e) ... In attracting the best people to manage its industries?	8.8	40.3	42.5	7.7
f) ... In attracting the best people to work in manufacturing industries?	8.3	31.6	50.4	9.0
g) ... In making goods that people really want to buy?	22.1	22.1	51.2	3.9
h) ... In keeping good relations between management and other employees?	11.3	35.0	45.9	7.1
i) ... In training employees in new skills?	15.2	35.4	41.7	7.0

- 37B -

N = 1410		Skip to
ASK ALL		
	SECTION SEVEN	
	Now I'd like to ask you a few questions about the countryside.	
	CARD Z	
95.a)	On this card are some activities people do in their leisure time. Have you taken part in any of these leisure activities in the last four weeks?	
	Yes 58.6	Q.96 b)
	No 41.1	
	IF NO AT a)	
b)	Can you remember when you last did any of these activities in the countryside? IF YES: How long ago was that?	
	PROBE FOR CORRECT CODE	
	Within past month 0.9	
	1-3 months ago 5.6	
	4-6 months ago 10.0	
	7-12 months ago 14.8	
	More than one year ago 6.4	
	No, can't remember 2.9	
	ASK ALL	
96.a)	Do you think the countryside generally is much the same as it was twenty years ago, or do you think it has changed? IF CHANGED: Has it changed a bit or a lot?	
	Much the same 20.3	Q.97
	Changed a bit 21.4	b)
	Changed a lot 55.2	
	(Don't know) 2.7	Q.97
	IF CHANGED A BIT OR A LOT (CODES 2 OR 3 AT a)	
b)	Do you think the countryside generally has changed for the better or worse?	
	Better 12.2	
	Worse 56.2	
	(Better in some ways/worse in others) 7.9	
	Don't know 0.2	

(INTERVIEWER REFERENCE ONLY)

> **CARD Z**   Q.95a,b
>
> In the last four weeks have you ...
>
> ... been for a drive, outing or picnic in the countryside
>
> ... been for a long walk, ramble or hike (of more than 2 miles) in the countryside
>
> ... visited any historic or stately homes, gardens, zoos or wildlife parks in the countryside
>
> ... gone fishing, horse riding, shooting or hunting in the countryside
>
> .... visited seacoast or cliffs

N = 1410		Skip to
ASK ALL		
97.	Are you personally concerned about things that may happen to the countryside, or does it not concern you particularly? IF CONCERNED: Are you very concerned, or just a bit concerned?	
	Very concerned 44.2	
	A bit concerned 32.7	
	Does not concern me particularly 23.3	
	Don't know 0.1	

- 38B -

ASK ALL
CARD AA

98.a) Which, if any, of the things on this card do you think is the greatest threat to the countryside; if you think none of them is a threat, please say so. RECORD ONE ONLY IN COL. a) BELOW

b) And which do you think is the next greatest threat? RECORD ONE ONLY IN COL. b)

	(a) Greatest threat	(b) Next greatest
Motorways and road building	11.1	11.0
Industrial pollution	32.4	21.0
Removal by farmers of traditional landscape, such as hedgerows, woodlands	10.6	12.0
Tourism and visitors	1.0	1.9
Litter	8.8	11.8
Urban growth and housing development	15.5	12.4
Use of chemicals and pesticides in farming	17.9	26.0
NONE OF THESE	1.1	1.6
Don't know	1.1	1.6

CARD BB

99.a) Modern farming methods have meant it now takes less land to produce the same amount of food.
On this card are some ways that land no longer needed for farming might be used. Which do you think would be the best use, and which next best? RECORD IN APPROPRIATE COLUMNS A AND B BELOW

b) And which do you think would be the worst way to use this land? RECORD ONE ONLY IN COLUMN C BELOW

	A Best	B Next best	C Worst
Pay farmers to return to methods of farming which need more land	9.6	7.0	15.5
Plant forests of pine and conifers for timber and woodlands	10.5	11.2	4.3
Plant forests of oak and beech for timber and woodlands	20.2	24.3	0.6
Provide places for countryside recreation, such as riding and golf	6.6	11.9	7.5
Create national parks and wildlife reserves	37.6	25.9	1.1
Develop new housing areas	6.8	5.0	37.5
Develop new areas for rural industries	5.1	10.1	24.9
NONE OF THESE	0.6	0.8	2.4
Don't know	2.3	2.9	5.2

- 39B -

N = 1410

		Skip to
100.a) **ASK ALL**		
Which political party's views on the environment would you say come closest to your own views?		
DO NOT PROMPT		
ONE CODE ONLY	Conservative	15.5
	Labour	11.8
	Liberal	4.0
	SDP/Social Democrat (Alliance)	3.2
	Green Party/Ecology Party	2.6
Other (SPECIFY) _____		6.0
	Don't know	0.3
	None	53.3
		2.7
b) **CARD CC**		
Are you, or anyone in your household, a member of any of the groups, clubs or organisations listed on this card?		
IF YES: Which ones? **YES - MEMBER OF:**		
	National Trust	8.7
	Royal Society for the Protection of Birds	4.5
	Other wildlife or countryside protection group	3.9
	Countryside sports/leisure organisation	6.7
	NO - NONE OF THESE	79.9
101.a) INTERVIEWER: CODE FROM OBSERVATION AND CHECK WITH RESPONDENT		
Can I just check, would you describe the place where you live as being ... **READ OUT** ...		
	... in a big city,	9.2 → b) & c)
	in the suburbs or outskirts of a city,	29.1 → c)
	in a small city or town,	36.3
	in a <u>country</u> village or town,	20.4 → c)
	or - in the countryside?	4.4 → Q.102
	Don't know	0.1
IF RESPONDENT LIVES IN CITY, SUBURBS, OR SMALL CITY/TOWN (CODES 1-3 AT a).		
b) Have you <u>ever</u> lived in the countryside, or in a country village or town - for instance, when you were a child or at some time before now?	Yes	30.6
	No	43.7
IF RESPONDENT LIVES IN CITY, SUBURBS, OR ANY CITY/VILLAGE/TOWN (CODES 1-4 AT a).		
c) About how far do you live from the nearest <u>open</u> countryside that you can visit or walk in? Please do not include city parks.		
IF NOT SURE, PROBE **FOR ESTIMATE**	Less than ½ mile (15 mins. walk)	34.9
	½, up to 1 mile (15-30 mins. walk)	15.3
	Over 1 mile, up to 3 miles	18.3
	Over 3 miles, up to 10 miles	18.2
	Over 10 miles	6.9
	Don't know	1.3

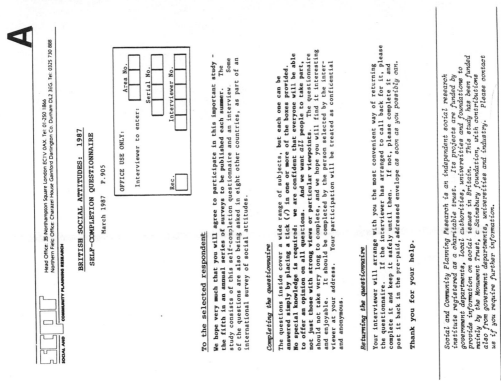

A

SOCIAL AND COMMUNITY PLANNING RESEARCH

Head Office: 35 Northampton Square London EC1V 0AX Tel: 01-250 1866
Northern Field Office: Charazel House Gainford Darlington Co. Durham DL2 3EG Tel: 0325 730 888

BRITISH SOCIAL ATTITUDES: 1987

SELF-COMPLETION QUESTIONNAIRE

March 1987   P.905

OFFICE USE ONLY:

Interviewer to enter:

Area No.

Serial No.

Interviewer No.

Rec.

To the selected respondent

We hope very much that you will agree to participate in this important study -
the fifth in an annual series of surveys to be published each summer.   The
study consists of this self-completion questionnaire and an interview.   Some
of the questions are also being asked in eight other countries, as part of an
international survey of social attitudes.

Completing the questionnaire

The questions inside cover a wide range of subjects, but each one can be
answered simply by placing a tick (✓) in one or more of the boxes provided.
No special knowledge is required: we are confident that everyone will be able
to offer an opinion on all questions.   And we want *all* people to take part,
not just those with strong views or particular viewpoints.   The questionnaire
should not take very long to complete, and we hope you will find it interesting
and enjoyable.   It should be completed by the person selected by the interviewer at your address.   Your participation will be treated as confidential
and anonymous.

Returning the questionnaire

Your interviewer will arrange with you the most convenient way of returning
the questionnaire.   If the interviewer has arranged to call back for it, please
complete it and keep it safely until then.   If not, please complete it and
post it back in the pre-paid, addressed envelope *as soon as you possibly can.*

Thank you for your help.

*Social and Community Planning Research is an independent social research
institute registered as a charitable trust.   Its projects are funded by
government departments, local authorities, universities and foundations to
provide information on social issues in Britain.   This study has been funded
mainly by the Monument Trust, c Sainsbury foundation, with contributions
also from government departments, universities and industry.   Please contact
us if you require further information.*

N = 1281		- 1 -			OFFICE USE ONLY

1. From what you know or have heard, please tick a box for *each* of the items below to show whether you think the National Health Service in your area is, on the whole, satisfactory or in need of improvement.

PLEASE TICK ONE BOX ON EACH LINE

	In need of a lot of improvement	In need of some improvement	Satis- factory	Very good	Don't know
a. GPs' appointment systems	11.3	35.6	40.2	10.5	0.9
b. Amount of time GP gives to each patient	6.9	25.8	51.9	13.7	0.5
c. Being able to choose which GP to see	8.0	20.5	50.2	19.6	0.5
d. Quality of medical treatment by GPs	5.9	20.2	49.5	22.6	0.5
e. Hospital waiting lists for non-emergency operations	43.1	43.6	9.3	0.9	1.4
f. Waiting time before getting appointments with hospital consultants	45.5	37.9	12.3	1.2	1.1
g. General condition of hospital buildings	15.0	37.9	34.4	9.7	0.8
h. Hospital casualty departments	18.1	35.9	33.6	9.1	1.4
i. Staffing level of nurses in hospitals	34.5	40.3	18.6	3.5	1.3
j. Staffing level of doctors in hospitals	26.0	44.3	23.4	3.1	1.2
k. Quality of medical treatment in hospitals	5.6	24.4	48.9	18.5	1.1
l. Quality of nursing care in hospitals	4.2	17.2	41.7	34.5	0.8

N = 1281	- 2 -

2. In the last two years, have you or a close family member ...

PLEASE TICK ONE BOX ON EACH LINE

	Yes	No
... visited an NHS GP?	95.0	4.3
... been an out-patient in an NHS hospital?	66.8	31.4
... been an in-patient in an NHS hospital?	47.1	50.6
... visited a patient in an NHS hospital?	76.3	22.4
... had any medical treatment as a <u>private</u> patient?	13.7	84.3

Please continue......

- 3 -

N = 1281

3. Please tick one box to show how much you agree or disagree with each of these statements about secondary schooling.

PLEASE TICK ONE BOX ON EACH LINE

	Agree strongly	Agree	Neither agree nor disagree	Disagree	Disagree strongly	Don't know
a) Formal exams are the best way of judging the ability of pupils.	8.6	35.9	17.0	31.2	6.5	0.1
b) On the whole, pupils are too young when they have to decide which subjects to specialise in.	11.2	51.8	15.9	18.9	1.2	0.4
c) The present law allows pupils to leave school when they are too young.	4.5	20.7	21.0	49.2	4.1	0.2
d) So much attention is given to exam results in Britain that a pupil's everyday classroom work counts for too little.	18.6	51.6	12.4	15.4	1.3	0.2

4. From what you know or have heard, please *tick one box on each line* to show how well you think state secondary schools nowadays...

PLEASE TICK ONE BOX ON EACH LINE

	Very well	Quite well	Not very well	Not at all well	Don't know
a) ... prepare young people for work?	1.8	27.4	54.4	14.9	0.6
b) ... teach young people basic skills such as reading, writing and maths?	10.4	46.2	31.4	11.0	0.2
c) ... bring out young people's natural abilities?	3.2	31.7	48.8	15.2	0.5

- 4 -

N = 1281

5. From what you know or have heard, please tick one box for each statement about state secondary schools now compared with 10 years ago.

PLEASE TICK ONE BOX ON EACH LINE

	Much better now than 10 years ago	A little better	About the same	A little worse	Much worse now 10 years ago	Don't know
a) On the whole, do you think school-leavers are better qualified or worse qualified nowadays than they were 10 years ago?	11.7	24.8	25.6	21.2	15.3	0.6
b) Do you think teachers are better paid or worse paid nowadays than they were 10 years ago?	30.5	24.9	19.4	14.3	9.4	0.8
c) And do you think classroom behaviour is better or worse nowadays than it was 10 years ago?	0.3	1.9	10.4	26.8	59.3	0.5

	Much more now than 10 years ago	A little more	About the same	A little less	Much less than 10 years ago	Don't know
d) Do you think parents have more respect or less respect for teachers nowadays than they did 10 years ago?	1.3	3.9	22.8	41.4	29.9	0.2
e) And do you think pupils have more respect or less respect for teachers nowadays than they did 10 years ago?	0.3	1.9	9.5	31.6	56.0	0.2
f) Do you think teachers are more dedicated to their jobs or less dedicated nowadays than they were 10 years ago?	1.4	4.3	33.5	35.9	24.1	0.4
g) And, on the whole, do you think the job of a state secondary school-teacher is more difficult or less difficult nowadays than it was 10 years ago?	32.2	29.9	15.7	10.4	11.2	0.2

OFFICE USE ONLY

| N = 1281 |

- 5 -

6. There has been a lot of debate among teachers about how British schools should cater for children whose parents come from other countries and cultures. Do you think in general that schools with many such children should ...

PLEASE TICK ONE BOX ON EACH LINE

	YES	NO	Don't know
... provide them with special classes in English if they require them?	80.2	18.8	0.2
... provide them with separate religious instruction if their parents request it?	36.9	62.1	0.2
... allow those for whom it is important to wear their traditional dress at school?	44.9	54.1	0.2
... allow them to study their mother tongue in school hours?	17.0	82.2	0.2
... teach them about the history of their parents' country of origin and its culture?	40.2	58.3	0.2
... teach all children about the history and culture of these countries?	73.7	25.1	0.2

7. Please tick one box for each statement to show how much you agree or disagree with it.

PLEASE TICK ONE BOX ON EACH LINE

	Agree strongly	Agree	Neither agree nor disagree	Dis-agree	Disagree strongly	Don't know
A. Social workers should put the child's interests first even if it means taking a child away from its natural parents.	28.4	50.1	12.7	6.5	1.3	0.2
B. Social workers have too much power to interfere with people's lives.	7.8	23.7	39.3	25.8	2.7	0.1
C. The welfare state makes people nowadays less willing to look after themselves.	12.0	40.3	18.6	24.1	4.4	-
D. People receiving social security are made to feel like second class citizens.	15.1	34.5	20.7	26.0	3.0	0.2
E. The welfare state encourages people to stop helping each other.	7.4	32.5	22.5	32.5	4.1	0.2
F. Doctors should be allowed to give contraceptive advice and supplies to young people under 16 without having to inform parents.	6.8	24.0	8.6	33.7	26.1	0.2

| N = 1281 |

- 6 -

8a) Central government provides financial support to housing in two main ways:

First, by means of allowances to low income tenants.
Second, by means of tax relief to people with mortgages.

On the whole, which of these three types of family would you say benefits **most** from central government support for housing?

PLEASE TICK ONE BOX

Families with high incomes	40.2
Families with middle incomes	20.2
Families with low incomes	36.2
No difference	0.1
Don't know	1.2

b) Which of these three views comes closest to your own on the sale of council houses and flats to tenants?

PLEASE TICK ONE BOX

Council tenants **should not** be allowed to buy their houses or flats	9.5
Council tenants **should** be allowed to buy but **only** in areas with no housing shortage	27.8
Council tenants **should generally** be allowed to buy their houses or flats	61.1
Don't know	0.5

9. Which of the following statements do you think are generally true and which false?

PLEASE TICK ONE BOX ON EACH LINE

	True	False	Don't know
Council tenants pay low rents	28.4	66.3	1.4
Councils give a poor standard of repairs and maintenance	65.0	30.7	1.6
Council estates are generally pleasant places to live	33.9	60.9	1.5

N = 1281

- 7 -

10. People in Britain often talk about the differences between the North and the South.

a) How about employment prospects generally - are they ...
PLEASE TICK ONE BOX

... better in the North,	0.8
better in the South,	84.1
or - is there no real difference?	13.7
Don't know	0.8

b) How about people wanting to set up their own businesses - are there ...
PLEASE TICK ONE BOX

... more opportunities in the North,	5.2
more opportunities in the South,	53.8
or - is there no real difference?	38.8
Don't know	1.3

c) How about young people buying their first home - do they have ...
PLEASE TICK ONE BOX

... a better chance in the North,	50.9
a better chance in the South,	20.3
or - is there no real difference?	26.8
Don't know	1.2

d) How about standards of education - are they ...
PLEASE TICK ONE BOX

... better in the North,	6.7
better in the South,	20.7
or - is there no real difference?	69.7
Don't know	1.8

e) And how about the National Health Service - is it ...
PLEASE TICK ONE BOX

... better in the North,	5.1
better in the South,	16.6
or - is there no real difference?	74.9
Don't know	2.3

OFFICE USE ONLY

N = 1281

- 8 -

11. Do you think that trade unions in this country have too much power or too little power?
PLEASE TICK ONE BOX

Far too much power	17.4
Too much power	30.2
About the right amount of power	31.9
Too little power	10.6
Far too little power	2.0
Can't choose	7.4

12. How about business and industry? Do they have too much power or too little power?
PLEASE TICK ONE BOX

Far too much power	5.7
Too much power	20.0
About the right amount of power	47.7
Too little power	10.8
Far too little power	1.2
Can't choose	13.6

13. And what about the government, does it have too much power or too little power?
PLEASE TICK ONE BOX

Far too much power	16.9
Too much power	26.7
About the right amount of power	43.9
Too little power	4.7
Far too little power	0.8
Can't choose	6.2

14. What do you think the government's role in each of these industries and services should be?
PLEASE TICK ONE BOX ON EACH LINE

	The government should			
	Own it	Control prices and profits but not own it	Neither own it nor control its prices and profits	Can't choose
A. Electricity	26.3	42.2	22.9	7.4
B. Local public transport	18.9	36.5	35.4	7.3
C. Gas	26.3	40.0	24.4	7.0
D. Banking and insurance	6.6	29.2	51.2	10.8
E. The car industry	8.1	25.0	53.7	11.2
F. The telephone system	23.1	38.5	29.2	7.8

OFFICE USE ONLY

- 9 -

| N = 1281 |

15. Here are a number of circumstances in which a women might consider an abortion. Please say whether or not you think the law should allow an abortion in each case.

PLEASE TICK ONE BOX ON EACH LINE

	Should abortion be allowed by law?		Don't know
	Yes	No	
The women decides on her own she does not wish to have the child	53.9	43.5	0.5
The couple agree they do not wish to have the child	58.7	37.9	0.6
The woman is not married and does not wish to marry the man	56.2	40.0	0.5
The couple cannot afford any more children	57.5	38.6	0.6
There is a strong chance of a defect in the baby	89.1	8.5	0.5
The woman's health is seriously endangered by the pregnancy	93.6	3.6	0.5
The woman became pregnant as a result of rape	93.3	4.2	0.7

16. Suppose a married couple want to have their own child, but cannot have one. Should the law allow or not allow them to use each of the methods below? Please assume in each case that it is the only method open to them on medical advice.

PLEASE TICK ONE BOX ON EACH LINE

	It should be		Don't know
	Allowed by law	Not allowed by law	
They try to have a child by artificial insemination, using the husband as donor	89.0	8.5	0.6
They try to have a child by artificial insemination, using an anonymous donor	49.6	46.7	0.5
They try to have a child by having their own 'test-tube' embryo implanted	85.3	11.6	0.6
They find a 'surrogate' mother who agrees, without payment, to bear a child for them (by artificial insemination, using the husband as a donor)	35.7	60.8	0.5
They find a 'surrogate' mother who is paid to bear a child for them (by artificial insemination, using the husband as donor)	22.5	74.2	0.5

17. Which of these statements comes closest to your views on the availability of pornographic magazines and films?

PLEASE TICK ONE BOX

They should be banned altogether	38.0
They should be available in special adult shops but not displayed to the public	42.4
They should be available in special adult shops with public display permitted	8.1
They should be available in any shop for sale to adults only	8.2
They should be available in any shop for sale to anyone	1.1
Don't know	0.1

- 10 -

| N = 1281 |

18. Would you say that opportunities for university education are, in general, better or worse for women than for men?

PLEASE TICK ONE BOX

Much better for women	1.1
Better for women	1.1
No difference	75.5
Worse for women	10.2
Much worse for women	0.8
Can't choose	11.1

19. How about job opportunities for women: do you think they are, in general, better or worse than job opportunities for men with similar education and experience?

PLEASE TICK ONE BOX

Much better for women	1.4
Better for women	4.1
No difference	33.7
Worse for women	49.2
Much worse for women	4.6
Can't choose	6.7

20. And how about income and wages: compared with men who have similar education and jobs - are women, in general, paid better or worse than men?

PLEASE TICK ONE BOX

Women are paid much better	0.1
Women are paid better	0.9
No difference	27.0
Women are paid worse	60.2
Women are paid much worse	5.5
Can't choose	6.2

OFFICE USE ONLY

N = 1281

- 11 -

21. For each of the jobs below, please tick a box to show whether you think the job is particularly suitable for men only, particularly suitable for women only, or suitable for both men and women equally?

PLEASE TICK ONE BOX ON EACH LINE

	Particularly suitable for men	Particularly suitable for women	Suitable for both equally
Social worker	1.0	15.0	83.1
Police officer	36.5	0.5	62.4
Secretary	0.6	54.1	44.3
Car mechanic	67.3	0.6	31.0
Nurse	0.4	31.4	67.3
Computer programmer	3.9	1.9	93.0
Bus driver	40.0	0.5	58.5
Bank manager	28.2	0.6	70.2
Family doctor/GP	5.7	0.8	92.5
Local councillor	7.2	0.9	91.0
Member of Parliament	9.6	0.5	89.2

22. People's views about whether a woman ought to work or not often change according to her circumstances.

Please tick one box on each line to show which is closest to your view a woman in the following circumstances?

PLEASE TICK ONE BOX ON EACH LINE

	She ought to go out to work if she's fit	It's up to her whether to go out to work or not	She should only go out to work if she really needs the money	She ought to stay at home
a) A married woman whose children have all left school	8.0	81.7	8.6	1.2
b) A married woman whose children are all at school	2.3	50.0	31.5	15.1
c) A married woman with children under school age	0.7	19.5	22.2	56.7
d) A married woman with no children	23.2	70.0	5.5	0.5
e) A single woman with no family responsibilities	69.8	27.5	1.9	0.1

N = 1281

- 12 -

23. Please tick one box for *each* statement below to show how much you agree or disagree with it.

PLEASE TICK ONE BOX ON EACH LINE

	Agree Strongly	Agree Slightly	Neither Agree nor Disagree	Disagree Slightly	Disagree Strongly	Don't know
a) A husband's job is to earn the money; a wife's job is to look after the home and family.	23.5	24.1	19.1	13.0	19.8	0.1
b) A woman and her family will all be happier if she goes out to work.	2.8	10.8	39.7	27.4	18.8	0.1
c) Women shouldn't try to combine a career and children.	13.0	19.0	22.2	27.2	18.9	0.1
d) In times of high unemployment married women should stay at home.	14.1	17.9	19.5	24.5	23.3	0.1
e) A job is all right but what most women really want is a home and children.	13.6	22.7	21.5	21.2	20.5	0.1
f) If the children are well looked after, it's good for a woman to work.	16.5	39.3	27.9	10.6	4.9	0.1
g) Most married women work only to earn money for extras, rather than because they need the money.	13.9	30.8	15.7	23.0	15.9	0.1
h) If a woman takes several years off to look after her children it's only fair her career should suffer.	6.2	23.2	25.3	23.9	20.2	0.2
i) Married women have a right to work if they want to, whatever their family situation.	31.4	31.1	15.3	13.0	8.5	0.1
j) Having a job is the best way for a woman to be an independent person.	26.5	33.1	24.5	9.4	5.7	0.1

OFFICE USE ONLY

N = 1281

- 13 -

24. Now a few questions about the disease called AIDS.

Please tick one box to show which is closest to your views about the following statement:

Within five years AIDS will cause more deaths in Britain than any other single disease.

PLEASE TICK ONE BOX

It is highly exaggerated	10.8
It is slightly exaggerated	26.9
It is more or less true	60.3
Don't know	0.4

25. Please tick one box for each statement to show how much you agree or disagree with it.

PLEASE TICK ONE BOX ON EACH LINE

	Agree strongly	Agree	Neither agree nor disagree	Disagree	Disagree strongly	Don't know
a) Most people with AIDS have only themselves to blame.	23.8	33.4	14.6	20.6	6.8	0.2
b) The National Health Service should spend more of its resources on giving better care to people dying from AIDS.	7.9	34.0	28.7	22.8	5.3	0.2
c) Official warnings about AIDS should say that some sexual practices are morally wrong.	31.2	35.4	13.1	14.3	5.1	0.1
d) Within the next five years doctors will discover a vaccine against AIDS.	4.2	30.5	44.9	16.3	2.7	0.4
e) AIDS is a way of punishing the world for its decline in moral standards.	9.6	18.6	25.1	24.1	21.9	0.1
f) AIDS is a tragedy for young people because it surrounds their sex lives with fear.	20.7	42.6	16.8	15.5	3.7	0.1

OFFICE USE ONLY

N = 1281

- 14 -

26a) Please tick one box to show which best describes the sort of work you do.

(If you are not working now, please tick a box to show what you did in your last job.)

PLEASE TICK ONE BOX

Farmer or farm manager	1.1
Farm worker	1.1
Skilled manual work (for example: plumber, electrician, fitter, train driver, cook, hairdresser)	14.4
Semi-skilled or unskilled manual work (for example: machine operator, assembler, postman, waitress, cleaner, labourer)	26.1
Professional or technical work (for example: doctor, accountant, school teacher, social worker, computer programmer)	18.5
Manager or administrator (for example: company director, manager, executive officer, local authority officer)	9.0
Clerical (for example: clerk, secretary)	15.2
Sales (for example: commercial traveller, shop assistant)	8.2
(Never had a job)	2.9

b) Are you self-employed or do you work for someone else as an employee?

(If you are not working now, please answer about your last job)

PLEASE TICK ONE BOX

Self-employed	10.1
Employee	80.2
(Never had a job)	2.9

c) As your position at work, are you (or were you) ...

PLEASE TICK ONE BOX

... a supervisor or foreman of manual workers,	13.5
a supervisor or foreman of non-manual workers,	15.3
or - not a supervisor or foreman?	61.4

OFFICE USE ONLY

N = 2493

- 15 -

27. Please tick *one* box for *each* statement below to show how much you agree or disagree with it.

PLEASE TICK ONE BOX ON EACH LINE	Agree strongly	Agree	Neither agree nor disagree	Disagree	Disagree strongly	Don't know (OFFICE USE ONLY)
a. Government should redistribute income from the better-off to those who are less well off.	14.9	30.0	20.1	26.2	7.2	0.1
b. Big business benefits owners at the expense of workers.	12.3	38.8	24.7	18.9	3.2	0.3
c. Ordinary working people do not get their fair share of the nation's wealth.	17.5	46.8	17.3	14.8	2.0	0.2
d. There is one law for the rich and one for the poor.	25.5	40.4	14.1	16.1	2.6	0.1
e. Management will always try to get the better of employees if it gets the chance.	18.7	42.2	17.8	17.6	2.2	0.1
f. Young people today don't have enough respect for traditional British values.	18.6	47.9	20.5	10.3	1.9	-
g. People who break the law should be given stiffer sentences.	36.7	42.9	15.1	4.0	0.9	-
h. People should be allowed to organise public meetings to protest against the government.	15.0	45.8	26.3	9.7	2.4	0.2
i. For some crimes, the death penalty is the most appropriate sentence.	42.6	31.1	8.8	9.8	7.0	-
j. People should be allowed to publish leaflets to protest against the government.	14.7	43.4	28.4	10.4	2.2	0.2

N = 2493

- 16 -

PLEASE TICK ONE BOX FOR EACH STATEMENT	Agree strongly	Agree	Neither agree nor disagree	Disagree	Disagree strongly	Don't know (OFFICE USE ONLY)
k. Schools should teach children to obey authority.	31.8	51.5	10.5	5.2	0.4	-
l. People should be allowed to organise protest marches and demonstrations.	9.0	44.5	29.1	13.3	3.0	0.1
m. The law should always be obeyed, even if a particular law is wrong.	9.1	36.5	23.5	25.8	3.7	-
n. Censorship of films and magazines is necessary to uphold moral standards.	19.9	51.2	13.9	11.6	2.6	-
o. The government should spend more money on welfare benefits for the poor, even if it leads to higher taxes.	16.3	38.3	22.8	19.3	2.6	-
p. Around here, most unemployed people could find a job if they really wanted one.	7.8	33.2	16.3	31.4	10.2	0.2
q. Many people who get social security don't really deserve any help.	6.9	24.2	23.7	33.7	10.9	-
r. Most people on the dole are fiddling in one way or another.	6.6	25.4	28.1	31.4	8.0	0.1
s. If welfare benefits weren't so generous people would learn to stand on their own two feet.	7.8	25.1	21.3	31.6	13.7	-

- 17 -

N = 2493

28. Please tick one box for each statement to show how you feel about training for people in work.
PLEASE TICK ONE BOX ON EACH LINE

	Agree strongly	Agree	Neither agree nor disagree	Dis-agree	Disagree strongly	Don't know (OFFICE USE ONLY)
a) Most employers are unwilling to pay for better training for their staff.	8.4	43.2	24.7	20.2	1.3	0.2
b) People who get training at work find their jobs more interesting.	14.0	70.8	10.1	3.1	0.1	0.1
c) Having well-trained staff benefits employers more than workers.	10.9	38.0	26.4	21.7	1.0	0.2
d) People who get training at work end up with better pay.	6.2	50.4	26.0	14.2	0.8	0.2
e) Training at work is really only for young people or people starting new jobs.	2.6	14.9	12.8	57.0	10.6	0.2
f) The government ought to help employers pay for the training of their staff.	8.8	42.1	21.6	22.8	2.7	0.2

29. The government these days pays for a number of schemes for unemployed people.

First, please tick one box to show how much you agree or disagree with each of these statements about government training schemes for school-leavers.
PLEASE TICK ONE BOX ON EACH LINE

Government training schemes for school-leavers.....	Agree strongly	Agree	Neither agree nor disagree	Dis-agree	Disagree strongly	Don't know
a) ... are a good way of giving young people better job prospects?	9.8	50.5	14.7	18.9	3.9	0.2
b) ... benefit employers more than the young people taking part?	17.2	38.9	21.7	19.2	0.7	0.5
c) ... are a bad substitute for proper job-experience?	15.4	36.5	20.7	23.6	1.3	0.4
d) ... are a good way for young people to get training after they leave school?	6.5	54.9	16.5	17.0	2.9	0.3

And now tick one box to show how much you agree or disagree with each of these statements about government employment schemes for people other than school-leavers.

	Agree strongly	Agree	Neither agree nor disagree	Dis-agree	Disagree strongly	Don't know
e) Government employment schemes are a waste of taxpayers' money.	6.6	15.0	26.2	45.7	3.7	0.4
f) The government should provide more schemes for unemployed people to do work that is useful to society.	16.3	62.8	11.4	6.4	0.9	0.2
g) The government should do more to encourage unemployed people to set up their own businesses.	11.7	53.4	23.3	8.1	0.9	0.3

- 18 -

N = 1281

30. Here are a number of things which might help to reduce unemployment in Britain. Please tick a box to show for each whether you would support or oppose it.
PLEASE TICK ONE BOX ON EACH LINE

	Support strongly	Support	Oppose	Oppose strongly	Don't know
A. Lower the retirement age to create more jobs for younger people	29.9	52.1	14.8	2.1	0.1
B. Shorten the working week and reduce the earnings of those in paid work	2.7	14.7	63.8	16.8	0.2
C. Introduce job sharing schemes so that two part-timers share one full-time job	6.0	35.6	43.4	12.5	0.6
D. Restrict over-time working	12.7	41.0	35.9	8.1	0.4

31. Employers have to consider many things before deciding what to pay employees. Please tick one box to show which should be most important and one box to show which should be next most important, in deciding the level of pay of an employee.
PLEASE TICK ONE BOX UNDER MOST IMPORTANT AND ONE BOX UNDER NEXT MOST IMPORTANT

	Should be most important	Should be next most important
The age of the employee	2.3	4.9
The performance of the individual employee	48.9	17.5
How long the employee has been with the firm	2.1	17.4
The employee's family commitments	1.6	2.9
The going rate for the job	18.5	23.9
What the firm says it can afford	3.2	7.5
Don't know	0.2	0.2

32. New kinds of technology are being introduced more and more in Britain: computers and word processors, robots in factories and so on. Please tick one box to show what effect you think this technology will have over the next five years?
PLEASE TICK ONE BOX

It will increase the number of jobs available	7.8
It will reduce the number of jobs available	71.3
It will make no difference to the number of jobs available	19.3
Don't know	0.6

	OFFICE USE ONLY

N = 1281

- 19 -

33a) Do you think that the introduction of new technology in Britain over the next five years will ...

PLEASE TICK ONE BOX

... make work more interesting,	40.8
make work more boring,	33.4
or - will it make no difference to work?	24.0
Don't know	0.6

b) And will it ...

PLEASE TICK ONE BOX

... make life more difficult,	13.6
make life easier,	60.6
or - will it make no difference?	23.6
Don't know	0.7

c) Please tick one box to show whether you agree or disagree with the following statement: The government should do more to encourage the spread of new technology in Britain.

PLEASE TICK ONE BOX

Agree strongly	21.4
Agree	45.6
Neither agree nor disagree	24.7
Disagree	5.9
Disagree strongly	0.8
Don't know	0.4

34. To help us plan better in future, please tell us about how long it took you to complete this questionnaire?

PLEASE TICK ONE BOX

Less than 15 minutes	2.8
Between 15 and 20 minutes	15.9
Between 20 and 30 minutes	30.2
Between 30 and 45 minutes	26.9
Between 45 and 60 minutes	13.7
Over one hour	9.1

THANK YOU VERY MUCH FOR YOUR HELP!

Please keep the completed questionnaire for the interviewer if he or she has arranged to call for it. Otherwise, please post it as soon as possible in the pre-paid, addressed envelope provided.

B

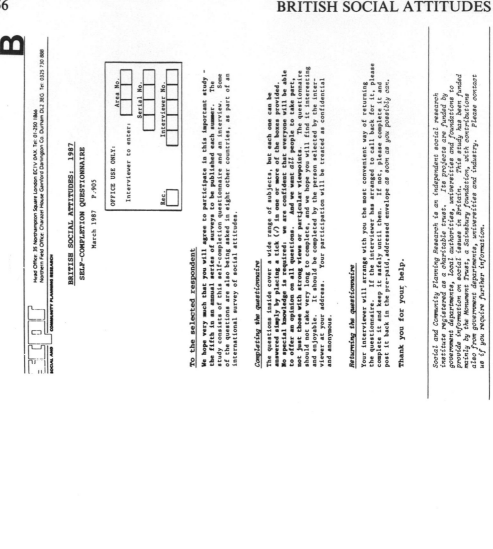

SOCIAL AND COMMUNITY PLANNING RESEARCH

Head Office: 35 Northampton Square London EC1V 0AX Tel: 01-250 1866
Northern Field Office: Charazel House Gainford Darlington Co. Durham DL2 3EG Tel: 0325 730 888

BRITISH SOCIAL ATTITUDES: 1987
SELF-COMPLETION QUESTIONNAIRE

March 1987   P.905

To the selected respondent

We hope very much that you will agree to participate in this important study - the fifth in an annual series of surveys to be published each summer. The study consists of this self-completion questionnaire and an interview. Some of the questions are also being asked in eight other countries, as part of an international survey of social attitudes.

Completing the questionnaire

The questions inside cover a wide range of subjects, but each one can be answered simply by placing a tick (/) in one or more of the boxes provided. No special knowledge is required: we are confident that everyone will be able to offer an opinion on all questions. And we want *all* people to take part, not just those with strong views or particular viewpoints. The questionnaire should not take very long to complete, and we hope you will find it interesting and enjoyable. It should be completed by the person selected by the interviewer at your address. Your participation will be treated as confidential and anonymous.

Returning the questionnaire

Your interviewer will arrange with you the most convenient way of returning the questionnaire. If the interviewer has arranged to call back for it, please complete it and keep it safely until then. If not, please complete it and post it back in the pre-paid, addressed envelope as soon as you possibly can.

Thank you for your help.

Social and Community Planning Research is an independent social research institute registered as a charitable trust. Its projects are funded by government departments, local authorities, universities and foundations to provide information on social issues in Britain. This study has been funded mainly by the Monument Trust, a Sainsbury foundation, with contributions also from government departments, universities and industry. Please contact us if you require further information.

- 1 -

N = 1212

To begin, we have some questions about opportunities for getting ahead ...

1. Please tick one box for each of these to show how important you think it is for getting ahead in life ...

First, how important is coming from a wealthy family?

a) PLEASE TICK ONE BOX

Essential	4.1
Very important	16.4
Fairly important	33.3
Not very important	30.0
Not important at all	13.9
Can't choose	1.6

b) Having well-educated parents?
PLEASE TICK ONE BOX

Essential	3.3
Very important	23.5
Fairly important	45.1
Not very important	19.5
Not important at all	7.3
Can't choose	0.9

c) Having a good education yourself?
PLEASE TICK ONE BOX

Essential	23.4
Very important	48.4
Fairly important	23.8
Not very important	2.8
Not important at all	0.7
Can't choose	0.5

d) Ambition?
PLEASE TICK ONE BOX

Essential	37.6
Very important	41.8
Fairly important	16.7
Not very important	2.1
Not important at all	0.7
Can't choose	0.5

Please continue ...

OFFICE USE ONLY

- 2 -

N = 1212

e) Natural ability - how important is that for getting ahead in life?
PLEASE TICK ONE BOX

Essential	14.4
Very important	42.6
Fairly important	37.3
Not very important	4.0
Not important at all	0.7
Can't choose	0.8

f) Hard work - how important is that?
PLEASE TICK ONE BOX

Essential	35.7
Very important	47.8
Fairly important	13.7
Not very important	1.4
Not important at all	0.7
Can't choose	0.3

g) Knowing the right people?
PLEASE TICK ONE BOX

Essential	13.0
Very important	26.4
Fairly important	40.7
Not very important	16.8
Not important at all	2.7
Can't choose	0.2

h) Having political connections?
PLEASE TICK ONE BOX

Essential	2.1
Very important	4.8
Fairly important	13.7
Not very important	47.7
Not important at all	28.3
Can't choose	3.3

OFFICE USE ONLY

- 3 -

N = 1212

i) A person's race - how important is that for getting ahead in life?

PLEASE TICK ONE BOX

	OFFICE USE ONLY
Essential	2.6
Very important	13.6
Fairly important	30.8
Not very important	31.3
Not important at all	18.2
Can't choose	3.4

j) A person's religion?

PLEASE TICK ONE BOX

Essential	1.9
Very important	3.4
Fairly important	8.5
Not very important	39.7
Not important at all	45.3
Can't choose	0.9

k) The part of the country a person comes from?

PLEASE TICK ONE BOX

Essential	1.0
Very important	6.3
Fairly important	20.6
Not very important	40.7
Not important at all	30.1
Can't choose	1.2

l) Being born a man or a woman - how important is that?

PLEASE TICK ONE BOX

Essential	1.8
Very important	9.5
Fairly important	21.5
Not very important	32.3
Not important at all	30.2
Can't choose	4.2

Please continue ...

- 4 -

N = 1212

m) A person's political beliefs, how important are they for getting ahead in life?

PLEASE TICK ONE BOX

	OFFICE USE ONLY
Essential	0.9
Very important	4.0
Fairly important	18.4
Not very important	47.6
Not important at all	26.3
Can't choose	2.5

2. Please tick a box to show how much you agree or disagree with the following statement:

The way things are in Britain, people like me and my family have a good chance of improving our standard of living.

PLEASE TICK ONE BOX

Strongly agree	4.4
Agree	31.4
Neither agree nor disagree	29.1
Disagree	26.6
Strongly disagree	5.0
Can't choose	3.2

3. Some people earn a lot of money while others do not earn very much at all ...

In order to get people to work hard, do <u>you</u> think large differences in pay are ...

PLEASE TICK ONE BOX

Absolutely necessary	13.5
Probably necessary	47.6
Probably not necessary	21.8
Definitely not necessary	12.4
Can't choose	4.3

- 5 -

N = 1212

4. Do you agree or disagree with each of these statements?

PLEASE TICK ONE BOX ON EACH LINE

	Strongly agree	Agree	Neither agree nor disagree	Disagree	Strongly disagree	Can't choose
a) People would not want to take extra responsibility at work unless they were paid extra for it.	22.9	58.3	8.6	8.7	0.5	0.4
b) Workers would not bother to get skills and qualifications unless they were paid extra for having them.	18.6	50.4	10.7	17.7	1.8	0.3
c) Inequality continues because it benefits the rich and powerful.	22.6	36.0	15.9	16.5	2.5	5.3
d) No-one would study for years to become a lawyer or doctor unless they expected to earn a lot more than ordinary workers.	24.3	44.5	9.4	18.5	2.1	0.6
e) Large differences in income are necessary for Britain's prosperity.	4.3	21.6	24.0	37.7	8.5	3.4
f) Allowing business to make good profits is the best way to improve everyone's standard of living.	10.2	42.7	19.2	21.2	3.0	2.8
g) Inequality continues to exist because ordinary people don't join together to get rid of it.	7.8	31.3	20.7	28.2	5.4	5.6

Please continue ...

- 6 -

N = 1212

5. We would like to know what you think people in these jobs actually earn.

Please write in how much you think they usually earn each year, before taxes.

(Many people are not exactly sure about this, but your best guess will be close enough. This may be difficult, but it is important, so please try.)

Please write in how much they actually earn each year, before tax

a) First, about how much do you think a bricklayer earns?	£ 9,000	MEDIAN
b) A doctor in general practice?	£ 20,000	MEDIAN
c) A bank clerk?	£ 8,000	MEDIAN
d) The owner of a small shop?	£ 10,000	MEDIAN
e) The chairman of a large national company?	£ 60,000	MEDIAN
f) A skilled worker in a factory?	£ 10,000	MEDIAN
g) A farm worker?	£ 6,000	MEDIAN
h) A secretary?	£ 7,000	MEDIAN
i) A city bus driver?	£ 8,000	MEDIAN
j) An unskilled worker in a factory?	£ 6,000	MEDIAN
k) A cabinet minister in the national government?	£ 30,000	MEDIAN

N = 1212

- 7 -

6. Next, **what do you think people in these jobs ought to be paid** - how much do you think they should earn each year before taxes, regardless of what they actually get?

Please write in how much they should earn each year, before tax

a) First, about how much do you think a bricklayer should earn? .... £ 10,000 MEDIAN

b) A doctor in general practice? .... £ 20,000 MEDIAN

c) A bank clerk, how much should s/he earn? £ 8,500 MEDIAN

d) The owner of a small shop? .... £ 11,000 MEDIAN

e) The chairman of a large national company? .... £ 35,000 MEDIAN

f) A skilled worker in a factory? ...... £ 10,000 MEDIAN

g) A farm worker? .... £ 8,000 MEDIAN

h) A secretary? .... £ 8,500 MEDIAN

i) A city bus driver? .... £ 8,500 MEDIAN

j) An unskilled worker in a factory? ... £ 7,000 MEDIAN

k) A cabinet minister in the national government? .... £ 24,000 MEDIAN

Please continue ...

N = 1212

- 8 -

7. Please show how much you agree or disagree with each statement....
PLEASE TICK ONE BOX ON EACH LINE

	Agree strongly	Agree	Neither agree nor disagree	Disagree	Disagree strongly	Can't choose
a) Differences in income in Britain are too large.	25.4	48.8	12.3	9.5	1.4	2.0
b) It is the responsibility of the government to reduce the differences in income between people with high incomes and those with low incomes.	20.5	42.0	12.3	19.1	3.0	2.5
c) The government should provide more chances for children from poor families to go to university.	31.0	51.0	10.8	5.3	0.5	0.7
d) The government should provide a job for everyone who wants one.	23.1	34.2	16.7	19.3	3.2	2.5
e) The government should spend less on benefits for the poor.	0.7	3.6	12.1	52.6	28.9	0.9
f) The government should provide a decent standard of living for the unemployed.	17.2	46.8	17.4	12.5	3.3	1.7
g) The government should provide everyone with a guaranteed basic income.	19.7	39.3	13.0	21.7	3.7	1.9

OFFICE USE ONLY

N = 1212

- 9 -

8. Generally, how would you describe taxes in Britain today ...

(We mean all taxes together, including national insurance, income tax, VAT and all the rest.)

a) First, for those with high incomes, are taxes ...

PLEASE TICK ONE BOX

Much too high	7.1
Too high	16.9
About right	32.7
Too low	30.7
Much too low	9.0
Can't choose	2.6

b) Next, for those with middle incomes, are taxes ...

PLEASE TICK ONE BOX

Much too high	8.3
Too high	31.3
About right	52.3
Too low	4.8
Much too low	0.4
Can't choose	2.0

c) Lastly, for those with low incomes, are taxes ...

PLEASE TICK ONE BOX

Much too high	37.4
Too high	46.8
About right	12.3
Too low	0.6
Much too low	0.2
Can't choose	1.9

9. Do you think that people with high incomes should pay a larger share of their income in taxes than those with low incomes, the same share, or a smaller share?

PLEASE TICK ONE BOX

Much larger share	19.2
Larger	54.9
The same share	20.7
Smaller	1.3
Much smaller share	-
Can't choose	2.9

Please continue ...

N = 1212

- 10 -

10. In all countries there are differences or even conflicts between different social groups. In your opinion, in Britain how much conflict is there between ...

PLEASE TICK ONE BOX ON EACH LINE

	Very strong conflicts	Strong conflicts	Not very strong conflicts	There are no conflicts	Can't choose
a) Poor people and rich people?	13.2	37.6	39.2	5.0	3.6
b) The working class and the middle class?	3.5	15.6	62.3	13.2	3.2
c) The unemployed and people with jobs?	8.2	29.4	43.2	12.2	4.0
d) Management and workers?	5.2	43.5	37.5	3.9	3.4
e) Farmers and city people?	4.3	21.2	45.1	21.2	5.9
f) Young people and older people?	1.0	28.9	43.4	14.3	4.5

11. In our society there are groups which tend to be towards the top and groups which tend to be towards the bottom. Below is a scale that runs from top to bottom. Where would you put yourself on this scale?

PLEASE TICK ONE BOX

Top	0.8
	1.6
	4.9
	11.4
	29.3
	18.5
	12.7
	9.7
	3.2
Bottom	3.5
Don't know	0.5

12. Please think of your present job (or your last one if you don't have one now). If you compare this job with the job your father had when you were 16, would you say that the level or status of your job is (or was) ...

Much higher than your father's	16.4
Higher	29.7
About equal	25.9
Lower	16.6
Much lower than your father's	4.2
(I never had a job)	2.4
(Never knew father/father never had a job)	1.9
Don't know	0.6

OFFICE USE ONLY

- 11 -

N = 1212

13.a) Here is a list of different types of jobs. Which type did your father have when you were 16?

(If your father did not have a job then, please give the job he used to have.)

PLEASE TICK ONE BOX

Professional and technical (for example: doctor, teacher, engineer, artist, accountant)	9.0
Higher administrator (for example: banker, executive in big business, high government official, union official)	4.4
Clerical (for example: secretary, clerk, office manager, bookkeeper)	7.3
Sales (for example: sales manager, shop owner, shop assistant, insurance agent)	7.8
Service (for example: restaurant owner, police officer, waiter, barber, caretaker)	4.7
Skilled worker (for example: foreman, motor mechanic, printer, tool and die maker, electrician)	22.1
Semi-Skilled worker (for example: bricklayer, bus driver, cannery worker, carpenter, sheet metal worker, baker)	19.4
Unskilled worker (for example: labourer, porter, unskilled factory worker)	12.3
Farm (for example: farmer, farm labourer, tractor driver)	5.8
(Never knew father/father never had job)	2.7
Don't know	0.1

b) Was your father self-employed, or did he work for someone else?

PLEASE TICK ONE BOX

Self-employed, had own business or farm	17.4
Worked for someone else	74.3
(Never knew father/father never had job)	2.6
Don't know	0.1

Please continue ...

- 12 -

N = 1212

14.a) And how about your first job - the first job you had after you finished full-time education?

(Even if that was many years ago, we would still like to know about it.)

PLEASE TICK ONE BOX

Professional and technical (for example: doctor, teacher, engineer, artist, accountant)	12.4
Higher administrator (for example: banker, executive in big business, high government official, union official)	0.5
Clerical (for example: secretary, clerk, office manager, bookkeeper)	22.3
Sales (for example: sales manager, shop owner, shop assistant, insurance agent)	12.6
Service (for example: restaurant owner, police officer, barber, waitress, caretaker)	6.0
Skilled worker (for example: foreman, motor mechanic, printer, seamstress, electrician)	12.4
Semi-skilled worker (for example: bricklayer, bus driver, cannery worker, carpenter, sheet metal worker, baker)	8.9
Unskilled worker (for example: labourer, porter, unskilled factory worker)	17.1
Farm (for example: farmer, farm labourer, tractor driver)	3.2
(Never had a job)	2.8

b) Were you self-employed, or did you work for someone else?

PLEASE TICK ONE BOX

Self-employed, had own business or farm	1.9
Worked for someone else	88.8
(Never had a job)	2.7

OFFICE USE ONLY

- 13 -

N = 1212

OFFICE USE ONLY

15.a) And how about your job now?
(If you are not working now, please tell us about your last job.)
PLEASE TICK ONE BOX

Professional and technical (for example: doctor, teacher, engineer, artist, accountant) 18.0

Higher administrator (for example: banker, executive in big business, high government official, union official) 2.9

Clerical (for example: secretary, clerk, office manager, bookkeeper) 17.4

Sales (for example: sales manager, shop owner, shop assistant, insurance agent) 11.7

Service (for example: restaurant owner, police officer, waitress, barber, caretaker) 8.5

Skilled worker (for example: foreman, motor mechanic, printer, seamstress, electrician) 13.7

Semi-skilled worker (for example: bricklayer, bus driver, cannery worker, carpenter, sheet metal worker, baker) 9.7

Unskilled workers (for example: labourer, porter, unskilled factory worker) 10.5

Farm (for example: farmer, farm labourer, tractor driver) 1.7

(Never had a job) 2.9

b) Are you self-employed, or do you work for someone else?
PLEASE TICK ONE BOX

Self-employed, have own business or farm 10.4

Work for someone else 78.5

(Never had a job) 2.9

Please continue ...

- 14 -

N = 1212

16. Do you think big businesses or small businesses are generally better at each of these things, or is there no difference?
PLEASE TICK ONE BOX ON EACH LINE

	Big businesses are better	Small businesses are better	There is no difference	OFFICE USE ONLY Don't know
Inventing new products	51.9	20.5	23.4	0.7
Making well-designed products	28.1	38.0	29.3	0.7
Investing in new machinery and technology	79.4	6.0	10.0	0.8
Attracting the best people to work in them	59.7	15.5	20.2	1.1
Making goods that people really want to buy	22.8	35.4	37.3	0.8
Keeping good relations between management and other employees	6.3	74.2	15.6	0.8
Training employees in new skills	52.4	22.5	20.3	0.9
Paying their employees a fair wage	39.5	23.1	32.9	1.0
Charging fair prices for their products	22.0	37.4	36.3	0.8
Caring about their customers	4.4	72.2	19.6	0.7

17. Who do you think benefits most from the profits made by British firms?
PLEASE TICK ONE BOX

Mainly their owners or shareholders 68.3
Mainly their directors and managers 20.8
Mainly their employees 3.2
The public generally 6.0
Don't know 0.2

- 15 -

| N = 1212 |

18. Please tick one box for each statement to show how much you agree or disagree with it.

PLEASE TICK ONE BOX ON EACH LINE

	Agree Strongly	Agree	Neither Agree nor Disagree	Disagree	Disagree Strongly	Don't know
a). Consumers are given too little protection by the law.	11.7	42.3	25.0	18.3	0.6	0.2
b). Too much of industry's profits go abroad.	13.5	39.8	31.1	12.1	0.6	0.7
c). We would all be better off if British firms made bigger profits.	14.0	43.7	22.4	16.3	1.2	0.3
d). Britain's economy can prosper without manufacturing industry.	1.9	3.6	12.6	57.4	21.4	0.4
e). British firms make too much profit.	3.3	13.3	31.0	43.3	5.4	0.5
f). Britain's schools fail to teach the kind of skills that British industry needs.	20.4	49.8	15.9	9.9	1.5	0.5
g). Employees who have shares in their companies tend to work harder.	13.5	57.9	17.4	8.4	0.8	-
h). The less profitable British industry is, the less money there is for governments to spend on things like education and health.	12.9	52.2	19.1	11.6	0.9	0.7
i). British people should try to buy British goods even when they have to pay a bit more for them.	16.9	45.2	17.0	17.6	2.0	-

19. Please tick one box on each line to show your views on government help for industry. Remember that if you say 'definitely' or 'probably', it might require an increase in income tax to pay for it.

Do you think the government should ...

PLEASE TICK ONE BOX ON EACH LINE

	Definitely	Probably	Probably not	Definitely not	Don't know
... help industry pay for research into new products?	25.7	37.2	26.0	8.1	0.3
... help pay for new factories in areas of high unemployment?	44.6	41.5	9.0	2.4	0.2
... help industry pay for the cost of replacing out-dated machinery and equipment?	19.5	32.5	35.0	10.1	0.3
... help industry pay the wages of people working in declining industries?	14.0	24.4	42.7	16.0	0.4
... give people grants to start their own businesses?	38.4	46.8	8.8	3.4	0.2
... give firms more help in selling goods abroad?	34.4	42.1	16.2	4.5	0.4
... help industry pay for training employees in new skills?	36.3	42.4	15.9	3.0	0.3

- 16 -

| N = 1212 |

20. Listed below are some of Britain's institutions. From what you know or have heard about each one, can you say whether, on the whole, you think it is well run or not well run?

PLEASE TICK ONE BOX ON EACH LINE

	Very well run	Well run	Not very well run	Not at all well run	Don't know
The National Health Service	3.3	32.0	49.3	14.2	0.1
The press	1.8	37.3	41.9	15.1	0.4
Local government	1.0	28.2	52.3	14.4	0.4
The civil service	3.0	42.7	40.4	9.5	0.6
Manufacturing industry	2.3	45.2	42.7	4.7	1.0
Nationalised industries	3.3	29.5	47.5	14.0	1.2
Banks	29.4	61.5	4.4	1.1	0.5
The trade unions	3.6	23.6	48.5	20.0	0.7
The BBC	12.1	54.9	23.1	7.1	0.3
Independent TV and radio	18.3	64.4	11.6	2.5	0.4
The police	13.1	53.1	24.8	6.3	0.2
The 'City of London' Stock Exchange	17.5	57.5	13.8	3.9	1.9
The 'City of London' generally	9.8	52.0	25.2	5.9	1.9
Universities	5.2	59.5	26.4	4.4	1.1
State schools	1.4	28.6	49.8	17.0	0.5

21. Suppose a large company had to choose between:
- doing something that improves pay and conditions for its staff,
or - doing something that increases profits.

PLEASE TICK ONE BOX FOR a) AND ONE BOX FOR b)

	Improve pay and conditions for staff	Increase profits	Don't know
a) Please tick one box to show which choice you think most large companies would generally make?	17.9	79.8	0.2
b) Now please tick one box to show which choice you would make if it was up to you to decide?	68.7	27.6	0.6

N = 1212

- 17 -

22. Now suppose a large trade union had to choose between:
- doing something that improves an industry's long-term chances of survival,
or - doing something that improves the present pay and conditions of the union's members.

PLEASE TICK ONE BOX FOR a) AND ONE BOX FOR b)

	Improve long-term chance of survival	Improve present pay and conditions	OFFICE USE ONLY Don't know
a) Please tick one box to show which choice you think most large trade unions would generally make?	40.8	56.7	0.4
b) Now please tick one box to show which choice you would make if it was up to you?	78.7	18.1	0.4

23. And suppose a large hospital had to choose between:
- doing something that makes life a bit easier for patients,
or - doing something that makes life a bit easier for doctors.

PLEASE TICK ONE BOX FOR a) AND ONE BOX FOR b)

	Make life easier for patients	Make life easier for doctors	Don't know
a) Please tick one box to show which choice you think most large hospitals would generally make?	63.9	33.8	0.6
b) Now please tick one box to show which choice you would make if it was up to you?	80.2	16.7	0.8

24. Different institutions or groups have a lot of influence over governments; others have less.
From what you know or have heard, how much say do you think each of these groups generally has in what a Conservative government does?

PLEASE TICK ONE BOX ON EACH LINE

	A lot of say	Quite a bit of say	Very little say	No say at all	Don't know
a) Manufacturing industry	12.9	41.4	36.8	5.0	0.9
b) The 'City of London'	34.1	43.8	14.8	2.7	1.3
c) The trade unions	5.3	14.9	47.7	27.8	0.9
d) The police	11.4	39.1	38.2	7.5	0.9
e) School-teachers	3.5	13.6	55.6	23.5	0.8
f) Farmers	6.4	25.4	43.9	20.5	0.8

N = 1212

- 18 -

25. And how much say do you think each of these groups generally has in what a Labour government does?

PLEASE TICK ONE BOX ON EACH LINE

	A lot of say	Quite a bit of say	Very little say	No say at all	OFFICE USE ONLY Don't know
a) Manufacturing industry	13.6	47.3	30.4	4.4	1.2
b) The 'City of London'	10.3	42.1	36.1	6.4	1.8
c) The trade unions	50.5	36.1	7.2	2.1	1.0
d) The police	5.7	29.7	50.3	9.9	1.3
e) School-teachers	10.2	37.7	39.0	8.8	1.1
f) Farmers	4.3	26.1	50.8	14.6	1.3

26. And suppose the Alliance parties were in government. How much say do you think each of these groups would have in what the government might do?

PLEASE TICK ONE BOX ON EACH LINE

	A lot of say	Quite a bit of say	Very little say	No say at all	Don't know
a) Manufacturing industry	10.2	53.5	27.5	3.1	2.0
b) The 'City of London'	14.0	50.4	25.6	4.0	2.3
c) The trade unions	5.7	33.9	48.1	6.8	2.0
d) The police	6.8	43.6	37.6	6.3	1.9
e) School-teachers	5.5	40.7	40.2	8.3	1.8
f) Farmers	4.5	34.1	45.1	10.7	2.0

N = 1212

- 19 -

27. 'The City' of London is often called the financial centre of Britain.

Please tick one box on each line to show how much you agree or disagree with each of these statements about 'The City'.

	Agree strongly	Agree	Neither agree nor disagree	Dis-agree	Disagree strongly	Don't know
a) The success of 'The City' is essential to the success of Britain's economy.	22.1	51.3	16.5	7.1	0.5	0.8
b) 'The City' can be relied on to uncover dishonest financial deals without government intervention.	4.4	26.4	31.4	27.2	7.5	1.1
c) The government should encourage as many ordinary people as possible to buy shares in British firms.	14.1	46.9	24.7	8.5	3.2	0.9
d) Too many 'City' institutions go for quick profits at the expense of long-term investment in British industry.	19.1	45.6	26.3	5.3	0.7	1.2

28. How serious an effect on our environment do you think each of these things has?

PLEASE TICK ONE BOX ON EACH LINE

	Very serious	Quite serious	Not very serious	Not at all serious	Don't know
Noise from aircraft	7.2	26.5	55.6	8.4	0.2
Lead from petrol	33.8	51.3	12.0	1.0	0.1
Industrial waste in the rivers and sea	60.4	35.0	2.9	0.2	0.1
Waste from nuclear electricity stations	59.6	23.4	12.9	2.1	0.2
Industrial fumes in the air	43.7	43.8	9.9	0.6	0.1
Noise and dirt from traffic	24.8	48.3	23.6	1.7	0.1
Acid rain	50.0	35.6	10.6	1.5	0.3

N = 1212

- 20 -

29.a) Which one of these three possible solutions to Britain's electricity needs would you favour most?

PLEASE TICK ONE BOX

We should make do with the power stations we have already	24.9
We should build more coal-fuelled power stations	48.3
We should build more nuclear power stations	22.2
Don't know	0.6

b) As far as nuclear power stations are concerned, which of these statements comes closest to your own feelings?

PLEASE TICK ONE BOX

They create very serious risks for the future	36.9
They create quite serious risks for the future	26.8
They create only slight risks for the future	24.4
They create hardly any risks for the future	8.2
Don't know	0.5

30.a) Which one of these two statements comes closest to your own views?

PLEASE TICK ONE BOX

Industry should be prevented from causing damage to the countryside, even if this sometimes leads to higher prices	83.1
OR	
Industry should keep prices down, even if this sometimes causes damage to the countryside	12.8
Don't know	0.4

b) And which of these two statements comes closest to your own views?

PLEASE TICK ONE BOX

The countryside should be protected from development, even if this sometimes leads to fewer new jobs	60.0
OR	
New jobs should be created, even if this sometimes causes damage to the countryside	34.5
Don't know	0.7

OFFICE USE ONLY

N = 1212   - 21 -

31. Here are some statements about the countryside. Please tick one box for each to show whether you agree or disagree with it.

PLEASE TICK ONE BOX ON EACH LINE

	Agree strongly	Agree	Dis-agree	Disagree strongly	OFFICE USE ONLY Don't know
A. Modern methods of farming have caused damage to the countryside.	17.4	50.3	26.8	1.5	0.3
B. If farmers have to choose between producing more food and looking after the countryside, they should produce more food.	4.8	30.8	54.2	6.2	0.6
C. All things considered, farmers do a good job in looking after the countryside.	8.9	65.0	20.0	2.5	0.4
D. Government should withhold some subsidies from farmers and use them to protect the countryside, even if this leads to higher prices.	6.9	44.4	41.7	2.5	0.8

32. Which of these two statements comes closest to your own views?

PLEASE TICK ONE BOX

Looking after the countryside is too important to be left to farmers - government authorities should have more control over what's done and built on farms	37.9
OR	
Farmers know how important it is to look after the countryside - there are enough controls and farmers and farmers should be left to decide what's done on farms	43.7
Can't choose	14.8

33. Please tick one box on each line to show how you feel about ...

PLEASE TICK ONE BOX ON EACH LINE

	It should be stopped altogether	It should be dis-couraged	Don't mind one way or the other	It should be encour-aged
... Increasing the amount of countryside being farmed	8.9	45.8	31.3	9.2
... Building new housing in country areas	15.3	48.6	21.7	10.9
... Putting the needs of farmers before protection of wildlife	15.4	56.8	16.2	7.6
... Providing more roads in country areas	9.9	45.6	27.3	13.2
... Increasing the number of picnic areas and camping sites in the countryside	3.9	16.2	27.9	48.6

N = 1212   - 22 -

34. Please tick one box on each line to show whether you agree or disagree with each of the following statements.

PLEASE TICK ONE BOX ON EACH LINE

	Agree strongly	Agree	Neither agree nor disagree	Dis-agree	Disagree strongly	OFFICE USE ONLY Don't know
A. New housing should be built in cities, towns and villages rather than in the countryside.	25.6	56.5	11.3	4.1	0.3	0.1
B. It is more important to keep green-belt areas than to build new homes there.	28.2	49.4	12.3	7.2	0.6	-
C. Planning laws should be relaxed so that people who want to live in the countryside may do so.	5.0	28.9	22.8	35.1	5.6	0.3
D. Compared with other users of the countryside, farmers have too much say.	5.3	24.5	39.2	26.2	2.1	0.1
E. The beauty of the countryside depends on stopping too many people from visiting it.	2.5	11.3	20.5	54.4	8.5	0.1

35. Here is a list of predictions. For each one, please say how likely or unlikely you think it is to come true within the next ten years?

PLEASE TICK ONE BOX FOR EACH PREDICTION

	Very likely	Quite likely	Not very likely	Not at all likely	OFFICE USE ONLY Don't know
Acts of political terrorism in Britain will be common events	14.8	44.9	33.2	4.0	0.6
Riots and civil disturbance in our cities will be common events	15.8	50.2	27.7	3.3	0.6
There will be a world war involving Britain and Europe	2.3	8.5	56.0	29.4	0.9
There will be a serious accident at a British nuclear power station	12.2	39.9	36.8	7.9	0.7
The police in our cities will find it impossible to protect our personal safety on the streets	20.6	43.1	29.4	3.6	0.6
The government in Britain will be overthrown by revolution	2.2	5.9	42.3	46.6	0.6
A nuclear bomb will be dropped somewhere in the world	6.0	22.2	39.3	29.3	0.7

Subject index